# ANNALS of DYSLEXIA

VOLUME XLVIII                                        1998

*Annals of Dyslexia* is listed in *Current Contents/Social and Behavioral Sciences* (CC/ S&BS), the Social Sciences Citations Index ©(SSCI™), and *Chicoral Abstracts to Reading and Learning Disabilities*. Microfilm and photocopies are available from University Microfilms International.
Annotated and indexed by the ERIC Clearinghouse on Handicapped and Gifted Children for publication in the monthly print index *Current Index to Journals in Education* (CIJE) and the quarterly index, *Exceptional Child Education Resources* (ECER).

# Officials of The International Dyslexia Association

## Officers

Gordon F. Sherman, Ph.D.,
*President*

Leonore Ganschow, Ed.D.
*Vice-President*

Joyce Kassouf
*Vice-President*

Harley A. Tomey, III
*Vice-President*

Nancy Hennessy
*Branch Council Chair*

G. Emerson Dickman, Esq.
*Secretary*

William Clingman
*Treasurer*

## Board of Directors

Marilyn Jager Adams, Ph.D.
Winston C. Addis, Ph.D.
Stanley J. Antonoff, D.D.S.
Susan Brady, Ph.D.
Grant B. Farrell
Jeffrey W. Gilger, Ph.D.
Charles W. Haynes, Ed.D.
Aleatha Kimbrough, Ph.D.

Susan Walker Kowen, Esq.
Lorna N. Kaufman, Ph.D.
Betty S. Levinson, Ph.D.
Louisa Cook Moats, Ed.D.
Joyce S. Pickering, M.A.
Lewis M. Roch, III
James G. Ward, Jr., M.D.

## Council of Advisors

Dirk J. Bakker, Ph.D.
Arthur L. Benton, M.D.
John B. Bigelow
Milton Brutten, Ph.D.
Jeanne S. Chall, Ph.D.
Regina Cicci, Ph.D.
Aylett Royall Cox
Drake D. Duane, M.D.
Helene Durbrow
Leon Eisenburg, M.D.
Albert M. Galaburda, M.D.
Alice H. Garside

Rosa A. Hagin, Ph.D.
Eleanor Thurston Hall
Jeannette J. Jansky, Ph.D.
Lucia R. Karnes, Ph.D.
Diana Hanbury King
Edith Klasen, Ph.D.
Carl Kline, M.D.
Carolyn Kline
Alice Koontz
Che Kan Leong, Ph.D.
Richard L. Masland, M.D.
Zdenek Matejek, Ph.D.

John McLeod, Ph.D.
Ralph D. Rabinovitch, M.D.
Margaret Byrd Rawson
Sylvia O. Richardson, M.D.
Paula Dozier Rome
Roger E. Saunders
Archie A. Silver, M.D.
Lucius Waites, M.D.
Mary Helen Robinson-Wells
Dorothy B. Whitehead
Leon J. Whitsell, M.D.

Executive Director, J. Thomas Viall

## Branches of The International Dyslexia Association

**Arizona**
Arizona Branch
**California**
Central California Branch
Inland Empire Branch
Los Angeles Branch
Northern CA Branch
Orange County Branch
San Diego Branch
**Canada**
British Columbia Branch
**Colorado**
Rocky Mountain Branch
**D.C. Capital Area**
D.C. Capital Branch
**Florida**
Florida Branch
**Georgia**
Georgia Branch

**Hawaii**
Hawaii Branch
**Illinois**
Illinois Branch
**Indiana**
Indiana Branch
**Iowa**
Iowa Branch
**Israel**
Israel (Branch-in-Formation)
**Kansas**
Kansas/Western Missouri (Branch-in-Formation)
**Louisiana**
Louisiana Branch
**Maryland**
Maryland Branch
**Michigan**
Michigan Branch
**Mississippi**
Mississippi Branch

**Nebraska**
Nebraska Branch
**New England Area**
New England Branch
**New Jersey**
New Jersey Branch
**New York**
Buffalo Branch
New York Branch
Suffolk Branch
**North Carolina**
North Carolina Branch
**Ohio**
Central Ohio Branch
Northern Ohio Branch
Ohio Valley Branch
**Oklahoma**
Oklahoma Branch
**Oregon**
Oregon Branch
**Pennsylvania**
Philadelphia Branch

**South Carolina**
South Carolina Branch
**Southwest**
Southwest Branch (NM, West TX)
**Tennessee**
Tennessee Branch
**Texas**
Austin Branch
Dallas Branch
Houston Branch
**Upper Midwest**
Upper Midwest Branch (MN, ND, SD, Manitoba)
**Virginia**
Virginia Branch
**Washington**
Puget Sound Branch
**Wisconsin**
Wisconsin Branch

The International Dyslexia Association Branches publish local newsletters and hold at least one public meeting per year (conference, workshop, etc.). You may request that your name be placed on any branch mailing list to receive notification of scheduled events. New members are automatically affiliated with the nearest branch, but our members may affiliate with the branch of their choice. For additional information about branches, please contact The International Dyslexia Association at 8600 LaSalle Rd., Chester Bldg./Suite 382, Baltimore, MD 21286-2044 • Telephone (410) 296-0232 • Fax (410) 321-5069. Web page: http://www.interdys.org

The International Dyslexia Association
Chester Building/Suite 382
8600 LaSalle Road
Baltimore, MD 21286-2044

Printed in the United States of America

Notice

Members of The International Dyslexia Association receive *Annals of Dyslexia*
without charge. Additional copies of this issue are available from The
International Dyslexia Association at $15.00 each for members and $18.00 each
for nonmembers plus 20% for postage and handling. Send orders prepaid to
the address above.

Cover design: Joseph M. Dieter, Jr.
Compositor: Type Shoppe II Productions, Ltd.
Printer: Port City Press

ISSN 0736-9387

# ANNALS OF DYSLEXIA

Volume XLVIII                                                    1998

## Contents

Instructions for Contributors

# FOREWORD

The *Annals of Dyslexia* is an interdisciplinary peer-reviewed journal published by The International Dyslexia Association, Founded in Memory of Samuel T. Orton. The focus of the journal is on the understanding, prevention, and remediation of reading disability. Although primary emphasis is placed on original research articles, we also publish significant reviews and well-documented reports of effective practice. We invite submissions to the journal from members of the Association as well as from other researchers, educators, and clinicians concerned with reading acquisition and reading disability.

The papers in this year's volume truly live up to our stated goals—and our new name. They are international (including four papers from the United Kingdom and the Netherlands), they are interdisciplinary (several involve collaborations between researchers, clinicians, and policy makers), and they rely on scholarship, basic research, and intervention studies to more effectively understand, identify, educate and advocate for persons with reading difficulties. Orton's influence is especially evident in the opening papers.

For their assistance in reviewing manuscripts, I am grateful to the dedicated Editorial Associates and Editorial Advisory Board; additional—and much appreciated input—was provided by M. Adams, N. Badian, M-L Bat-Hayim, J. Birsh, P. Bowers, B. Byrne, J. Carlisle, A. Faber, B. Foorman, L. Ganschow, S. Gathercole, M. Henry, J. Javorsky, J. Lerner, S. Nittrouer, R. Olson, A. Pollatsek, L. Reed, H. Reiff, D. Sawyer, D. Shankweiler, B. Sheffield, R. Sparks, M. Studdert-Kennedy, R. Treiman, J. Torgesen, and B. Wise. The Publications Committee of the IDA has provided guidance and support to the journal, as have Cindy Ciresi and Tom Viall from the Baltimore office. I count myself lucky to be assisted by Sharon Ringgold and Abigail Struthers, who have been flexible, gracious, prompt, and thoughtful through the many many stages of the editorial process. Type Shoppe II Productions has taken on larger responsibilities this year, and I thank them for making that transition so smooth.

If you wish to submit a manuscript to the *Annals of Dyslexia*, you must do so by January 15 to receive consideration for publication in the following year. A copy of Information for Contributors is included in the back of this volume or may be obtained by writing to: The International Dyslexia Association, Chester Building/Suite 382, 8600 LaSalle Road, Baltimore, Maryland 21286-2044. Individual copies of papers in the current or prior issues (including those from the Bulletin of the Orton Society) are available at the same address. The cost is $4.00, including postage and handling.

*Editor*

# THE 1997 SAMUEL T. ORTON AWARD PRESENTED TO C. WILSON ANDERSON, JR.

*by Joan Stoner and Arlene Sonday*

Each year the International Dyslexia Association, formerly known as the Orton Dyslexia Society, has given its highest award to an individual who has made outstanding and far-reaching contributions. This year that recipient is C. Wilson Anderson Jr.

Wilson is a *visionary*. Although dyslexia was recognized by parents and by many in medicine, research, and private education, teacher trainers in universities and educators in public schools were slow to consider identification and intervention for students with dyslexia. Wilson's public school background prepared him for the task of expanding awareness of dyslexia in public school settings where so very many students were unable to learn basic skills.

Wilson also displayed vision in his efforts to expand the reach of the Orton Dyslexia Society. As a member of the Upper Midwest Branch, he participated in outreach programs that resulted in new branches in Nebraska, Wisconsin, and Iowa. He is among those currently organizing the new Kansas-Western Missouri Branch.

Wilson has provided and continues to provide *leadership*. For the Upper Midwest Branch of The Orton Dyslexia Society, he worked tirelessly on many committees; he served on the Board of Directors, as an officer, and as president. He continued to co-chair conference committees by long distance telephone even as he was completing his Master's Degree in Special Education at Augustana College in South Dakota. On the National level, Wilson served on the Board of Directors of the Orton Dyslexia Society for six years. He served two terms as Vice President and, from 1988 to 1992, two terms as the ninth President of the Society. He has continued to be active on the Board as a past president.

As the first president of the Society to come from a public school background., Wilson was invited to the White House by Barbara Bush to meet with leaders of other organizations to discuss learning disabilities. He received the General Educator of the Year Award from Minnesota ACLD and the Outstanding Leadership award from the Upper Midwest Branch. He is listed in Who's Who in the Midwest and is the subject of the book The Runaway Learning Machine by James Bauer.

As president and negotiator of the Robbinsdale Federation of Teachers, as president of the Orton Dyslexia Society, and as a teacher, Wilson has had many occasions to serve as a *mediator*. Many of us have witnessed these skills in action as he invariably "took the high road", smoothed ruffled feathers, and brought seemingly irreconcilable views and individuals to common ground.

Wilson is an *educator*. For 28 years (in the Robbinsdale, Minnesota, School District), he taught junior and senior high school English and social studies. When he witnessed the difference in a student who had the benefit of instruction from the Rochester Reading Center, Wilson was inspired to seek training in the Orton-Gillingham approach with Paula Rome and Jean Osman. From 1989 to 1994 he worked as an LD Specialist and Teacher Educator at the Menninger Clinic in Topeka, Kansas, while he was also president of The Orton Dyslexia Society.

Wilson's talents as a teacher have benefited many. He serves on the Board of Trustees of Kildonan School in New York, and on the Advisory Councils at Pine Ridge Academy in Vermont, Camperdown Academy in South Carolina, the Brehm School in Illinois, and the Greenhills School in South Carolina. He holds adjunct faculty appointments at Washburn University in Kansas, and at Wayne State College in Nebraska. He is a member of the Advisory Board of the Dyslexia Specialist Program at Fairleigh-Dickinson University in New Jersey.

Wilson is a Fellow in the Academy of Orton-Gillingham Practitioners and Educators. As a consultant, he continues to present countless workshops, courses, and lectures in which he simultaneously instructs teachers, individuals with dyslexia, their parents, administrators, and colleagues. He has published articles and materials and helped write and produce videos to aid students, teachers, and parents.

As an *advocate*, Wilson has been extraordinarily generous with his time, ideas, materials, and money. If Wilson sees someone in need, he tries to help. He continues to receive phone calls from former students and families across the country for guidance and encouragement.

Wilson serves as a *mentor* to colleagues and individuals in ways that extend beyond his professional connections. Whether stopped in the hall or elevator, or called on the phone, he is willing to listen and offer suggestions.

An incurable *optimist*, Wilson always believes the best about people and finds they rarely fail to meet his expectations. No roadblock or temporary setback limits his ability to find a favorable resolution in arranging a course, teaching a student, organizing a group, or completing a project.

Everyone who knows him considers Wilson a *friend*. He has a special ability to relate to kids of all ages. He has them laughing and chatting moments after he meets them; teenagers know they have met someone whom they can trust. The magic extends to all of us since those teens will trust any of us recommended by Wilson.

Wilson will long be remembered for his organization of classic Minnesota potlucks for the staff of Robbinsdale High School, the Children's Division at the Menninger Clinic, the couples'club, or the students and families of his summer workshops and courses.

Finally, although it is not one of the qualities listed on the plaque, Wilson is a punster. His presentations are punctuated with anecdotes and his one-liners have broken the tension in many serious discussions. About 6 weeks after his son, Matthew, was born, Wilson was asked about the new baby. "Oh, he's just fine," Will said, "and he knows all of his short vowels, especially /a/."

Wilson, on behalf of the International Dyslexia Association, we are pleased to offer you this plaque which reads:

The Samuel T. Orton Award
presented to

*C. Wilson Anderson, Jr.*

*Visionary*

*Leader*

*Mediator*

*Educator*

*Mentor*

*Advocate*

*Optimist*

*Friend*

*The International Dyslexia Association*
*Founded in memory of Samuel T. Orton*
*November 14, 1997*

# ACCEPTANCE OF THE SAMUEL T. ORTON AWARD
## NOVEMBER 14, 1997, MINNEAPOLIS

*C. Wilson Anderson, Jr.*

Thank you. I am honored, flattered, humbled and, believe it or not, somewhat embarrassed by being chosen to receive this award.

When Eleanor Hall accepted this award in San Diego, she said, "I think that this has something to do about age!" When Sally Childs accepted this award in New York, she said, "Isn't it wonderful having young people discover what we have known all along!"

I say, "Because of this award, finally, I am going to be published in Annals, but I do worry that no one will read it!"

I am deeply indebted to so many people who have been so warm and gracious about sharing what they have learned and who have not used their various positions in the Society for financial gain. One of the great things about this organization is that presenters and leaders are approachable, generous, and knowledgeable.

One such warm and generous person is Margaret Rawson and she has been so patient with me since she met me in 1967. Several times she has taken me to the "Quaker version" of the wood shed. One time I was lamenting to her regarding the ignorance that is still out there even after all the work that the Society has been doing. She reached over, patted my hand and said, "Wilson, the issue is not ignorance; it is presumed knowledge!"

I would first like to recognize the Nevin Huestad Foundation which, in 1967, provided me a grant so I could take the training offered by Paula Rome and Jean Osman. The grant was for $500.00 at a time I was earning $6,000 per year. I also have a list of over 10,000 of my close and personal friends that I would like to thank, but I painfully remember the Orton Conference in Rochester, Minnesota. Because of my love and respect for this audience, I have narrowed my list down quite a bit. If you are not on the short list, rest assured that you are on the long list! Here is the short list:

I want to thank Roger Saunders for his willingness to let a Midwest public school teacher present at an Orton Conference and for his steadfast friendship and mentorship over the years. I want to recognize the efforts of Paula and Howard Rome, Jean

Osmon, Regina Cicci, Alice Koontz, Bill Ellis, Emmie Flynn, Dorothy Whitehead, Pricilla Vail, Alice Ansara, Tori Greene, Rosa Hagin, Mary Lee Enfield, Paul and Pat Williams, Carl and Carolyn Kline, Marcia Henry who did a magnificent job as president during two very tough years, Sylvia Richardson, Ro Bowler, Drake Duane, Bob and Eleanor Hall, Dick and Molly Masland, Catherine Angle, Maureen Landry, Cheri Didie, Georgette and Emerson Dickman, Margery Roth, Lucia Karnes, and Iris Spano, for their advice and support. I would like to thank several current and former Branch Presidents, Mike Ryan, Billie Hill, Grant Farrell, Stan Antoff, Sophie Gibson, and Rosemary Williams, for their friendship and support. A big thank you goes to Anna Ramey, Gloria Davis, Harley Tomey, Martha Renner, and Le Ganschow for their gifts of these wonderful annual conferences. I'd like to recognize colleagues Elli Cross, Joan Stoner, Arlene Sonday, and my former Menninger partners, Michele Berg, Trudy Stegelman, and Carleen Franz.

Over the years I had the pleasure of knowing several Orton legends who were and are anything by shy about expressing their views, Ramalda Spalding, Beth Slingerland, Aylette Cox, June Orton, Renee Herman, Gil Schiffmann, Sally Childs, Jane McClelland, and Nina Traub. Finally, I give thanks to my students who taught me how to teach them when my training failed me.

There are two very special people who have come to the aid of the society on several critical occasions who have not, in my opinion, been properly recognized, and to whom, I feel the association owes its very existence today. In an emergency Len Hartwig stepped in as Treasurer and later Elly Hartwig stepped in as Executive Director. Len and Elly have my gratitude and heartfelt thanks for their devotion above and beyond the call of duty.

I also want to thank the National Office Staff, especially Cindy Ciresi. I admire the work of Tom Viall our Executive Director.

I have been the only president of this organization who was a public school teacher. As President, I pushed as hard as I could for cooperation between like-minded National organizations. Our reward was Mrs. Bush speaking to us in Washington DC. We are now seeing the results of our push for cooperation! I also pushed for collaborative efforts between the Orton-Gillingham Approach, Slingerland, MTA, Academic Language Therapy Association, Spalding, Herman, and Lindamood-Bell—not only so each house would be strong, but also so each house would have a partnership with and under the umbrella of International Multisensory Structured Language Education Council (IMSLEC). As we all became friends, in Kansas City and other places around the United States, we realized our commonalties and appreciated our differences. We began to see that internecine warfare was fruitless; the public enemy of "presumed knowledge" was too big. To all of you involved in this movement, I say a huge thank you for a difficult job well done. However, I beg all of you to respect our differences and hark back to the hypothetical question posed to either Orton or Gillingham, "Which way is right?" Their response will always be another question, "What will work to ensure the pupil is successful?"

Bob Nash, Director of Project Success at the University of Wisconsin in Oshgosh once told me that coming to the Orton Conferences was like returning to the well, not only to quench our thirst, but also to understand and to be understood. Reid Lyon says that 47% of American children need our knowledge and our skills. Dr. Orton was right and is right! The research is coming our way. Let's use the power of our well, and use the power of each other to take on the giant task that we must accomplish. The time is right, the time has to be now!

I am bothered by our new phrase used on our stationery, "Founded in memory of Samuel T. Orton." If all of you check your bylaws you will discover that we were founded in 1949 to *continue* the work of Samuel T. Orton and we are doing just that through the brilliant work of the NIH, Louisa Moats, Susan Brady, Gordon Sherman, Al Galaburda, and the late Norman Geschwind! It is all of this collective work which gives us the scientific, research-based weapons with which to fight the enemy of "Presumed Knowledge!"

The late Marion Welshman, in one of her Baltimore presentations, kept using the phrase "hangers-on." Finally I asked, "What are hangers-on?" She replied that these are the people who love us so much that they allow us to do what we think needs to be done!

I have been extraordinarily blessed beyond what I ever dreamed and any person deserves. I could not have done any of this without my wife Polly, our daughter Emily and her husband Kevin, our daughter Jennifer and her fiancé Tim, our son Matthew and his wife Kelly, and my almost 86 year old father and administrative assistant, Dr. C. Wilson Anderson.

In conclusion, I want to tell a story that Gil Schiffmann told me. There was an old man who was the last survivor of the great Johnstown, PA flood. All this man could talk about was what it was like to be the last survivor of the Johnstown flood. It got to the point that as he would wander around, people would run and hide because they did not want to hear him tell that story again! Finally, the Lord in his infinite wisdom took him to heaven. When he met St. Peter, he was asked if he wanted anything. He said, "Yes, I always wanted to tell people what it was like to be the last survivor of the Johnstown flood." St. Peter assembled all of heaven to hear the story. Whole language teachers put down their big books, coaches put down their pieces of chalk, Orton-Gillingham teachers put rubber bands around their sound packs, and all of heaven settled in to listen to this story. St. Peter introduced the speaker, and as St. Peter yielded the microphone, he said, "Noah is in the audience!"

There are many Noahs in this audience who are every bit if not more deserving of this wonderful award than I. It is just that my turn has come now, Thank you!

# PART I
## The Orton Tradition: Influences
## Past and Present

In the opening chapter of this volume, Marcia Henry reflects positively on the continuing influence that Orton has exerted on how we define, identify, and treat dyslexia, evident even in what some might consider "new" perspectives. In chapter 2, T. R. Miles and colleagues are much less sanguine about the shifts in definition and research focus in the years since Orton. The carefully considered perspectives of these highly influential leaders on either side of the Atlantic are both informative and thought-provoking.

The issue of how to define and remediate dyslexia is controversial, to say the least. Although basic research studies have shed much light on these topics in recent years, these papers remind us that we have a way to go to close the gap between clinical intuition, research-based diagnosis, and optimal treatment. At the same time, the three papers that begin this volume also demonstrate the great value that derives from the extensive communication between researcher and clinician.

Marcia Henry, author of chapter 1, has served as teacher, teacher trainer, and researcher. Most importantly, as leader of the International Dyslexia Association, she has served as consensus builder between clinicians, researchers, educators and policy makers. Her informative paper about the life and legacy of Samuel Orton reminds us that his dual roles as clinician and scientist are mutually informative. She urges us, as we work to contain the messiness with clean scientific definitions, to continue to address the complex needs of actual learners. She suggests that effective clinically-based interventions be acknowledged and undertood, even as research is used to shape new methods of instruction. In short, she asks that as a community, we work from both ends—that observation and clinical expertise be used to guide research and hypotheses and that research and hypotheses guide practice. It is this interface that defines IDA and it is clear from her articulate paper why it is that Henry was such a powerful force in furthering efforts in both research and practice.

In the United Kingdom, one of the most influential individuals at the nexus of research and practice is T. R. Miles. In the study described in chaper 2, Miles, M. Haslum and T. Wheeler applied two different definitions of dyslexia to calculate a gender ratio for dyslexia in an epidemiological sample of ten-year olds. Using a clinically based diagnosis derived from the Bangor Dyslexia Test, Miles et al. finds a strong preponderance of boys to girls (4.5 to 1); using a definition of reading disability that excludes clinical indicators other than "poor reading in relation to intelligence", they find a much smaller preponderance of boys to girls (1.7 to 1). The question that Miles et al. consider in their thoughtful discussion is whether the inclusion of classic "clinical" features identifies a unique form of dyslexia that is not present in all poor readers. The discussion leads directly to an empirical question well worth investigating, opening a dialog between research and practice.

The final paper in this section, by A. Fawcett, C. H. Singleton and L. Peer (head of the British Dyslexia Association) is almost celebratory in nature. It describes the collaborative efforts of researchers, educators, and politicians who have worked together to enact into law screening measures which will identify youngsters at an early age who are at risk for reading failure. Two research-based measures designed for this purpose are motivated and described. These efforts were successful: the British government has adopted universal assessment of preschool skills predictive of reading disability. What is impressive in this particular collaboration is the manner in which researchers and policy-makers have joined forces at multiple levels, providing a model for the kind of marriage needed to advance the understanding, prevention and remediation of reading disability to which the IDA and its sister organizations are dedicated.

# Structured, Sequential, Multisensory Teaching: The Orton Legacy

*Marcia K. Henry*

San Jose State University

*This manuscript is based on The Samuel Torrey Orton and June Lyday Orton Memorial Lecture, presented by Marcia K. Henry at the 48th Annual Conference of the International Dyslexia Association. The paper provides a selective biography of Samuel T. Orton, discusses his educational ideas and how they came to be, and considers how current educational research validates much of Orton's early thinking.*

I think it is extremely important, as The Orton Dyslexia Society, founded in memory of Samuel T. Orton, holds its 48th annual conference with its new name, The International Dyslexia Association (IDA), that we reflect on just who Samuel Orton was, what his educational ideas were, and how current educational research validates much of Orton's early thinking.

Samuel Orton was foremost a scientist. Most of his writing deals with the neurobiological concepts and theories surrounding dyslexia. In this paper, however, I concentrate on the educational aspects of Orton's work. Let me first mention that for many years there has been criticism of Orton's theory and practice, primarily because there was so little research carefully documenting his instruction and its consequences. In Minneapolis in 1978, during the 29th annual ODS conference, I was part of a panel that included Bob Nash of the University of Wisconsin at Oshkosh, Aylett Cox of Dallas, Lucia Karnes of Winston-Salem, and Maynard Reynolds of the University of Minnesota. The rest of us extolled the virtues of the Orton-Gillingham approach from

Annals of Dyslexia, Vol. 48, 1998
ISSN 0736-9387

our clinical experiences, but Dr. Reynolds reminded us, forcefully, that "anecdotal evidence is easily dismissed." He kept asking us where the scientific studies were that might verify our claims. His concern was shared by Dr. Carl Kline, whose 1977 paper in The Bulletin of The Orton Society was titled "Orton-Gillingham Methodology: Where Have All of the Researchers Gone?"

In this paper I hope to present evidence that supports the efficacy of instructional approaches derived from Orton's pioneering work. But, I first digress to introduce you to Samuel Torrey Orton: the scientist, the physician, the educator, the man.

## A BIOGRAPHICAL SKETCH

Orton was a pathologist, neuropathologist, neurologist, and psychiatrist. He was born October 15, 1879, in Columbus, Ohio, where his father, a geology professor, later presided as the first president of Ohio State University. Sam went to elementary school in Columbus, and later graduated from the Taft School in Watertown, Connecticut.

Orton received a B.S. degree from Ohio State and an M.D. from the University of Pennsylvania, followed by an M.A. in Education from Harvard. In the early 1900s, he served as a pathologist in Massachusetts, Ohio, and Montana, and held teaching positions in neuropathology at Harvard and in neurology at Clark University. A highlight of his career was studying with Dr. Alois Alzheimer in Breslau, Germany. He returned to the United States to become Pathology and Clinical Director of the Pennsylvania Hospital for Mental Diseases.

In 1917, while still at the hospital, Orton read Hinshelwood's manuscript on "Congenital Word Blindness" and was intrigued by the discussion of reading problems in bright children. His interest in this paper was a first step toward his work with children having, what Orton later called, "strephosymbolia." This most apt term was formed from the Greek roots meaning "twisted" and "symbols" and describes the types of errors frequently made in reading and writing by the children to whom it applies.

In 1919 Orton was urged to come to Iowa to build and direct a psychopathic hospital system for the state and head the Department of Psychiatry at the University of Iowa Medical School. The laboratory unit where he spent so much of his time was later dedicated in his name.

Through a Rockefeller Foundation grant, Orton set up the first mobile health unit in the state of Iowa, and it was through this project in Greene County that he met MP. MP was aged 16 years, 2 months with a mental age of 11 years, 4 months, and an IQ of 71. Orton noted the following in his meeting with MP following the psychological testing: ". . . I was strongly impressed with the feeling that this estimate did not do justice to the boy's mental equipment, and that the low rating was to be explained by the fact that the test is inadequate to gage [sic] the equipment in a case of such a special disability. Further, it was easily seen that while he was unable to recall the visual impressions of words clearly enough to recognize them in print, he did make facile use of visual imagery of objects of rather complex type. I asked him, for example, questions concerning the adjustment of bearings in the V type automobile engine which required a good visualizing power for answer, and his replies were prompt and keen" (Orton 1925, p. 584).

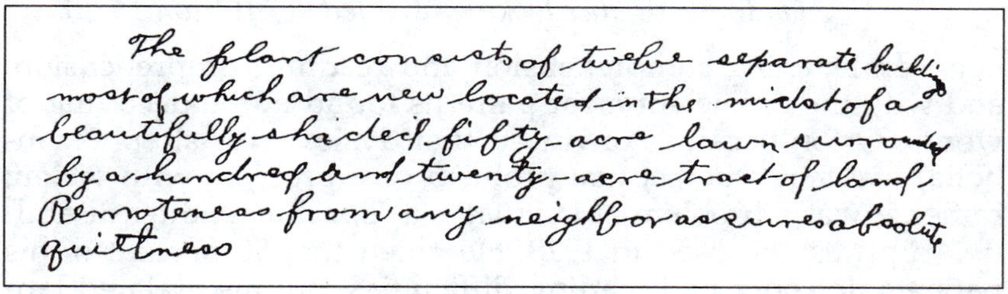

Figure 1. *MP's copying from text. "The plant consists of twelve separate buildings most of which are now located in the midst of a beautifully shaded fifty-acre lawn surrounded by a hundred and twenty-acre tract of land. Remoteness from any neighbor assures absolute quietness" (Orton 1925, p. 586).*

Orton was fascinated that while MP could read only at a primary grade level, his copying was nearly perfect (see figure 1). Orton concluded that MP's ". . . visual equipment was adequate to receive correct impressions of the stimuli and to translate them into one form of motion copying" (1925, p. 592). Clearly, this was not a visual defect. In contrast to his facility with copying, MP took over six minutes to read a similar passage consisting of 60 words in three sentences, and he made many errors. His errors in writing from dictation were also numerous (see figure 2). Orton suggested that MP had faulty sound association. Although he knew alphabet letters by name, "there was striking lack of association of certain letter sounds with the corresponding letter form"(1925, p. 589).

Orton went on to study other similar cases while working at the mental health clinic. He was fascinated with the discrepancy

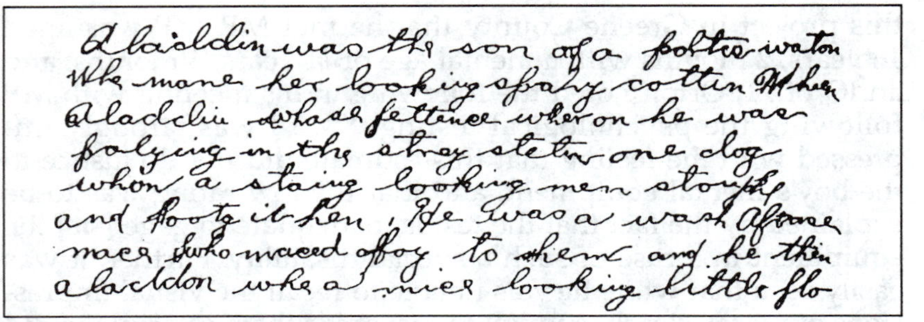

Figure 2.    MP's writing to dictation. This should read: "Aladdin
             was the son of a poor widow who made her living spin-
             ning cotton. When Aladdin was fifteen years old he was
             playing in the street one day when a strange-looking man
             stopped and looked at him. He was a wicked African
             magician who needed a boy to help him, and he thought
             Aladdin was a nice looking little fellow" (Orton 1925).

between listening comprehension and reading comprehension,
and with the consistent error patterns found in the decoding of
words. Orton became convinced that dyslexia (or strephosymbolia) was not a perceptual problem or a problem with vision;
rather, it was a problem of language, a "specific reading disability," a phrase he used in 1928. He noted that 50 percent of his
patients not only had reading difficulties, but also related language disorders including problems with receptive and expressive language, passage comprehension, spelling, and
composition. He later concluded that ". . . in a considerable proportion of cases of the reading disability there is evidence of difficulty acquiring other functions. . ., for example, disorders in
speech, special disability in spelling, special disability in writing, failure to acquire skilled movements with normal ease and
accuracy, difficulty in learning foreign languages after English
has been mastered. . . . " (1939, p. 60).

It is important to remember that Orton was not working in
isolation. He was fortunate to have assistants who were among
the greats in early cognitive and language research and practice.
Among the colleagues he hired for his work in Iowa were
Lauretta Bender, Marion Monroe, Donald Durrell, and June
Lyday. Neither did he have the luxury of focusing exclusively
on the scientific aspects of his research. In going through the
Orton files at Columbia, I was struck by the complete responsibility he took for those under his supervision. He dealt with
both academic and nonacademic issues among his colleagues
and staff such as harassment, plagiarism, politics, substance

abuse, and overriding all, budget constraints. Finally, Orton did not isolate himself from the community affected by his studies. As I studied the Orton Collection at Columbia University, I was moved by his willingness to speak to all kinds of audiences: the medical faculty, the local service clubs, the PTA, and students at local high schools.

Orton always spoke of the strengths of his patients, not only the weaknesses. His recurring theme was that the problem is not with the children: all are teachable with appropriate instruction. In a talk in 1924 to Marshalltown High School students, he asserted that, "Heredity and early environment determine limits only. That is, they determine potentialities or raw material, if you will, not its product." Orton's ideas were strongly influenced by the pluralistic theories of William James, the renowned psychologist. In speaking to a group of Oskaloosa teachers he noted that the failure to acquire reading is a disability rather than a defect. "This means we do not look upon them as deficiences which cannot be cured but rather as special handicaps requiring special methods or often simply more careful and painstaking application of usual methods."

The late Norman Geschwind paid tribute to Dr. Orton's work in Iowa by writing "Why Orton Was Right," published in the 1982 *Bulletin*. In this paper, Geschwind talked of the validity of many of Orton's scientific theories on dyslexia. Geschwind noted that in his original description of cases in 1925, Orton drew several major conclusions, a number of them specifically dealing with language and with instruction. These conclusions related to normal visual perception in dyslexics, the location of the disorder in the brain, and the prevalence of mirror writing, ambidexterity, and left-handedness among dyslexic individuals. The link between dyslexia and laterality became a personal fascination for Orton, who was extremely interested in "lefties." He collected pictures of left-handers such as Babe Ruth, Harpo Marx, Michelangelo and other artists, athletes, and celebrities. Geschwind himself, in research with Peter Behan (Geschwind 1983; Geschwind and Behan 1982), observed a much higher incidence of left-handedness in the dyslexic population than the nondyslexic population, although this finding has been difficult to replicate in more recent studies.

Geschwind also collected data consistent with Orton's theories about the relationship of stuttering to dyslexia (three of Orton's original 15 cases involved stuttering), and reiterated Orton's claim that dyslexia could not be studied or understood isolated from accompanying conditions. Orton had declared that poor handwriting, left-handedness, inverted letters, and stuttering ". . . all went together in severe cases" (1933 letter).

Geschwind credited Orton with observing the high rate of related disorders in the families of his patients such as the frequent clumsiness associated with dyslexia, and the accompanying poor spelling. Of spelling, Orton remarked "Spelling forms an almost insuperable obstacle to the strephosymbolic child. . . . These children can often learn to spell words by rote memory but this is apt to be very short lived. . . ." (1937, p. 84).

It is especially noteworthy, given today's emphasis on early speech, early identification, and phonological awareness, that Orton noted the frequency with which dyslexic children evidenced slowness in the acquisiton of spoken language. Orton also often inferred that, as Geschwind put it, "dyslexics themselves are frequently endowed with high talents in many areas"(1982, p. 21). Orton also emphasized the social/emotional aspects of dyslexia, a common concern today of psychiatrists (Kline 1978; Rome 1971) and psychologists (Rawson 1988; Ryan 1994).

Albert Galaburda, Gordon Sherman, and others continue to conduct brain research of the sort initially developed by Orton and Geschwind. New findings of brain structure and function can only add to our knowledge of dyslexia, and may lead to even more effective teaching strategies. Presaging current opinions, Orton believed that the cause of dyslexia undoubtedly had a biologic basis, but thought the treatment should be educational, such as teaching aspects of the structure of the English language. As early as 1925, six years before he began his work with Anna Gillingham, Orton tentatively suggested that ". . . the logical training for these children would be that of extremely thorough repetitive drill on the fundamentals of phonic association with letter forms both visually presented and reproduced in writing, until the correct associations were built up and the permanent elision of the reversed images and reversals in direction was assured" (1925, p. 614).

Orton relied on the ideas conveyed by Grace Fernald and Helen Keller in 1921, when they wrote as follows about several cases they studied: ". . . lip and hand kinaesthetic elements seem to be the essential link between the visual cue and the various associations which give it word meaning. In other words, it seems to be necessary for the child to develop a certain kinaesthetic background before he can apperceive the visual sensations for which the printed words form the stimulus. Even the associations between the spoken and the printed word seem not to be fixed without the kinaesthetic links" (Fernald and Keller 1921, p. 376).

As Orton's interest in intervention grew, his personal life also underwent change. The first Mrs. Orton, Mary Follett Orton, died after a long illness in September, 1926. In 1928 Orton married a former social worker on his staff, June Lyday, who became his professional partner as well as his wife.

After leaving Iowa in 1928 because of differences of opinion in "administration and business policies . . . far out of harmony with [his] ideals for the teaching of medicine and for research . . . ," and loss of research funding, Orton moved back to Columbus where he wrote many articles and reports related to the Iowa research projects. The Ortons then moved to New York where together they began a private practice in "neurology, psychiatry, and specific language disabilities." Orton also served as neuropathologist at the New York Neurological Institute and professor of neurology and neuropathology at the College of Physicians and Surgeons at Columbia University. He became president of the American Psychiatric Association in 1929 and later headed the Association for Research in Nervous and Mental Diseases.

It was at the Neurological Institute that Dr. Orton designed the Language Research Project, again funded by the Rockefeller Foundation, and where he and Anna Gillingham became acquainted. Working with Dr. Paul Dozier, Dr. Edwin Cole, and Dr. Earl Chesher, they immersed themselves in the study and treatment of specific language disability. Gillingham, a psychologist at New York's Ethical Cultural School, had read of Orton's theories of cerebral dominance and strephosymbolia, and of his interest in both diagnosis and instruction. They began their professional collaboration in 1931.


## THE ORTON-GILLINGHAM TECHNIQUE

Let us look briefly at the Orton-Gillingham technique itself. Orton had requested that Gillingham organize the instruction to conform to his neurological hypotheses. He wanted the instruction carefully structured but not programmed, and it was to be adaptable to individual needs. Mrs. Orton, in an interview in 1974 with Margaret Rawson, said that while Orton gave Anna Gillingham the principles of organization, she took the ball and ran with it. "She organized the material or put the language into some sort of rational organization for use in teaching and that, I think, was her great contribution for the state-of-the art."

Gillingham and her colleague, Bessie Stillman, insisted that children with specific reading difficulties could not "learn to read by 'sight word' methods, even when these are later reinforced by 'functional,' 'incidental,' 'intrinsic' or 'analytical' phonics, based on 150-200 learned words, or by tracing procedures (suggested by Fernald) such as are sometimes employed." They noted that their technique ". . . is based upon the constant use of associations of all of the following: how a letter or word looks, how it sounds and how the speech organs or the hand in writing feels when producing it" (Gillingham and Stillman 1956, p. 17).

In their manuals, Gillingham and Stillman direct the teacher to assist children in making numerous visual, auditory, and kinesthetic-tactile linkages as portrayed by their "language triangle." For example, a child first sees a letter, then traces it, and says the letter name and/or sound. Or, the sound is made by the teacher and the name is given by the pupil.

Correct letter formation is emphasized while children are learning the letters and their corresponding sounds. Children with dyslexia often persist in reversing letters or transposing letters within words, and knowing how to form the letters helps in correcting the reversals. For example, to assist children in correcting reversals, teachers point out different order of strokes for letter formation (see figure 3).

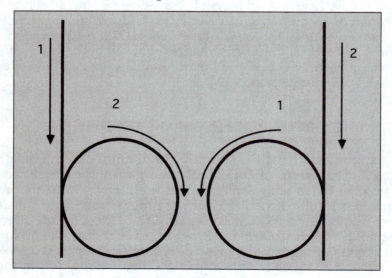

*Figure 3.     Letter-formation for b and d.*

June Orton described Dr. Orton's two basic principles for re-training as:

1. "Training for simultaneous association of visual, auditory, and kinesthetic language stimuli—in reading cases, tracing and sounding the visually presented word and maintaining consistent direction by following the letters with the fingers during the sound synthesis of syllables and words"; and

2. "Finding such units as the child can use without difficulty in the field of his particular disability and directing the training toward developing the process of fusing these smaller units into larger and more complex wholes"(1966a, p. 131).

Margaret Rawson's thoughtful description of this approach embraces these two principles. "Dyslexic students need a different approach to learning language from that employed in most classrooms. They need to be taught, slowly and thoroughly, the basic elements of their language—the sounds and the letters which represent them—and how to put these together and take them apart. They have to have their writing hands, eyes, ears, and voices working together in conscious organization and retention of their learning" (personal correspondence).

Gillingham and Stillman wrote four editions of their Manual, the first bound edition in 1936 (affectionately called "Old Brown"), and then later editions in 1946 (Old Blue), 1956 (Red), and 1960 (Green). The writing of the final green edition was prompted by Dr. Dozier to bring the manual into conformity with the new *Webster's Dictionaries*.

In 1935 Gillingham and Stillman left New York to set up a Gillingham program at the Punahoe School in Honolulu where they trained Beth Slingerland and worked closely with her for two years. Gillingham and Stillman returned to New York in 1938 and continued their work, training teachers, establishing programs, and managing the distribution of their materials.

In *Perspectives* (Fall, 1997), Mary Helen Robinson Wells, who worked directly with the Ortons in 1939 and 1940, writes of the remarkable partnership they established. She tells of Orton's genuine concern for each child, parent, and teacher who came to him for help, and remembers him ". . . as a brilliant pioneer in his profession and a warm sympathetic human being, keenly aware of and interested in everything and everyone" (p. 8).

Between 1939 and 1944, with his third Rockefeller grant in hand, Orton concentrated his research on children with special difficulty in learning motor skills. During this time, he lost several research assistants to World War II, and brought Katrina de Hirsch from England to work with him.

Dr. and Mrs. Orton continued their partnership until 1948 when Dr. Orton died from complications after a fall at HWIMSY, the vacation home he had built—and whimsically named—himself.

About a year after Dr. Orton's death, Mrs. Orton organized an invitational memorial dinner at the Croyden Hotel, where plans for an Orton Society in his memory were discussed. The first annual business meeting of the Society was held in 1950. By then, Mrs. Orton had joined the Bowman Gray Medical School in North Carolina, and with Dr. Lloyd Thompson, had founded the language clinic.[1]

## RESEARCH VALIDATION OF ORTON'S APPROACH

With this background in mind, let us turn to the research issues surrounding Orton's educational approach. Jeanne Chall, on receiving the Samuel T. Orton Award in 1996, said: ". . . it was not until my research for The Great Debate that I became aware of his (Orton's) exceptional achievements in the study of reading and reading disabilities. That a physician was able to delve so deeply into the theories of reading and language development was unusual enough. But, that he found an effective educational treatment for reading disability and also a means for preventing it was rare indeed" (Chall, 1997, p. xv).

Chall also reflected on what Orton's reaction would be to current practices. "I often wonder what he would say about what is happening in reading today. I think he would be content to know that his theories and insights had been confirmed many times by the research in reading, by clinical experience, and by student achievement. But, I think he would also be saddened by our making the same mistakes again and again and again" (Chall, 1997, p. xv).

Notice that Chall refers not only to reading research and to clinical experience, but also to student achievement. For even when statistical controls are not provided, it is the gains that we see in student achievement, and the related gains in self-esteem, that motivate us to continue teaching dyslexic students.

[1] Bessie Stillman died in 1947, and Anna Gillingham continued her professional career until her death in 1964. June Lyday Orton kept teaching and writing until her death on March 12, 1977.

As Chall also reminds us, we cannot overlook some outstanding studies based on current clinical practice. Although clinical and case studies are not readily accepted by the scientific community, to ignore them altogether would miss the importance of the work of Margaret Rawson and many others. Indeed, the Rawson (1965, 1995) longitudinal study was based on an early hypothesis of Orton's (1928), that ". . . the reading disability forms a graded series in severity; that it is not generically related to general mental retardation, and. . . that proper methods of retraining, if started early enough, may be expected to overcome the difficulty" (J. L. Orton, 1966b, p. 65). Orton himself studied 175 children who bore out his conviction that ". . . these cases form a series graded in severity from the mild case in which spontaneous correction occurs under the ordinary teaching system to the extreme case in which practically no reading facility is acquired without special instruction" (J. L. Orton, 1966b, p. 66).

Rawson rank-ordered the boys at Rose Valley between 1930 and 1947 according to her Language Learning Facility Scale, based on Orton's continuous scale of severity in the presence of the language difficulty factor. She concluded that dyslexic boys are not necessarily poor academic and occupational risks, and in fact, are as capable of equally high levels of achievement as nondyslexics when they receive adequate instruction. Her follow-up report, some 40 to 55 years after her initial testing, verified these conclusions.

I also call your attention to a collection entitled "Clinical Studies of Multisensory Structured Language Instruction for Students with Dyslexia and Related Disorders" (McIntyre and Pickering 1996). These clinical studies document results of instructional techniques influenced by Samuel Orton, and I recommend them especially to clinicians and teachers. The studies focus on Orton-Gillingham and its offspring including Alphabetic Phonics, Herman, Project Read, Slingerland, Spalding, Wilson, and others. In the same volume, Sylvia Richardson provides a review of the history of multisensory instruction for those wanting a complete picture of this type of intervention.

One important clinical effort involves the Project Read work begun in the Bloomington Public Schools by two outstanding educators, Mary Lee Enfield and Tori Green. Enfield's (1976) doctoral dissertation on Project Read, "An Alternate Classroom Approach to Meeting Specific Learning Needs of Children with Reading Problems," showed that children with specific language disability could achieve or exceed grade level in reading and spelling, in the regular classroom, when taught by general education teachers trained in her classroom adaptation of the Orton-Gillingham approach. Follow-up studies by Enfield (1988), Greene (1991), and Stoner (1991) showed similar results. The best news—for teachers, students, parents, and the district—was that there was a significant reduction in the number of children requiring tutoring or special education services.

Whereas numerous case and clinical studies have demonstrated the effectiveness of structured multisensory approaches for many children, few long-term prospective studies had been conducted. This was corrected beginning in 1965 when the National Institutes of Health (NIH) expressed interest in funding reading research. In 1985 the Health Research Extension Act resulted in a new charge to the National Institute of Child Health and Human Development (NICHD) to improve the quality of reading research by conducting longitudinal, experimental studies. Reid Lyon has led the NICHD reading research effort by coordinating over 100 researchers in medicine, psychology, and education at approximately 14 centers around the country. By establishing detailed sampling requirements and increasing scientific rigor, Lyon and his team have produced a growing body of highly replicable findings in the area of early reading acquisition and reading difficulties. These findings have been reported in over 2,000 refereed journal articles since 1965.

Many of these articles have provided scientific evidence for what many of us know from clinical work. First, as Orton predicted 70 years ago, dyslexia has a biological basis. Second, and again supporting Orton's early theories, dyslexia often occurs with other disorders, such as social adjustment, attention deficit, and problems in written expression. Third, the great majority (over 80 percent) of children diagnosed as having learning disabilities also have primary problems in reading. Importantly, we find that the most reliable indicator of a reading problem is an inability to decode single words, and this inability is probably due to a problem with phonological, specifically phonemic, awareness. Persons with dyslexia lack the speed and accuracy to decode words fluently. This problem of decoding also affects the dyslexic child's reading comprehension. I might add that Orton made similar observations over 70 years ago.

Approximately three years ago, NICHD began funding research directly related to intervention. Several groups have now published numerous articles related to their preliminary analyses. I will try to summarize some of the NICHD research as well as other studies that relate to some of the premises held by Samuel Orton.

Dr. Orton, too, was interested in the precursors to specific language disabilities. He noted that problems in early language acquisition often foretold later problems with written language. This has been substantiated by numerous research projects.

Hollis Scarborough (1998) has completed a meta-analysis of numerous studies on early correlates and predictors of reading disability. She divides her data into categories for "Print-specific knowledge/skills" and "Non-print-specific abilities." Scarborough notes that "Not surprisingly, measures of skills that are directly related to reading and writing—including knowledge about letter identities, about letter-sound relationships, and about the mechanics and functions of book reading—have yielded the highest simple correlations with subsequent reading scores. Each of these predictors, on its own, has typically accounted for about 21–31 percent of the variance in later reading achievement. Among the other measures studied, four stand out as the strongest predictors of reading, each accounting for about 18–24 percent of the variance in later achievement scores: confrontation naming (expressive vocabulary), general language ability, sentence/story recall, and phonological awareness. Somewhat weaker effects (10–17 percent of reading variance) have been obtained for another six predictors, all measures of general ability and various narrower facets of language skill. Weaker average correlations have been obtained for the nine other kindergarten abilities that have been examined, including speech production and perception, visual and verbal short-term memory measures, and other nonverbal abilities"(Scarborough 1998, pp. 91–92).

I do want to remark on the factor of phonemic awareness because this appears to be the center of current research. Clearly, as Scarborough shows us, there are other factors to consider seriously, but the benefits of phonological awareness training is clear. To my knowledge, Orton did not use the term "phonological awareness" but did remark on the fact that many of his patients lacked an understanding of the role sounds play in words, and had difficulty with understanding letter-sound relationships. Numerous studies support the work begun almost 30 years ago by Isabelle Liberman and Donald Shankweiler. The NICHD research teams converge on one research finding: all conclude that phonological awareness (primarily phonemic awareness) is necessary for reading acquisition.

Once children enter school, usually eager and willing to learn to read, they need to learn the alphabetic code. Yet some children do not: they fail to learn strategies for decoding unfamiliar words. Educators in California were abashed as they looked at 1994–1995 school year test scores and found that 40 percent of California fourth graders were reading significantly below grade level. Two California Task Forces, one led by Bill Honig (who as Superintendent of Public Instruction had brought whole language/literature-based instruction to the state in 1987), led the way in demanding basic skill instruction in phonemic awareness and phonics, not only for dyslexic students, but for all students. Honig's recommendations (Honig 1996) were largely based on NICHD data.

Orton, too, believed that decoding (word recognition) was the leading problem for dyslexic children, and urged early intervention. Long before Honig, Orton saw the connection between teaching method and ability to learn to read. As early as 1928, Orton wrote that most of the referrals to the mobile unit came from the school district where ". . . the children were not permitted to learn the alphabet and hence to attempt phonetic syntheses of words until they had learned 90 words by sight" (p. 1099). Later researchers, notably Linnea Ehri (1989) and Bob Calfee (1983), made similar points regarding the crucial role of instruction in the development of reading. Ehri noted the importance of teaching to provide beginning readers with a full knowledge of the spelling system: the orthographic and phonological connections. She urged us to perfect the way we teach children to read and spell. Calfee stated that most children with reading disability "reflect an instructional dysfunction rather than a constitutional shortcoming of the child" (Calfee 1983, p. 26). I must add that this "dysteachia" is not because teachers do not want to teach children to read, but because so many teacher preparation programs do not prepare them to teach reading adequately.

Brady and Moats, in their position paper on teacher preparation adopted by the Board of The International Dyslexia Association (1997), urge informed instruction; that is, instruction based on research findings. They conclude that ". . . both research results and teaching practice indicate that children profit from instruction in reading that is explicit, systematic, and sequential" (p. 9). I believe we can safely add the term "multisensory" to that statement.

Do we have research that validates such teaching? The evidence presented below represents the work of NICHD researchers, several of whom have described their intervention research in *Perspectives* (Fall 1997).

In Houston, Barbara Foorman and her team used "Alphabetic Phonics," developed by Aylett Cox, as one experimental treatment condition. They conclude that, "In a study with 113 second and third graders identified with reading disabilities, children who received an Orton-Gillingham, synthetic phonics approach [Alphabetic Phonics] outperformed children receiving a combined synthetic/analytic phonics approach or a sight-word approach in the development of literary related skills" (Foorman, Francis, Beeler, Winikates, and Fletcher 1997, p. 63). I was especially interested in whether or not the Foorman teachers in the synthetic approach stressed the multisensory pathways in the intervention, especially the kinesthetic-tactile. Foorman, in a personal correspondence (September, 1997), responded that "The Alphabetic Phonics training provided to our teachers through the Neuhaus Center here in Houston does emphasize kinesthetic-tactile modality. They are consistent in letter formation."

In Florida, Torgesen and his colleagues (1995, 1997) have been conducting both prevention and remediation studies. The Torgesen team use the multisensory Lindamood Auditory Discrimination in Depth approach, which they call the Phonological Awareness Plus Synthetic Phonics (PASP) as one treatment condition. While early analyses revealed that the Lindamood program results in significantly greater progress in word attack (nonsense word reading) and phonological awareness, there were no differences among the treatment groups in whole word reading accuracy or fluency.

Two factors might bear on these results. First, while the Lindamood program emphasizes the importance of the kinesthetic-speech pathway in careful articulation of speech sounds, it does not emphasize the kinesthetic-tactile for letter formation. Lindamood (personal communication) does give value to specific tactile exercises with letters for children for whom writing is a real problem. Torgesent et al. suggest that some children may require even more intensive decoding instruction "involving units of word structure larger than the single phoneme" (Torgesen, Wagner, and Rashotte 1997, p. 232).

The Torgesen intervention also resulted in no differences in reading comprehension among the treatment groups. I suggest that while phonological awareness training alone is a necessary but not sufficient condition for success in decoding, decoding ability alone is probably not necessarily a sufficient condition for success in comprehending a passage. Perhaps future research will consider the strategies for intervention in comprehension as well as in decoding. For example, do teachers make the distinction between narrative and expository text, and teach the elements of story versus exposition? Do they differentiate between the levels of rhetorical structure and functional structure in expository paragraphs? Are text features such as bold print, headings, and graphics emphasized? Do students learn to predict and summarize material they are reading through webs, matrices, hierarchies, story graphs, and other graphic organizers?

Returning to the topic of decoding, few other studies have looked as specifically as Foorman's and Torgesen's at the association between the various sensory modalities. Felton (1993) at Bowman Gray identified 81 kindergartners as at-risk for reading disability. These students were placed in groups of eight in regular classrooms, either meaning emphasis (context group) or code emphasis (code group). She found that the code emphasis group earned higher mean scores at the end of Grade 1 in reading phonetically regular and irregular real words, reading nonsense words, passage comprehension, and spelling predictable and unpredictable words. At the end of second grade, the code group was significantly better at reading phonetically regular polysyllabic real words as well as decoding nonsense words. Based on these findings, Felton concluded that the following elements are critical to the success of a beginning reading program for at-risk children:

• provide direct instruction in language analysis;
• provide direct teaching of the alphabetic code;
• teach reading and spelling in coordination;
• provide intensive reading instruction; and
• teach for automaticity.

Reid Lyon, speaking in late September to a joint conference of the Wisconsin Branch of IDA, Wisconsin LDA, and the Medical College of Wisconsin noted that some students in the NIH intervention projects had not made adequate progress in reading. Approximately 5 percent of children initially performing in the lowest 10th–15th percentile on measures of phoneme awareness and word recognition tasks do not make substantial gains, even in synthetic code programs that include phonemic awareness training. We may infer that these children have more severe disability and require even more intensive intervention, consistent with Orton's continuous scale of severity.

Professor Laura Fredrick (1997) of Georgia State University, appearing before the Committee on Education and the Workforce of the U.S. House of Representatives, presented the six principles of effective reading instruction based on current research:

1. Begin teaching phonemic awareness at an early age.
2. Teach each sound-spelling correspondence explicitly.
3. Teach frequent, highly regular sound-spelling relationships systematically.
4. Show children exactly how to sound out words.
5. Use connected, decodable text for children to practice the sound-spelling relationships they learn.
6. Use interesting stories to develop language comprehension.

She lamented that few teachers are well prepared to teach these principles.

Few of the NIH studies are specifically investigating the effects of the various treatments on spelling. Based on other studies that have looked at spelling (Enfield 1976; Henry 1988, 1989; Oakland, Black, Stanford, Nussbaum, and Balise 1998), we can expect that the gains in spelling will be less dramatic than in reading.

Nor have NIH-funded studies systematically evaluated the role of handwriting instruction as a factor in improving reading and spelling. Studies by Berninger and her team at the University of Washington (Berninger, in press) are an exception, looking at several aspects of language arts instruction. They screened nearly 700 first graders and identified 144 children with handwriting problems. Children were randomly assigned to one of five handwriting treatments or to a control group. Treatment groups included copy, motor imitation, numbered arrow cues, memory retrieval, and numbered arrow cues + memory retrieval. The latter treatment was most effective in improving handwriting and compositional fluency. This treatment, however, was not combined with specific teaching of letter-sound correspondences as it is in an Orton-Gillingham approach.

Lyon (September 1977) remarked that we probably know only 30 percent of what there is to know about reading acquisition and teaching reading. We should all encourage more research in reading and the related language arts. As the NIH studies continue, my hope is that researchers will look more closely at associating the three basic modalities useful in learning to read and spell. It is clear that some children will need more intensive one-on-one instruction, not only reading, but also in spelling and writing.

In this paper, I have only mentioned a few of the many American researchers who are designing and completing intervention studies. There are many others investigating reading processes and instruction throughout the world: In Great Britain—Maggie Snowling, Charles Hulme, Uta Frith, Lynnette Bradley, Peter Bryant, and Usha Goswami. In Scotland—Gavin Reid, In Wales—Elaine and Tim Miles. In Scandinavia—Torleiv Hoien. In Norway—Bente Hagvedt. In Sweden—Ingvar Lundberg and Jan Alms. In Denmark—Carston Elbro and Kjeld Johannsen. In Finland—Heikki Lytonnen. In The Netherlands—Dirk Bakker and Kees von den Bos. In Germany—Renate Valtin and Edith Klasen. In the Czech Republic—Zdenek Matecjek. People all over the world are trying to find the most effective programs for children with dyslexia. And, because of the Internet, we can all keep up with one another's work. E-mail and the Internet have become a standard means of communication for those of us interested in cross-cultural research on language and reading. Orton, an innovator himself, would be delighted that this new technology, in both medicine and education, can be used to so effortlessly transmit new findings, theoretical concepts, and instructional ideas.

Although all of this research is of extreme importance, and will hopefully result in better teacher preparation for teachers in both regular and special education (and, therefore, in better teaching), we can neither neglect nor discard the voices of dyslexics themselves. Samuel Orton would be so very proud of his former client, Delos Smith. He would have loved to know computer whiz and writer, Tom West; author, Carolyn Janover; investment banker, Charles Schwab; sculptor Malcolm Alexander; young poet Samantha Abeel; businessman and author, John Corcoran; British actress, Susan Hampshire; physician, Garth Vaz; mountain climber, Ellie Hawkins; opera singer, Patrick Blackwell; polar explorer, Ann Bancroft; artist P. Buckley Moss; neuroscientist Annette Jenner; the "boys" from Rose Valley; and the many other productive, successful, and creative dyslexics among us today.

I doubt that Orton ever met the late Russell Varian, born in 1898, but they would have been immediate compatriots. Long after discovering the klystron microwave tube in 1937, used first by Britain to spot German bombers and crucial in the Allied struggle against the Luftwaffe in World War II, Russell Varian participated in a study on creativity. In that study, he reminisced about his childhood in Palo Alto and remembered, "In my youth I did get knocked around a bit . . . and my particular difficulties with reading, writing, spelling, and the whole package of skills related to visual symbiology of language added to this . . . Because of these factors, I did have somewhat of an inferiority complex and a fear of the judgment of other people, although I always knew full well that I saw so much more in the world about me than the people who were inclined to call me stupid, that there wasn't much comparison" (Varian 1983, p. 45).

Russell's wife, in her insightful biography on the Varian brothers, *The Inventor and the Pilot* (1983) noted that Dr. Percy Davidson, a Stanford University professor who was experimenting with phonetics in teaching reading, began working with Russell. Dorothy Varian concluded that ". . . if it hadn't been for Dr. Davidson, Russell might have been illiterate all his life" (p. 45).

## SUMMARY

Current research on written language instruction validates many of the principles established by Orton and his colleagues almost three-quarters of a century ago, regarding a phonetic basis for reading instruction within a structured, sequential, multisensory model. This instruction must be based on learning the structure of English and its alphabetic code, and contain phonologically-based training. Although the importance of teachers knowing and understanding the structure of English becomes clear, Moats (1994) concluded that, regrettably, most teachers do not have this knowledge.

In my own doctoral dissertation (Henry 1988), and having taught the Orton-Gillingham approach for 25 years, I designed a model for consideration (see figure 4).

My research concluded that if teachers organize an integrated decoding/spelling curriculum in this fashion, and teach the few spelling rules corresponding to each cell in a multisensory way, their students will be well on their way to reading and spelling. In this model, the three structural patterns become the strategies available to attack unfamiliar words. Readers cannot rely on phonics alone, as sounding letter-by-letter works only for one syllable at a time. We need to access strategies for dividing longer words into syllables, and for recognizing the morpheme or meaning units in words (the prefixes, suffixes, and roots). As approximately 90 percent of English words come from Anglo-Saxon, Romance, or Greek origins, it is also useful to contrast words by the characteristics of their origin (pointing out the scientific nature of Greek based words and the use of special spellings such as "ch", "ph", and "y", as in *chlorophyll*).

|  | LETTER-SOUND CORRESPONDENCE | SYLLABLE PATTERNS | MORPHEME PATTERNS |
|---|---|---|---|
| ANGLO-SAXON | <u>Consonants</u><br>mad   step   that<br><u>Vowels</u><br>pin/pine  part  coin | rabbit   silver  hobo<br><br>cabin   turtle   poem | hardware   railroad<br>like<br>unlike<br>unlikel;y |
| ROMANCE | schwa:<br>direction<br>spatial<br>excellent | inter-<br>intra<br>-ity | construction<br>erupting<br>conducter |
| GREEK | phonograph<br>scholar<br>sympathy | hyper<br>micro | microscope<br>chloroplast<br>physiology |

Figure 4.    *Framework for curriculum and instruction based on word structure and word origin.*

I also want to encourage the teaching of decoding and spelling, systematically and explicitly, beyond Grade 2 or 3. The NICHD studies are mostly early intervention studies, but many older children need programs as desperately as their younger brothers and sisters.

Decoding and spelling should be taught throughout the grades until all aspects of language structure have been covered. Obviously, first and second graders will not be ready for the Latin and Greek word roots so necessary in upper-grade reading. Figure 5 illustrates a grade-by-grade sequence for instruction, beginning with phonological awareness, and moving

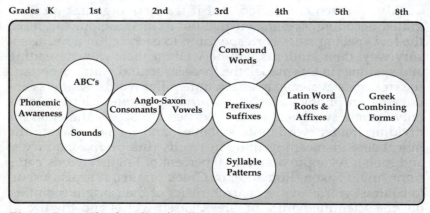

Figure 5.    *The decoding/spelling continuum: A sequence for instruction.*

on to letter-sound correspondences, syllable patterns, compound words, and Anglo-Saxon, Latin, and Greek affixes and roots (Henry 1997). I am pleased to say that Olson and Wise, and their colleagues at the University of Colorado, are studying the effects of specific types of instruction for reading and spelling on students in the upper elementary grades, and that Berninger and her team at the University of Washington are looking at intervention in secondary school.

To summarize what Orton and current research might emphasize about effective intervention for children with dyslexia, we know that we must start by stimulating and encouraging oral language. Prior to former schooling, we can informally begin some phonological awareness training. We need to articulate words clearly, in order to enhance children's awareness of speech patterns, of phonemes, and of the placement of the tongue and of other muscles of the mouth and throat.

We must then begin introducing the alphabetic code because not all children master the code without help. We must explicitly teach children the alphabet itself and point out the difference in upper and lower case letters. We can then teach the common letter patterns, or graphemes, along with the corresponding sounds, or phonemes. We should reinforce these patterns with both kinesthetic-speech and kinesthetic-motor patterns as we secure the "feel" of making the sound or letter in memory. We teach children to synthesize sounds for reading, and to analyze them for spelling.

As we teach the structure of English spelling, we need to incorporate the few corresponding spelling rules. And we should follow a continuum for integrated decoding and spelling instruction throughout the elementary school years and into middle and high school.

The University of Colorado team states it nicely: "Students with reading disabilities will probably need direct instruction and much practice on automaticity, on learning to be flexible with the vowel sounds and stress in sounding out words, and on spelling, writing, and reading for understanding to have all these skills transfer into strong and successful reading and writing" (Wise, Olson, and Ring 1997, p. 271).

Toward the end of his career, Orton was the ultimate scientist. In his last publication, in 1946, Orton maintained his open-minded, never doctrinaire, position as he noted: "Whether or not our theory is right, I do not know, but I do know that the methods of retraining which we have derived from that viewpoint have worked. I do not claim them to be a panacea for reading troubles of all sorts, but I do feel that we understand the blockade which occurs so frequently in children with good minds, and which results in the characteristic reading disability of the strephosymbolic type of childhood" (1946, p. 25).

The words of Paul Irvine, writing about Samuel Orton in *Pioneers in Special Education* (1969) seem especially appropriate: "Samuel Torrey Orton: With brilliant tenacity, he sought solutions to the perplexities and the dilemmas posed by children who should but could not read. Seeking specific determinants and causes, he never lost sight of the total child. Hewing to a medical etiology, his remedial approaches were by and large educational. His voice, uncertainly and hesitantly heard in his day, rings clear and vibrant in ours" (p. 317).

## ACKNOWLEDGMENTS:

My appreciation to Paula Rome and Jean Osman, my teachers and mentors, for their generosity of spirit and cooperation over almost 40 years. I want to thank Lucia Karnes, Paula Rome, and Roger Saunders for the insights and information they provided about both Samuel Torrey Orton and June Lyday Orton. Special thanks go to Margaret Rawson for her generosity in sharing her knowledge through her personal archives, reports, correspondence, and library.

*References*

Berninger, V. W. in press. Specific reading and writing disabilities in young children: Assessment, prevention, and intervention. In B. Y. L. Wong, ed., *Learning about Learning Disabilities*, 2nd ed. San Diego: Academic Press.

Brady, S., and Moats, L. 1997. *Informed instruction for reading Success: Foundations for teacher preparation*. Baltimore, MD: The Orton Dyslexia Society.

Calfee, R. C. 1983. The mind of the dyslexic. *Annals of Dyslexia* 33, 9–28.

Chall, J. 1996. Acceptance of S. T. Orton Award, 47th Annual Conference, *The Orton Dyslexia Society*, Boston, MA.

Ehri, L. 1989. The development of spelling knowledge and its role in reading acquisition and reading disability. *Journal of Learning Disabilities* 22, 356–65.

Enfield, M. L. 1976. An alternate classroom approach to meeting special learning needs of children with reading problems. Unpublished doctoral dissertation, University of Minnesota, Minneapolis.

Enfield, M. L. 1988. The quest for literacy. *Annals of Dyslexia* 38, 8–21.

Fernald, G. M., & Keller, H. 1921. The effect of kinesthaetic factors in the development of word recognition in the case of non-readers. *Journal of Educational Research*, 4, 355-377.

Felton, R. H. 1993. Effects of instruction on the decoding skills of children with phono-logical-processing problems. *Journal of Learning Disabilities* 26(9), 583–89.

Foorman, B. R., Francis, D. J., Beeler, T., Winikates, D., and Fletcher, J. M. 1997. Early in-terventions for children with reading problems: Study designs and preliminary findings. *Learning Disabilities* 8, 63–71.

Fredrick, L. D. 1997. Statement of Laura D. Fredrick. Paper presented to Committee on Education and the Workforce, United States House of Representives at The Hearing on Teachers: The Key to Helping America Read, September 3, Washington, DC.

Geschwind, N. 1982. Why Orton was right. *Annals of Dyslexia* 32, 13–30.

Geschwind, N. 1983. Biological associations of left-handedness. *Annals of Dyslexia* 33, 29–40.

Geschwind, N., and Behan, P. 1982. Left-handedness: Association with immune disease, migraine, and developmental learning disorder. *Proceedings of the National Academy of Science*, 79, 5097–5100.

Gillingham, A., and Stillman, B. W. 1956. *Remedial Training for Children with Specific Disability in Reading, Spelling and Penmanship*, 5th Ed. Bronxville, NY: Anna Gillingham.

Greene, J. F. 1991. Systematic phonology: The critical element in teaching reading and language to dyslexics. Paper presented to the 18th Scientific Conference of the Rodin Remediation Academy, Bern, Switzerland. Published in McIntrye & Pickering, 1996, pp. 173–79.

Henry, M. K. 1988. Understanding English orthography: Assessment and instruction for decoding and spelling. *Dissertation Abstracts International* 48, 2841-A. (University Microfilms No. 88–00,951).

Henry, M. K. 1989. Children's word structure knowledge: Implications for decoding and spelling instruction. *Reading and Writing: An Interdisciplinary Journal* 2, 135–52.

Henry, M. K. 1997. The decoding/spelling continuum. *Dyslexia: An International Journal of Research and Practice* 3(3), 178–89.

Honig, B. 1996. *Teaching our Children to Read*. Thousand Oaks, CA: Corwin Press.

Irvine, P. 1969. Pioneers in special education: Samuel T. Orton. *Journal of Special Education* 3(4), 317.

Kline, K. L. 1977. Orton-Gillingham methodology: Where have all the researchers gone? *Bulletin of the Orton Society* 27, 82–87.

Kline, K. L. 1978. Developmental dyslexia in adolescents: The emotional carnage. *Annals of Dyslexia* 28, 160–74.

McIntryre, C., and Pickering, J. 1995. *Clinical Studies of Multisensory Structured Language Education for Students with Dyslexia and Related Disorders*. Salem, OR: International Multisensory Structured Language Education Council.

Moats, L. 1994. The missing foundation in teacher education: Knowledge of the struc-ture of spoken and written language. *Annals of Dyslexia* 44, 81–102.

Oakland, T., Black, J., Stanford, G., Nussbaum, N., and Balise, R. R. in press. An evalua-tion of the dyslexia traning program: A multisensory method for promoting reading in students with reading disabilities. *Journal of Learning Disabilities* 31, 140–47.

Orton, J. L. 1966a. The Orton-Gillingham approach. In J. Money, ed., *The Disabled Reader: Education of the Dyslexic Child*. Baltimore: Johns Hopkins Press.

Orton, J. L. Ed. 1966b. *"Word-blindness" in school children and other papers on strephosymbo-lia*. (Monograph 2). Pomfret, CT: The Orton Society, Inc.

Orton, S. T. 1925. 'Word-blindness' in school children. *Archives of Neurology and Psychiatry* 14, 581–615.

Orton, S. T. 1928. Specific reading disability - Strephosymbolia. *The Journal of the American Medical Association* 90, 1095–99.

Orton, S. T. 1929. The "sight reading" method of teaching reading, as a source of reading disability. *Journal of Educational Psychology* 20, 135–43.

Orton, S. T. 1937. *Reading, Writing, and Speech Problems in Children.* New York: Norton.

Orton, S. T. 1946. Some disorders in the language development of children. Proceedings of Child Research Clinic Conference, The Woods Schools, 23–28.

Rawson, M. B. 1965. *Developmental Language Disability: Adult Accomplishments of Dyslexic Boys.* Frederick, MD: Hood College.

Rawson, M. B. 1988. *The Many Faces of Dyslexia.* Baltimore, MD: The Orton Dyslexia Society.

Rawson, M. B. 1995. *Dyslexia Over the Lifespan: A 55-year Longitudinal Study.* Cambridge, MA: Educators Publishing Service.

Rome, H. D. 1971. The psychiatric aspects of dyslexia. *Bulletin of The Orton Society* 21, 64–70.

Ryan, M. 1994. *The Other Sixteen Hours: The Social and Emotional Problems of Dyslexia.* Baltimore, MD: The Orton Dyslexia Society.

Scarborough, H. 1998. Early identification of children at risk for reading disabilities: Phonological awareness and some other promising predictors. In B. Shapiro, P. Accardo, and A. Capute, eds. *Specific Reading Disability: A View of the Spectrum.* Timonium, MD: York Press.

Stoner, J. 1991. The potential for at-risk students to learn to read in groups contrasted under traditional and multisensory reading instruction. *Reading and Writing: An Interdisciplinary Journal* 3, 19–30.

Torgesen, J. K. 1995. Phonologically based reading disabilities: Approaches to prevention and remediation. *Thalamus* 15, 26–27.

Torgesen, J. K., Wagner, R. K., and Rashotte, C. A. 1997. Prevention and remediation of severe reading disabilities: Keeping the end in mind. *Scientific Studies in Reading* 1(3), 217–34.

Varian, D. 1983. *The Inventor and the Pilot.* Mountain View, CA: Mayfair.

Wise, B. W., Olson, R. K., and Ring, J. 1997. Teaching phonological awareness with and without the computer. In C. Hulme and M. Snowling, eds., *Dyslexia: Biology, Cognition and Intervention.* London: Whurr Publishers.

# Gender Ratio in Dyslexia

*T. R. Miles*

School of Psychology, University of Wales,
Bangor, United Kingdom


*M. N. Haslum*

University of the West of England,
Bristol, United Kingdom


*T. J. Wheeler*

University College,
Chester, United Kingdom

*This paper is based on a study carried out in Great Britain on a national sample of 11,804 ten-year olds. The first section describes an attempt to pick out cases of "specific developmental dyslexia" (Critchley 1970), a constellation or syndrome of difficulties which some believe to be recognizable clinically. When specified criteria for dyslexia were used, 269 children qualified as dyslexic (2.28 percent of the sample). These included 223 boys and 46 girls, for a ratio of 4.51 to 1. Two possible difficulties in interpreting these data are discussed, and a defense is offered of the criteria used.*

*Since some recent research papers report a gender ratio much nearer 1:1 (Shaywitz et al. 1990; Wadsworth et al. 1992; Lubs et al. 1993), those papers were examined for possible differences in procedure; it was found that the definition of dyslexia they used was "poor reading in relation to intelligence." We carried out a further analysis on our own data using the same criterion. Of the 494 children who qualified as dyslexic on the*

Annals of Dyslexia, Vol. 48, 1998

basis of discrepancy criteria alone (4.19 percent of the sample), 314 were boys and 180 were girls for a ratio of 1.69 to 1. It seems, therefore, that the apparent differences in gender ratio reported in the literature have arisen because different criteria for dyslexia have been used.

We argue that the definition based on clinical criteria leads to a more powerful taxonomy and that the widespread equation of "dyslexia" with "poor reading" is a hindrance to progress.

## INTRODUCTION

It has traditionally been supposed that there are many more dyslexic males than females (Hinshelwood 1917; Hallgren 1950; Hermann 1959; Critchley 1970; Goldberg and Schiffman 1972; Hier 1980; Finucci and Childs 1981). More recently, however, this imbalance has been called into question (Shaywitz et al. 1990; Wadsworth et al. 1992; Lubs et al. 1993).

The data presented in this paper are in agreement with traditional accounts in finding a preponderance of males when clinically based criteria for dyslexia are applied. These criteria include not only poor reading and spelling in relation to general intelligence, but also such clinical indices as uncertainty over left and right (a phenomenon first noted by Dr. Samuel Orton) or difficulty in the recall of auditorily presented digits. On the other hand, if a diagnosis of dyslexia is based solely on measures of reading and intelligence, making what we argue to be an unwarranted equation of dyslexia with specific reading retardation, we also found the gender ratio to be closer to 1:1.

For ease of communication, we shall distinguish between "specific developmental dyslexia" (SDD), a condition diagnosed on multiple criteria of a clinical kind (Critchley 1970), and "specific reading retardation" (SRR) (Rutter and Yule 1975), which refers to poor reading in relation to intelligence.[1]

The data which form the basis of the present paper were collected in 1980 and relate to 11,804 ten-year olds. This body of data will be referred to in what follows as the "British Births Survey." The size of the sample and the fact that it targets a complete population has provided a unique opportunity for an

---

[1] The expression "SDD" is new to the present paper: in earlier papers the participants were described simply as "dyslexic". In the present context, however, this would be question-begging—as would the expressions "genuine dyslexic", "proper dyslexic", etc.,—since the question of the relative merits of the SDD and SRR concepts is precisely what is at issue. The expression SRR can be treated as equivalent to what in the United States is termed RD (reading disability).

investigation of dyslexia. The following publications have already appeared: Miles and Haslum (1986); Haslum (1989); Miles (1991); Miles, Haslum, and Wheeler (1993, 1996, 1997); Miles, Wheeler, and Haslum (1994). Analyses of the data are ongoing and further papers are in preparation.

The primary objective of the dyslexia component of the research was to find a formula which, if consistently applied across the cohort, would pick out those children showing strong evidence of SDD. The underlying assumption was that children with dyslexia can be recognized by persons with relevant clinical experience including doctors, teachers, psychologists, parents, and many individuals who are themselves dyslexic. We also assumed that the early pioneers—Hinshelwood (1917), Orton (1937/1989), Hallgren (1950), Hermann (1959), and Critchley (1970)—were talking about the same group of children. Our research goal, therefore, was to sharpen the definition of the concept that these early researchers referred to without radically changing it. To adapt some wise words used in a different context by the philosopher, Sidgwick (1922), "A definition may be given . . . which will be accepted by all competent judges as presenting, in a clear and explicit form, what they have always meant by the term, though perhaps implicitly and vaguely. In seeking such a definition we may, so to speak, clip the ragged edge of common usage, but we must not make excision of any considerable portion" (p. 264).

To put the matter another way, our intention was to *operationalize* clinical judgments of SDD. We hoped not only to specify operations which would distinguish children with SDD from others with literacy problems, but to show that the differences between them were important and could be used as the basis for a meaningful taxonomy (classificatory principle).

## PARTICIPANTS AND METHOD

The data for the analyses presented in this paper are taken from the ten-year follow up of the British Births Survey including all live births which occurred in England, Wales, and Scotland between April 5th and 11th 1970 (Chamberlain et al. 1975; Chamberlain et al. 1978). This was the third of the British national perinatal longitudinal studies. The study of the 1970 cohort at around birth, and the nationwide follow-up studies at age five (Osborn et al. 1984; Butler et al. 1986) and at age ten (Butler et al. 1982a, 1982b) have been extensively described.

Children were traced at the age of ten by the use of three processes. The research team held manual indices on the children from the birth survey, the nationwide five-year follow up, and a seven-year follow up that had traced an additional 1917 children not contacted at age five. A computer file was set up for all known living children in the cohort. The cohort children were flagged at the Office of Population Census and Surveys and the cohort team was automatically informed of deaths and migrations.

For the ten-year study, children were traced through Family Practitioner Committee records. The Area Health Authority (public health nurses) contacted families requesting consent to participate in the follow up, and interviewed the parents or parent figure.

The children were also traced through school records. Trace forms were sent to every Local Education Authority and independent primary or middle school in England, Scotland, and Wales (Northern Ireland was omitted from the five-, seven-, and ten-year follow-up studies). The schools provided the name, address, and date of birth of the children; they also provided the name of the parent or guardian who was then sent a letter requesting participation in the educational part of the survey.

In addition to the educational testing, school doctors took medical histories, carried out general physical examinations, and tested motor coordination; hearing and visual acuity were also tested. Health visitors interviewed parents to collect structured medical, family, and social histories; and mothers completed behavior scales and skills scales about their children. Classroom teachers also rated the children's behavior and skills, administered educational tests, and commented on their educational needs.

The present paper is limited to a selection of the educational data which were obtained by classroom teachers when the children were ten years old; data were scored by members of the research team. The tests of achievement included a word recognition test which involved the reading of single words out of context, a test of reading comprehension (the Shortened Edinburgh Reading Test, later published by Hodder and Stoughton in 1985), and a spelling test in the form of a dictation. (See Appendix I for details about the tests.)

In selecting appropriate measures of intelligence, we took into account clinical experience and research evidence specific to children with SDD (compare Miles 1996). As a result of the so-called ACID profile (weakness at the Arithmetic (A), Coding

(C), Information (I), and Digit Span (D) sub-tests of the Wechsler Intelligence Scale for Children) global IQ scores of SDD children tend to be depressed (see, for instance, Miles and Ellis 1981). SDD children also show uneven profiles on the British Ability Scales (BAS) (Elliott, Murray, and Pearson 1979, 1983). For example, Thomson (1982) reports that at three different ages, persons with dyslexia performed consistently well on the Similarities and Matrices subtests, and consistently poorly on Recall of Digits and Speed of Information Processing.[2] For these reasons, we assessed intelligence in the present study by using the combined score on the Similarities and Matrices subtests. In the Similarities test, the child has to explain how three things are alike, then produce a fourth of the same kind (for example, given *horse*, *cow*, and *sheep*, a child should respond "they are animals", and produce a fourth such as *pig*). The Matrices test was of the standard variety: the child had to recognize relationships between figures and then choose, from a number of alternatives, the correct figure to fill a vacant space. To provide a common measure for comparison, the scores on the word recognition and spelling tests, and the combined score on the Similarities and Matrices, were standardized so as to give a mean of 100 and a standard deviation of 15; they were not normalized.

To supplement these measures of achievement and general cognitive function, we also presented four tasks which our clinical experience had suggested were indicative of specific developmental dyslexia (Miles 1993). These included the Recall of Digits subtest from the BAS (Elliott et al. 1979, 1983), and three subtests from the Bangor Dyslexia Test (Miles 1982, 1997), such as Left-Right (which involves items like "point to my right ear with your left hand"), Months Forwards (where the months of the year have to be recited in forward order), and Months Reversed (where they have to be recited in reverse order). Resources did not allow for the Bangor Dyslexia Test to be given in full, and the items chosen were those which could most easily and reliably be administered by classroom teachers. (Appendix II presents relevant items from the Bangor Dyslexia Test and instructions for scoring.)[3] Since our intention was to

---

[2] These subjects were assessed at Aston University where research on dyslexia (in the SDD sense) was being pioneered. Although the words "specific reading difficulty" appear in the title of his paper, Dr. Thomson (personal communication) has assured us that the children in this study met traditional criteria for dyslexia.

[3] The two Memory for Digits items (forwards and reversed) from the Bangor Dyslexia Test would have been largely superfluous since the Recall of Digits subtest from the British Ability Scales had already been included.

use the BAS Recall of Digits subtest alongside the Bangor Dyslexia Test, rather than as a measure of intelligence, these scores were converted so that, like the Bangor items, they too could be scored as "plus", "zero", or "minus."[4]

## CRITERIA FOR SDD

In selecting criteria for SDD, we took the view that defining dyslexia as "poor reading in relation to intelligence" was not so much wrong as incomplete. Children can be poor readers for many different reasons, including lack of motivation or absence from school. To classify such children as dyslexic, which implies some kind of biological basis for their difficulties, seems at variance with traditional usage and unlikely to lead to any worthwhile taxonomy. On this point, we quote the words of Galaburda (1992):

> Lumping together all children with discrepancies between reading skills and intelligence makes no more sense than lumping together all persons with high blood pressure (p. 279).

Our task, within the resources available, was to try to identify children who would have been recognized as classic cases of dyslexia (in the SDD sense) had a fuller assessment been possible. Since SDD is widely agreed to involve difficulty with the *decoding* aspects of reading and writing, we chose to assess reading using the single word recognition test rather than the Edinburgh Reading Test, which relies more heavily on comprehension. We also decided that more importance should be attached to weakness in spelling than to weakness in reading.

To pick out poor readers, each child's word recognition score was regressed on his or her combined score on the Similarities and Matrices items. To obtain the best fit for the regression lines, outliers beyond 1.5 standard deviations from the mean were excluded; the equations were recalculated on the remainder and then refitted to the entire population. Residual scores (observed −predicted) were then calculated for each individual. Those children whose residuals were between

---

[4] The decision was taken to score this item in relation to intelligence. This was done by converting the standardized Recall of Digits scores into z-scores (referred to as z.RD, RD meaning Recall of Digits) and creating z-scores on the combined Similarities-Matrices score (referred to as z.SM, SM meaning Similarities and Matrices). For each individual, a value was determined (z.RD minus z.SM) and the mean and standard deviation were calculated. If a result was less than −1.5 SD it was scored as plus; if it lay between −1 and −1.5 it was scored as zero, and if it was greater than −1 it was scored as minus.

1.0 and 1.5 standard deviations below prediction were described as "moderate underachievers"; those whose residuals were outside 1.5 standard deviations below prediction were described as "severe underachievers." The procedure was repeated for spelling scores. As a result, it was possible to identify "normal achievers" at both word recognition and spelling, and to distinguish them from "moderate underachievers" and "severe underachievers."

Our emphasis on spelling was based on our own clinical experience. We knew, in particular, that by the age of ten-years, some children, who in other respects showed clear signs of SDD, were nevertheless reasonably adequate readers (Miles 1993, Chapter 8). Not only did Naidoo (1972) find it necessary to distinguish dyslexics who were poor at both reading and spelling from those who were poor at spelling only, but it is clear that many college students with dyslexia struggle with essay writing, note-taking, or the memorization of formulae without finding reading itself to be a significant problem. In establishing criteria for SDD, just as we hoped to avoid the risk of false positives (children who were poor readers for predominantly environmental reasons such as the absence of opportunity or poor teaching) so, too, did we wish to avoid false negatives—children who failed to come out as "dyslexic" by SRR criteria because they were adequate readers but who were clinically dyslexic in other ways.

We took the view, based on our clinical experience, that any ten-year old whose spelling was adequate could not be regarded as a "classic" case of dyslexia of the sort we were looking for; normal achievement at spelling was therefore a counterindicator to SDD, whatever the child's performance at reading. In contrast, a child who was severely underachieving at spelling was eligible for the SDD group regardless of his or her reading skills, given evidence that some SDD children could be adequate readers In addition, we stipulated that a child who was both a severe underachiever at reading *and* a moderate underachiever at spelling was also eligible to belong to the SDD group. This stipulation was made on the grounds that the two underachievements combined give rise to a different situation from that which would have held if either had occurred on its own. These criteria may seem complex, but they do no more than reflect the complexity of any specification based on clinical judgment. For ease of communication, children who were either severe underachievers at spelling or severe underachievers at reading *and* moderate underachievers at spelling will be referred to in what follows simply as "underachievers."

To eliminate the risk of false positive (children, who despite poor reading or spelling in relation to intelligence, did not seem to show the typical signs of SDD), we relied on three subtests from the Bangor Dyslexia Test (Left-Right, Months Forward, and Months Reversed), along with the Recall of Digits subtest from the British Ability Scales. These additional items, based originally on clinical experience, were used to supplement the existing information by supporting, or failing to support, the claim that the typical SDD pattern of difficulties was present. It has been argued by Miles (1993, p. 23) that a diagnosis of dyslexia is, in effect, a "bet." One is arguing on the basis of a limited number of signs that further manifestations will be forthcoming, and if it turns out they are not forthcoming, then the diagnosis was mistaken.

Because clinical experience had convinced us that there are a variety of dyslexia-related conditions, including so-called *formes frustes* (Critchley and Critchley 1978, Chapter 9), as well as individuals who, despite some literacy problems, did not present as typical cases of SDD, we created three categories of children with specific literacy difficulties in relation to their intelligence. These comprised: (1) those who on the basis of the supplementary items would probably, but not certainly, have displayed further signs of SDD had more data been available (the so-called "classic" cases); (2) those who were marginal; and (3) those who, as far as we could tell, did not appear to be showing typical signs of SDD. We shall refer to the first group as underachievers A, to the second as underachievers B, and to the third as underachievers C. On a probability basis, we hypothesized that the underachievers A group contained more SDD children than the underachievers B group, which in turn contained more SDD children than the underachievers C group.

Those who advocate the SDD concept are logically committed to showing that SDD children are different, not only from normal achievers but from other underachievers as well. The category of underachievers C was created so as to make possible this comparison; if no differences were found between underachievers A and underachievers C, the SDD concept would be weakened. This procedure meets the scientific requirement of generating a falsifiable hypothesis (compare Popper 1963).

The reason for creating the underachievers B group was different. It was inevitable in a survey on the scale of the British Births Survey—where the amount of information that could be collected about any one individual was limited—that there would be some children about whom a decision one way or the other regarding SDD was problematic. Clearly, such children were not normal achievers; on the other hand, we did not wish to risk contamination of our data by including doubtful cases either in the underachievers A (SDD) group or in the under-achievers C group. The creation of a separate group avoided both these risks.

It was also decided, after considerable thought, not to treat children as eligible for inclusion in the SDD group if there was any doubt about their level of intellectual functioning. This was done, not because we believed on *a priori* grounds that such children could not be dyslexic, but simply to avoid the unnecessary complications to which limited intellectual ability might give rise. Given the number of children available, it seemed desirable to choose a relatively high cutoff point rather than run the risk of contaminating our data with complications which could simply be the consequence of low intellectual ability. For this reason, it was decided to accept as eligible for inclusion in the SDD group only those children with a standard score of 90 or above on the combined results of the Similarities and Matrices tests.

The SDD children (underachievers A) were then defined as those children of adequate intellectual ability who satisfied *both* the criteria for underachievement specified above *and* had at least two positive indicators or at least three zeros on the supplementary items. (Further specification of what this means is found in Appendix II). Underachievers B (the buffer group) were defined as those who, on the supplementary items, had either a positive indicator and a zero or two zeros, whereas underachievers C were defined as those who had at most a single positive indicator or a single zero. It should be noted that the three groups all satisfied the same criteria for underachievement and that they differed only with respect to their performance on the supplementary items.

Our procedure was not intended to provide a method for determining the overall prevalence of SDD. As was indicated above, the intention was to specify criteria by which the clearest and most obvious cases of SDD could be picked out and to provide two further groups for comparison.

The above description of our procedure emphasizes in an interesting way the difference between a specification based on clinical judgment and one based simply on a statistical cutoff point. If one is trying to identify a given condition, it may well be that many individuals outside a particular statistical cutoff point do in fact exemplify the condition; still, the cutoff point does not *define* the condition. Therefore, in the present case, a cutoff point which separated severe underachievers at word recognition from other children might well, if used on its own, have captured a significant number of SDD children. However, it still would not have provided a definition of SDD.

Another interesting feature of a clinical judgment is the use of concepts such as "either–or", "unless", and "both–and" to reflect how a diagnosis is made. Typically, condition A is present if *some* of symptoms V, W, X, Y, and Z are present, or if *both* symptom Y *and* symptom Z are present. In some cases it may be necessary to add the proviso "*unless* symptom M is present" in which case symptom M is described as a "counterindicator." The diagnosis as a whole is made on the basis of a coherent *pattern* of symptoms, and the presence of a counterindicator may indicate that the "fit" to this pattern is less than adequate.

In the present study, we used both disjunctive concepts (SDD entails underachievement at *either* spelling *or* word recognition) and conjunctive concepts (SDD entails *both* a particular level of underachievement *and* sufficient positive indicators on the supplementary items); normal achievement at spelling was treated as a counterindicator. In contrast, the SRR concept depends on a statistical cut-off point, and it is unambiguous whether or not an individual belongs to a particular group. Although the tidiness of the SRR classification may find favor with those who operate primarily in statistical terms, the SDD concept appeals to those of us who have wrestled with the problems and complexities of clinical diagnosis. We suspect that lumping everything together that falls on one side of a statistical boundary is unlikely, on its own, to point to a worthwhile taxonomy. What we have used in the present study is information based on statistical boundaries (scores on the word reading and spelling residuals) *combined with* information based on the results of the supplementary items derived from clinical judgment. We believe that the combination of the two methods provides a more powerful research tool than either method alone.

The present procedure differed from a simple discrepancy-based approach as follows:

- tests of intelligence were chosen which, we believed, would not put SDD children at a disadvantage (Thomson 1982);
- spelling scores were used as well as reading scores;
- single word reading was tested rather than reading comprehension; and

- clinically-based supplementary items from the Bangor Dyslexia Test, and the Recall of Digits from the British Ability Scales, were included as further evidence for the presence or absence of SDD.

## RESULTS AND DISCUSSION

Data were available on 11,804 children, 5,995 boys and 5,809 girls.[5] For reasons indicated above, it was decided to divide the children into four subgroups: the three groups of under-achievers, defined earlier, and the rest of the cohort. Table I gives the gender ratios (adjusted to take into account the pre-ponderance of boys in the cohort) for each subgroup. It is clear from this table that the underachievers A (SDD) group con-tained many more boys than girls, by a ratio of 4.51 to 1. Moreover, since the gender ratios are different in the three groups, the decision to define the SDD children as a distinctive group receives some measure of support.

**TABLE I. GENDER RATIOS FOR THE DIFFERENT SUBGROUPS**

| | Total $n$ | Male | Female | Ratio of boys to girls | Ratio adjusted for slight preponderance of boys in total cohort |
|---|---|---|---|---|---|
| Underachievers A (SDD) | 269 | 223 | 46 | 4.85 | 4.51 |
| Underachievers B (buffer) | 221 | 163 | 58 | 2.81 | 2.72 |
| Underachievers C (others) | 417 | 243 | 174 | 1.40 | 1.31 |
| Rest of Cohort | 10,897 | 5,366 | 5,531 | 0.97 | 0.94 |
| Total Cohort | 11,804 | 5,995 | 5,809 | 1.03 | |

[5] The full cohort for whom educational data were available comprised 12,905 children, 6,685 boys (51.8%) and 6,220 girls (48.2%). Inevitably, in a survey of this magnitude, data sets were sometimes incomplete; for 1,101 cases (8.53 % of the total sample) missing data made it impossible either to confirm or ex-clude SDD. These 1,101 cases were made up of 690 boys and 411 girls. Given that our 269 SDD children constituted 2.28% of the total sample, it is possi-ble that there might have been about 25 additional SDD children (2.28% of 1,101) had full data sets been available. Given the excess of boys in the miss-ing data, it seems unlikely that among the hypothesized SDD children there would have been an excess of girls. Even on this unlikely hypothesis, how-ever, the overall gender ratio among the SDD children would not have been seriously affected.

Before we proceed further, it is necessary to consider whether the predominance of boys in the SDD group could have been a statistical artifact, one which had arisen not for any reason connected with dyslexia, but because there was an imbalance in gender ratios on the four supplementary items.

Table II shows the total numbers and gender ratios of those who came out plus, zero, and minus on each of the four supplementary items. At first glance, this result seems damaging to our thesis because on Months Forward, 2,430 boys out of a total of 6,482 (37.60%) earned a plus or a zero, compared to 932 girls out of a total of 6,060 (15.38%). It was possible, therefore, that the apparent strong gender bias derived from our choice of a supplementary item, independent of a child's status in relation to dyslexia. Moreover, since the selection procedure for underachievers C guaranteed that most of this group would be successful on Months Forward, it is possible that the relatively small preponderance of boys in group C was an artifact of that single item.

To find out if this was indeed the case, we calculated the gender ratio among the SDD children, this time relying on the other three supplementary items. Because there were four items in all (call them ABCD), there were four possible estimates of gender ratio when any three of them were used in combination (ABC, ABD, ACD, BCD). The outcome of this analysis is shown in table III. Clearly, even when the Months Forward item is discounted, the 4:1 boy to girl ratio still holds up; any three supplementary items out of the four generate a similar gender ratio.

TABLE II. NUMBERS OF BOYS AND GIRLS SCORING
DYSLEXIA POSITIVE, DYSLEXIA ZERO, AND DYSLEXIA MINUS ON
THE FOUR SUPPLEMENTARY ITEMS

| | Dyslexia Positive | | | Dyslexia Zero | | | Dyslexia Negative | | |
|---|---|---|---|---|---|---|---|---|---|
| | Boys | Girls | Ratio | Boys | Girls | Ratio | Boys | Girls | Ratio |
| Recall of Digits | 1,903 | 1,858 | 1.24 | 2,356 | 2,294 | 1.03 | 1,958 | 1,965 | 1.00 |
| Left-Right | 756 | 652 | 1.1 | 688 | 1758 | 1.16 | 4,990 | 4,770 | 1.05 |
| Months Forward | 788 | 183 | 4.31 | 1,642 | 749 | 2.19 | 4,032 | 5,128 | 0.78 |
| Months Reversed | 1,078 | 537 | 2.01 | 2,063 | 1,512 | 1.36 | 3,110 | 3,968 | 0.78 |

Note. Use has been made in the above table of all available information on the supplementary items, including those cases where complete data sets were not available; for this reason the row totals add up to more than 11,804.

**TABLE III. GENDER RATIOS WHEN EACH OF THE FOUR SUPPLEMENTARY ITEMS\* IS EXCLUDED IN TURN**

| Combination | No. picked | No. of boys | No. of girls | Ratio | Ratio adjusted for slight preponderance of boys in total cohort |
|---|---|---|---|---|---|
| A B C | 65 | 56 | 9 | 6.22 | 6.00 |
| A B D | 88 | 73 | 15 | 4.87 | 4.54 |
| A C D | 183 | 156 | 27 | 5.78 | 5.42 |
| B C D | 194 | 164 | 30 | 5.47 | 5.10 |
| ABCD | 269 | 223 | 46 | 4.85 | 4.51 |

\* A = Recall of Digits, B = Left-Right, C = Months Forward,
D = Months Reversed

## A FURTHER ANALYSIS, USING SRR CRITERIA

For the next analysis, we looked at the gender ratio when the supplementary items were excluded. One of the things that concerned us when we first read the papers by Shaywitz et al. (1990), Wadsworth et al. (1992), and Lubs et al. (1993) was that their results were at variance, not only with the earlier literature but also with ordinary experience. For example, when we spoke about this new evidence to head teachers of schools for dyslexic children, they found it extremely hard to credit. In their initial paper, Shaywitz et al. (1990) drew a distinction between research-identified and school-identified children. They reported that only in the case of school-identified children was there any significant imbalance in gender ratio. Their suggested explanation was that teachers perceived boys as being more disruptive than girls, and were therefore more likely to refer them as having special problems (p. 1002). The preponderance of boys reported in the literature could therefore be explained in terms of selection bias.

This interpretation is hard to square with data from Miles (1993; see especially p. 25); of the 223 individuals referred to him and selected as classic cases of dyslexia, 182 were male and 41 female (ratio 4.4:1). This was indeed a clinic population, which means that referral bias cannot be categorically excluded. If the referral bias hypothesis is right, however one would have to assume that boys are much more disruptive than girls not only at school but also in the home. We find it surprising that our previous detailed documentation (Miles 1993) has revealed so much about the dyslexic pattern of difficulties and so little about disruptiveness. We think it is possible that many of the children referred through the school system in the Shaywitz et al. study were recognized by their teachers as having what in this paper we have called SDD, and therefore in need of special help.

Thus our next step was to take special note of the procedures adopted by Shaywitz et al. (1990) and consider possible ways in which their procedures differed from ours. What we found was that they had relied only on reading and intelligence measures, and had excluded spelling tests and anything corresponding to our supplementary items. We thought it would be interesting to carry out a further analysis of our own data using SRR as the criterion for dyslexia rather than SDD.

We had available to us, as part of the British Births Survey, a reading test which we did not use in picking out children with SDD. This was the Edinburgh Reading Test primarily a test of reading comprehension. We did not use it because clinical experience told us that SRR children could sometimes be strong at comprehension and that accurate attention to detail was less important in text reading than in a test of single word reading. For present purposes, however, where a measure of poor reading in relation to intelligence was needed independently of any clinical experience we might have of the field, we decided that the Edinburgh Reading Test was entirely suitable and would form a good basis for comparing the SRR concept with the SDD concept. In particular, we wanted to know if the gender ratio would be any different on the two definitions.

To provide residuals on the Edinburgh Reading Test, we again measured intelligence by taking the combined score on the Similarities and Matrices tests. A regression equation was calculated in the same way as before, and those whose residuals were more than 1.5 standard deviations below prediction were classified as severe underachievers. The numbers of boys and girls who satisfied this criterion are given in table IV.

It can be seen from this table that 494 children came out as severe underachievers, of whom 314 were boys and 180 were girls (adjusted ratio 1.63:1). Clearly, if dyslexia is defined in terms of SRR, it is not the case that there are many more affected boys than girls. What is also clear is that conflicting re-

**TABLE IV. GENDER RATIO OF SEVERE UNDERACHIEVERS WHEN DYSLEXIA IS IDENTIFIED IN TERMS OF SRR (EDINBURGH READING TEST)**

| Total | No. of boys | No. of girls | Ratio | Ratio adjusted for slight preponderance of boys in total cohort |
|-------|-------------|--------------|-------|-----------------------------------------------------------------|
| 494   | 314         | 180          | 1.74  | 1.63                                                            |

ports in the literature have arisen because different criteria for dyslexia were being used.

## DISCUSSION

The purpose of this paper was to define operationally what we believe has been meant traditionally by the term dyslexia (SDD) and to distinguish it from reading disability/specific reading retardation. When SDD is defined using clinically derived criteria specifying low spelling (and/or reading) together with clinically significant weaknesses on the Bangor Dyslexia Test, gender ratios were 4.5 to 1. In contrast, when criteria for SRR (involving only a significant weakness in reading in relation to IQ) were applied to the very same sample, gender ratios were much closer to 1:1.

One objection to the SDD criterion refers to a potential gender bias in one of the Bangor items. We ruled this out as unable to explain the extreme preponderance of boys. A second, and more basic, objection to our procedure for defining SDD concerns the possibility that the choice of items in the Bangor Dyslexia Test is itself affected by an unwarranted reliance on clinical judgment without proper scientific justification. The great drawback to decisions based on clinical judgment ("I know one when I see one") is that they involve the risk of perpetuating a misleading stereotype. For example, there is reason to suspect that some clinical psychologists may have misled themselves and others by putting forward, with unjustifiable confidence, somewhat speculative interpretations of responses to the Rorschach inkblot cards. The possibility needs therefore to be faced that the concept of SDD, as operationalized by the Bangor Dyslexia Test, is open to the same objection.

Let us press the argument further. Stereotypes, it might be said, tend to become confirmed as descriptions of the alleged condition appear in the popular press. As a result, people recognize the said condition as applying to their children, their pupils, or themselves. They then ask to be assessed by "experts" who regard the referrals as further evidence that their views are correct, thus reinforcing the stereotype! Could it be that the choice of items in the Bangor Dyslexia Test was itself influenced by this misleading stereotype?

If this objection is valid it would apply, of course, both to the Bangor Dyslexia Test in its full version and to the items selected from it which were used in the present study. In what follows we shall refer to evidence from both sources.

The first point to make is that the SDD concept, although not a new one in terms of the clinical experience of the early pioneers, has not been operationalized previously. Because it is impossible to validate our measure of SDD without *other* measures of SDD to compare it to, arguments in support of the SDD concept have to be of a different kind. Our aim therefore is not to demonstrate conclusively that the SDD concept provides a valid taxonomy, but instead to cite an accumulation of research findings on the Bangor Dyslexia Test which in the absence of the SDD concept would be difficult to explain away.

Now it should be noted that acceptance by the scientific community of a particular taxonomy does not normally depend on a single experiment or on one kind of evidence; rather, advances are achieved when there are interlocking pieces of evidence that cannot otherwise easily be explained away. Not only do all the pieces of evidence demand explanation in their own right; more importantly, when they are taken in conjunction a much stronger structure emerges, while at the same time alternative explanations become progressively more uncomfortable.

The first relevant evidence derives from data from the British Births Survey published by Miles (1993) showing that items from the Bangor Dyslexia Test accounted for a sizable proportion of the variance on word recognition and other academic measures of spelling, mathematics, and pictorial comprehension. Sample tables shown in appendix III illustrate the significance of the Bangor items even when controlling for intelligence. Clearly, these "dyslexia indicators" are associated with academic success apart from their association with general intelligence. In fact, in a separate analysis of the same data set, Miles, Haslum, and Wheeler (1997) found that SDD children differ from normal achievers *and* the underachievers C group on some (but not all) of a 72-item mathematics test.

Additional support for the utility of the Bangor Dyslexia Test derives from evidence that children believed to be dyslexic (in the SDD sense) on clinical grounds scored more pluses on the Bangor Test (positive indicators of dyslexia) than did suitably matched controls (Miles 1993, pp. 56–57). Similarly, Oviedo (1996), when she translated the Bangor Dyslexia Test into two Spanish languages, Castilian and Galician, found a difference in the number of positive indicators, not only between children diagnosed as dyslexic and normal readers but (to a lesser extent, although still at a statistically significant level) between those diagnosed as dyslexic and poor readers believed *not to be* dyslexic.

It is important to note that poor performance on the Bangor items is not a simple function of reading level. For example, children selected on the basis of poor spelling scored more positive indicators on the Bangor Dyslexia Test than did younger children matched for spelling age (Miles 1993, Chapter 27). Similar results were found in Greece (Miles 1993, Chapter 28); and there was also some supporting evidence from Germany and Japan (Miles 1993, Chapters 29 and 30).[6]

The Bangor Dyslexia Test also has some intriguing distributional attributes. For example, in an early analysis of the results from the British Births Survey (Miles and Haslum 1986) when we attempted to pick out SDD children by means of a dyslexia index that included the supplementary items used in the present study, there was unambiguous evidence of an excess of children at the dyslexia end of the distribution. If allegedly positive indicators of SDD occur simply in accordance with normal variation, their frequencies will conform to the Poisson distribution. Interestingly, Miles and Haslum (1986) did find a Poisson distribution among discrepantly *good* readers and spellers, confirming the widely held view that indicators of SDD occur in many people from time to time on a random basis; however, among the discrepantly *poor* readers and spellers, there was significant departure from the Poisson distribution.

The final evidence in support of the Bangor Dyslexia Test is theoretical plausibility. It is now recognized that a central feature in dyslexia (however defined) is a weakness at the phonological level; and if the items in the Bangor Dyslexia Test are examined from this point of view (Miles 1993, Chapter 25), it seems clear they are precisely the kinds of items which those with a weakness at the phonological level might find difficult. Although a clinical hunch was the reason for the choice of these items in the first place, there is now a degree of theoretical justification for them which did not exist when the test was first published.

At a more speculative level, there is now good reason for supposing that SDD may be associated with minor malfunctioning of the cerebellum (Nicolson, Fawcett, and Dean 1995; Nicolson et al. 1996). If, as suggested by Thach (1996), one of the functions of the cerebellum is to make possible the use of motor sequences as an aid to memorizing, persons with minor cerebel-

---

[6] The co-authors of Chapter 26 were T. R. Miles, M. N. Haslum, and T. J. Wheeler; of Chapter 27, T. R. Miles and S. A. Turner Ellis; of Chapter 28, T. R. Miles and Andriana Kasviki; of Chapter 29, T. R. Miles and Claudia de Wall; and of Chapter 30, T. R. Miles, Jun Yamada, and Adam Banks.

lar deficiencies should perform such sequences relatively less efficiently. Thach makes his point as follows:

> Beginning with babbling in infancy, we proceed through "rote learning" of nursery rhymes, nonsense poems, and jingles without necessarily understanding them. . . . We can listen to what we say in order to get at what we otherwise can't remember. For example, "Thirty days hath September . . . " allows us to remember how many days there are in each month. . . . One can suggest that recitation of the alphabet, multiplication tables, are similar (p. 429).

What Thach says about recitation of the alphabet and about tables also could apply to the memorization of the months of the year, providing an intriguing theoretical justification for why the clinically derived Months Forward item may be a useful indicator of SDD.[7]

It does not, of course, follow from these considerations that the claims of those researchers who have made poor reading the central concept of dyslexia are therefore discredited. It is more than likely that their selection procedures picked up many children who were both poor readers *and* showed other signs of SDD, particularly in those studies where the participants were chosen from prosperous communities where environmental deprivation played only a minor part. The objection to their procedure is not that it is inherently flawed but that it leads to the presence of an unnecessary amount of "noise." It can still be claimed that the research findings contribute to a powerful taxonomy even though this can more usefully come under the general explanatory principle of SDD. One can therefore say that SDD has a biological basis (Galaburda and Livingstone 1993), that it is sometimes inherited (Pennington 1991), and that it is often the consequence of difficulties at the phonological level (Catts 1989; Rack 1994). Certain researchers (Tallal, Miller, and Fitch 1993; Merzenich et al. 1996) also believe that some of the clinical manifestations of dyslexia are the consequence of a biologically based difficulty in responding accurately to auditory input presented at very rapid speeds, although some of these claims have been called into question (Studdert-Kennedy et al. 1994–1995). These are all live research issues which are interrelated through the SDD concept.

---

[7] Recitation of multiplication tables is one of the items in the Bangor Dyslexia Test, although it was not used in the British Births Study. In the Bangor-Hiroshima Dyslexia Test (Miles 1993, Chapter 30, and pp. 259–60 ), which is modeled closely on the original Bangor Test, one of the items is to say the alphabet (syllabary) backwards.

Without this concept, however, there is no logical justification for making such a connection. Those who define dyslexia in terms of SRR are forced to say that some poor readers *also* display these other manifestations, but unless one goes beyond the SRR concept there is no logical commitment to look for an overall explanation.

A view similar to that of the present authors was put forward by Scarborough (1991), who wrote:

> Instead of casting the preschool characteristics of dyslexic children as "precursors" and the reading problems of these children as "outcome", it might be more helpful to view both as successive, observable symptoms of the same condition. . . . While the educational goal may be to explain reading difficulty for its own sake, the neuropsychological goal is to define the nature of the fundamental difficulty that manifests itself most evidently, but not solely, as underachievement in reading (p. 38-39).

We would even go further, and query Scarborough's use of the expression "most evidently." An alternative is to say that lateness in learning to read is a fairly common manifestation (although not an invariable one) of this underlying condition, and we would wish to argue that unless the underlying condition is present (whatever it may be) the term dyslexia should not be used. Those who assume that dyslexia can be equated by definition with poor reading are depriving themselves of a taxonomy which appears, in the light of the latest research evidence, to be one of considerable power. (For similar views see also Nicolson et al. 1996; Frith 1997).

It is true, of course, that the concept of SRR has the merit of simplicity in contrast to the concept of SDD, since it requires no elaborate operationalization of clinical judgments. Arguably, however, it may be more appropriate to view "reading" as a "starter" concept; and in that case, like "memory", "intelligence", and "learning", it not only broadly delineates a research area but also covers a "mixed bag" of somewhat diverse phenomena.

On the other hand, if the SDD criteria are correct, the procedure adopted by the SRR researchers has effectively buried the SDD children in a much wider population of children who, at a given time, were underachieving at reading. Although it seems that he may have been ignored, Critchley (1970) warned against this risk over a quarter of a century ago:

Throughout the world, instances of developmental dyslexia tend to be submerged within the larger population of bad readers, and so their specificity may escape detection. . . . To what extent these groupings represent a melange of the educationally inadequate, the intellectually deficient, the emotionally disturbed, the infirm of purpose, and the genuine dyslexics, has never been determined (p. 94-95).

In further papers (1992, 1994) Shaywitz et al. refer to the studies of Rutter, Tizard, and Whitmore (1970) and of Rutter and Yule (1975). The following passage merits detailed discussion:

Traditionally dyslexia has been viewed as a specific categorical entity that affects a small, circumscribed group of children and that is invariable over time. Classically, this group of individuals, often referred to as having specific reading retardation (SRR) (Rutter, Tizard, and Whitmore 1970), has been envisioned as primarily male and as qualitatively distinct from other poor readers (Shaywitz et al. 1994, p. 13).

We question, however, whether the authors' subdivision into categorical and dimensional models does justice to the complexity of the situation. Certainly some concepts are *purely* categorical: one cannot, for instance, have a mild touch of pregnancy. There are many others, however, where within a broad diagnostic label there is considerable diversity. If, therefore, it is asked whether dyslexia is a categorical or a dimensional concept, one may perhaps query whether it has to be unambiguously one or the other. As was pointed out earlier, the dyslexics in table I (underachievers A) were characterized as those about whose dyslexia there was little doubt.

It should also be pointed out that Rutter and his colleagues took particular care *not* to use the word dyslexia. They chose instead the expression specific reading retardation precisely because they did not wish to commit themselves to the theoretical superstructure which the word dyslexia seemed to imply.

If the two concepts, dyslexia and specific reading retardation (SDD and SRR) meant the same thing like, for example, rubella and German measles, the matter would have been unimportant: a claim about the one would in that case have also been a claim about the other. As things are, however, there is a problem of communication. Like Rutter and his colleagues, Shaywitz et al. picked out children who were poor readers in relation to their intelligence; unlike them, however, they then proceeded to call such children dyslexic. The fact that Rutter and Yule obtained different results, e.g. more boys than girls, and relative stability of diagnosis, is, of course, an interesting phenomenon in its own right. A possible explanation is that the Isle of Wight, where their study took place, is a relatively prosperous area where one might expect a relatively larger proportion of SDD children in comparison with children who were underachieving through lack of educational opportunity. This suggestion, however, cannot be more than speculative.

Had Shaywitz et al. (1992) treated SDD and SRR as different concepts, they would then have said, not "that dyslexia may represent the lower tail of a normal distribution of reading ability" (p. 145), but that certain statistical procedures show this to be true of SRR. They also say (1992) that "only 7 of the 25 children (28 percent) classified as having dyslexia in grade 1 would also be classified as having dyslexia in grade 3" (p. 145). It makes sense that there should be this instability of diagnosis in the case of children with SRR, since reading is clearly a skill that can be taught. There is ample evidence, however, from both sides of the Atlantic, both experimental (Miles 1986) and personal (Simpson 1980; Hampshire 1981; Fenwick Stuart 1988; Ganschow, Lloyd-Jones, and Miles 1994; Gilroy and Miles 1995; Rawson 1995), that if the word dyslexia is given its traditional sense, some of the difficulties experienced by dyslexics persist into adulthood. The Shaywitz et al. studies do nothing to refute this. Moreover, if such people can read adequately it would be necessary for those who equate dyslexia with poor reading to refer to them as "compensated" dyslexics; this could have the unfortunate consequence of their current needs being overlooked.

## CONCLUDING REMARKS

The main purpose of this paper was to report on the gender ratio in dyslexia. In the course of writing the paper, however, wider theoretical issues emerged, and one particularly far-reaching source of apparent disagreement was revealed. The claim by Shaywitz et al. that there are nearly as many dyslexic girls as boys needs to be considered in the context of their other claims, in particular the claims that full stability of diagnosis is lacking in dyslexia and that dyslexics simply represent one tail of a normal distribution of reading ability. If, as commonly happens, researchers pick out children who have difficulty with reading in relation to their intelligence, and then regard themselves as entitled to make statements about dyslexia in the traditional sense, the world at large will assume that certain things are true of dyslexia in the traditional sense which, in fact, are true only of specific reading retardation.

The words "in the traditional sense" are important here. Those who speak of "dyslexics" are implicitly claiming to be part of a tradition which began in Britain with Morgan (1896) and Hinshelwood (1917), was significantly advanced in the United States by Orton (1937/1989), and was later taken up in Scandinavia by Hallgren (1950), Hermann (1959), and in Britain by Critchley (1970). Although these writers sometimes appear to place what we feel is an undue emphasis on poor reading, it is clear that poor reading *simpliciter* was not their main interest. For example, the paper by Morgan contains an interesting list of spelling errors, and Hinshelwood makes clear that he is talking about "a pathological condition" (1917, p. 40), whereas, there need be nothing pathological about being a poor reader. Orton's book refers specifically to "reading, *writing and speech* problems" (authors' italics); Hallgren, who speaks, like Morgan and Hinshelwood, of "congenital word blindness"—and gives the alternative description "specific dyslexia"—clearly has SDD children in mind, while Critchley (1981) writes:

> The etymology of the term "dyslexia" expresses admirably a difficulty–not in reading–but in the use of words, how they are identified, what they signify, how they are handled in combination, how they are pronounced, and how they are spelt. . . . The term "specific reading retardation" is . . . not appropriate as it indicates an isolated symptom, whereas developmental dyslexia is a complex syndrome (p. 2).

We therefore ask that the word dyslexia be used only in its traditional sense, to refer to a family of lifelong manifestations that show themselves in many ways other than poor reading. We would even argue that the criterion of poor reading typically applies only between the ages of about five and fourteen years, because one cannot be a poor reader below the age of five years, and by age fourteen, many who formerly had reading problems can read more or less adequately. It would make for better communication if those who wish to limit their studies to reading did not use the word dyslexia at all.

Finally, we stress that the issue is not simply one of avoiding misunderstanding. The reason for investigating SDD as opposed to SRR is that the concept of SDD represents a more powerful taxonomy, one which links together converging evidence from a number of different research areas. Identification of dyslexia with poor reading or specific reading retardation neglects this taxonomy and is, therefore, in our view, a hindrance to the advancement of scientific knowledge.

Address for correspondence: Professor T. R. Miles, School of Psychology, University of Wales, Bangor LL57 2DG, Wales, United Kingdom. Fax: 01248 383842. e-mail: t.r.miles@bangor.ac.uk

Requests for reprints: Professor T. R. Miles, School of Psychology, University of Wales, Bangor LL57 2DG, Wales, United Kingdom.

## References

Butler, N. R., and Golding, J. 1986. *From Birth to Five. A Study of the Health and Behaviour of Britain's 5-year olds.* Oxford: Pergamon Press.

Butler, N. R., Haslum, M. N., Barker, W., et al. 1982a. *Child Health and Education Study. First Report to the Department of Education and Science on the 10-year Follow-up.* University of Bristol: Department of Child Health.

Butler, N. R., Haslum, M. N., Stewart-Brown, S., et al. 1982b. *Child Health and Education Study. First Report to the Department of Health and Social Security on the 10-year Follow-up.* University of Bristol: Department of Child Health.

Catts H. W. 1989. Phonological processing deficits and reading disabilities. In: A. G. Kamhi and H. W. Catts, eds, *Reading Disabilities: A Developmental Language Perspective.* Boston: Little Brown.

Chamberlain, R., Chamberlain, G., and Howlett, B., et al. 1975. *British Births 1970. Vol. 1. The First Week of Life.* London: Heinemann.

Chamberlain, G., Phillip, E., Howlett, B., et al. 1978. *British Births 1970. Vol. 2. Obstetric Care.* London: Heinemann.

Critchley, M. 1970. *The Dyslexic Child.* London: Heinemann.

Critchley, M. 1981. Dyslexia: an overview. In: G. Th. Pavlidis and T. R. Miles, eds. *Dyslexia Research and Its Applications to Education.* Chichester: Wiley.

Critchley, M., and Critchley, E. A. 1978. *Dyslexia Defined.* London: Heinemann.

DeFries, J. C., Stevenson, J., Gillis, J. J., and Wadsworth, S. J. 1991. Genetic etiology of spelling deficits in the Colorado and London twin studies of reading disability. In: B. F. Pennington, ed., *Reading Disabilities: Genetic and Neurological Influences.* Dordrecht: Kluwer.

Elliott, C. D., Murray D. J., and Pearson L. S. 1979, 1983. *The British Ability Scales.* Windsor: NFER-Nelson.

Fenwick Stuart, M. 1988. *Personal Insights into the World of Dyslexia.* Cambridge, MA: Educators Publishing Service.

Finucci, J. M., and Childs, B. 1981. Are there really more dyslexic boys than girls? In: A. Ansara, N. Geschwind, A. M. Galaburda, M. Albert, and M. Gartrell, eds., *Sex Differences in Dyslexia.* Towson, MD: Orton Dyslexia Society.

Frith, U. 1997. Brain, mind and behaviour in dyslexia. In: C. Hulme and M. Snowling, eds., *Dyslexia: Biology, Cognition and Intervention.* London: Whurr.

Galaburda, A. M. 1992. Correspondence in *The New England Journal of Medicine* 327, 4.

Galaburda, A. M., and Livingstone, M. 1993. Evidence for a magnocellular deficit in dyslexia. In: P. Tallal, ed., *Annals of the New York Academy of Sciences* 70–81.

Ganschow, L., Lloyd-Jones, J., and Miles, T. R. 1994. Dyslexia and musical notation. *Annals of Dyslexia* 44:185–202.

Gilroy, D. E., and Miles, T. R. 1995. *Dyslexia at College*. (2nd rev. ed.). London: Routledge.

Goldberg, H. K., and Schiffman, G. 1972. *Dyslexia: Problems of Reading Disabilities*. New York: Grune & Stratton.

Hallgren, B . 1950. Specific dyslexia (congenital word blindness). A clinical and genetic study. *Acta Psychiatrica et Neurologica* Suppl.65:i-xi and 1287.

Hampshire, S. 1981. *Susan's Story*. London: Sidgwick & Jackson.

Haslum, M. N. 1989. Predictors of dyslexia? *Irish Journal of Psychology* 10(4):622–30.

Hermann, K. 1959. *Reading Disability: A Medical Study of Word-Blindness and Related Handicaps*. Copenhagen: Munksgaard.

Hier, D. B. 1980. Sex differences in hemispheric specialisation: Hypothesis for the excess of dyslexia in boys. *Bulletin of the Orton Society* 29:74–83.

Hinshelwood, J. 1917. *Congenital Word-Blindness*. London: H. K. Lewis.

Lubs, H. A., Rabin, M., Feldman, E., Jallad, B. J., Kushch, A., and Gross-Glenn, K. 1993. Familial dyslexia: Genetic and medical findings in eleven three-generation families. *Annals of Dyslexia* 43, 44–60.

Merzenich, M. M., Jenkins, W. M., Johnston, P., Schreiner, C., Miller, S. L., and Tallal, P. 1996. Temporal processing deficits of language-learning impaired children ameliorated by training. *Science* 272:77–80.

Miles, T. R. 1982, 1997. *The Bangor Dyslexia Test*. Wisbech, Cambridge: Learning Development Aids.

Miles T. R. 1986. On the persistence of dyslexic difficulties into adulthood. In: G. Th. Pavlidis and D. F. Fisher, eds., *Dyslexia: Its Neuropsychology and Treatment*. Chichester: Wiley.

Miles, T. R. 1991. Towards a prevalence figure for dyslexia. In: M. Snowling and M. Thomson, eds., *Dyslexia: Integrating Theory and Practice*. London: Whurr.

Miles, T. R. 1993. *Dyslexia: The Pattern of Difficulties*. (2nd rev. ed.) London: Whurr.

Miles, T. R. 1994. A proposed taxonomy and some consequences. In: A. J. Fawcett and R. I. Nicolson, eds., *Dyslexia in Children: Multidisciplinary Perspectives*. Hemel Hempstead: Harvester Wheatsheaf.

Miles, T. R. 1996. Do dyslexic children have IQs? *Dyslexia: An International Journal of Research and Practice* 2(3):175–78.

Miles, T. R., and Ellis, N. C. 1981. A lexical encoding deficiency II: Clinical observations. In: G. Th. Pavlidis and T. R. Miles, eds., *Dyslexia Research and Its Applications to Education*. Chichester: Wiley.

Miles, T. R., and Haslum, M. N. 1986. Dyslexia: Anomaly or normal variation? *Annals of Dyslexia* 36:103–17.

Miles, T. R., Haslum, M. N., and Wheeler, T. J. 1996. Handedness in dyslexia: Should this be routinely recorded? *Dyslexia Review* 8(2):7–9.

Miles, T. R., Haslum, M. N., and Wheeler, T. J. 1997. Dyslexia and mathematics: Evidence from a large-scale survey. Paper delivered at the 4th International Conference of the British Dyslexia Association, York.

Miles, T. R., Wheeler, T. J., and Haslum, M. N. 1994. Dyslexia and the middle classes. *Links* 2 1(2):17–19.

Morgan W. P. 1896. A case of congenital word-blindness. *British Medical Journal* 2:1378.

Naidoo, S. 1972. *Specific Dyslexia*. London: Pitman.

Nicolson, R. I., Fawcett, A. J., and Dean, P. 1995. Time estimation deficits in developmental dyslexia: Evidence of cerebellar involvement. *Proceedings of the Royal Society of London, B*. 259, 43–47.

Nicolson, R. I., Fawcett, A. J., Maclagan, F., and Dean, P. 1996. Poster presented at the 47th international conference of the Orton Dyslexia Society.

Norusis, M. J. 1983. *Introductory Statistics Guide.* Chicago: SPSS Inc.

Orton, S. T. 1937/1989. *Reading, Writing, and Speech Problems in Children.* Austin, TX: PRO-ED.

Osborn, A. F., Butler, N. R., and Morris, A. C. 1984. *The Social Life of Britain's Five-year Olds: A Report on the Child Health and Education Study.* London: Routledge & Kegan Paul.

Oviedo, P. O. 1996. *Adaptacion del Test de Dislexia Bangor al Castellano y al Gallego.* Tesis de Licentiatura, Universidad de Santiago de Compostela, Spain.

Pennington, B. F. (ed.) 1991. *Reading Disabilities: Genetic and Neurological Influences.* Dordrecht: Kluwer.

Popper, K. R. 1963. *Conjectures and Refutations.* London: Routledge & Kegan Paul.

Rack J. 1994. Dyslexia: The phonological deficit hypothesis. In: A. J. Fawcett and R. I. Nicolson, eds., *Dyslexia in Children: Multidisciplinary Perspectives.* Hemel Hempstead: Harvester Wheatsheaf.

Rawson, M. B. 1995. *Dyslexia Over the Lifespan: A Fifty-Five-Year Longitudinal Study.* Cambridge, MA: Educators Publishing Service.

Rutter, M., Tizard, J., and Whitmore, K. 1970. *Education, Health and Behaviour.* Huntington, NY: Robert E. Krieger.

Rutter, M., and Yule, W. 1975. The concept of specific reading retardation. *Journal of Child Psychology and Psychiatry* 16:181–97.

Scarborough, H. 1991. Antecedents to reading disability: Preschool language development and literacy. Experiences of children from dyslexic families. In: B. F. Pennington, ed., *Reading Disabilities: Genetic and Neurological Influences.* Dordrecht: Kluwer.

Shaywitz, S. E., Shaywitz, B. A., Fletcher, J. M., and Escobar, M. D. 1990. Prevalence of reading disability in boys and girls. *Journal of the American Medical Association* 264(3), 998–1002.

Shaywitz, S. E., Escobar, M. D., Shaywitz, B. A., Fletcher, J. M., and Makuch, R. 1992. Evidence that dyslexia may represent the lower tail of a normal distribution of reading ability. *New England Journal of Medicine* 326(3), 145–50.

Shaywitz, S. E., Fletcher, J. M., and Shaywitz, B. A. 1994. A new conceptual model for dyslexia. In: A. J.Capute, P. J. Accardo, and B. K. Shapiro, eds., *Learning Disabilities Spectrum.* Baltimore: York Press.

*Shortened Edinburgh Reading Test.* 1985. Sevenoaks, Kent: Hodder & Stoughton.

Sidgwick, H. 1922. *Methods of Ethics.* London: Macmillan.

Simpson, E. 1980. *Reversals.* London: Gollancz.

Studdert-Kennedy, M., Liberman, A. M., Brady, S. A., Fowler, A. E., Mody, M., and Shankweiler, D. F. 1994–1995. Lengthened formant transitions are irrelevant to the improvement of speech and language impairments. *Haskins Laboratories Status Report on Speech Research.*

Tallal, P., Miller, S., and Fitch, R. H. 1993. Neurobiological basis of speech: A case for the preeminence of temporal processing. In: P. Tallal, ed., *Annals of the New York Academy of Sciences* 70–81.

Thach, W. F. 1996. On the specific role of the cerebellum in motor learning and cognition. Clues from PET activation and lesion studies in man. *Behavioural and Brain Sciences* 19,3, 411–31.

Thomson, M. E. 1982. The assessment of children with specific reading difficulties (dyslexia) using the British Ability Scales. *British Journal of Psychology* 73:461–78.

Wadsworth, S. J., DeFries, J. C., Stevenson, J., Gilger, J. W., and Pennington, B. F. 1992. Gender ratios among reading-disabled children and their siblings as a function of parental impairment. *Journal of Child Psychology and Psychiatry* 33:1229–39.

# APPENDIX I.

## Word Recognition and Spelling Tests Used in the British Births Survey

### a. Diagnostic Reading

Please ask the child to read out each of the words on the list at the end of this paragraph. The words should be read *from left to right* in each line. As the child reads each word, please note incorrect pronunciation (or refusal to attempt the word) on the appropriate list in the Educational Score Form.

| | | | | |
|---|---|---|---|---|
| PLAY | SHARP | LIST | OLD | JUMPING |
| BEFORE | SOON | OPEN | SLY | GROUND |
| CHILDREN | DITCH | MOUTH | AIR | SPEAKING |
| LOW | EVERYONE | MISCHIEF | FRIENDLY | BECAUSE |
| STRANGE | FAREWELL | MEADOW | FRIGHTENED | TOWARDS |
| BEAUTY | ADVENTURE | ALTOGETHER | THISTLE | AUTUMN |
| GRACIOUS | OCEAN | QUARRELSOME | NEIGHBOURHOOD | JEALOUSY |
| DELICIOUS | SOVEREIGN | MANUFACTURE | IDLENESS | POPULATION |
| ACQUAINTANCE | PALEST | CEREMONY | MONUMENTAL | ACKNOWLEDGE |
| THREATEN | BURIAL | LEAGUE | NEVERTHELESS | TRIUMPHANT |
| ROGUE | RUINOUS | DENY | ORIGINAL | CONSEQUENCES |
| REVERENCE | CHEQUE | PYRAMID | VEHICLE | EMPHASISE |
| LIEUTENANT | BENEFICIAL | PIETY | ENDEAVOUR | SUSCEPTIBLE |
| SACRIFICIAL | ANTICIPATE | IDIOTIC | AREA | HEROIC |
| DIAMETER | FACILITY | CYNICAL | ANALYSIS | PICTURESQUE |
| SOLICITOR | INACCURACY | STRATAGEM | PERSUASIVE | MANOEUVRES |
| PREFERENCE | TYRANNY | CATASTROPHE | OPAQUE | DECISIVE |
| MISCELLANEOUS | RECIPE | PRECIPITOUS | PNEUMONIA | CALIBRE |
| MAUSOLEUM | OCCIPITAL | FACETIOUS | TSETSE | NAUSEA |
| RHETORIC | UNANIMITY | HEINOUS | FORTUITOUS | DESULTORY |

### b. Writing and Spelling:

Please dictate the following to the child, at a speed suited to the child's pace of writing. If the child cannot write a word and asks how to spell it, say: "Just try to write it as best you can", and repeat the sentence containing the problem word. Do not repeat a particular sentence more than once. However, if the child asks for a repetition of the imaginary words in the middle of the passage, those words may be repeated twice. Please note the time taken by the child to complete the writing of the passage, in the appropriate space on the Educational Score Form.

*I often visited my aunt. She lived in a magnificent house opposite the gallery. I remember her splendid purple curtains. She wrote poetry. The problem was nobody could understand it. Her latest poems had words like prunty, slimber, grondel, blomp. I wanted to laugh but I had to pretend to like them. However, I really like the special refreshment. There was blue juice, cake and biscuits. When I left, my stomach was full and I was happy and contented.*

# APPENDIX II.

### Three Items from the Bangor Dyslexia Test (Miles 1982, 1997)

*Note.* These items constituted three of the four supplementary items as described in the main text. The fourth supplementary item was the Recall of Digits from the British Ability Scales (Elliott et al. 1979/1983).

The following written instructions were given to the teachers in the British Births Survey:

**Naming Body Parts: The Left-Right Test**
Seat the child at a table opposite you. Read each instruction clearly to the child, taking care to look straight ahead. Do not look at his/her or your hands. For item 3 onward, put both your hands on the table, palms down, fingers pointing toward the child.
Please tick the appropriate boxes on Page 9 of the Educational Score Form for the child and the observer. If the child corrects his/her response, please record the final response.

1. *Show me your right hand.*
2. *Show me your left ear.*
3. *Which is MY right hand?* (Put both hands on the table.)
4. *Touch my left hand with your right hand.*
5. *Point to my right ear with your left hand.*
6. *Touch my right hand with your right hand.*
7. *Point to my left ear with your right hand.*
8. *Touch my right hand with your right hand.*
9. *Touch my left hand with your left hand.*

Additional information about whether the child corrects his initial response, asks for the question again, or echoes the question would be most helpful.

**Sequential Recall—Months of the Year**
Please ask the child to say the months of the year in order and record the response on Page 9 of the Educational Score Form.

*1. Say the months of the year.* (Record response on the Educational Score Form.)

*2. Now say them backwards.* (Record response on the Educational Score Form.)

Write down the initial letter of each month as it is said, indicate long pauses with dots. For example, if a child pauses after August and inverts September and October but then corrects them, the entry would read:

J F M A M J J A ... O S, no S O N D

Please record all corrections. Also record any queries about the importance of order, e.g., "Do I have to say them in order?"

## APPENDIX II. (continued)

**Instructions for scoring, given in the manual for the Bangor Dyslexia Test, are as follows:**

### Left-right (body parts)

Score as plus:

1. Two errors or more
2. Consistent mirror image of correct answer
3. Subject turns in his seat (real or imagined)

Score as zero:

1. Report of earlier difficulty over left and right and/or report of special strategy (referring to watch, scar, "the hand I write with", etc.)
2. Hesitation in working out the answer in at least two items
3. Any two examples of echoing the question or asking for it to be repeated (e.g., "My left with your right, was it?")
4. One error

### Months Forward

Score as plus:

1. Any two or more omissions
2. Any two or more inversions (for example, "October, September" for "September, October")
3. Any uncertainty where to start
4. Any query about the importance of order (for example, "Do I have to say them in order?")

Score as zero:

1. Any two corrections
2. Any one omission (for example, leaving out September)
3. Any one inversion
4. Any report of earlier difficulty or special tuition

### Months Reversed

Score as plus:

1. Any two or more omissions
2. Any two or more inversions

Score as zero:

1. Any two corrections
2. Any special strategies, (for example, saying the months forward under his breath)
3. Any one omission
4. Any one inversion

Note that in both months forward and months reversed a single corrected error is scored as minus.

# APPENDIX III.
**Extracts from Tables 26.3 and 26.4 of** *Dyslexia: The Pattern of Difficulties*
**(Miles 1993).**

These two tables show the relationship between (supposed) dyslexia indicators and educational performance (table 26.3) and educational underachievement (table 26.4). The technique used was that of stepwise regression (for an
account of this technique see Norusis 1983). The first column in each case
shows the regression coefficients. These indicate how much the word recognition test score (in this example) changes for unit increase in the variables in
the equation. Thus it can be seen from the analysis that there is a much greater
change associated with Recall of Digits and Months Reversed than there is for
the others. Column 2 shows that these two items were accounting in conjunction for 13.87% of the variance. It can also be seen that whereas the gender of
the child has an influence on word recognition performance (a positive value
indicating that girls had higher scores than boys), it is tiny compared with the
influence of the (supposed) dyslexia indicators. Further analysis (not given
here) showed similar effects for spelling, spelling residuals, the Edinburgh
Reading test, and a mathematics test.

| Extracts from Table 26.3 | | | |
|---|---|---|---|
| | Regression coefficient | Explained variance(%) | Change (%) in explained variance |
| *Word recognition test* | | | |
| **Recall of Digits** | −0.29 | 8.53 | 8.53* |
| **Months Reversed** | −0.27 | 13.89 | 5.34* |
| **Left-Right test** | −0.15 | 14.99 | 1.11* |
| **Months Forwards** | −0.21 | 15.93 | 0.96* |
| **Gender** | 0.02 | 15.99 | 0.06+ |

A further analysis was then carried out using the word recognition and
spelling residuals, i.e. removing the influence of intelligence. The results were
as follows:

| Extracts from Table 26.4 | | | |
|---|---|---|---|
| | Regression coefficient | Explained variance(%) | Change (%) in explained variance |
| *Word recognition test* | | | |
| **Months Reversed** | −0.18 | 3.08 | 3.08* |
| **Recall of Digits** | −0.17 | 5.32 | 2.24* |
| **Months Forwards** | −0.16 | 6.12 | 0.80* |
| **Left-Right test** | −0.05 | 6.16 | 0.04* |

*p<0.001
+p<0.005

# Advances in Early Years Screening for Dyslexia in the United Kingdom

*A. J. Fawcett*

Dept. of Psychology, University of Sheffield, United Kingdom

*C. H. Singleton*

Dept. of Psychology, University of Hull, United Kingdom

*L. Peer*

British Dyslexia Association, Reading, United Kingdom

*In this article, we describe two United Kingdom (UK) screening tests for dyslexia: the Dyslexia Early Screening Test (DEST) and the Cognitive Profiling System (CoPS 1), both normed and designed to be administered by teachers to children four years and older. We first outline the political context in the UK, which for the first time, makes the use of such tests viable. We then outline the research programs behind and the components of each test; reliability and validity are also discussed. Information is presented on the tests in use. We conclude that tests such as these have the potential to identify children as at risk before they fail, halting the cycle of emotional and motivational problems traditionally associated with dyslexia. Both tests are appropriate for use in the United States, and initial reactions from the education sector have been favorable.*

Annals of Dyslexia, Vol. 48, 1998
Copyright© 1998 by The International Dyslexia Association
ISSN 0736-9387

# INTRODUCTION

For many years, it has been the hope of applied dyslexia researchers to develop a screening test able to identify children as at risk for dyslexia before they fail to learn to read, that is, by age six years or younger. There is no doubt that such a screening procedure, if feasible, would be of immense help. Research has shown clearly that the earlier the intervention, the easier it is for a child with dyslexia to learn to read, and the less danger there is of psychological trauma. But despite the clear value of early screening for dyslexia, and despite excellent research in the area (e.g., Scarborough 1991; Badian 1994; Fawcett, Pickering, and Nicolson 1993; Singleton 1988; Singleton and Thomas 1994), until recently viable measures have not been available in any English-speaking country.

We believe that the time is now right for the acceptance of such screening tests, and in this article we present our reasons for optimism, namely, that the current political backdrop in the United Kingdom ensures, for the first time, that such tests are educationally acceptable. Information for this section is based on the work of Lindsay Peer, Education Director for the British Dyslexia Association. We go on to describe two early screening tests which are currently available in the UK: *the Dyslexia Early Screening Test* (DEST), designed at the University of Sheffield by Nicolson and Fawcett; and the *Cognitive Profiling System* (CoPS 1), designed at the University of Hull by Singleton, Thomas, and Leedale.

# THE POLITICAL BACKGROUND IN THE UNITED KINGDOM

We believe that in the UK, we have found a practical catalyst for change in the form of diagnostic tests for all at school entry. These tests have been designed and tested by psychologists for use by teachers or classroom assistants. In a joint project targeting research into practice, the British Dyslexia Association (BDA) ran trials of the early identification packages described in this article, providing in-service training in four education authorities (districts). The BDA is in some ways comparable to the International Dyslexia Association, serving as the UK's voluntary umbrella organization to coordinate action for people with dyslexia of all ages. However, in the UK, there are no funds dedicated to dyslexia research, whereas in the United

States (US) substantial annual funding is provided by the National Institutes of Health. Consequently, research in the UK tends to be scattered in different university departments, which typically compete for access to funding that is largely provided by charities rather than by the government. The dyslexia research units in Sheffield and Hull have been conducting research on dyslexia for more than a decade. The only links between the two units are the common concern they share for people with dyslexia, and the fact that both units have independently created preschool screening tests for dyslexia. These tests are unique in the UK in that they test a *range* of skills; a number of excellent tests available for this age group evaluate disparate skills. Before the current project was conceived, CoPS 1 and the prototype DEST had been designed by their respective authors, and the BDA was sufficiently enthusiastic about the broad opportunities which these tests presented to suggest that they should be tried out nationwide. The project was backed by British Telecom, BBC TV, and the Honourable Lord Walker. It has proved highly successful overall, judging from the response of the education authorities and teachers involved in the evaluation. In fact, the reaction has been so encouraging that the Teacher Training Agency has recently directed extra funding to the BDA for dissemination of these packages into higher education institutions so that trainee teachers can be taught to use them. This paper represents a rare collaboration between independent research groups with the goal of informing our American readers about the options available for screening children with dyslexia and other learning difficulties.

In Britain, there has been a great deal of pressure on the government to implement educational change, leading to a system whereby children with dyslexia, who have different learning needs, can be identified and supported at an early age. Children in the UK start school either in the term in which their fifth birthday falls, or as a "rising 5" entering the reception class at age 4.5 years. Teaching of letter sounds begins in the first week of school, and by the second term, it is expected that the children will come to grips with simple CVC words. All children are expected to have their first reading book by the end of the first year, and many children will have taken off with their reading by this time. Formal reading instruction is, therefore, initiated considerably sooner in the UK than in the US, where it typically starts with six-year olds in Grade 1. Consequently, the British regime provides especially good opportunities to identify any problems during the first year of school. Moreover, unlike in the US where educational decisions are made by each individual state, educational policies in the UK are created at the national level. It is therefore possible, in principle, to introduce sweeping reforms.

A major factor in the success of early years screening tests was the 1993 Education Act which, linked with the 1994 Code of Practice, clearly placed dyslexia on the mainstream school agenda. Paragraph 3.60 states:

**Specific Learning Difficulties (for example, Dyslexia)**
Some children may have significant difficulties in reading, writing, spelling or manipulating numbers, which are not typical of their general level of performance. They may gain some skills in some subjects quickly and demonstrate a high level of ability orally, yet may encounter sustained difficulty in gaining literacy or numeracy skills. Such children can become severely frustrated and may also have emotional and/or behavioural difficulties.

The *Code of Practice on the Identification and Assessment of Special Educational Needs* (Department for Education 1994) provides a significant clarification in terms of identifying and supporting children with special educational needs of all types, including specific learning difficulties such as dyslexia. It reflects the current ethos in education in the UK, which has moved away from teaching children with special educational needs in special schools toward integration into mainstream schooling. In order to achieve this, the burden has been placed on schools for the first time to identify and support children with special educational needs in the early years of school. The Code of Practice defines special educational needs as "a learning difficulty which calls for special educational provision" (§2.1); it suggests that about 20 percent of children will have special educational needs at some time, but the vast majority of these can be met by appropriate support within the child's school, with outside help where necessary (§2.2). This 20 percent will be made up of children with a range of special educational needs, including physical and sensory deficits and low intelligence, as well as specific learning difficulties (including dyslexia). Approximately 2 percent will have needs of such severity or complexity that they require an assessment for a "statutory statement of special educational needs." Note that as outlined above, this 2 percent includes children with special needs of all types. However it is now generally accepted that 4 percent of all children will be severely dyslexic (Badian

1984), and approximately 6 percent mildly or moderately dyslexic. The Code of Practice, then, prescribes formal assessment for only a limited subgroup of children with the most severe dyslexia.

The "Statutory Assessment" requires advice from the child's parents and from a number of professionals from educational, medical, psychological, and social services. Statutory Assessment is the fourth stage in the recommended procedure for identification and remediation of special educational needs. Schools must first identify children with difficulties and provide a course of structured remediation before any statutory assessment processes can be set in motion. The first three stages of the process involve early identification (at around age five years) and then support within the school by either the classroom teacher, the school's special educational needs coordinator, or external specialists. The Code provides a valuable summary of these early stages:

> **2.119** In summary, schools should adopt a staged response to children's special educational needs and:
> - employ clear procedures to identify and register children whose academic, social or emotional development is giving cause for concern
> - identify children's areas of weakness which require extra attention from their teachers or other members of staff
> - develop, monitor, review and record, in consultation with parents and involving the child as far as possible, individual education plans designed to meet each child's identified needs. Such plans should in clude written information about:
>   - individual programmes of work
>   - performance targets
>   - review dates, findings and decisions
>   - parental involvement in and support for the plans
>   - arrangements for the involvement of the child
>   - information on any external advice or support
> - assess children's performance, identifying strengths as well as weaknesses, using appropriate measures so that the rate of progress resulting from special educational provision can be assessed
> - call upon specialist advice from outside the school to inform the school's strategies to meet the child's special educational needs in particular, but not necessarily only, at stage 3.

A guide for educators follows on the use of a five-stage support process derived from these guidelines. In essence, this system is meant to act as a funnel, by identifying children with mild, moderate, and severe problems, with the goal of providing in-school support targeted to remediate those problems. This early intervention should leave only a small core of children (2 percent) whose problems prove intractable, and who might need further support from outside the school system.

In theory, the Code of Practice has made it possible for teachers to identify all levels of dyslexia and other learning difficulties, and to put an individual education plan (IEP) into practice immediately. In some schools, this has worked very well. In practice, however, many teachers are worried by the requirements of the Code of Practice. They are aware that they have neither the necessary expertise to identify children with dyslexia or other special educational needs, nor the resources and skills to provide appropriate support for these children in a large classroom setting. In fact, many teachers would argue that the main impact of the Code of Practice lies in demanding an extra layer of administration from them. Typically, teachers were asked to prepare an IEP, without the benefit of additional financial resources to allow them to implement such a plan efficiently. The overall effect of this was that only those children with the greatest need were allocated extra resources through stage 5 of the process, under a Statement of Educational Needs. This is a formal and legally binding fully diagnostic assessment which provides protection for the child with special educational needs. Such a statement is reserved for children with the most pervasive problems, and its creation is a lengthy process, typically not completed until the age of eight or nine years. It is designed to specify exactly what type of support is necessary and how many hours support will be delivered weekly to ensure that children overcome their difficulties. The progress of children who hold a statement is monitored annually, in a formal meeting including parents, teachers, psychologists, and other interested professionals. Support for statemented children is expensive, and makes heavy demands on limited special-educational-needs resources, in that it is based largely on one-to-one teaching. It is, therefore, far more cost-effective to comply with the Code of Practice by identifying problems early and providing support before problems become entrenched.

In conclusion, only those children with the most severe impairments receive outside help in the early stages of the Code of Practice. Unfortunately for the remaining children, who show only mild to moderate difficulties, there are few resources left to meet their special educational needs. In reality, despite its good intentions, the Code of Practice often leaves the situation for children with special educational needs largely unchanged, serving only to hold teachers accountable, for the first time, for the failure of their pupils.

The reasons for difficulties in effective implementation of the Code of Practice are manifold. A particular problem lies in the fact that only a limited number of personnel are available to meet special educational needs despite escalating demand for early-years support. Teachers interact with children on a daily basis, so are well placed to notice any difficulties encountered. However, in order to obtain support for their children, traditionally they have needed to draw on the skills of educational psychologists who are already overcommitted. In the early stages of the Code of Practice, schools which were unable to meet the needs of their dyslexic pupils countered that their major problem lay in accessing the local authority educational psychologist for assessment of their children's needs. This complaint is merely the culmination of many years of frustration for teachers, caused by the need to wait for an educational psychologist to confirm their findings. This situation became untenable once the Code of Practice placed the burden to identify and support children through the early stages of assessment entirely on teachers. The majority of teachers are not fully trained to recognize dyslexia and other learning difficulties. Development of screening tests, specifically designed to be delivered by personnel largely untrained in psychometric testing (which became generally available in 1996), provided one solution to this problem. Naturally enough, teachers make ideal deliverers of screening tests because they are able to obtain a representative performance from even the youngest children. It could be said that screening tests have provided teachers with the tools necessary to undertake the assessments they are now routinely expected to deliver.

## SCREENING FOR DYSLEXIA IN THE UNITED KINGDOM

Fortunately, two early screening tests which fulfill the criteria for identifying primary school children at risk for difficulties have recently been published in the UK. Both the *Dyslexia Early Screening Test* (DEST) and the *Cognitive Profiling System* (CoPS 1) have been specifically tuned to the 1994 Code of Practice. These tests adopt a similar approach in quantifying strengths as well as weaknesses. Both tests are designed to be administered in the first term of school, with the goal of identifying children at risk of failure, before they fall behind their peers. Similarly, both tests are designed to be more accessible to young children than is the lengthy psychometric testing traditionally employed for diagnosis of dyslexia. In the UK, diagnosis would typically involve a full IQ test (the WISC-III, Wechsler 1991 or BAS II, Elliott 1996), an educational history, plus standardized tests of single word reading, spelling and the reading of connected text (including speed, accuracy, and comprehension). A test of free writing is frequently included, and on occasion, a personality test. A diagnostic screen of this type would take approximately three to four hours to complete. By contrast, a skilled tester can deliver the DEST in about 20 minutes, with each subtest taking only minutes to complete. CoPS 1 takes slightly longer to administer, about 45 minutes per child. It can be seen that both tests represent a significant advance in cost effectiveness when compared to traditional diagnostic measures.

It should be noted that the DEST and the CoPS 1 are not intended to replace traditional diagnosis, but rather to identify children at risk of failure for a range of different reasons, and provide pointers to the need for further assessment. The tests differ somewhat in their emphasis and in their research base, picking up different themes within the recommendations of the Code of Practice. The DEST covers a wide range of skills, including theoretically derived tests of motor skill and speed, as well as tests of phonological skills and memory. CoPS 1, by contrast, concentrates more exclusively on tests of phonological skills and memory. The DEST is designed to be inexpensive, self-contained, accessible to all schools without the need for special equipment; it can be interpreted by the teachers themselves. The CoPS 1, on the other hand, is delivered in computer format. It is necessarily more expensive to purchase, and should be interpreted by a psychologist. Neither test is designed for use or interpretation by parents. The tests are alike in that they both screen for a variety of learning difficulties, in addition to dyslexia, and provide a profile of skills which can form the basis of an Individual Education Plan (IEP). Interest in the tests is increasing, and both have been translated into a number of languages. Users of both CoPS 1 and the DEST report how useful they are finding these tests to be (see the report of the Special Needs Research Center 1998).

The authors of this article share expertise in dyslexia at all ages, developed over careers spanning a combined total of more than half a century. We have hands-on knowledge of both children and adults with dyslexia, and of the educational and emotional havoc that this disability can wreak. Consequently, it has long been our dream to produce a test to identify children with dyslexia before they fail. We consider that there have been at least three good reasons for the difficulties in establishing a successful early school test. First is the difficulty of designing and validating an early screening test. This involves not only choosing appropriate subtests but also demands longitudinal testing with a three-year lag between design, results, and revisions. The second obstacle is the high cost of administering screening tests, which traditionally have involved lengthy evaluations of each child by educational psychologists. The idea of testing an entire cohort of six-year olds at one time seemed almost hopelessly overambitious. The third, and in our view the most important, challenge is the hidden problem of the method of diagnosing dyslexia.

The kernel definition for many years has been that dyslexia is a disorder in reading. Consequently, a child needed to fail at reading for several years before it was possible to diagnose dyslexia. In our view, this over reliance on reading has led to intractable practical and theoretical difficulties in the understanding and diagnosis of dyslexia (Fawcett 1990; Singleton 1988; Nicolson 1996). Consider a simple applied case. A dyslexic child who is diagnosed with reading problems at age eight and given appropriate reading support may effectively overcome the reading difficulties and be reading at or above age level on tests of single word reading. Technically, the child is no longer dyslexic and no longer eligible for support, even if reading performance remains labored, and problems persist with the phonological skills underpinning reading. When some Local Education authorities have adhered too rigidly to this understanding of dyslexic impairments, there was no means to address these continued weaknesses. Even in the well-compensated dyslexic, deficits may still show up in the fluency of skills, particularly in reading unfamiliar words, in spelling, in working under time pressure, in short-term memory, and in general organizational skills (Augur 1985; Miles 1993). Current studies of dyslexia document the breadth of deficits, which may change with experience.

# THE DYSLEXIA EARLY SCREENING TEST
# (NICOLSON AND FAWCETT 1996)

## RESEARCH BASIS FOR THE DEST

In developing the DEST, the traditional scientific method of investigation was adopted, checking the performance of children with dyslexia across a wide range of ages and tasks including motor skill, speed of processing, and cognitive skills.

Recently, a wealth of evidence has been amassed for difficulties across a wide range of skills in dyslexia. This evidence is presented in detail in a book edited by Fawcett and Nicolson (1994) (see the chapters by Rack, Stein, Lovegrove, and Fawcett and Nicolson). However, these investigations typically examined single skills with a small group of dyslexics and controls, and failed to indicate the relative severity of the deficits. In order to investigate multiple skills in one sample, the Sheffield team administered a battery of over 50 tests to each child to assess reading, spelling, phonological skill, motor skill, memory, speed of processing, and balance. To check the effects of age, we tested 8-, 12-, and 16-year olds with and without dyslexia, but matched on general cognitive variables. The children with dyslexia performed significantly worse than their same-age controls on most of our tasks, and significantly worse even than their reading-level controls on tests of phoneme segmentation, picture naming speed, word flash (speeded reading), bead threading, blindfold balance, and dual task balance. Furthermore, 90 percent of the children with dyslexia showed marked impairments (performance at least one standard deviation below that of the controls) on at least two out of three tasks (dual task balance, segmentation, and picture naming speed) chosen to span the range of skills (Nicolson and Fawcett 1994).

The results from Nicolson and Fawcett (1994) were augmented by a predictive study of development of these same skills in children between four and six years of age (Pickering 1995). The Pickering study followed the progress of 110 nursery-school children and 30 siblings of persons with dyslexia; seventy-one and 20, respectively, of the original participants, were available for follow up two years later. Seventeen of these nursery-school children (24 percent) showed problems in literacy at age six or seven; 68 percent of those 17 showed a mild general learning disability (IQ 70–88). Only two children were clearly dyslexic. Initial testing of the siblings (who were somewhat older than the nursery-school children) revealed that the majority showed no evidence of problems; only four showed evidence of dyslexia. Moreover, despite our best efforts to retain our group of dyslexics' siblings, the three boys with the most clear-cut difficulties moved out of the area without leaving a forwarding address (possibly because their parents were also dyslexic?). Attrition of sample is one of the major problems in a study of this type, which attempts to follow children longitudinally, testing annually. Factor analysis was not possible on this data because of the high ratio of tests to children. However, children with dyslexia and slow learners showed problems in rhyming and motor skill speed at Phase 1, and the dyslexic group showed problems in phonological discrimination and copying. Deficits in these tests had been predicted from our work (and that of others) with children known to be dyslexic. Note however, that at this stage, the tests used were largely computer-based, and too lengthy to form a successful screening battery. We therefore refined the tests further, confident that in our converging research we had identified those tests likely to prove most useful in identifying problems of all types. Rather than evaluate these tests further in a second predictive study which would require a further four years of research, we decided that the time was right to start collecting norms. This would give us sufficient data to identify the normal range of scores on the various subtests of the DEST, which we needed in order to check whether the children were deemed to be at risk.

This article is not the place to address the full theoretical rationale for the DEST. Suffice it to say that the Sheffield approach confirmed the presence of severe phonological difficulties in the dyslexic panels at all ages, in line with a wealth of evidence of the importance of phonological skill in early reading (for a review of the area, see Bradley and Bryant 1983; Fowler 1991; Hatcher, Hulme, and Ellis 1994; Rack 1985; for the impact of training on phonological awareness skills, see Ball and Blachman 1991; Tangel and Blachman 1992; Felton 1994). Nevertheless, it is important to ensure that a wide enough range of potential deficits are covered in a screening test to keep pace with any theoretical changes. An excellent example of this is the meticulous approach adopted by Badian (1994), who has progressively refined her screening battery based on insights gleaned during her 15-year research program. Her original battery involved extensive specialist testing, and included three main categories of test: language, pre-academic, and visual motor. At that time, however, the seminal role of phonological skill had not yet been recognized. Subsequently, in order to improve the identification of children with difficulties, Badian (1994) augmented her standard battery with tests of phonological awareness, naming speed, and orthographic processing. The addition of these three new tests increased the success rate of the battery, accounting for 41 percent of the variance in reading/spelling at age seven years. This battery was good at identifying those children who were successful, with an overall hit rate of 91 percent, but even with the addition of the new tests, only 58 percent of the at risk children had confirmed reading difficulties at age seven years.

It would appear, therefore, that even tests involving extensive specialist testing (and hence not feasible for large-scale screening) are only moderately successful in identifying children likely to suffer from literacy difficulties. It is this rather disappointing level of cost-effectiveness that has dissuaded education authorities from implementing large-scale screening procedures. The major risk in developing such tests lies in deciding which tasks to include and which to leave out. In subsequent years, the authors may wish they had included a broader range of measures, which at the time of test development may not have been fully supported, just as phonological deficits were overlooked in earlier research. Naturally the emphasis here must be on including tests on which there is a consensus in the research community. Nevertheless, we were keen to augment the primitive skills tests with any recent theoretical developments in dyslexia. Therefore, measures of phonological skill, memory, knowledge, and motor skill were augmented by two additional types of measures. Tests of cerebellar function were derived from research suggesting that mild cerebellar dysfunction may underlie many dyslexic deficits (Fawcett, Nicolson, and Dean 1996). Measures of temporal order processing (Tallal et al. 1993) were based on the proposal that difficulties in rapid temporal processing of auditory information may underlie the phonological difficulties shown by dyslexic children. The Sheffield team propose to modify the next edition of the DEST if any measures fail to identify children with difficulties.

## SCREENING FOR DYSLEXIA

Before a cost-effective screening procedure could be developed, it was necessary to address the issue of how to reduce the cost of testing each individual child. By this stage, the DEST had moved away from its original computerized format so as not to demand expensive equipment not routinely available within the school system. Moreover, the Sheffield team had noted that while some teachers were enthusiastic in endorsing the use of computers, others were reluctant, and many lacked the necessary skills or motivation to use computers on a regular basis. In the DEST system for early screening for dyslexia, screening is undertaken by the school teacher (or school health professional) with the whole cohort of children tested at age five in much the same way that all children are screened for eyesight, hearing, and tooth decay. Those identified as at risk can be immediately supported in school, and those who still fail to progress may then be referred for further assessment, and an appropriate remediation program be developed. This screening ➤ assessment ➤ support approach can be adopted for screening at school for older children and for adult screening.

## COMPONENTS OF THE DEST, SCORING, AND INTERPRETATION

The above analysis led to the construction of the Dyslexia Early Screening Test (DEST) designed to identify children at risk of failure, and to produce an individual profile of performance which provides pointers to remedial intervention. The intention was that the measures adopted would cover a sufficiently wide range of skills in which the Sheffield team, and other researchers, had found impairment, to give positive indicators of difficulty. Naturally, the measures selected were based on those with the greatest severity and highest incidence in the general population of children with dyslexia (Nicolson and Fawcett 1994) (see table 1). The Sheffield team chose to augment tests of phonological skill with tests of clumsiness on the basis of research outlined above (Fawcett, Nicolson, and Dean 1996). The choice of measures has also been tuned to the requirements of the Code of Practice, §3.60-3.63, which requires that for the initial stages in statementing, there be ". . . clear, recorded evidence of clumsiness, significant difficulties of sequencing or visual perception; deficiencies in working memory; or significant delays in language functioning" (§3:61iii). This does not mean that dyslexia cannot be diagnosed without evidence of deficits in any of these areas. Rather, these are areas which the Code of Practice has identified as potential evidence for specific learning difficulties, in children who show problems in the early stages of literacy which are not typical of their general level of performance, or their high level of oral ability. It should be noted here, of course, that the DEST was designed to screen not only for dyslexia but also for learning difficulties of all types, including language delay and general intellectual impairment.

| | Test | Description |
|---|---|---|
| | **TABLE 1. SUBTESTS IN THE DEST (4.5–6.5 YEARS)** | |
| Test 1 | Rapid Naming | Time taken to name 40 simple outline pictures. |
| Test 2 | Beads | Number of beads threaded in 30 seconds. |
| Test 3 | Phonological Discrimination | Ability to detect subtle differences in spoken words (such as *fin* versus *thin*). |
| Test 4 | Postural Stability | How much the child wobbles when pushed gently in the back with a cali brated testing device. Standard test of cerebellar function (balance). |
| Test 5 | Rhyme Detection/ Alliteration | Ability to decide whether or not two spoken words rhyme, and to identify the first sound in a word. Standard tests of phonological awareness. |
| Test 6 | Digit Span | Ability to recall a series of digits in the order spoken. A test of working memory. |
| Test 7 | Digits | Ability to name individual digits. A straightforward test of knowledge. |
| Test 8 | Letters | Ability to name individual letters. |
| Test 9 | Sound Order | Ability to decide which of two sounds was presented first, as the time between onset of the two is steadily decreased. |
| Test 10 | Shape Copying | Ability to copy a series of shapes. |

Over one hundred schools nationwide participated in the pilot study of the prototype DEST; the schools evaluated the tests for ease of administration and returned their data and comments to the Sheffield team. On the basis of these comments, modifications were made to the instructions and tests of muscle tone, and processing speed were omitted from the final version because they were difficult for teachers to administer, and required complex equipment. Each subtest was designed to be fun, to take no more than a couple of minutes to administer, and to include a practice to ensure that the child understands what is required. Phonological skills include phonological discrimination (after Bishop 1985), rhyming (a simplified version of Bradley and Bryant 1978; 1985), and alliteration. Speed tests include rapid automatized naming (Denckla and Rudel 1976); the motor skill tasks include bead threading and copying. The test of cerebellar function (Fawcett, Nicolson, and Dean 1996) is postural stability (the degree of imbalance caused by a gentle push in the back). The knowledge tests are digit and letter naming. In addition, the battery was augmented with a simplified version of the Tallal sound order test (Tallal et al. 1993), devised by the Sheffield team and requiring judgment of the order of a mouse squeak and a duck quack. Each subtest may provide an independent positive indicator of dyslexia, but it is recommended that the profile as a whole be used to indicate whether or not a child is at risk of failure.

The scoring procedure allows the tester to identify whether each child is at risk, without further reference to psychological expertise. It follows the simple but clear positive indicator system introduced by Miles in the Bangor Dyslexia Test (1982). Age-based norms have been developed such that on each subtest a child is scored either "−−" (high risk), "−" (moderate risk), or "0" (neutral). Scores of "+" or "++" indicate above average performance. The individual scores for each subtest may then be combined to derive an at-risk quotient (ARQ) for each child, with an ARQ of 0.9 or greater providing strong evidence of being at risk, and an ARQ of 0.6 or greater indicating mild evidence of risk. At-risk children may then be referred to educational psychologists for full psychometric assessment of their needs. A skyline or profile chart may also be completed from the DEST which allows the pattern of the positive indicators of difficulty to be highlighted. This leads to suggestions for remediation, forming an Individual Education Plan, as specified in the Code of Practice. At-risk scores in areas such as rhyming call for remediation; digit span weaknesses suggest memory difficulties; discrimination weaknesses may derive from hearing problems. Other areas of weakness, such as cerebellar impairment, are less directly related to school work but may be useful for diagnosis rather than remediation. An example of the DEST in use, with a child whose parents were concerned about his progress, is presented in figure 1. The DEST results here indicate strong risk with support needed in language and motor skills. Particularly poor scores on discrimination indicate the need for further assessment of hearing.

The value of the approach was assessed by asking the teachers involved to comment on how well the children picked out as at risk corresponded to their own prior judgments. Nineteen schools who contributed data to the norms completed and returned an informal questionnaire. All those participating considered the approach potentially valuable, and many commented that for some children, the DEST confirmed and

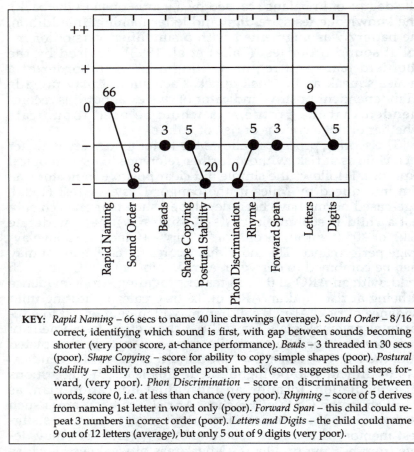

**KEY:** *Rapid Naming* – 66 secs to name 40 line drawings (average). *Sound Order* – 8/16 correct, identifying which sound is first, with gap between sounds becoming shorter (very poor score, at-chance performance). *Beads* – 3 threaded in 30 secs (poor). *Shape Copying* – score for ability to copy simple shapes (poor). *Postural Stability* – ability to resist gentle push in back (score suggests child steps forward, (very poor). *Phon Discrimination* – score on discriminating between words, score 0, i.e. at less than chance (very poor). *Rhyming* – score of 5 derives from naming 1st letter in word only (poor). *Forward Span* – this child could repeat 3 numbers in correct order (poor). *Letters and Digits* – the child could name 9 out of 12 letters (average), but only 5 out of 9 digits (very poor).

*Figure 1.* *Case Study of a child age 5 years 5 months, exhibiting language delay, lethargy, head injury. Outcome: – – 3, – 5, total (2 x 3) + 5 =11. ARQ 1.1.*

strengthened their judgments; for other children, it alerted them to problems that they had previously not noticed. On a scale of 1 to 4, where 1 = not useful and 4 = extremely useful, the DEST was allocated a mean score of 3.33. However, two schools commented that the DEST was less useful for children older than six and one-half years. It did not identify two children known to be dyslexic; despite having achieved average scores on many of the subskills of reading, they were still unable to read. This led us to alter the age range for which we recommended the DEST. Of the teachers sampled in this questionnaire, 85 percent indicated that they found the test useful in revealing areas of difficulty for their children generally, as well as for detecting more profound problems for children with special educational needs. The + and ++ categories enabled testers to identify areas of strength as well as weakness; this proved particularly useful in schools where the caliber of the intake is generally low as it allowed children with strengths to receive appropriate support to achieve their potential. Furthermore, the test format was appropriate to the target sample: teacher feedback indicated that few children suffered anxiety in doing the tests, most children had no difficulty completing the tests in one session, and both children and teachers enjoyed taking part. Feedback from the schools participating in norm collection suggests that over 90 percent would like to see the DEST introduced as routinely as the current eye test. After norm collection was completed, the DEST was also involved in the BDA and British Telecom initiative for Early Identification and Intervention, which trained local education authorities in the use of screening tests. Four training days were undertaken by the authors, but overall, the DEST proved easily accessible to teachers without the need for specific training in its use. A report on DEST and CoPS1 in use, is available from the Special Needs Research Center 1998.

Originally, the DEST was designed for children up to the age of seven years, but as outlined above, the pilot data suggested that by this age, tests of literacy are necessary to differentiate children with reading problems. The Sheffield Dyslexia Screening Test (DST, 6:6-16:5) was therefore modified to make it appropriate for this age range. The DEST and DST (UNITED KINGDOM versions) were published in the spring of 1996. The DEST has been normed on approximately 1000 (unselected) children; the DST was normed on 860 children, including 60 diagnosed with dyslexia. Norms for the DEST have been calculated for children at six-monthly intervals because pre-reading skills develop so rapidly at this stage. This means that the comparison groups for the norms are based on about 250 children at each age bracket, drawn from a range of backgrounds. Currently, around 2,500 copies of the DST and DEST are in use in schools throughout the UK and in other English-speaking areas of the world.[1]

---

[1] In acknowledgment of the pervasive nature of dyslexia, a screening test for adults with dyslexia (the Dyslexia Adult Screening Test [DAST], Fawcett and Nicolson 1998) has recently been normed, both for students and for the general population.

## THE VALIDATION STUDY

Having collected the norms for the DEST, the major outstanding requirement was to undertake a longitudinal predictive study where the progress of the five-year-old cohort was followed through to the age of seven so as to identify which of those identified as at-risk at age five do indeed turn out to be dyslexic. In March 1997, 97 children who had been tested on the DEST in October 1994 (mean CA 5:4), were retested on WORD Reading and Spelling (at mean CA 7:9).[2] The group represented a range of scores on the DEST and included all children originally screened in Sheffield who had remained in their original school. When screening the children at age five, our criteria for categorizing a child as at-risk for dyslexia or other learning difficulties was a score of 1.0 or greater on the DEST. For this group of children, the hit rate was 15/20 children, and the false positive rate 5/75. Our criterion was thus reasonably successful in identifying children who would later show problems, but it is possible to improve the hit rate with slight retrospective modifications to the criteria. By applying a DEST cutoff of 0.9, and defining our reading deficit outcome as a deficit of 10+ months, we obtained a hit rate of 90 percent. As evident in figure 2, those children showing the highest evidence of risk on the DEST came out with the largest reading age deficit. Correlational and other statistical analyses revealed significant differences between scores of the children in the at-risk group, and the no-risk group on all subtests of the DEST. (The shape-copying subtest was not available for this cohort; we intend to replace this subtest with a visual test for the next edition of the DEST). Digit names, rhyming, digit span, and rapid naming were the most highly correlated with reading ability at age eight, with correlations of 0.701, 0.615, 0.520, and -0.443, respectively, with the ARQ (at risk quotient) correlating at 0.64. However, the ARQ correlated most highly overall with reading *deficit* at age eight, $r = 0.675$, with the next highest correlation being digit naming, $r = 0.442$. This suggests that the combined ARQ score on the DEST at age five is more useful than scores on the individual subtests in terms of identifying those children who will show reading difficulty at age eight.

In this validation study, a false-positive rate of 12 percent was obtained, with eight of the children incorrectly predicted to

[2] This cohort of children were selected for ease of access for the Sheffield team, forming the complete cohort of children tested by the team in two schools in the Sheffield region.

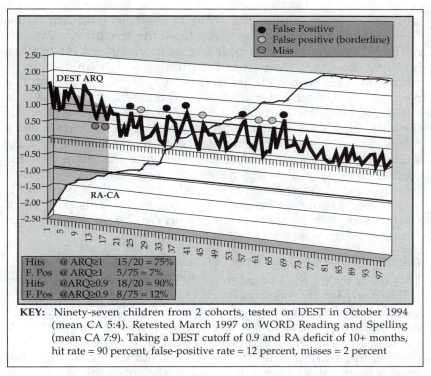

KEY:  Ninety-seven children from 2 cohorts, tested on DEST in October 1994
      (mean CA 5:4). Retested March 1997 on WORD Reading and Spelling
      (mean CA 7:9). Taking a DEST cutoff of 0.9 and RA deficit of 10+ months,
      hit rate = 90 percent, false-positive rate = 12 percent, misses = 2 percent

*Figure 2.    Validation study (DEST). Scatterplot of DEST At-Risk
              Quotient versus Reading Age Deficit.*

be at risk by the DEST when we modified the at-risk score from
1.0 to 0.9. In our view, it is advantageous to have a cutoff score
which identifies the majority of children at risk even at the ex-
pense of being slightly overinclusive. Some structured early support would be beneficial to most children, regardless of whether
they were strongly at risk of failure. Only two children who
showed mild evidence of risk were missed on this analysis, leading to a false-negative rate of only 2 percent. This led us to suggest that a category of mild risk should be introduced to include
children with ARQ scores of 0.6 or greater. These results suggest
that the predictive validity of the DEST is high overall, and can
be increased by introducing a category of mild risk.

From an experimental viewpoint, it would have been ideal
if schools were not made aware of any potential difficulties, so
that differential treatment of children identified as at-risk on
the DEST would not influence the outcome at age seven. On
the other hand, it would have been unethical not to provide the

support needed to help the child to learn to read normally. Consequently, feedback was given to all the schools involved in norm collection, and with tests expressly designed for teacher interpretation, it is clear from the profiles which children have problems, and in which areas those problems lie.[3] In fact, a member of the Sheffield team provided remedial training to four of the eight children who later fell into the false-positive group in the validation study. Interestingly enough, these children clearly fulfilled the criteria for reading deficit at the start of the training study, about six months before the retest (see Maclagan 1998 for further details). Following systematic intervention over a ten-week period, these children had caught up with their peers sufficiently to drop out of the reading deficit group. This pilot work suggests that short-term intervention can be successful with young children who are at risk of reading failure.

## USING THE DEST FOR SUPPORT

This leads to the final point from the Sheffield group. Screening children to identify their risk levels must lead naturally to remediation targeted to their areas of weakness. The DEST is designed to be readministered after six months, and it is therefore recommended that the DEST profile be kept with the child's records in order to quantify the development of skills following remediation. In a recent, carefully designed study with matched control groups, a new cohort of 62 6-year olds were identified as at risk on the basis of a standardized test of reading (the WORD test of single word reading), and subsequently received reading assistance in small groups (Nicolson et al. in press). The WORD test is useful in this context because it starts from the prereading level. For example, the child is shown a picture of the sun, and asked to find the word from 4 presented which starts with the same sound as "sun"). Children were also screened on the DEST and given the British Picture Vocabulary Scales (BPVS) (Dunn, Dunn, and Whetton 1982). In the approach adopted, the classroom teachers selected the bottom half of their classes for screening. There were a total of four participating schools, located in two different geographic areas, with one school in each area drawing from a

---

[3] Of course, it might be suggested that if the school has knowledge of deficits in individual children, they are bound to intervene and this may contaminate the research design. It seems likely that all longitudinal educational research in the UK will face the problems of this type now that the government is focusing on Literacy *Hour*. Literacy has become *the* major issue, every school is now required to present a Literacy *Hour* daily, and any children with problems are likely to receive intensive help, particularly in a school where parents are concerned and push for results.

largely middle-class background and the other from a lower socioeconomic background. The approach proved highly effective, such that 40 of the 62 trained children were reading single words at the 90th percentile or better for their age. It was also highly cost-effective, given a total dedicated teacher time of only 3.5 hours per child. However, about one quarter of the trained group (just over 10 percent of the total cohort) remained problem readers. The likelihood of being a problem reader was thus greater for older children (confirming the need for early support) and for children with high scores on the Dyslexia Early Screening Test.

In summary, a screening→ assessment→ support system would be of immense value to all those involved in education, and especially in helping students with learning difficulties. Theoretical work in the Sheffield lab and elsewhere identified a range of measures which can predict dyslexia with reasonable accuracy. Two thirty-minute screening tests—the DEST and DST— were constructed to be used from 4.5 years up; these serve as the first stage in the screening → assessment → support system. The screening tests fit naturally within the existing UK Code of Practice framework and are also appropriate for use in the US and other English-speaking countries. The tests lead naturally to early support, on the "stitch in time" principle, forming the basis of an Individual Education Plan for each child.

## COPS 1 COGNITIVE PROFILING SYSTEM

CoPS 1 Cognitive Profiling System is a fully computerized psychometric assessment system for use with children aged 4 years 0 months through 8 years 11 months (Singleton, Thomas, and Leedale 1996, 1997). The purpose of CoPS 1 is to identify children's cognitive strengths and weaknesses, which can give an early indication of who is at risk for dyslexia and other learning difficulties. However, the information generated by CoPS 1 is also valuable in enabling the teacher to recognize the learning styles of all children in the age range. This can assist the teacher to differentiate teaching so that it addresses individual educational needs more appropriately. CoPS 1 was used by 85 schools participating in the Early Intervention Project carried out by the British Dyslexia Association in the United Kingdom during 1996-1997.

CoPS 1 is designed to be used by teachers, psychologists, and other appropriately trained and qualified persons working in education or related professions. Although CoPS 1 is straightforward to administer, interpretation of the results requires expertise in education and/or psychology; it is not designed for use by parents or untrained personnel. The CoPS 1 tests yield a graphical profile of the child's cognitive strengths and weaknesses, based on standardized norms. The graphic profile may be printed out, if desired, and used in consultation with psychologists and other educational specialists to help formulate an individual learning program.

CoPS 1 ideally should be used for screening all children at the time of school entry, or as soon as is convenient thereafter. When used in this way, it can identify many children who are likely to encounter significant difficulties in developing literacy skills but who might otherwise pass undetected at that stage. The problems experienced by such children may then be addressed swiftly and before these children have been discouraged by failure. CoPS 1 can also be used for the assessment of any child between the ages of four and nine who has encountered difficulties in learning. In such cases, CoPS 1 can help to reveal underlying cognitive causes of learning difficulties so that these may be taken into account when devising educational plans.

## THE RATIONALE FOR COMPUTER-BASED ASSESSMENT

Since the principal aim of the research behind CoPS 1 was to investigate techniques which teachers could use with ease and confidence to identify dyslexia in young children, the mode of delivery of the assessment tasks was important. There were three main reasons for choosing the computer to deliver these tests. First, the precision, objectivity, and flexibility of the computer made it an appropriate and effective tool for assessing cognitive strengths and limitations. Computer-based assessment techniques are now widely used in psychology (Bartram 1989) and education (Singleton 1997b), and the feasibility of computerized assessment of dyslexia has previously been demonstrated (Fawcett and Nicolson 1994; Hoien and Lundberg 1989; Inouye and Sorenson 1985; Seymour 1986; Singleton 1991).

Second, computer-based assessments require minimal training of the administrator, so busy teachers can utilize the system quickly without the need for lengthy or costly training. It would not be feasible for educational psychologists to carry out universal screening for dyslexia (even with the availability of a computer-based system) because there are insufficient human and financial resources to support this.

Third, compared to conventional assessment, computer-based assessment has been shown to be more attractive and less threatening to young children. In practice, the activities can be made enjoyable for young children who are thereby highly motivated to do the tasks. This contrasts with the resistance that is often encountered by an educational psychologist when trying to assess young children (Singleton 1997b).

## THE RESEARCH BASIS FOR COPS 1

Singleton (1987, 1988) outlined a cognitive model for the early diagnosis of dyslexia based an assessment of underlying strengths and weaknesses in abilities that are known to underpin the learning process, particularly in phonology and memory. The criteria on which conventional procedures are typically based (intelligence–attainment discrepancy and exclusion of social disadvantaging factors) biases identification toward relatively bright, middle-class children. Dyslexic children of lower ability and/or from less advantaged home backgrounds may be overlooked. Singleton (1994) argues that *early* identification can be established by reference to cognitive precursors, such as phonological awareness (Hulme and Snowling 1992; Snowling 1995) and memory (Beech 1997).

Over the period 1990-1996, researchers in the Department of Psychology, at the University of Hull carried out a longitudinal study of a representative sample of almost 400 children from 24 schools. At the beginning of the study, these children were all five years old. A total of 27 different computer tests were created in order to assess a wide range of cognitive abilities that are especially important in the early stages of literacy development, and that are believed to be valid indicators of dyslexia (Singleton and Thomas 1994). These tests, which are in the form of games with colorful graphics, animation, and high-quality digitized speech, included measures of visual and verbal memory, sequencing, phonological awareness, naming speed, auditory discrimination, and visual-perceptual analysis. These computer tests were administered to all the children in the sample; over the next four years their literacy, numeracy, and intellectual development was tracked using a variety of standardized psychological measures. The follow-up data were then used to determine which of the computer tests were the most effective predictors of dyslexia and other difficulties in literacy. The eight computerized tests which gave the most satisfactory results were selected and consolidated into a software package incorporating a pupil-registration system, facility for on-screen graphical profiling, and printout of results in both percentile and z-score formats. The whole suite was given the name *CoPS 1 Cognitive Profiling*

*System* (Singleton, Thomas, and Leedale 1996). The system was subsequently standardized on a new sample of over 800 children in the UK (Singleton, Thomas, and Leedale 1997). The components of CoPS 1 are shown in table 2.

The results of the longitudinal study showed that the selected computer tests gave a satisfactory prediction of at-risk status for children later found to be experiencing literacy difficulties and dyslexia (Singleton 1996). Correlational, regressional, and discriminant function analyses were carried out on the data when the children were eight years old. The highest correlations between the computerized tests at five years and reading ability (single word recognition) at age eight were in auditory sequential working memory (CoPS 1 *Races* test[4]; $r = 0.56$), phonological awareness (CoPS 1 *Rhymes* test; $r = 0.52$), auditory discrimination (CoPS 1 *Wock* test; $r = 0.44$) and visual sequential memory (CoPS 1 *Zoid's Friends* test; $r = 0.39$). A test of application of phonic rules administered at age eight also correlated significantly with these measures, with the highest correlation coefficient being 0.73 for the com-

TABLE 2. THE COMPOSITION OF THE COPS 1 SUITE OF COMPUTERIZED TESTS

| Name of Test | Principal Cognitive Mode | Principal Processing Skills Being Assessed |
|---|---|---|
| Zoid's Friends | Visual † | Sequential Memory (colors) |
| Rabbits | Visual | Sequential Memory (spatial + temporal) |
| Toybox | Visual † | Associative Memory (shape + color) |
| Zoid's Letters | Visual † | Sequential Memory (symbols) |
| Zoid's Letter Names | Auditory/Verbal | Associative Memory (symbols + names) |
| Races | Auditory/Verbal | Sequential Memory (names) |
| Rhymes | Auditory/Verbal | Phonological Awareness (rhyming) |
| Wock | Auditory/Verbal | Auditory Discrimination |
| Clown | Visual | Color Discrimination (supplementary test) |

† indicates that a verbal encoding strategy may augment visual strategies.

---

[4] These tests are "games" and are generally referred to by their names to avoid the complexities of the different aspects of visual sequential and verbal memory assessed by each.

puterized test of auditory discrimination (CoPS 1 *Wock* test). All these correlations were significant at the $p < 0.01$ level or better. Stepwise multiple regression analyses showed that the CoPS 1 *Rhymes* and *Races* tests administered at age five together accounted for 48 percent of the variance in reading ability at age eight; this can be compared to only 23 percent of the variance attributable to verbal intelligence in a study reported by Thomas et al. 1997.

Discriminant function analysis also produced encouraging results in a sample of 49 children who had completed the full CoPS 1, including the original tests and the follow-up at all stages. The sample was divided into two groups: eight year olds who attained scores more than 1 standard deviation below the mean on the *British Ability Scales* Word Recognition Test, and those scoring above this level. The overall prediction rate of CoPS 1 tests delivered at age five was found to be 96 percent, with a false-negative rate of 16.7 percent and a false-positive rate of only 2.3 percent, both of which are within acceptable limits (Singleton 1997a); this discriminant function is significant at a probability of $p < 0.03$. By contrast, a simple word recognition test given at age six was not found to predict reading difficulty at age eight nearly as well; although this measure generated a false-positive rate of only 3.3 percent, it resulted in a massive false-negative rate of 82.1 percent. In other words, early reading progress does not always guarantee later success. This is particularly pertinent in cases of those dyslexic children who are able to apply visual strategies for whole-word recognition in the early stages of learning to read, but who then fall behind as they get older because weaknesses in phonological processing and/or auditory memory hinder the acquisition of effective phonic reading skills. Comparison with other screening devices widely used in the UK also showed that CoPS 1 performed very favorably. For example, investigation of the Aston Index (Newton and Thompson 1982) has revealed 47 percent false-positives and 21 percent false-negatives (Kingslake 1982). Limitations of CoPS 1 are the time to administer the tests (45 minutes for all the tests, although it is possible to use a subset of tests), and the difficulty of interpreting some complex profiles (although this becomes much easier with practice).

## COPS 1 IN PROFESSIONAL PRACTICE

When interpreting CoPS 1 results and making recommendations for educational action, two fundamental educational strategies need to be kept in mind: (1) remediation of cognitive weaknesses, and (2) differentiated teaching in literacy. These two approaches should be *complementary* rather than *contradictory*. Many cognitive abilities which are especially important for early literacy (such as phonological awareness and auditory discrimination) generally improve with practice. Where CoPS 1 reveals limitation in these skills, the teacher knows where and with which students to give remediation. However, the objective of CoPS 1 is not only the identification of specific cognitive weaknesses to be targeted for remediation, but also to give the teacher insights into the child's pattern of cognitive strengths and weaknesses. This enables the teacher to make the literacy learning program for the child more *individualized*, such as instigating a structured multisensory phonics teaching program for children who display weaknesses in phonological awareness and auditory sequential memory (which will show up as low scores on the CoPS 1 *Rhymes* and *Races* tests). The best overall approach is usually one which attempts to remedy weaknesses, while simultaneously building on strengths. Many dyslexic children have strengths in visual memory, which can be utilized in developing alternative strategies for learning.

Occasionally, more unusual profiles are revealed. For example, a boy (MP) aged five years seven months was assessed with CoPS 1 because he was making very poor progress in literacy despite apparently being of at least average intelligence (a fact later confirmed in psychological assessment). His CoPS 1 profile (see figure 3) showed extremely low scores on the visual tests, and on *Wock* (auditory discrimination). MP's teachers had already recognized his auditory discrimination difficulties, which were subsequently ameliorated by surgery, and, in fact, had attributed his reading problems entirely to poor auditory discrimination, not realizing that he also had poor visual memory.[5] This was uncovered as a major factor in his difficulties in word recognition at that stage, which relied largely on whole-word strategies. An advantage of CoPS 1 is that it allows the teachers to uncover the cognitive causes of the child's difficulties without having to wait for assessment by a psychologist, which can lead to delays in making appropriate educational provision.

---

[5] Although some of the visual tests can involve an element of verbal labelling, the rabbits test is the equivalent of a Corsi blocks test, which involves clicking on a sequence of holes from which the rabbit jumps out. This is a visual memory span task, starting with two holes, and becoming more complex if the child is successful, which is not amenable to verbal labelling.

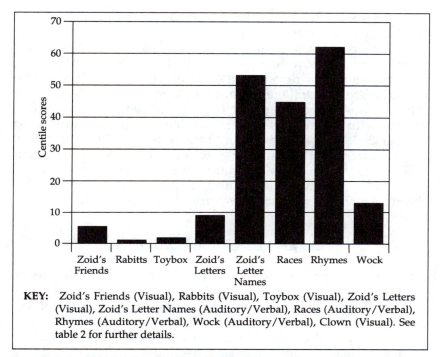

KEY:   Zoid's Friends (Visual), Rabbits (Visual), Toybox (Visual), Zoid's Letters (Visual), Zoid's Letter Names (Auditory/Verbal), Races (Auditory/Verbal), Rhymes (Auditory/Verbal), Wock (Auditory/Verbal), Clown (Visual). See table 2 for further details.

*Figure 3.    CoPS 1 Profile for MP (age 6 years 3 months).*

## CONCLUSIONS ON COPS 1

This research has shown that computer-based assessment of cognitive skills underlying literacy development can be a practical and cost-effective solution to the problem of early identification of children at risk of literacy difficulties and dyslexia. The CoPS 1 suite of tests is advantageous not only because it is easy to administer, but because young children find the computer activities enjoyable, a fact which overcomes many of the inherent difficulties experienced when trying to assess cognitive skills at this age.

The English version of CoPS 1 is currently in use in over 1,000 schools in the UK and elsewhere in the world. A survey of 85 schools using CoPS 1 as part of the Early Intervention Project carried out by the British Dyslexia Association, revealed a high degree of teacher satisfaction with the system (BDA 1997): 94 percent of the schools reported the CoPS 1 was "very useful" or "moderately useful." The main advantages of the system cited by teachers were that it identified strengths and weaknesses, had particular value in *early* identification, could give confirmation to a teacher who already suspected a problem, appealed to children, and was easy to use.

Since CoPS 1 is a diagnostic and assessment tool with fairly wide utility, it is now being used in the UK by teachers working both with typically developing children and with children who have dyslexia, ADHD, autism, or moderate to severe learning difficulties. A Swedish version (KoPS) was developed in collaboration with researchers at ReLS, Bollnäs, Sweden, and is used in over 200 schools and centers in Sweden (Ohlis et al. 1996). Versions in various other languages are now being explored, and the research team is currently working on the development and validation of a similar computerized assessment system for children aged 9 years 0 months through 15 years 11 months.

## OVERALL CONCLUSIONS

As a consequence of the availability of these screening tests, teachers for the first time have felt empowered to identify children with problems on norm-based tests, and to use this information to make suggestions for appropriate provision. The tests have facilitated the work of teachers at all levels of competence in special needs, from those who needed some clear guidance on how to proceed to those who were well aware of which children needed help, and used the norms to back up their professional judgment. Reaction to both the tests have been good, and the majority of schools who evaluated the tests have elected to continue using them. Demand for the tests is increasing.

Recent changes in the government in the UK have brought to power a party committed to an improved education system. This has led to the production of the 1997 Green Paper (a discussion document for education) which is the most in-depth examination of special needs education in the UK since the 1978 Warnock report. This renewed focus on special needs is largely attributable to a Secretary of State for Education who is himself blind; he is the father of two dyslexic boys, and so has a very real appreciation of the problems. At the same time, publicity has mounted on falling standards in literacy in the UK, in particular for boys, who the literature suggests may be more prone to dyslexic-type difficulties. Consequently, the pressure to make changes in the Special Needs provision efficiently and cost-effectively has never been stronger.

For the first time, there exists a strong political will in the UK to improve standards overall, with the introduction of innovations such as baseline testing and the Literacy Hour. Fortunately enough, we have the tools at hand to facilitate these initiatives. Lindsay Peer, on behalf of the British Dyslexia Association, has argued for a second tier of baseline screening, using tests such as the DEST and CoPS1 in the second term of school. The idea behind this is to identify children who have not made the expected progress in their first term at school; that is, children with mild and moderate difficulties, as well as those severe cases who can be identified in preschool. We believe that, together, we have provided the tools to make a significant contribution to the understanding, diagnosis, and remediation of developmental dyslexia and other learning difficulties, in the UK and in other English-speaking countries.

## ACKNOWLEDGMENTS

We acknowledge with gratitude the contributions of Prof. Rod Nicolson, at the University of Sheffield, Department of Psychology to the research outlined in this article. We also acknowledge the contribution of Dr. Susan Pickering at the University of Bristol, Department of Psychology, for contributions from her Ph.D. study. The research was supported by grants from British Telecom, the BBC, Lord Walker, the Psychological Corporation, the Leverhulme Trust, the British Dyslexia Association and the University of Hull. We are particularly grateful to the teachers and children in schools in the UK, nation-wide, for their support in the project.

*References*

Augur, J. 1985. Guidelines for teachers, parents and learners. In M. Snowling, ed., *Children's Written Language Difficulties*. Windsor: NFER Nelson.

Badian, N. A. 1994. Preschool prediction: Orthographic and phonological skills and reading. *Annals of Dyslexia* 44, 3–25.

Ball, E. W., and Blachman, B. A. 1991. Does phoneme segmentation training in kindergarten make a difference in early word recognition and developmental spelling. *Reading Research Quarterly* 26, 49–66.

Bartram, D. 1989. Computer-based assessment. In P. Herriot, ed., *Handbook of Assessment in Organisations*. London: Wiley.

Beech, J. R. 1997. Assessment of memory and reading. In J. R. Beech and C. Singleton, eds., *The Psychological Assessment of Reading*. London: Routledge, pp. 143–60.

Bishop, D. 1985. Spelling ability in congenital dysarthria: Evidence against articulatory coding in translating between graphemes and phonemes. *Cognitive Neuropsychology* 2, 229–51.

Bradley, L., and Bryant, P. E. 1978. Difficulties in auditory organization as a possible cause of reading backwardness. *Nature* 271, 746–47.

Bradley, L., and Bryant, P. E. 1983. Categorising sounds and learning to read: A causal connection. *Nature* 301, 419–21.

Bradley, L., and Bryant, P. E. (1985). *Rhyme and Reason in Reading and Spelling.* International Academy for research in learning disabilities series. Michigan: University of Michigan Press.

British Dyslexia Association 1997. CoPS 1 *Cognitive Profiling System: An evaluation of its use in the British Dyslexia Association Early Intervention Project.* Hull: University of Hull.

Code of Practice 1994. Code of Practice on the identification and assessment of special educational needs. DFE and Welsh offices, HMSO: London.

Denckla, M. B., and Rudel, R. G. 1976. Rapid 'Automatized' naming (R.A.N.). Dyslexia differentiated from other learning disabilities. *Neuropsychologia* 14, 471–79.

Dunn, L. M., Dunn, L. M., and Whetton, C. 1982. *The British Picture Vocabulary Scale.* NFER-Nelson, Windsor.

Elliott, D 1996. *British Ability Scales II.* Windsor, NFER-Nelson.

Fawcett, A. J. 1990. A *Cognitive Architecture of Dyslexia.* Unpublished Ph.D. thesis, University of Sheffield.

Fawcett, A. J., and Nicolson, R. 1994. Computer-based diagnosis of dyslexia. In C. H. Singleton, ed., *Computers and Dyslexia: Educational Applications of New Technology.* Hull, UK: Dyslexia Computer Resource Centre, University of Hull.

Fawcett, A. J., and Nicolson, R. I. Eds. 1994. *Dyslexia in Children: Multidisciplinary Perspectives.* London: Harvester Wheatsheaf.

Fawcett, A. J., and Nicolson, R. I. 1996. *The Dyslexia Screening Test.* The Psychological Corporation, London.

Fawcett, A. J., and Nicolson, R. I. 1998. *The Dyslexia Adult Screening Test.* The Psychological Corporation, London.

Fawcett, A. J., Pickering, S., and Nicolson, R. I., 1993. Development of the DEST test for the early screening for dyslexia. In S. F. Wright and R. Groner, eds., *Facets of Dyslexia and its Remediation.* Amsterdam: Elsevier Science Publishers B. V.

Fawcett, A. J., Nicolson, R. I., and Dean, P. 1996. Impaired performance of children with dyslexia on a range of cerebellar tasks. *Annals of Dyslexia* 46, 259–83.

Felton, R. H. 1994. Effects of instruction on decoding skills in children with phonological processing problems. *Journal of Learning Disabilities* 26, 583–90.

Fowler, A. E. 1991. How early phonological development might set the scene for phoneme awareness. In S. A. Brady and D. P. Shankweiler, eds., *Phonological Processes in Literacy.* Hillsdale, NJ: Lawrence Erlbaum Associates.

Hatcher, P., Hulme, C., and Ellis, A. W. 1994. Ameliorating early reading failure by integrating the teaching of reading and phonological skills. *Child Development.*

Hoien, T., and Lundberg, I. 1989. A strategy for assessing problems in word recognition among dyslexics. *Scandinavian Journal of Educational Research* 33, 185–201.

Hulme, C., and Snowling, M. 1992. Deficits in output phonology: an explanation of reading failure? *Cognitive Neuropsychology* 9, 47–72.

Hurford, D. P. 1990. Assessment and remediation of a phonemic discrimination deficit in reading disabled second and fourth graders. *Journal of Experimental Child Psychology* 50, 396–415.

Inouye, D. K., and Sorenson, M. R. 1985. Profiles of dyslexia: The computer as an instrument of vision. In D. B. Gray and J. K. Kavanagh, eds., *Biobehavioural Measures of Dyslexia.* Parkton, MD: York Press.

Kingslake, B. 1982. The predictive (In) Accuracy of On-entry to school screening procedures when used to anticipate learning difficulties. *Special Education* 10, 23–26.

Maclagan, F. 1998. Screening and remediation for children with learning difficulties. Unpublished PhD thesis, University of Sheffield.

Miles, T. R. 1982. *The Bangor Dyslexia Test*. Cambridge: Learning Development Aids.

Miles, T. R. 1993. *Dyslexia: The Pattern of Difficulties*. London: Whurr.

Newton, M. J., and Thompson, M. E. 1982. *The Aston Index* (Revised) Wisbech, UK: LDA.

Nicolson, R. I., and Fawcett, A. J. 1994. Comparison of deficits in cognitive and motor skills among children with dyslexia. *Annals of Dyslexia* 44, 3–26.

Nicolson, R. I., and Fawcett, A. J. 1996. *The Dyslexia Early Screening Test*. The Psychological Corporation, London.

Nicolson, R. I. 1996. Developmental Dyslexia: Past, Present and Future. *Dyslexia: An International Journal of Research and Practice* 2, 190–208.

Nicolson, R. I., Fawcett, A. J., Moss, H., Nicolson, M. K., and Reason, R. in press. An Early Reading Intervention Study: Evaluation and Implications. *British Journal of Educational Psychology*.

Ohlis, K., Singleton, C. H., Thomas, K. V., and Leedale, R. C. 1996. *KoPS Kognitif Profilerings System*. Stockholm: LIAB-Laromedia.

Pickering, S. J. 1995. The early identification of dyslexia. Unpublished PhD thesis; University of Sheffield.

Rack, J. 1985. Orthographic and phonetic coding in normal and dyslexic readers. *British Journal of Psychology* 76, 325–40.

Scarborough, H. 1991. Antecedents to reading disability: Preschool language development and literacy experiences of children from dyslexic families. *Reading and writing* 3, 219–33.

Seymour, P. H. K. 1986. *Cognitive Analysis of Dyslexia*. London: Routledge and Kegan Paul.

Singleton, C. H. 1987. Dyslexia and cognitive models of reading. *Support for Learning* 2, 47–56.

Singleton, C. H. 1988. The early diagnosis of developmental dyslexia. *Support for Learning* 3, 108–21.

Singleton, C. H. 1991. Computer applications in the diagnosis and assessment of cognitive deficits in dyslexia. In C. H. Singleton, ed., *Computers and Literacy Skills*. Hull: Dyslexia Computer Resource Centre, University of Hull.

Singleton, C. H. 1994. Computer applications in the identification and remediation of dyslexia. In D. Wray, ed., *Literacy and Computers: Insights from Research*. Widnes: United Kingdom Reading Association.

Singleton, C. H. 1996. Computerised Screening for Dyslexia. In G. Reid, ed., *Dimensions of Dyslexia*, Vol. 1. Edinburgh: Moray House Publications.

Singleton, C. H. 1997a. Screening for early literacy. In J. Beech and C. H. Singleton, eds., *The Psychological Assessment of Reading*. London: Routledge.

Singleton, C. H. 1997b. Computerised assessment of reading. In J. Beech and C. H. Singleton, eds., *The Psychological Assessment of Reading*. London: Routledge.

Singleton, C. H., and Thomas, K. V. 1994. Computerised screening for dyslexia. In C. H. Singleton, ed., *Computers and Dyslexia: Educational Applications of New Technology*. Hull: Dyslexia Computer Resource Centre, University of Hull.

Singleton, C. H., Thomas, K. V., and Leedale, R. C. 1996. *CoPS 1 Cognitive Profiling System: DOS Edition*. Beverley, East Yorks, UK: Lucid Research Limited.

Singleton, C. H., Thomas, K. V., and Leedale, R. C. 1997. *CoPS 1 Cognitive Profiling System: Windows Edition*. Beverley, East Yorks, UK: Lucid Research Limited.

Snowling, M. J. 1995. Phonological processing and developmental dyslexia. *Journal of Research in Reading* 18 (2)132–38.

Special Needs Research Center. 1998. *Impact of CoPS1 and DEST on teaching in primary schools*. Report for the British Dyslexia Association, Department of Education, University of Newcastle.

Tallal, P., Miller, S., and Fitch, R. H. 1993. Neurobiological basis of speech—A case for the pre-eminence of temporal processing. *Annals of the New York Academy of Sciences* 682, 27–47.

Tangel, D. M., and Blachman, B. A. 1992. Effect of phoneme awareness instruction on kindergarten children's invented spelling. *Journal of Reading Behaviour* 24, 233–61.

Thomas, K. V., Singleton, C. H., Leedale, R. C., Plant, R. R., and Horne, J. K. 1997. *Computer-based identification of dyslexia and special educational needs.* Paper presented at the 25th Anniversary Conference of the British Dyslexia Association, University of York, UK.

Wechsler, D. 1991. *Wechsler Intelligence Scale for Children III (WISC III).* San Antonio, TX: The Psychological Corporation.

# PART II
## Consequences and Correlates of Dyslexia: Beyond Phoneme Awareness

Phoneme awareness is a powerful conceptual achievement—both for the would-be reader and for the scientist seeking to understand the crucial links between spoken and written language. But it has long been recognized by both researchers and practitioners (1) that success in phoneme awareness depends crucially on other more basic factors; and (2) that other factors may also contribute to the reading difficulties of some children. We are pleased to publish this year four papers that consider correlates of reading difficulty that are not easily subsumed under the construct of phoneme awareness.

Chapters 4 and 5 are longitudinal studies of rapid serial naming, which is one of the most reliable and consistent (if least understood) long-term predictors of reading disability. By tracking students through the elementary school years, both provide valuable information about the developmental course of rapid naming skills and the association between rapid naming and other literacy-related skills over time. The normative data on naming presented in chapter 4 by M. Meyers and her colleagues will serve as a valuable resource to clinicians; their kindergarten results should also add to our understanding of the factors that influence naming speed. In kindergarten, the letter/number naming advantage (over object/color naming) is strongly tied to alphabet recitation accuracy; by first grade the letter/number advantage is no longer a useful index of any literacy measure. The data from H. Scarborough make clear just how important and stable naming is as a predictor of reading success. Even when collected at Grade 2, individual differences in naming speed account for variability in 8th grade reading above and beyond what can be explained by phoneme awareness. Scarborough's and other recent studies suggest ways that assessment in schools can easily be expanded to more accurately predict who would benefit most from intervention.

The preliminary study by Jaarsma and colleagues in chapter 6 investigates a much less studied phenomenon—the association betwen reading difficulties and difficulties in learning labels for musical notes. Jaarsma and colleagues note a number of parallels between the reading of text and the reading of music; their data suggest that at least some poor readers have weaknesses with sound-symbol correspondences that do not require explicit analysis of words into phonemes. It is a phenomenon worth pondering and studying in greater depth.

The final chapter in part II, by Cornelissen and Hansen, takes up the possibility that some (though by no means most) reading difficulties stem from visual processing impairments. The specific hypothesis is that deficits at the magnocellular level result in an unstable visual image, leading to exhanges among features across letters, shifts of letter order within words, and shifts of words within a line. Their paper begins with evidence that adult poor readers are slightly less able to detect coherent motion among moving dots on a computer screen than are adult skilled readers. It goes on to relate weaker performance on the motion detection task to a greater number of errors in a lexical decision task tapping susceptibility to letter reversals. Cornelissen and Hansen's second study focuses on children and reveals a nonlinear association between weak motion detection and letter reversal errors in a word reading task. Although the findings are subtle, this provocative paper makes an unusually clear presentation of the argument and should generate discussion among those trying to make links between neurobiology and behavior.

# Longitudinal Course of Rapid Naming in Disabled and Nondisabled Readers

*Marianne S. Meyer*

*Frank B. Wood*

*Lesley A. Hart*

*Rebecca H. Felton*

Wake Forest University School of Medicine

*The Rapid Automatized Naming Test (Denckla and Rudel 1974) was studied cross-sectionally in an sample of kindergartners (n = 342) at-risk for reading disability (Study 1), and longitudinally in an n = 160 epidemiological normal sample of children tested in first, third, fifth, and eighth grades (Study 2). Study 1 showed faster absolute naming speeds for those with near perfect untimed alphabet recitation, but the stronger and more orderly relation (at r = .31, p < .0001) was between three levels of alphabet recitation accuracy and the relative number/letter naming speed advantage (ratio of mean number/letter naming speed minus mean color/object naming speed over mean color/object naming speed). In Study 2, the number/letter advantage was already strongly present by first grade, and did not increase significantly thereafter, but absolute naming times improved steadily across grades in an exponential decay function. In this sample, the relative number/letter advantage was not related to reading level. However, the absolute color/object naming speed was strongly related*

Annals of Dyslexia, Vol. 48, 1998
Copyright© 1998 by The International Dyslexia Association
ISSN 0736-9387

*to reading level and vocabulary across grades. Norms for the Rapid Automatized Naming Test based on the epidemiological normal sample tested in Grades 1, 3, 5, and 8 are presented in the appendix.*

## INTRODUCTION

In 1974 Denckla and Rudel, noting the relationship between acquired alexia and childhood dyslexia, developed the Rapid Automatized Naming Test (RAN), which required rapid sequential naming of printed colors, numbers, objects, and letters. Two years later, they reported that deficits in rapid sequential naming differentiated children with dyslexia from learning disabled students without dyslexia and from normal controls (Denckla and Rudel 1976). At about the same time, LaBerge and Samuels (1974) proposed an information processing model that posited that good reading requires not only accurate, but also automatic, retrieval so that the reader's attention can be focused on meaning and content. Both sets of investigators considered automatic, rapid, and accurate retrieval an important component of skilled reading. These researchers laid the groundwork for much of the current research on rapid naming deficits which are increasingly considered to be among the underlying cognitive correlates of dyslexia.

Although there have been numerous subsequent studies on rapid naming and its role in reading acquisition, most of these studies have been either cross sectional or have followed children for only a few years. Moreover, studies have varied in their choice or preference within the four stimulus categories of the original RAN (Wolf, Bally, and Morris 1986; Lovett 1987; Walsh, Price, and Cunningham 1988; Bowers, Steffy, and Tate 1988; Badian, McAnulty, Duffy, and Als 1990; Cornwall 1992; Badian 1993; Ackerman and Dykman 1993; Torgesen, Wagner, and Rashotte 1994; Fawcett and Nicholson 1994; and Korhonen 1995). To date, no study has specifically addressed the longitudinal course of rapid serial naming over the elementary school years, nor have norms been collected for large groups of dyslexic versus nondisabled readers over an extended period of time.

Beginning with Denckla and Rudel (1976), many studies have shown that a slowed rate of rapid naming is a strong correlate of dyslexia. Findings differ on the relative sensitivity of the four rapid naming stimuli. Lovett (1987) found in a group of primarily nine to eleven year olds that naming speed deficits for all RAN stimuli differentiated fluent normal readers from readers weak in both rate and/or accuracy. When Lovett looked separately at readers who were slow and those who were inaccurate, both groups exhibited a comparable degree of disadvantage on colors, objects, and numbers, but not on letters. Based on these findings, Lovett suggested that accuracy disabled readers have a selective problem with accessing letter names in addition to a general deficit in naming speed for visual stimuli. Our recent findings (Meyer, Wood, Hart, and Felton 1998), based on color/object and number/letter composites, show that both graphological (letters and numbers) and nongraphological (colors and objects) naming speeds are equally sensitive to, and predictive of, sight word identification in third through eighth graders. Others also show this generality (Cornwall 1992; Fawcett and Nicholson 1994; Korhonen 1995). Other investigators find graphological stimuli to be more sensitive measures. For example, Wolf, Bally, and Morris (1986) found that kindergarten rate of response, for both graphological and nongraphological stimuli, predicts impaired readers from average readers in Grade 2. However, by second grade, only the speed of naming of letters and numbers—the graphological symbols—predicted Grade 2 reading level. Consistent with the Wolf et al. findings are those of Bowers, Steffy, and Tate (1988) who looked only at colors and numbers. Bowers et al. (1988) found that number naming, but not color naming, contributed significantly to the variance in sight word identification ($p <.001$) and word attack skills ($p < .05$) among eight- to eleven-year-old referred students.

Recently, a two-factor theory (Bowers and Wolf 1993; Wolf and Bowers 1997; Wolf and Obregon 1997) has suggested that a rapid naming deficit may be distinct and separable from a phonological processing deficit which most investigators agree is a powerful and persisting predictor of dyslexia (Stanovich 1988; Wagner and Torgesen 1987; Shankweiler and Liberman 1989; Adams 1990). Consistent with a two factor theory, Biddle (1996) suggested that within groups of dyslexic children, those with rapid naming ("rate") deficit may follow a different developmental path than those with phonological deficits.

Congruent with the deficit (as opposed to a maturational lag) model, differences in the rate of rapid naming are evident as early as kindergarten, persist through school, and continue to characterize adults diagnosed as dyslexic in childhood (Felton, Naylor, and Wood 1990; Flowers 1993; Korhonen 1995). Furthermore, a rapid naming appears to have considerable predictive power for concurrent and future reading achievement. Blachman (1984) found that rapid sequential color naming in kindergarten was strongly correlated with a kindergarten child's ability to identify upper and lower case letters. Felton and Brown (1990) found that rapid naming weaknesses identified in at-risk kindergarten children predicted their reading level in first grade and later. Felton (1992) reported a stepwise regression analysis showing that letter naming in kindergarten in particular was the most potent predictor of first grade reading. In a similar vein, Badian (1995) found that untimed letter naming (not rapid naming) in kindergarten was a strong predictor of reading level through sixth grade. Interestingly, rapid naming deficits seem specifically to predict deficits in sight word identification and in speed and accuracy of prose reading, but seem unrelated to reading comprehension (Wolf 1990; Torgeson, Wagner, Simmons, and Laughon 1990; Bowers and Swanson 1991; Cornwall 1992 ). Two large sample longitudinal studies showed rapid naming to be an especially strong long-term predictor of eighth-grade single-word reading within groups of poor reading third graders (Meyer, Wood, Hart, and Felton 1998). Furthermore, the evidence of generalizability across stimulus types notwithstanding, there is a face valid reason to think that at least letter naming would reflect mastery of the alphabet and possibly exposure to print (Stanovich 1986), so the longitudinal emergence of relative gains in letter/number naming speed would be a particularly important issue, particularly if this were shown to be related to reading performance.

## OVERALL METHOD

The present study documents the longitudinal course of rapid naming in kindergarten, elementary, and middle-school students. Data were obtained from two different groups within the same urban school system, identified at different stages of their educational careers. The first group included kindergartners rated by teachers as average, below average, and very poor in terms of expected future reading acquisition. (Those rated above average or superior were excluded.) The second group included randomly selected, normally distributed students (an appropriate random portion of whom were poor readers) ascertained in first grade and followed longitudinally through eighth grade.

## DEPENDENT MEASURES

The principal dependent measures for all of the above sample were the RAN tests developed by Denckla and Rudel (1974). On the RAN, children are required to name, as rapidly as possible, items presented visually on the four different charts. Each individual chart contains 50 items consisting of five different items presented in horizontal rows of ten items per row and randomly repeated. Stimulus sets are as follows:

(a) **colors**—red, yellow, green, blue, and black;

(b) single digit **numbers**—2, 4, 6, 7, and 9;

(c) line drawings of **objects**—key, scissors, umbrella, watch, and comb; and

(d) high-frequency lower case **letters**—o, a, s, d, and p.

Each test is scored for the seconds it takes to name each of the items on an individual chart in left-to-right and top-to-bottom sequence.

To introduce the task, children (or adolescents or adults) are told that we want to see how fast they can name some things with which they are familiar. The color chart is presented first, and the examiner points to each color on the chart and asks, "What color is this?" to determine if the child can identify the colors correctly. If the child can identify them correctly, the examiner then says, "Now I want you to start here (point) at the top of this chart and name the colors in this row (point), then the next row (point) all the way to the bottom as fast as you can without making mistakes and without skipping any." This same procedure is followed for the three subsequent charts (numbers, objects, letters). In each case, the examiner makes certain, before starting the timer, that the child can identify the stimuli accurately. Note that in the case of the object chart, the subject can choose to identify the watch as either a watch or a clock, but must consistently use that word throughout or it is counted as an error. The time it takes to complete the chart is recorded and the child's responses, including any uncorrected errors, are noted. Although errors are not corrected, the child is allowed to correct his or her own errors spontaneously. The time it takes for spontaneous self-correction is counted in the total time. At most, the total task requires 10 minutes, but by mid-elementary school, children often take less than 5 minutes.

To facilitate analysis, RAN raw scores were combined into a color and object composite (COLOBJ) and a letter and number composite (NUMLET). The composite letter/number and color/object scores were calculated as the mean of their respective component scores. We and others (Denkla and Rudel 1974; Wolf, Bally, and Morris 1986; Badian et al. 1991; and Korhonen 1995) have shown that numbers and letters require almost equal time to complete at all age levels. Colors and objects require a longer time to complete, with objects typically requiring approximately a third again as much time as colors. These two composites were chosen because numbers and letters are both printed symbols, whereas objects and colors are not. Therefore, number/letter scores are, on their face, more likely to reflect the impact of early learning to read, including alphabet mastery, whereas color/object scores are less obviously related to prior alphabet or reading mastery itself. Color/object composite scores might then be seen as "purer" measures of naming speed whereas number/letter composite scores might reflect more of a combination of "pure" naming speed and fluency acquired by means of exposure to alphabet or print.

Consistent with the above analysis, an informative way to represent the distinctiveness of the two composites was to report the color/object composite (COLOBJ) as one major dependent variable, representing naming speed that is uncontaminated by print stimuli; and a ratio score (RATIO) that expresses the extent to which the number/letter composite exceeds the color/object composite. This ratio score thus represents the relative number/letter advantage. The second variable isolates and represents the particularly lexical, print-related component distinct from the general naming speed component. RATIO is calculated as the quotient of number/letter (NUMLET) speed minus color/object (COLOBJ) speed over color/object (COLOBJ) speed. Speed is defined as the number of items named per second. Because there are 50 items, speed is 50 divided by the total number of items named. Speed is different from time which is simply the number of seconds required to name all 50 items.[1] The statistical alternative to this RATIO construct is to take NUMLET speed as a de-

---

[1] It is appropriate to express the arithmetic difference between NUMLET and COLOBJ as a quotient over COLOBJ, since the size of the arithmetic difference is not independent of the absolute speed of either variable. See Harshman and Krashen 1972 for an early treatment of this question in the context of laterality indices. In the present case, because of the theoretical assumption that COLOBJ represents the purer measure of absolute speed, we use it alone in the denominator of the quotient instead of using the sum of COLOBJ and NUMLET.

pendent measure with COLOBJ speed partialled out by co-variance.

Since the raw rapid naming scores are measured as seconds to complete the page of stimuli, and since such measures are naturally positively skewed, we used the reciprocal of the time measure in seconds, thereby converting it to a speed measure.

## STUDY 1—KINDERGARTEN SAMPLE

### PARTICIPANTS

Participants for Study 1 were drawn from all the kindergarten classes in the eight schools in our local public school system. During their kindergarten year, all children had been exposed to the Writing to Read program developed by IBM, but had not been taught using basal readers. Letter identification and letter recognition, alphabet recitation, and sound-symbol correspondence had also been taught using the Houghton-Mifflin kindergarten curriculum and Alphatime. In the spring of the year, all students were ranked by their teachers for their ability to master basic reading skills, using categories of superior, above-average, average, below average, or very poor. No criterion, other than expected reading acquisition and mastery, was given to the teachers. Because these kindergartners were initially tested as part of an intervention study on teaching methods for at-risk readers, those who were rated as superior or above average in potential for reading success, and those who scored below a standard score of 80 on the recently administered Otis-Lennon Mental Ability Test (Otis and Lennon 1968), were not included in the study.

Of the 469 children remaining in the sample after these exclusions, permission was obtained to evaluate 365 children; 355 were subsequently tested on an individually administered battery of reading readiness tests which included the Rapid Naming Test. Thirteen of these children could not recognize lower case letters or single digit numbers on the RAN, and were, therefore, not included in the analysis. The remaining 342 children, whose average age was 6.13 (SD 0.39) and who were rated as average, below average, or poor in reading potential by their teachers, had a mean Otis Lennon IQ of 107.11 (SD 12.34). Gender and race were reflective of the public school population from which this sample was drawn (53 percent female; 24 percent minority). We do not have data about the subsequent achievement scores of all of these 342 students.

## RESULTS

For this total group of 342 kindergartners, rated by their teachers as average or below average in reading potential, the time to name letters/numbers was already faster than the time to name color/objects, although the variances did overlap considerably. (Number/letters mean = 63.0, $SD$ = 20.0; colors/objects mean = 76.2, $SD$ = 18.0.) Therefore, a number/letter advantage already exists in the second half of the kindergarten year. To test the hypothesis that a number/letter advantage will emerge as alphabet mastery is achieved, we compared the number/letter advantage to concurrent level of alphabet mastery. Alphabet recitation, measured here by having children orally recite the alphabet from memory without reference to print, is one of the most elemental and commonly rehearsed of all kindergarten skills. Note that it is an untimed measure and relies on knowledge, not speed. However, like the RAN, alphabet recitation relies on automaticity of response when fully achieved, despite the fact that it is an untimed measure. It is, therefore, the underlying automatic nature of both tasks which unites them.

Those children whose alphabet knowledge was so minimal that they did not recognize the RAN stimuli had already been excluded, but within the remaining sample of 342, a considerable range of alphabet recitation ability was found. Children were divided into three categories (limited, moderate, perfect) based on the number of letters in the alphabet that they could recite. Although the vast majority recited most of the alphabet in sequence, correct order was not a requirement of the task.

Orderly changes in rapid naming performance were found across the three alphabet recitation groups (see figure 1). Specifically, the poorest "limited" recitation group ($n$ = 24) took almost exactly the same time to name colors/objects and numbers/letters. The middle or "moderate" group ($n$ = 56) took 10 seconds less to name numbers/letters compared to colors/objects, although color/object naming was no faster than in the poorest group. The "perfect" group, who could recite the alphabet almost flawlessly, showed a relative time advantage of slightly more than 14 seconds in favor of letter/number naming. Their times to name both classes of stimuli was also significantly faster than the times of the first two groups. In terms of the major dependent measures described in the Methods, RATIO (the relative number/letter advantage) showed an orderly increase across the three alphabet recitation groups, with the extreme groups differing significantly at $p < .01$. COLOBJ (the absolute color/object speed) was different between the extreme groups and between the middle and high alphabet recitation groups, at $p < .01$. Neither gender, age, or race accounted for differences in alphabet recitation accuracy across the three groups. RATIO, but not COLOBJ, was significantly correlated with the continuous measure of alphabet recitation accuracy at $r = .31$, $p < .0001$, and this correlation was also independent of Peabody Picture Vocabulary standard score.

In brief, poor alphabet reciters (limited group) showed no number/letter with RATIO scores near zero. Children with better alphabet recitation performance (moderate and perfect groups) showed a letter/number advantage, and this advantage was itself proportional to their alphabet recitation ability. Even in kindergarten, then, the number/letter composite may be reflective of prior achievement and exposure to alphabet, if not exposure to print (Cunningham and Stanovich 1990). Alternatively, there could be chronic individual deficiencies in the ability to automatize, despite equal amounts of exposure (Bowers 1993).

At the same time, another effect is also apparent: particularly good alphabet recitation (again, operationalized as accuracy, not speed) is associated with color/object naming speed in the absolute. On its face, this relationship is less obviously related to alphabet mastery; it could reflect a more long-standing, perhaps congenital, ability. At minimum, the data seem to sug-

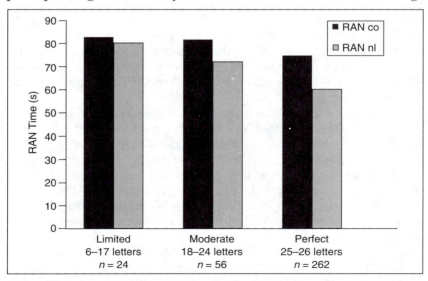

*Figure 1.* *Alphabet Recitation and Rapid Naming Rates in Kindergarten.*

gest two different mechanisms: absolute naming speed on the one hand, and relative number/letter advantage on the other.

Let us now examine the longitudinal "fate" of these two components over Grades 1 through 8 in an epidemiologically derived normal sample.

## STUDY 2—LONGITUDINAL SAMPLE

### PARTICIPANTS

A longitudinal sample of 160 students was derived from a larger, normally distributed, random sample of 485 students who were accessed in first grade. Since they were recruited in the same year as the sample in Study 1, they were then one year older and one year farther along than the previous Study 1 sample. The $n = 160$ subset, comprising the present sample, was tested in first, third, fifth, and eighth grades, and is virtually identical to the longitudinal sample in Meyer et al. (1998). Students were excluded who could not be tested in all four grades, but sampling was still stratified so as to ensure a normal distribution of reading ability in first grade (and, as it turned out, in the other grades as well). Students were also excluded if their Peabody Picture Vocabulary (PPVT-R) score was below 70 or above 130. The mean Woodcock Johnson reading standard score in first grade was 107.20 (SD 14.73); by eighth grade it was 102.66 (SD 12.48). The first grade PPVT-R score was 103.84 (SD 15.22). The demographics of this sample were appropriately representative of their public school system: males and females are equally represented, and race was 73 percent Caucasian and 27 percent African-American. All students were English-speaking.

Reading level was determined by measuring single-word reading which is usually considered the core defining weakness in reading disabled students (Stanovich 1986; Adams 1990; Olson et al. 1994; Beck and Juel 1995; Lyon 1995). Two measures of single-word reading in third grade were used to establish the three groups of readers: (1) *Woodcock-Johnson Psycho-Educational Battery*—Reading Cluster, (WJWID) (Woodcock and Johnson 1977); and (2) *Decoding Skills Test*-Part II: Phonetic Patterns, Real Words (DSTREAL) (Richardson and DiBenedetto 1985). The WJWID is norm referenced and requires identifying letters and both phonetically regular and irregular sight words within a five-second time limit. The DSTREAL is a criterion-referenced test, where participants read up to 60 phonetically regular words—

30 monosyllabic and 30 polysyllabic—chosen to represent common orthographic patterns. Normal-reading fifth graders get all of them right. Reading ability was defined on the basis of third grade rather than first grade tests. This allowed us to avoid first grade floor effects, particularly on WJWID.

The poorest reading group consisted of those scoring in the bottom 16 percent of the sample on both tests; this designation required raw scores of less than 29 on the WJWID and less than 38 on the DSTREAL. This converging requirement yielded 17 students at the lowest reading level which comprised 10.6 percent of our total sample at the time. A similar requirement that good readers score in the top 16 percent of the sample on both tests identified 13 top readers, comprising 8 percent of the total group. The remaining cases (who scored above the sixteenth percentile on at least one test and below the eighty-fourth percentile on at least one test) comprised the middle-level group with an $n$ of 130.

In order to obtain a fuller composite or overall measure of reading skill, we administered the other two subtests from the Woodcock Johnson: Word Attack and Passage Comprehension. These, together with Word Identification, yield an age-referenced standard score (Woodcock and Johnson 1977, p. 34). The Word Attack subtest requires untimed reading of a list of words defined as "letter combinations that are not actual words or are extremely low frequency words in the English Language." The Passage Comprehension subtest uses a cloze procedure that requires reading sentences that are missing a word and supplying a word that makes sense in the sentence or passage.

Finally, certain brief estimates of intelligence were taken. In first grade, we administered both the *Peabody Picture Vocabulary Test* (Dunn and Dunn 1981), a measure of receptive vocabulary knowledge, and *Raven's Colored Progressive Matrices* (Raven, Court, and Raven 1984), a nonverbal measure of reasoning by analogy. We administered the *Kaufman Brief Intelligence Test* (Kaufman and Kaufman 1990) to the eighth graders. According to its authors, the K-BIT's two subtests measure crystallized thinking (assessed by a two-part vocabulary task requiring word knowledge and verbal concept formation) and fluid thinking (assessed by a matrices which requires nonverbal reasoning to solve new problems).

## RESULTS

Table I shows rapid naming, reading, and vocabulary scores for the three reading level subgroups, and figure 2 shows the

TABLE I. READING, RAPID NAMING, VOCABULARY, AND ABILITY SCORES FOR THREE READING LEVELS.

| | Lower Group 0–11% n = 17 | | Middle Group 12–91% n = 130 | | Top Group 92–100% n = 13 | | Total n = 160 | |
|---|---|---|---|---|---|---|---|---|
| | X̄ | SD | X̄ | SD | X̄ | SD | X̄ | SD |
| **Woodcock Johnson Word Identification (WJWID)** | | | | | | | | |
| Grade 1 Raw | 16.4 | 2.0 | 22.8 | 5.1 | 31.6 | 6.7 | 22.8 | 6.0 |
| Grade 3 Raw | 25.2 | 1.7 | 33.6 | 2.9 | 40.4 | 3.3 | 33.3 | 4.4 |
| Grade 5 Raw | 32.8 | 2.1 | 39.3 | 3.6 | 44.8 | 2.8 | 39.0 | 4.3 |
| Grade 8 Raw | 36.7 | 2.3 | 42.7 | 3.2 | 46.9 | 2.2 | 42.4 | 3.8 |
| **Decoding Skills Test—Real Words (DSTREAL)** | | | | | | | | |
| Grade 1 Raw | 3.5 | 5.2 | 22.3 | 17.0 | 46.2 | 16.2 | 22.2 | 18.4 |
| Grade 3 Raw | 27.1 | 8.1 | 53.5 | 6.9 | 60.0 | 0.0 | 51.2 | 10.9 |
| Grade 5 Raw | 48.8 | 6.5 | 58.1 | 2.3 | 59.7 | 0.6 | 57.3 | 4.2 |
| Grade 8 Raw | 53.6 | 5.2 | 59.2 | 1.3 | 59.8 | 0.6 | 58.7 | 2.7 |
| **Color/Object—Rapid Naming (COLOBJ)** | | | | | | | | |
| Grade 1 | 79.3 | 19.9 | 64.4 | 14.1 | 54.7 | 11.6 | 65.2 | 15.5 |
| Grade 3 | 55.1 | 8.4 | 49.9 | 9.0 | 43.3 | 4.3 | 49.9 | 9.0 |
| Grade 5 | 46.9 | 6.1 | 42.1 | 6.9 | 38.2 | 4.3 | 42.3 | 6.9 |
| Grade 8 | 38.4 | 5.1 | 34.0 | 5.5 | 32.7 | 3.4 | 34.4 | 5.5 |
| **Number/Letter—Rapid Naming** | | | | | | | | |
| Grade 1 | 49.6 | 18.5 | 37.4 | 9.0 | 31.9 | 6.0 | 38.3 | 11.0 |
| Grade 3 | 32.8 | 6.5 | 28.0 | 5.5 | 23.3 | 4.2 | 28.2 | 5.9 |
| Grade 5 | 26.7 | 4.1 | 22.8 | 4.9 | 20.5 | 3.3 | 23.0 | 4.9 |
| Grade 8 | 22.8 | 4.2 | 20.3 | 4.3 | 18.5 | 4.0 | 20.4 | 4.3 |
| **Rapid Naming Ratio (RATIO)*** | | | | | | | | |
| Grade 1 | 0.38 | 0.15 | 0.41 | 0.12 | 0.41 | 0.07 | 0.41 | 0.12 |
| Grade 3 | 0.40 | 0.11 | 0.43 | 0.10 | 0.46 | 0.07 | 0.43 | 0.10 |
| Grade 5 | 0.43 | 0.06 | 0.46 | 0.08 | 0.46 | 0.07 | 0.45 | 0.08 |
| Grade 8 | 0.40 | 0.09 | 0.40 | 0.14 | 0.43 | 0.11 | 0.40 | 0.13 |
| | | | | | | | | |
| PPVT-R SS1** | 92.1 | 15.3 | 104.3 | 14.6 | 114.8 | 11.6 | 103.8 | 15.2 |
| RCPM Total 1*** | 18.4 | 4.0 | 21.3 | 5.1 | 26.5 | 5.8 | 21.4 | 5.4 |
| K-BIT VSS 8**** | 89.3 | 10.1 | 100.8 | 9.6 | 115.0 | 8.2 | 100.8 | 11.0 |
| K-BIT MSS 8***** | 100.9 | 9.6 | 104.1 | 11.2 | 115.2 | 10.7 | 104.6 | 11.4 |

*RATIO is calculated as the quotient of number/letter (NUMLET) speed minus color/object (COLOBJ) speed over color/object (COLOBJ) speed.
**Peabody Picture Vocabulary Test—Revised.
***Raven's Children Progressive Matrices.
****Kaufman Brief Intelligence Test—Verbal
*****Kaufman Brief Intelligence Test—Matrices.

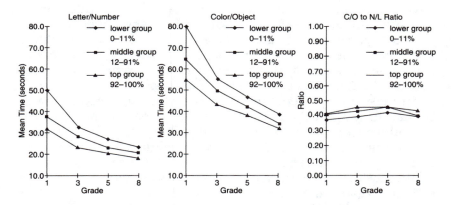

*Figure 2.    Growth curves for rapid automatized naming.*

growth curves of rapid naming for the three reading level sub-groups.

The growth curves show an obvious floor effect as naming speeds approach an asymptote by about eighth grade. Many of the subsequent observations noted below can be explained, at least in part, by this floor effect. First, there is a steady improvement of rate of responding over time, with the greatest improvement in rate occurring between first grade and third grade for all groups, marginally more so for the poor reading group than for the other groups. Second, with increasing age, there is a narrowing of the gap between the groups as they approach the eighth grade asymptote. Third, the number/letter advantage (RATIO) remains similar across Grades 1 through 8. Finally, naming speed is itself related to reading level, with the greatest difference between the normal and poor reading groups. Again, perhaps for reasons of a floor effect, the relationship is stronger in the early grades.

These fairly straightforward observations on the growth curves aside, the question then turns to the dissociation observed in Study 1 between absolute color/object naming speed (COLOBJ) and the relative number/letter advantage (RATIO) expressed as the quotient of the difference of NUMLET minus COLOBJ over COLOBJ. As the longitudinal curves in figure 2 show, naming speeds improve considerably over the eight grades, but RATIO does not. In the context of the findings of Study 1, showing the orderly relationship of RATIO to alphabet recitation knowledge, the implication of these growth curves is that much of the number/letter advantage expressed in the

RATIO measure is related to early processes in kindergarten and first grade, thereafter to show little change over time despite the considerable improvement in absolute color/object and number/letter naming speeds. The differential longitudinal course of these absolute and ratio measures reinforces the impression that they are separate mechanisms.

If these are two separate mechanisms, then it would be important to test whether or not they have separate relationships to reading achievement longitudinally. The present longitudinal data permitted that test to be formally conducted, to assess the extent to which variance in reading achievement was separately related to these two mechanisms. In consideration of the large sample size and the multiple analyses involved, alpha was set at $p = .01$. Correlations detailing the prediction of reading and brief IQ measures, from rapid naming scores at each grade level, are shown in table II. This table presents the absolute color/object naming scores and the absolute number/letter naming scores, along with the RATIO that expresses the degree of number/letter advantage, as defined above. Table II also shows the partial correlations involving NUMLET, where COLOBJ is partialled out by covariance (the outcome of a Type III sums of squares multiple regression analysis).

Table II clearly shows that the number/letter composite (NUMLET) is usually the strongest predictor of reading achievement. The color/object composite (COLOBJ) is almost as strong a predictor, however, so that the difference between them, i.e., the relative number/letter advantage (RATIO), is always weak and sometimes negative. RATIOs at any grade never account for as much as 4 percent of the variance and are never significant predictors at $p < .01$. Similarly, while there is some unique explanatory variance in NUMLET when COLOBJ is partialled out by covariance, the unique NUMLET variance tends not to be as great as the COLOBJ variance.

Of particular interest is the fact that the first and eighth grade verbal and nonverbal IQ estimates are dissociated in their relations to COLOBJ, NUMLET, and RATIO. The nonverbal tests—Raven's in first grade and K-BIT Matrices in eighth grade—are never significantly related to any naming variable. Moreover, eighth grade K-BIT Verbal IQ is usually marginally better predicted by COLOBJ at any grade than by NUMLET, and not at all by the unique NUMLET variance. First grade picture vocabulary, PPVT-R, is related to COLOBJ at each grade, but to NUMLET only concurrently at Grade 1. Within the limits of the content distinctions among the IQ estimates, therefore,

TABLE II.    PEARSON CORRELATIONS BETWEEN NAMING VARIABLES AND SELECTED READING AND IQ MEASURES.

| | WJWID 1 | WJWID 3 | WJWID 5 | WJWID 8 | WJSS 1 | WJSS 3 | WJSS 5 | WJSS 8 | PPVT-R | RCPM | KBV | KBM |
|---|---|---|---|---|---|---|---|---|---|---|---|---|
| COLOBJ 1 | **36** | **40** | **35** | **35** | **37** | **35** | **36** | **38** | **27** | 14 | **37** | 04 |
| COLOBJ 3 | 18 | **28** | **26** | **23** | **24** | **26** | **27** | **29** | **21** | 06 | **24** | 00 |
| COLOBJ 5 | **26** | **34** | **33** | **35** | **30** | **35** | **34** | **41** | **24** | 02 | **30** | -01 |
| COLOBJ 8 | **22** | **34** | **38** | **38** | **33** | **35** | **37** | **39** | **27** | 05 | **30** | 00 |
| NUMLET 1 | **46** | **40** | **39** | **38** | **48** | **38** | **38** | **40** | **26** | 07 | **34** | 05 |
| NUMLET 3 | **27** | **38** | **34** | **32** | **31** | **33** | **32** | **36** | 12 | -01 | **25** | -03 |
| NUMLET 5 | **26** | **36** | **39** | **38** | **34** | **37** | **36** | **41** | 13 | -09 | **27** | -05 |
| NUMLET 8 | **20** | **30** | **34** | **34** | **27** | **31** | **29** | **36** | 07 | -13 | **23** | -10 |
| RATIO 1 | -13 | -05 | -07 | -08 | -16 | -07 | -05 | -05 | -02 | 08 | -01 | 00 |
| RATIO 3 | -10 | -16 | -14 | -15 | -10 | -13 | -10 | -12 | 07 | 07 | -05 | 02 |
| RATIO 5 | -12 | -15 | -19 | -17 | -15 | -14 | -14 | -13 | 08 | 17 | -05 | 05 |
| RATIO 8 | -02 | -03 | -05 | -04 | -01 | -04 | -01 | -04 | 16 | 19 | 03 | 09 |
| PNUMLET 1 | **32** | **21** | **23** | **23** | **35** | **22** | **21** | **22** | 13 | -02 | 14 | 03 |
| PNUMLET 3 | **20** | **28** | **25** | **24** | **22** | **24** | **21** | **25** | 01 | -02 | 15 | -03 |
| PNUMLET 5 | 15 | 19 | 24 | 20 | 19 | 18 | 18 | 19 | -06 | -15 | 09 | -05 |
| PNUMLET 8 | 11 | 16 | 19 | 19 | 13 | 17 | 14 | **21** | -07 | -18 | 10 | -11 |

Notes: Significant values ($p < .01$) are bolded and underlined.

PNUMLET values are partial correlations involving NUMLET, with the respective (grade appropriate) COLOBJ values partialled out by covariance.

See Overall Method section for dicussion of RATIO definition.

COLOBJ as well as NUMLET are best interpreted as verbal, rather than as nonverbal or fluid skills.

Of interest also are the long-term predictive relations. COLOBJ in first grade is a somewhat better longitudinal predictor of reading than is COLOBJ at other grade levels, and COLOBJ in first grade predicts reading at all grade levels equally strongly. First grade NUMLET, on the other hand, is a particularly strong concurrent predictor of first grade reading, but its strength of prediction declines somewhat for subsequent years. The remarkable stability of the prediction by COLOBJ, selective to verbal skills, and its ability to predict subsequent reading as well as concurrent reading in first grade, may suggest a lesser role for experience and a greater role for a continuing, perhaps congenital, trait.

In brief, Study 2 shows the maintenance of the two separate mechanisms first identified in the kindergarten sample in Study 1: COLOBJ, or absolute color/object naming speed, improves to asymptote over the eight grades of school whereas RATIO, the relative advantage for number/letter speed over color/object speed, remains relatively constant across the eight grades of school. COLOBJ, especially in first grade, is by itself a strong predictor of subsequent reading performance and is a correlate and predictor of vocabulary or estimated verbal IQ. RATIO is not a strong correlate or predictor of reading.

## DISCUSSION

Taken together, Studies 1 and 2 suggest conclusions in three broad areas: kindergarten experience, development in Grades 1 through 8, and intervention implications.

First, it is a safe assumption that there is some period, however brief and early in kindergarten or even prekindergarten, when color/object and number/letter naming speeds (COLOBJ and NUMLET) are equally fast (or slow). However, the relative speed advantage of numbers/letters over colors/objects (RATIO) develops rapidly in kindergarten, is strong in first grade, and does not increase in magnitude thereafter. There are individual differences in the degree of this advantage, although almost all first graders have the advantage to some degree. It is difficult to avoid the conclusion, therefore, that the major determinants of the degree of the number/letter advantage tend to exert their effect in kindergarten or early first grade. These determinants could include exposure to print or alphabet, and to that extent, they could be environmental. There could, of course, be a more chronic individual trait difference in the ability to automatize new information, whether in alphabet recitation or in number/letter naming. However, since it a learned stimulus-response automaticity that is emerging at different levels of fluency, it is almost by definition an interactive and reciprocal process relating a prior predisposition to the current instructional situation. Both pre-existing traits and current environmental stimulation are almost certainly interacting to produce the kindergarten and first grade level of number/letter advantage. Indeed, the very speed of the emergence of the number/letter advantage, and its subsequent long term stability over eight grades of school, suggests a process that is amenable to environmental modification in that learning phase.

Second, in regard to the longitudinal sample, the general form of the growth curve for rapid naming rate holds for all students, regardless of reading ability, with the greatest growth in naming speed occurring between first and third grade, after the number/letter advantage has already been established. More important, the number/letter advantage itself has little further predictive or concurrent validity. This contrasts with the strong predictive effect of the absolute COLOBJ or NUMLET scores. The conclusion is inescapable that speed in general, not strongly dependent on the type of stimuli, is the important variable in the grade school years. That COLOBJ in first grade has predictive validity as strong as its concurrent validity suggests that something stable is measureable in first grade and is not much changed thereafter. In a separate paper (Meyer, Wood, Hart, and Felton 1998), we report that most of the predictive variance in rapid naming is within the group of poor readers, distinct from average or superior readers. This suggests that only some poor readers, especially those with the poorest prognosis, are constrained by their automaticity or fluency deficit. A chronic, possibly even congenital, trait affecting some initially poor readers is implied, and this trait becomes the background reality against which intervention efforts should be viewed.

Taken together, the above two considerations suggest that the implications for intervention are appropriately considered in the context of the reciprocal causation hypothesis (Stanovich 1986; Perfetti et al. 1987) which states that some skills both facilitate learning to read and result from reading itself. Cunningham and Stanovich (1990) invoke exposure to print as that mediating variable, and our Study 1 may represent a generalization of that concept to what could be described as "exposure to (hence mastery of) alphabet" in kindergarten. The Study 1 data do not rule out the possibility that interventions in kindergarten designed to increase exposure to print or alphabet could have an impact on reading related processes, in particular on the number/letter advantage. At the same time, it must be admitted that individual differences in the number/letter advantage, already well established by first grade, had little further impact on subsequent reading performance. If naturally occurring differences in kindergarten environment had a beneficial effect on the number/letter advantage, perhaps due to variations in exposure to print or alphabet, and if these persisted until first grade as the main component of the number/letter advantage, then the data from Study 2 suggest that this effect dissipates in subsequent grades with little long-term relation to reading achievement. Kindergarten interventions that would be successful in the long term might, therefore, have to exceed the best of the naturally occurring variations in kindergarten environments. The data suggest that kindergarten or first grade, not later grades, are the most productive times at which to intervene to enhance fluency.

One obvious next test of these implications would be to provide direct fluency training as early as kindergarten in an early effort to improve both absolute fluency and the number/letter advantage. Attempts to improve it would plausibly be made through consistent fluency training beginning in kindergarten with alphabet mastery and single-letter calling, and continuing in the school grades with a focus on fluent and automatic reading itself through sentence and passage repetition (such as the Repeated Readings method in Samuels 1987; Mathes, Simmons, and Davis 1992; Young, Bowers, and MacKinnon 1996; or the RAVE-0 method in Wolf and Obregon 1997). In the context of the reciprocal causation hypothesis, a continuous feedback mechanism might be imagined whereby even small gains in the number/letter advantage could result in improvements in reading and reading readiness, which, in turn, might cause further gains in fluency and so on for several grades of school. Bowers (1993) reports that repeated reading of a text causes more improvements in the passage reading fluency of children who are rapid namers than in that of slower namers even when initial text speed is controlled. This suggests not only differential rates of improvement among children but also the need to titrate the amount of fluency training provided (more for the less able). While the number/letter advantage has some relevance for the earliest years, as a possible marker of improvement, it is likely that more generalized improvements in fluency, across all categories of stimuli, would be the broader goal since speed itself across all classes of stimuli was the major correlate and predictor of reading in the grade school years.

Correspondence may be sent to: M. S. Meyer, Section of Neuropsychology, Wake Forest University School of Medicine, Medical Center Blvd., Winston-Salem, N.C. 27157-1043. e-mail: mmeyer@wfubmc.edu

## ACKNOWLEDGMENT

This study, part of a larger research project on dyslexia, was funded by the National Institute of Child Health and Human Development, Research Grant HD 21887-10. The participation of the Winston-Salem/Forsyth County Schools and their students is acknowledged with gratitude.

### *References*

Ackerman, P. T., and Dykman, R. A. 1993. Phonological processes, confrontational naming, and immediate memory in dyslexia. *Journal of Learning Disabilities* 26(9):597–609.

Adams, M. J. 1990. *Beginning to Read*. Cambridge, MA: MIT Press.

Badian, N. A. 1993. Phonemic awareness, naming, visual symbol processing, and reading. *Reading and Writing: An Interdisciplinary Journal* 5:87–100.

Badian, N. A. 1995. Predicting reading ability over the long term: The changing roles of letter naming, phonological awareness and orthographic processing. *Annals of Dyslexia* 45:79–96.

Badian, N. A., Duffy, F. H., Als, H., and McAnulty, G. B. 1991. Linguistic profiles of dyslexics and good readers. *Annals of Dyslexia* 41:221–45.

Badian, N. A., McAnulty, G. B., Duffy, F .H., and Als, H. 1990. Prediction of dyslexia in kindergarten boys. *Annals of Dyslexia* 40:152–69.

Beck, I. L., and Juel, C. 1995. The role of decoding in learning to read. *American Educator* 19: 8–12.

Biddle, K. R. 1996. Timing deficits in impaired readers: an investigation of visual naming speed and verbal fluency. Ph.D. Diss., Tufts University, Boston.

Blachman, B. 1984. Relationship of rapid naming ability and language analysis skills in kindergarten and first-grade reading achievement. *Journal of Educational Psychology* 76(4):610–22.

Bowers, P. G., Steffy, R., and Tate, E. 1988. Comparison of the effects of IQ control methods and naming speed predictors of reading disability. *Reading Research Quarterly* 23:304–9.

Bowers, P. G. 1993. Text reading rereading: Predictors of fluency beyond word recognition. *Journal of Reading Behavior* 25:133–53.

Bowers, P. G., and Wolf, M. 1993. Theoretical links among naming speed, precise timing mechanisms and orthographic skill in dyslexia. *Reading and Writing: An Interdisciplinary Journal* 5:69–85.

Bowers, P. G., and Swanson, L. B. 1991. Naming speed deficits in reading disability: Multiple measures of a singular process. *Journal of Experimental Child Psychology* 51:195–219.

Cornwall, A. 1992. The relationship of phonological awareness, rapid naming, and verbal memory to severe reading and spelling disability. *Journal of Learning Disabilities* 25:532–38.

Cunningham, A. E., and Stanovich, K. E. 1990. Assessing print exposure and orthographic processing skill in children: A quick measure of reading experience. *Journal of Educational Psychology* 82(4):733–40.

Denckla, M. B., and Rudel, R. G. 1974. Rapid automatized naming of pictured objects, colors, letters and numbers by normal children. *Cortex* 10:86–202.

Denckla, M., and Rudel, R. G. 1976. Rapid automatized naming (RAN): Dyslexia differentiated from other learning disabilities. *Neuropsychologia* 14:471–79.

Dunn, L. M., and Dunn, L. M. 1981. *Peabody Picture Vocabulary Test.* Circle Pines, MN: American Guidance Service.

Fawcett, A., and Nicholson, R. 1994. Naming speed in children with dyslexia. *Journal of Learning Disabilities* 27(10):641–46.

Felton, R. H., and Brown, I. S. 1990. Phonological processes as predictors of specific reading skills in children at risk for reading failure. *Reading and Writing: An Interdisciplinary Journal* 2:39–59.

Felton, R. H., Naylor, C. E., and Wood, F. B. 1990. Neuropsychological profile of adult dyslexics. *Brain and Language* 39:485–497.

Felton, R.H. 1992. Early identification of children at risk for reading disabilities. *Topics in Exceptional Children and Special Education* 12(2):212–29.

Flowers, D. L. 1993. Biological basis for reading disability: A review of work in progress. *Journal of Learning Disabilities* 26:575–82.

Lovett, M. W. 1987. A developmental approach to reading disability: Accuracy and speed criteria of normal and deficient reading skill. *Child Development* 58: 234–60.

Lyon, G. R., 1995. Toward a definition of dyslexia. *Annals of Dyslexia* 45:3–30.

Kaufman, A., and Kaurman, N. 1990. *Kaufman Brief Intelligence Test.* Circle Pines, MN: American Guidance Service.

Korhonen, T. 1995. The persistence of rapid naming problems in children with reading disability: A nine year follow-up. *Journal of Learning Disabilities* 28(4):232–39.

LaBerge, D., and Samuels, J. 1974. Toward a theory of automatic information processing in reading. *Cognitive Psychology* 6:293–323.

Mathes, P. G., Simmons, D. C., and Davis, B. I. 1992. Assisted reading techniques for developing reading fluency. *Reading, Research, and Instruction* 31(4):70–77.

Meyer, M. S., Wood, F. B., Hart, L., and Felton, R. H. 1998. Selective predictive value of rapid automatized naming within poor readers. *Journal of Learning Disabilities* 31(2):106–17.

Olson, R., Forsberg, H., Wise, B., and Rack, J. 1994. Measurement of word recognition, orthographic and phonological skills. In G.R. Lyon, ed., *Frames of Reference for the Assessment of Learning Disabilities: New Views on Assessment Issues.* Baltimore: Paul Brooks Publishing: 243–77.

Otis, A.S., and Lennon, R. T. 1968. *Otis-Lennon Mental Ability Test.* New York: Harcourt Brace Jovanovich.

Perfetti, C., Beck, I., Bell, L., and Hughes, C. 1987. *Merrill-Palmer Quarterly* 33(3):283–319.

Porter, R., and Hughes, L. 1983. Dichotic Listening to CV's: Method, Interpretation, and Application. In J. Hellige, ed., *Cerebral Hemispheric Asymmetry: Method, Theory, and Application.* New York: Praeger.

Raven, J., Court, J., and Raven, J. 1984 *Coloured Progressive Matrices*. London: H.K Lewis & Co. Ltd.

Richardson, E., and DiBenedetto, B. 1985. *Decoding Skills Test*. Los Angeles, CA: Western Psychological Services.

Samuels, S. J. 1987. Information processing abilities and reading. *Journal of Learning Disabilities* 20(1):18–22.

Shankweiler, D., and Liberman, I. Y. 1989. *Phonology and Reading Disability*. Ann Arbor, MI: The University of Michigan Press.

Snyder, L. S., and Downey, D. M. 1995. The serial rapid naming skills of reading disabled children. *Annals of Dyslexia* 45:31–50.

Stanovich, K. E. 1986. Matthew effects in reading: Some consequences of individual differences in the acquisition of literacy. *Reading Research Quarterly* 21:360–407.

Stanovich, K. E. 1988. Explaining the differences between the dyslexic and the garden-variety poor reader: The phonological-core variable-difference model. *Journal of Learning Disabilities* 21:590–612.

Torgesen, J. K., Wagner, R. K., and Rashotte, C. A. 1994. Longitudinal studies of phonological processing and reading. *Journal of Learning Disabilities* 27:276–86.

Torgesen, J. K., Wagner, R. K., Simmons, K., and Laughon, P. 1990 Identifying phonological coding problems in disabled readers: Naming, counting and span measures? *Learning Disabilities Quarterly* 13: 236–45.

Wagner, R. K., and Torgesen, J. K. 1987. The nature of phonological processing and its casual role in the acquisition of reading skills. *Psychological Bulletin* 101:192–212.

Walsh, D. J., Price, G., and Gillingham, M. G. 1988. The critical but transitory importance of letter naming. *Reading Research Quarterly* 23:108–22.

Wolf, M., Bally, H., and Morris, R. 1986. Automaticity, retrieval processes, and reading: A longitudinal study in average and impaired readers. *Child Development* 57:988–1000.

Wolf, M. 1990. The word retrieval deficit hypothesis and developmental dyslexia. Presented at American Educational Association Meetings, Boston, Mass.

Wolf, M. 1991. Naming speed and reading: The contribution of the cognitive neurosciences. *Reading Research Quarterly* 26:123–40.

Wolf, M., and Bowers, P. 1997. The "double-deficit hypothesis" for the developmental dyslexias. Unpublished paper, submitted for publication.

Wolf, M., and Obregon, M. 1997. The "double-deficit" hypothesis: Implications for diagnosis and practice in reading disabilities. In L. Putman, ed., *Readings on Language and Literacy*. Cambridge, MA: Brookline Books, 177–210.

Woodcock, R. W., and Johnson, M.B. 1977. *Woodcock-Johnson Psycho-educational Battery*. Allen, TX: DLM.

Young, A., Bowers, P., and MacKinnon, G. 1996. Effects of prosodic modeling and repeated reading on poor readers' fluency and comprehension. *Applied Psycholinguistics* 17: 59–84.

# APPENDIX

This study generates data that are usable as norms for Grades 1, 3, 5, and 8. They are presented here for the convenience of readers. It may be noted that the tests were repeated across grades on the same children, but this minimal practice effect is not expected to have any significant impact on the utility of these norms. Since the sample is of n = 160, then the 1st, 2nd, 98th, and 99th percentile estimates are naturally somewhat less reliable than the others. Given that principle, it is likely that the left or slow performing side of the table (in this case the 1st and 2nd percentile side), represents the direction of natural skewing of response times and may be somewhat more reliable than the right or fast performing side where the differences between percentiles in their accompanying raw scores are generally rather small. Our experience suggests that percentiles inclusive of the range from the 5th on the poor performing end to the 90th on the good performing end are both reliable and valid for clinical and research use. Interpretation naturally must take into account the IQ estimate exclusions reported in the text in the method section of Study 2.

Since the Rapid Automatized Naming Test is not commercially available, individuals interested in purchasing the test for a small fee can do so by contacting the Section of Neuropsychology, Wake Forest University School of Medicine, Bowman Gray Campus, Medical Center Boulevard, Winston-Salem, North Carolina, 27157-1043, or FAX 336-716-9810. Permission from the surviving author (Denckla) has been granted.

**APPENDIX TABLE A.   RAW SCORE PERCENTILE NORMS FOR RAN SUBTESTS AND COMPOSITES, FOR GRADES 1, 3, 5 AND 8.**

| | Percentiles | | | | | | | | | |
|---|---|---|---|---|---|---|---|---|---|---|
| | 1 | 2 | 5 | 10 | 25 | 50 | 75 | 90 | 95 | 99 |
| Colors | | | | | | | | | | |
| 1 | 90 | 78 | 70 | 60 | 51 | 44 | 40 | 42 | 38 | 33 |
| 3 | 65 | 56 | 53 | 48 | 42 | 37 | 33 | 35 | 32 | 29 |
| 5 | 54 | 49 | 45 | 40 | 36 | 32 | 28 | 29 | 27 | 23 |
| 8 | 41 | 39 | 37 | 33 | 29 | 26 | 23 | 25 | 22 | 20 |
| Objects | | | | | | | | | | |
| 1 | 188 | 117 | 103 | 86 | 73 | 61 | 53 | 56 | 51 | 44 |
| 3 | 97 | 82 | 71 | 62 | 54 | 48 | 44 | 45 | 42 | 36 |
| 5 | 73 | 63 | 59 | 53 | 47 | 41 | 38 | 39 | 35 | 32 |
| 8 | 58 | 51 | 48 | 43 | 37 | 34 | 30 | 32 | 28 | 18 |
| Numbers | | | | | | | | | | |
| 1 | 70 | 58 | 54 | 42 | 35 | 32 | 27 | 30 | 26 | 22 |
| 3 | 46 | 42 | 38 | 32 | 27 | 24 | 21 | 22 | 19 | 18 |
| 5 | 39 | 33 | 31 | 26 | 22 | 20 | 17 | 18 | 16 | 13 |
| 8 | 36 | 28 | 26 | 23 | 20 | 17 | 15 | 16 | 15 | 12 |
| Letters | | | | | | | | | | |
| 1 | 103 | 59 | 53 | 43 | 35 | 30 | 27 | 29 | 25 | 21 |
| 3 | 44 | 39 | 36 | 32 | 27 | 23 | 21 | 22 | 19 | 17 |
| 5 | 36 | 31 | 29 | 26 | 22 | 19 | 17 | 18 | 16 | 15 |
| 8 | 41 | 29 | 24 | 22 | 19 | 17 | 15 | 15 | 14 | 13 |
| COLOBJ (Mean) | | | | | | | | | | |
| 1 | 132 | 90 | 85 | 72 | 63 | 54 | 47 | 51 | 45 | 40 |
| 3 | 78 | 66 | 63 | 55 | 48 | 43 | 39 | 40 | 38 | 35 |
| 5 | 63 | 54 | 50 | 47 | 41 | 37 | 34 | 35 | 32 | 29 |
| 8 | 49 | 44 | 41 | 38 | 33 | 30 | 27 | 28 | 26 | 23 |
| NUMLET (Mean) | | | | | | | | | | |
| 1 | 79 | 58 | 51 | 42 | 36 | 31 | 27 | 29 | 26 | 22 |
| 3 | 43 | 39 | 36 | 31 | 27 | 23 | 21 | 22 | 20 | 18 |
| 5 | 35 | 32 | 29 | 26 | 22 | 19 | 18 | 18 | 16 | 15 |
| 8 | 34 | 28 | 25 | 22 | 19 | 17 | 15 | 16 | 14 | 13 |

Notes: Values entered are in whole seconds with decimal fractions truncated.

COLOBJ is the mean of times for colors and objects.

NUMLET is the mean for numbers and letters.

The left side of the above table is the low performing side.

**APPENDIX TABLE B.  SPEED (ITEMS NAMED PER SECOND) NORMS FOR RAN SUBTESTS AND COMPOSITES FOR GRADES 1, 3, 5 AND 8.**

| | | | | | Percentiles | | | | | |
|---|---|---|---|---|---|---|---|---|---|---|
| | 1 | 2 | 5 | 10 | 25 | 50 | 75 | 90 | 95 | 99 |
| **Colors** | | | | | | | | | | |
| 1 | .556 | .641 | .714 | .833 | .980 | 1.136 | 1.250 | 1.190 | 1.316 | 1.515 |
| 3 | .769 | .893 | .943 | 1.042 | 1.190 | 1.351 | 1.515 | 1.429 | 1.563 | 1.724 |
| 5 | .926 | 1.020 | 1.111 | 1.250 | 1.389 | 1.563 | 1.786 | 1.724 | 1.852 | 2.174 |
| 8 | 1.220 | 1.282 | 1.351 | 1.515 | 1.724 | 1.923 | 2.174 | 2.000 | 2.273 | 2.500 |
| **Objects** | | | | | | | | | | |
| 1 | .266 | .427 | .485 | .581 | .685 | .820 | .943 | .893 | .980 | 1.136 |
| 3 | .515 | .610 | .704 | .806 | .926 | 1.042 | 1.136 | 1.111 | 1.190 | 1.389 |
| 5 | .685 | .794 | .847 | .943 | 1.064 | 1.220 | 1.316 | 1.282 | 1.429 | 1.563 |
| 8 | .862 | .980 | 1.042 | 1.163 | 1.351 | 1.471 | 1.667 | 1.563 | 1.786 | 2.778 |
| **Numbers** | | | | | | | | | | |
| 1 | .714 | .862 | .926 | 1.190 | 1.429 | 1.563 | 1.852 | 1.667 | 1.923 | 2.273 |
| 3 | 1.087 | 1.190 | 1.316 | 1.563 | 1.852 | 2.083 | 2.381 | 2.273 | 2.632 | 2.778 |
| 5 | 1.282 | 1.515 | 1.613 | 1.923 | 2.273 | 2.500 | 2.941 | 2.778 | 3.125 | 3.846 |
| 8 | 1.389 | 1.786 | 1.923 | 2.174 | 2.500 | 2.941 | 3.333 | 3.125 | 3.333 | 4.167 |
| **Letters** | | | | | | | | | | |
| 1 | .485 | .847 | .943 | 1.163 | 1.429 | 1.667 | 1.852 | 1.724 | 2.000 | 2.381 |
| 3 | 1.136 | 1.282 | 1.389 | 1.563 | 1.852 | 2.174 | 2.381 | 2.273 | 2.632 | 2.941 |
| 5 | 1.389 | 1.613 | 1.724 | 1.923 | 2.273 | 2.632 | 2.941 | 2.778 | 3.125 | 3.333 |
| 8 | 1.220 | 1.724 | 2.083 | 2.273 | 2.632 | 2.941 | 3.333 | 3.333 | 3.571 | 3.846 |
| **COLOBJ** (Mean) | | | | | | | | | | |
| 1 | .379 | .556 | .588 | .694 | .794 | .926 | 1.064 | .980 | 1.111 | 1.250 |
| 3 | .641 | .758 | .794 | .909 | 1.042 | 1.163 | 1.282 | 1.250 | 1.316 | 1.429 |
| 5 | .794 | .926 | 1.000 | 1.064 | 1.220 | 1.351 | 1.471 | 1.429 | 1.563 | 1.724 |
| 8 | 1.020 | 1.136 | 1.220 | 1.316 | 1.515 | 1.667 | 1.852 | 1.786 | 1.923 | 2.174 |
| **NUMLET** (Mean) | | | | | | | | | | |
| 1 | .633 | .862 | .980 | 1.190 | 1.389 | 1.613 | 1.852 | 1.724 | 1.923 | 2.273 |
| 3 | 1.163 | 1.282 | 1.389 | 1.613 | 1.852 | 2.174 | 2.381 | 2.273 | 2.500 | 2.778 |
| 5 | 1.429 | 1.563 | 1.724 | 1.923 | 2.273 | 2.632 | 2.778 | 2.778 | 3.125 | 3.333 |
| 8 | 1.471 | 1.786 | 2.000 | 2.273 | 2.632 | 2.941 | 3.333 | 3.125 | 3.571 | 3.846 |

Notes: Values entered are the reciprocals of the entries in table I above, multiplied by 50 (the number of items named). They thus represent the speed expressed as items named per second.

The percentiles are reversed from table I, so that the left and right sides of the table remain the poor and good performing ends, respectively.

COLOBJ is the mean for colors and objects.

NUMLET is the mean for numbers and letters.

# Predicting the Future Achievement of Second Graders with Reading Disabilities: Contributions of Phonemic Awareness, Verbal Memory, Rapid Naming, and IQ

*Hollis S. Scarborough*

Brooklyn College of the City University of New York

*Concurrent and prospective correlations among reading, spelling, phonemic awareness, verbal memory, rapid serial naming, and IQ were examined in a longitudinal sample that was studied at Grade 2 and Grade 8. Substantial temporal stability of individual differences in all of these skills was seen over the six-year period between assessments. The strongest predictors of future reading and spelling outcomes were different for normally achieving second graders than for those who had been designated as having reading disabilities. For the former, Grade 2 literacy scores were the best predictors of later achievement. For the children with reading disabilities, however, prediction of most future reading and spelling skills was substantially improved by the inclusion of the cognitive-linguistic measures, particularly rapid naming.*

Individual differences in reading ability have consistently been shown to be very stable over time. On average, children who have difficulty learning to read in the early grades tend to remain relatively poor readers in the years that follow, and children who are very successful at the outset tend to remain at the top of the class. Hence, correlations between reading scores

Annals of Dyslexia, Vol. 48, 1998
Copyright© 1998 by The International Dyslexia Association
ISSN 0736-9387

taken one to six years apart have been quite substantial ($r$ = .63 to .86) in several large samples (e.g., Butler et al. 1985; Shaywitz et al. 1992). Similarly, it has typically been found that a majority of children who are judged to have reading disabilities (RD) at one age continue to meet the criteria for such a classification at later ages, and it is relatively uncommon for a child who is not considered to be RD in the early grades to later qualify for this designation (e.g., Badian 1988; Fergusson et al. 1996; Juel 1988; McGee, Williams, and Silva 1988; Satz et al. 1981).

Despite this rather strong degree of temporal stability, however, there remains considerable variability in reading achievement that is not accounted for simply by knowing a child's previous level of reading performance. In contrast to the overall trend, some children exhibit marked upward or downward shifts in achievement relative to their schoolmates. Some such changes, although predominantly small ones, are to be expected given that no test of achievement is entirely reliable (Fergusson et al. 1996). In addition, some classifications will inevitably change, given that dividing a continuous distribution of scores into two categories (RD or not) must occur at an arbitrarily selected cutoff point, and children whose scores are close to one side of the borderline on one occasion are likely to earn scores on the other side on another occasion (e.g., Shaywitz et al. 1992). Even so, it seems clear that real and meaningful shifts in reading ability can and do occur in some individual children. Some of these changes can result from differences in print exposure (e.g., Cunningham and Stanovich 1997). Little is known, however, about what strengths and weaknesses in reading-related cognitive and linguistic skills may also be associated with children's rates of progress in reading achievement over the long term.

In this study, the stability of individual differences in reading achievement was examined in a longitudinal sample in which reading skills were evaluated in the second and eighth grades (Scarborough 1989). In addition to determining how accurately the students' early achievement predicted their outcomes over the six-year interval, the analyses were designed to investigate the power of other kinds of measures to account for changes in reading status over time, particularly for children who had originally been designated as disabled readers. To that end, the set of predictors included not just reading and spelling scores, but also measures of more basic cognitive-linguistic skills—phonological awareness, verbal memory, rapid serial naming, and general verbal ability—that have been associated with reading ability differences in other samples (e.g., Ackerman and Dykman 1993;

Cornwall 1992; Hansen and Bowey 1994; Stone and Brady 1995; Wagner, Torgesen, and Rashotte 1994).

*Phonological awareness* was of interest because of its well-established theoretical and empirical relationship to reading acquisition (e.g., Adams and Bruck 1995; Brady and Shankweiler 1991; Byrne and Fielding-Barnsley 1989; Ehri and Wilce 1980; Liberman et al. 1974; Perfetti et al. 1987). In this particular sample, as in many others, differences in phonological awareness at age five years were reliably associated with reading abilities in second grade (Scarborough 1989), and it was hypothesized that such differences would continue to play a role in maintaining individual differences in achievement.

*Verbal memory* is another ability that has sometimes, although not always, been found to be weak in many children with reading difficulties (e.g., Brady 1991; Stone and Brady 1995). Although verbal memory, like phonological awareness, requires phonological processing of spoken input, there is evidence that memory and awareness do not tap a unitary dimension of skill (e.g., McDougall et al. 1994). Because reading at older ages typically involves sentences and texts of considerable length, high achievement may increasingly depend on a child's ability to retain material in memory as it is being read so that syntactic and semantic analyses necessary to comprehension can be performed.

*Rapid serial naming* was examined because it has been hypothesized that such tasks tap another fundamental kind of processing that, if deficient, can impede reading acquisition (e.g., Bowers and Wolf 1993; Wolf 1997). There is a large and growing body of evidence to suggest that rapid naming is well correlated with reading abilities (e.g., Ackerman, Dykman, and Gardner 1990; Bowers and Swanson 1991; Wolf 1991). In particular, the speeded nature of this task may make it particularly well suited for predicting reading at older ages when fluency and automaticity are expected to be attained.

Finally, the correlation between reading skill and *general intellectual ability* (IQ) is known to increase in strength over the elementary school years (e.g., Stanovich, Cunningham, and Cramer 1984). Although preschool IQ scores in this sample were not an important predictor of second grade outcomes (Scarborough 1989), it was hypothesized that IQ might make a stronger contribution to individual differences, particularly in reading comprehension, at older ages.

# METHOD

## PARTICIPANTS

All of the children had participated, from the age of two years, in a longitudinal study that began in 1980 (Scarborough 1989, 1991). All were of normal IQ, were monolingual speakers of English, and resided in several dozen different municipalities in and around central New Jersey. They were from working class to upper-middle class families (strata I through IV) according to Hollingshead and Redlich's (1958) five-tiered classification of socioeconomic status on the basis of parental education and occupation.

The original sample of 88 children included an at-risk group of 38 children who had at least one parent or older sibling with a reading disability. In many instances, there were also dyslexic individuals outside the immediate family. There was no such incidence of reading disability in the families of the other 50 children. It is important to note that children from affected families were deliberately overrepresented in the sample. This was done with the expectation that a larger proportion of these preschoolers would later develop reading problems than would be expected in a population-representative sample of this size. (For details of the recruitment of the sample and the assessment of familial risk, see Scarborough 1989.)

During the summer following the completion of Grade 2 (1986 for some children, 1987 for the remainder), 78 (89 percent) of the original 88 children, then eight years old, were located. Of these, 66 could be directly tested (31 from the at-risk group, 35 not at risk). For 12 others (3 at risk, 9 not), information about reading achievement was obtained from parents and schools. The sample was divided into RD and NRD subgroups on the basis of their reading achievement as described in detail previously (Scarborough 1989). The RD group included 24 children (22 of whom had been initially designated as at risk) and the NRD group included 54 (of whom 12 had a family history of dyslexia).

Six years later, when they completed Grade 8, 68 (87 percent) of the Grade 2 sample were again located. Of these, 64 could be directly tested. Only parental reports could be obtained for the four adolescents who declined to participate (two RD and two NRD).

The present analyses were based on the data for the 55 participants for whom test scores were available at both second and eighth grade. This sample includes 19 children from the RD subgroup (9 boys and 10 girls) and 36 from the NRD group (16 boys and 20 girls).

## MEASURES

*Reading.* At both grades, the word identification, word attack, and passage comprehension subtests of the *Woodcock-Johnson Psychoeducational Battery* (1978) were administered. Rasch-scaled *W* scores for the three subtests, and a composite score computed by averaging them, were analyzed.

*Spelling.* Nonstandardized spelling-to-dictation measures were used. At Grade 2, the list included 30 words from Treiman (1984), half of which were regularly spelled and half of which were "exception" words. The list at Grade 8 included 50 words taken from the materials developed by Bruck (1993) and Waters, Bruck, and Malus-Abramowitz (1988). The percentage of words correctly spelled was computed at each grade.

*Phonological Awareness.* At each age, a phoneme deletion task was administered, on which the child was asked to say what is left after the first/last sound is removed from a spoken monosyllable. To insure that the test items were correctly perceived, the children repeated each item before carrying out the requested deletion operation. At Grade 2, the stimuli consisted of 24 words, such as m/ice, s/mall, hou/se, and pas/te. At Grade 8, there were 24 pseudowords adapted from Bruck (1992) including v/oot, f/lib, chu/t, and bas/t. The percentage of correct responses was scored.

*Verbal Memory.* At each age, the children were asked to imitate a series of 25 exceedingly rare, phonologically complex words that were effectively pseudowords (for example, *sesquepedalian, funambulist,* and *arteriosclerosis*). The percentage of correctly repeated items was scored at each age.[1]

*Rapid serial naming.* In this task, children were asked to say the names of all items in a large visual array as quickly as possible. At Grade 2, the 6 x 8 array contained pictures of 48 common objects. At Grade 8, the standard 5 x 10 Colors and Objects arrays from the Rapid Automatized Naming Test (Denckla and Rudel 1976) were used. The total number of seconds was measured for each array. Although some studies have found that naming of color or object arrays is less closely tied to

---

[1] Another measure of verbal memory, the WISC-R (1989) Digit Span subtest, was also obtained at Grade 2. These scores were correlated with the repetition (.41) and phoneme deletion (.33) tasks, but not with any other measures ($r < .25$). Digit Span, therefore, was not included as a predictor in the multivariate analyses.

reading skill than naming of digit or letter arrays (Wimmer 1993; Wolf 1991), others have not found a difference in the strength of the association (Denckla and Rudel 1976; Meyer et al. 1998; Snyder and Downey 1995). Object naming was chosen for this study out of concern that reading skill and naming speed for alphanumeric symbols might reciprocally influence each other. Particularly for second graders with reading disabilities, performance might be hindered by weaknesses in letter/number knowledge.

IQ.   At Grade 2, the WISC-R was administered and Full-Scale IQ scores were computed. At Grade 8, following Sattler's (1992) guidelines, IQ was estimated from Information, Vocabulary, Arithmetic, Block Design, and Picture Arrangement subscores.

## PROCEDURES

At both second and eighth grade, each child was individually examined by a member of the research team during a single session lasting approximately 2.5 hours. Testing took place in the family's home, in the presence of one or both parents. The examiner was kept "blind" to the risk status of the child and, at Grade 8, to the adolescent's previous reading status and educational history. All sessions were recorded so that scoring could later be independently reviewed by another researcher. In addition to the measures described above, a variety of other tests and questionnaires was given at each age, but these will not be discussed in this report.

# RESULTS

## PRELIMINARY ANALYSES

Arc sine transformations were applied to the proportional scores (spelling, phonological awareness, verbal memory) prior to parametric statistical analyses. No other adjustments, such as for distributional irregularities (severe skewness, outliers, multimodality), were needed to meet the assumptions of the planned statistical tests. In addition, correlations of sex and socioeconomic status (SES) with the literacy outcome measures were examined to determine whether these demographic factors needed to be covaried in subsequent prediction analyses. At neither age were any of these correlations found to be significant ($r < .22$).

To obtain a composite measure of overall reading and spelling achievement at each age, the three Woodcock-Johnson subscores and the spelling score were entered into a principal components analysis. The single factor that was extracted from each analysis accounted for 70 percent of the variance in these measures at Grade 2 and 60 percent at Grade 8.

A summary of the sample's performance on all measures at Grade 2 and Grade 8 is provided in table I.

## CONCURRENT RELATIONSHIPS AMONG THE READING AND COGNITIVE MEASURES

Pearson correlations among the eight measures at each grade are shown in table II. Because a large number of significance tests were conducted, a conservative significance level of .01, two-tailed, was adopted in analyzing these relationships. Because IQ and phonemic awareness were each found to be correlated ($r = .29-.33$, $p < .05$) with SES at both second and eighth grade, partial correlations controlling for SES were also computed. These were virtually identical to the coefficients shown in table II, and, therefore, are not reported here.

With one exception, there were moderately strong correlations among all of the reading and spelling measures at both

### TABLE I.
### SUMMARY OF PERFORMANCE BY THE SAMPLE ON ALL MEASURES AT GRADE 2 AND GRADE 8.

| Measure | Grade 2 | | | Grade 8 | | |
|---|---|---|---|---|---|---|
| | *M* | *SD* | range | *M* | *SD* | range |
| Word Identification | 492.7 | 13.8 | 471–523 | 534.2 | 12.6 | 507–572 |
| Word Attack | 498.3 | 13.5 | 454–519 | 511.3 | 9.9 | 491–533 |
| Passage Comprehension | 492.8 | 12.1 | 466–514 | 524.6 | 8.8 | 505–542 |
| Reading Cluster | 494.6 | 11.3 | 467–514 | 523.3 | 8.1 | 505–544 |
| Spelling (% correct) | 65.1 | 16.0 | 24–98 | 79.0 | 10.1 | 48–96 |
| Phoneme Deletion (% correct) | 77.1 | 13.1 | 29–100 | 88.9 | 10.9 | 42–100 |
| Verbal Memory (% correct) | 74.6 | 14.3 | 43–100 | 82.3 | 11.2 | 56–100 |
| Rapid Serial naming (seconds) | 56.5 | 14.2 | 33–99 | 34.0 | 5.8 | 25–53 |
| Full-Scale IQ | 117.4 | 11.0 | 90–143 | 113.1 | 10.9 | 87–140 |

Note: $n = 55$

grades, with somewhat larger effects at Grade 2 (median $r$ = .62) than at Grade 8 (median $r$ = .525). Of particular note is that word attack and passage comprehension scores were unrelated at the older age, indicating a dissociation between these aspects of reading skill over time.

The cognitive-linguistic variables, on the other hand, were only weakly related to each other on both occasions. Consistent with the findings of previous studies, each was correlated with at least one measure of reading and/or spelling at Grade 2 and, except for rapid serial naming, at Grade 8. These findings suggest that phonemic awareness, verbal memory, rapid naming, and IQ each tap somewhat different reading-related skills.

## TEMPORAL STABILITY OF INDIVIDUAL DIFFERENCES IN COGNITIVE-LINGUISTIC ABILITIES

Even though different instruments were used at the two ages, considerable stability over a six-year interval was seen for the four cognitive-linguistic measures. The correlation between Grade 2 and Grade 8 scores were .49 for phoneme deletion, .66 for verbal memory, .51 for rapid serial naming, and .68 for IQ (all $p$ < .01). This suggests that each measure tapped a dimension of individual differences that remained quite stable during the school years, even though its relationships with various reading skills were somewhat different at the two grades as shown in table II.

---

**TABLE II.**
**CONCURRENT CORRELATIONS AMONG MEASURES AT GRADE 2 (BELOW THE DIAGONAL) AND GRADE 8 (ABOVE THE DIAGONAL).**

|  | Reading and Spelling | | | | Other Skills | | | |
|---|---|---|---|---|---|---|---|---|
|  | **1.** | **2.** | **3.** | **4.** | **5.** | **6.** | **7.** | **8.** |
| **Reading and Spelling** | | | | | | | | |
| 1. Word Identification | — | .53** | .52** | .64** | .28 | .41* | −.27 | .38* |
| 2. Word Attack | .66** | — | .06 | .54** | .47** | .22 | −.13 | .17 |
| 3. Passage Comprehension | .58** | .41* | — | .43* | .11 | .36* | −.01 | .50** |
| 4. Spelling | .70** | .70** | .48** | — | .40* | .38* | −.12 | .54** |
| **Other Skills** | | | | | | | | |
| 5. Phoneme Deletion | .42* | .40* | .35* | .45** | — | .02 | −.02 | .22 |
| 6. Verbal Memory | .39* | .39* | .18 | .47** | .18 | — | −.19 | .24 |
| 7. Rapid Serial Naming | −.30 | −.15 | −.18 | −.39* | −.19 | −.25 | — | −.14 |
| 8. Full-scale IQ | .48** | .25 | .46** | .27 | .31 | .28 | −.24 | — |

$*p$ < .01, two-tailed  $**p$ < .001
Note: $n$ = 55.

## TABLE III.
## CORRELATIONS OF GRADE 2 SCORES WITH GRADE 8 SCORES ON READING AND SPELLING MEASURES.

| At Grade 2 | At Grade 8 | | | | |
|---|---|---|---|---|---|
| | Word Identific'n | Word Attack | Passage Compreh'n | Spelling | Read/Spell Composite |
| Word Identification | .67** | .48** | .46** | .53** | .70** |
| Word Attack | .58** | .60** | .13 | .46** | .59** |
| Passage Comprehension | .51** | .19 | .41* | .51** | .54** |
| Spelling | .64** | .48** | .29 | .63** | .68** |
| Read/Spell Composite | .72** | .53** | .38* | .63** | .75** |

*$p < .01$, two-tailed  **$p < .001$

Note: $n = 55$.

## TEMPORAL STABILITY OF INDIVIDUAL DIFFERENCES IN READING AND SPELLING ABILITIES

Correlations between second and eighth grade reading and spelling scores are shown in table III. Along the diagonal, it can be seen that each measure showed significant stability of individual differences over the six-year interval between assessments, with the composite measure having the strongest correlation and the passage comprehension subtest having the weakest. Passage comprehension in Grade 8 was also predicted moderately well by Grade 2 word identification scores and by the composite measure, but not by earlier performance on word attack or spelling. Conversely, Grade 8 word attack scores were not predicted by second grade comprehension abilities. Word identification and spelling, however, were quite well predicted by each of the second grade measures, as was the eighth grade composite.

Classification of the participants as RD or NRD on the basis of their second grade reading abilities also showed the degree of stability that had been seen in previous research. In Grade 2, a cutoff of –1.5 SD below the mean reading cluster score for the not-at-risk sample, which was equivalent to a delay of one year or more in achievement, had been used to assign children to the two subgroups (Scarborough 1989). Figure 1 shows the bivariate distribution of reading cluster scores of the RD and NRD children at the two grades. In the graph, the second grade cutoff point is marked by a vertical dotted line. The points for the RD sample fall to the left of the line and those of the NRD fall to its right.

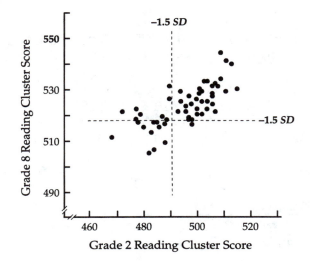

*Figure 1.* *Bivariate distribution of Grade 2 and Grade 8 Reading Cluster Scores (n = 55).*

At Grade 8, the cutoff point analogous to the second grade criterion is shown by the horizontal dotted line in the figure. The 11 cases with scores in the lower left quadrant and the 35 in the upper right quadrant are the children whose classifications remained the same at the two grades. The eight points in the upper left quadrant represent children whose reading improved enough to avoid (though often just barely) meeting the RD criterion in eighth grade, and the one child who fell in the lower right quadrant was not a disabled reader in second grade but did fall slightly below the cutoff six years later. In sum, 58 percent of the children who were originally assigned to the RD group, and 97 percent of those in the NRD group, had stable classifications over six years. It must be emphasized, however, that of the children whose classifications changed, all but two remained "borderline" cases (within a few points of the cutoff) in eighth grade, and the two who showed more impressive gains had been the highest achievers within the RD group in second grade.

## CAN MORE ACCURATE PREDICTIONS BE MADE BY TAKING OTHER FACTORS INTO ACCOUNT?

In a series of multiple regression analyses, the prediction of eighth grade reading was next examined in relation to the four cognitive-linguistic measures at Grade 2. For each outcome measure, the four new predictors were entered as a group, and the resulting multiple correlation was compared to the simple across-age prediction of that outcome measure by itself. Except for passage comprehension, it turned out that the Grade 8 scores were predicted as well or better by the corresponding Grade 2 score than by the combination of phoneme deletion, verbal memory, rapid serial naming, and IQ scores (.67 versus .61 for word identification; .60 versus .42 for word attack; .63 versus .58 for spelling; and .75 versus .66 for the composite variable). For passage comprehension, which was earlier noted to be the least temporally stable of the reading measures ($r$ = .41), the multiple correlation based on other variables was higher, but only slightly ($R$ = .49). In a subsequent hierarchical multiple regression analysis, when Grade 2 comprehension was entered first, the addition of the set of cognitive-linguistic measures at the second step did not result in a significant increase in the proportion of variance accounted for. Results similar to these were also obtained for the other reading and spelling outcome measures. It was clear from these analyses that knowing a second grader's phonemic awareness, verbal memory, rapid serial naming, and IQ scores did not yield a more accurate prognosis than simply knowing about the child's reading ability.

The foregoing analyses failed to take into account, however, an interesting feature of the data that can be seen in figure 1. Visual examination of the scatterplot suggested that the relationship between Grade 2 and Grade 8 reading cluster scores was not linear but was flatter along the lower portion of the Grade 2 distribution and steeper for the higher portion. In other words, it looked as though the prediction of eighth grade scores from second grade scores was much stronger within the NRD group than within the RD group. This observation was confirmed statistically[2], and across-age correlations for reading cluster scores were found to be very weak within the RD group ($r$ = .18) but quite strong within the NRD group ($r$ = .64), even though the ranges of scores at both ages were equivalent for the two subsamples. It would seem then that this difference in the size of the correlations is not simply an artifact of range restrictions. Given this indication that the predictability of future reading might be quite different for disabled readers than for other students, the series of multiple regression

---

[2] The addition of a quadratic term at the second step of a hierarchical multiple regression predicting Grade 8 from Grade 2 reading cluster scores resulted in a significant increase in $R^2$ from .51 to .56, $F(2,53) = 6.046$, $p = .017$.

analyses described above was repeated, this time separately for the two groups. The results are summarized in table IV.

For the larger NRD group, the results pretty much mirrored those for the entire sample, as one would expect. The multiple correlations based on the four cognitive-linguistic predictors were not much larger, if at all, than the simple across-age correlations of each reading measure with itself. Moreover, in subsequent hierarchical regressions, it was found that including the four additional predictors did not significantly increase the proportion of variance accounted for, beyond that predicted by the second grade measure of the dependent variable itself. In sum, the best predictors of future reading and spelling skills of the normally-achieving subsample were those skills themselves at the younger age.

For the RD group, the picture was dramatically different. First, the across-age correlations for the reading measures were much lower than the multiple correlations of Grade 8 reading with the four cognitive-linguistic factors (.43 versus .76 for the composite; .31 versus .75 for word identification; .51 versus .76 for word attack; .01 versus .38 for passage comprehension; and .61 versus .81 for spelling). It is not surprising, therefore, that when subsequent multiple regression analyses included the second grade reading measure at the first step, substantial additional proportions of variance were accounted for by including the cognitive-linguistic predictors, above and beyond the prediction of reading by itself (except for passage comprehension). The increase in $R^2$ was .42 ($p = .038$) for the reading/spelling composite, .46 ($p = .039$) for word identification, .31 ($p = .11$) for word attack, and .29 ($p = .068$) for spelling. These findings suggest that the accuracy of prognoses for children who have already developed a reading disability can be substantially improved by taking into account not just how poor the child's reading achievement is, but also some additional information about cognitive and linguistic abilities.

Which skills were most closely related to the eighth grade outcomes of the children who were designated as RD in second grade? Of the four cognitive-linguistic abilities that were analyzed in this study, rapid serial naming speed emerged as the most consistently useful predictor for the RD subsample, making a unique contribution to the prediction of their composite, word identification, word attack, and spelling scores, according to the beta weights from the regression analyses (table IV). It bears noting here that these relationships between rapid naming and later reading do not appear to have been inflated by any undue influence of extreme scores (outliers) as can occur in analyses of small samples. When Spearman rank order correlations (which are far less prone to such distortion) were computed, Grade 2 rapid naming speed remained well correlated with the Grade 8 composite ($r_s = -.60$), word identification (−.64), word attack (−.35), and spelling (−.58) measures. These coefficients are in close agreement with the Pearson correlations listed in table IV.

In contrast, phoneme awareness and verbal memory differences within the RD group at Grade 2 were only weakly related, if at all, to how much progress in reading these children made over the following six years, although phonemic awareness did make a contribution to the prediction of future spelling. Finally, along with rapid naming, IQ also contributed to the prediction

TABLE IV. PREDICTION OF GRADE 8 READING SKILLS FROM GRADE 2 PHONEME DELETION, VERBAL MEMORY, RAPID SERIAL NAMING AND IQ SCORES: RD VERSUS NRD SUBSAMPLES.

| Grade 8 Outcome Measure | Grade 2 Predictor(s) | RD Group (n = 19) | | | NRD Group (n = 36) | | |
|---|---|---|---|---|---|---|---|
| | | r | β | **R** | r | β | **R** |
| Read/Spell Composite | Phoneme Deletion | .28 | .35 | | .35* | .27 | |
| | Verbal Memory | .26 | −.05 | | .43** | .36* | |
| | Rapid Naming | −.61** | −.78** | | −.33* | −.19 | |
| | IQ | −.06 | −.43 | | .40** | .25 | |
| | All four | | | .76** | | | .64** |
| | Read/Spell Composite alone | .43* | | | .72*** | | |
| Word Identif'n | Phoneme Deletion | .24 | .31 | | .20 | .13 | |
| | Verbal Memory | .25 | −.06 | | .46** | .40* | |
| | Rapid Naming | −.62** | −.78** | | −.26 | −.16 | |
| | IQ | −.03 | −.39 | | .32* | .19 | |
| | All four | | | .75** | | | .56* |
| | Word Ident'n alone | .31 | | | .48* | | |
| Word Attack | Phoneme Deletion | .06 | .17 | | .17 | .15 | |
| | Verbal Memory | .26 | .09 | | .25 | .25 | |
| | Rapid Naming | −.39* | −.62** | | −.09 | −.01 | |
| | IQ | −.42* | −.71** | | .13 | .06 | |
| | All four | | | .76** | | | .32 |
| | Word Attack alone | .51* | | | .34* | | |

(Continues)

TABLE IV. PREDICTION OF GRADE 8 READING SKILLS FROM
GRADE 2 PHONEME DELETION, VERBAL MEMORY, RAPID SERIAL
NAMING AND IQ SCORES: RD VERSUS NRD SUBSAMPLES. *(cont.)*

| Grade 8 Outcome Measure | Grade 2 Predictor(s) | RD Group (*n* = 19) | | | NRD Group (*n* = 36) | | |
|---|---|---|---|---|---|---|---|
| | | *r* | *β* | **R** | *r* | *β* | **R** |
| Passage Compreh. | Phoneme Deletion | .11 | .05 | | .24 | .16 | |
| | Verbal Memory | −.05 | −.11 | | .28* | .20 | |
| | Rapid Naming | −.07 | .04 | | −.21 | −.11 | |
| | IQ | .36 | −.39 | | .39** | .30 | |
| | All four | | | .38 | | | .49 |
| | Passage Compreh. alone | .01 | | | .44* | | |
| Spelling | Phoneme Deletion | .38 | .45* | | .33* | .26 | |
| | Verbal Memory | .26 | .09 | | .20 | .14 | |
| | Rapid Naming | −.64** | −.81** | | −.26 | −.17 | |
| | IQ | .01 | −.39* | | .28 | .18 | |
| | All four | | | .81** | | | .45 |
| | Spelling alone | .61** | | | .50** | | |

*p < .05, two-tailed   **p < .01

of word attack and spelling outcomes, but surprisingly, this represented an *inverse* relationship with outcomes. In other words, it was the reading disabled children with slower naming speeds and *higher* IQs who were least able to read pseudowords and spell accurately in eighth grade.

## DISCUSSION

Considerable temporal stability of individual differences in reading achievement over a six-year period was found in this longitudinal sample. Few of the children who had been designated as reading disabled in second grade became more than low-average readers in adolescence, and of the rest, only one met the criterion for RD in eighth, but not second, grade. In both respects, these results are consistent with those from previous research with larger and more population-representative samples (e.g., Badian, 1988; Butler et al. 1985; Fergusson et al. 1996; Juel 1988; McGee et al. 1988; Satz et al. 1981; Shaywitz et al. 1992).

The main goal of the analyses, however, was to examine reading outcomes, not just in relation to previously measured reading skills, but also in relation to some more basic cognitive and linguistic abilities that have consistently been shown to correlate with, and prospectively predict, reading skills at younger ages: phonemic awareness, verbal memory, rapid serial naming speed, and IQ (e.g., Ackerman and Dykman 1993; Cornwall 1992; Hansen and Bowey 1994; Wagner, Torgesen, and Rashotte 1994). Correlational analyses of these measures yielded results that were quite consistent with previous findings in several respects. First, as expected, these four skills were indeed associated with reading abilities in the sample at both second and eighth grade. Second, individual differences in these abilities were found to have considerable temporal stability, consistent with previous evidence for moderate to high across-age correlations during the elementary school years for IQ (e.g.,Bloom 1964) and for phonemic awareness, verbal memory, and rapid serial naming (e.g., Wagner et al. 1997). Third, the intercorrelations among these four skills were quite low at both grades. Similar dissociations between these skills have been obtained in other samples (e.g., Bowers 1995; Bowers and Swanson 1991; Wimmer 1993). On the other hand, it is not uncommon for correlations to be observed among them (e.g., Cornwall 1992; Hansen and Bowey 1994; Wagner, Torgesen, and Rashotte 1994). To some extent, such results may be task specific; for example, correlations between phonemic awareness and memory measures tend to occur when memory-laden "oddity" tasks are used to assess phonemic awareness (Kyle and Oakhill 1998). In addition, the age and diversity of participants and/or the distribution of reading abilities in a sample may affect the strength of these kinds of associations. In any event, even when these measures are related to some extent, they usually account for some unique (as well as common) variance in reading in multivariate analyses, suggesting that they tap somewhat different reading-related abilities (e.g., Bowers 1993; Bowers, Steffy, and Tate 1988; McBride-Chang and Manis 1996; McDougall et al. 1994; Torgesen et al. 1997). The present findings are consistent with that conclusion.

It was hypothesized that, singly or in combination, these four stable and largely independent measures might serve as good predictors of future achievement in their own right, and might increase the accuracy of prognoses when used in conjunction with measures of reading and spelling. For predicting outcomes along the whole range of reading ability, however, it turned out that little was gained by taking into account children's cognitive and linguistic abilities in addition to their early reading and spelling scores. Even for reading comprehension, which was the least temporally stable aspect of reading ability, very little improvement in prediction accuracy was obtained by using the wider set of predictor measures. Similar results were obtained when only the NRD group was analyzed on its own. Apparently, by the end of the second grade, differences among children in phonemic awareness, verbal memory, rapid naming speed, and IQ have already made their contributions to determining individual differences in reading skill for normally achieving students whose subsequent degrees of success rest primarily on prior literacy skills themselves, and perhaps on other factors that were not examined here such as print exposure (Cunningham and Stanovich 1997).

From an educational perspective, however, making predictions about the future reading achievement of successful students is rarely a concern. Of greater interest is the prognosis for young schoolchildren who have fallen behind in learning to read. For these children, the present findings suggest that the severity of their reading disabilities may be less informative in predicting future improvement than their strengths and weaknesses in other areas. Somewhat surprising is that neither phonemic awareness nor verbal memory abilities in second grade were particularly useful for prognosis, although the former did make a modest contribution to the prediction of spelling outcomes. In contrast, differences in IQ, and especially in rapid serial naming speed at the younger age, provided the most information about future achievement in the RD subsample.

For the two literacy tasks that make the heaviest demand on knowledge of phoneme-grapheme correspondences, namely word attack (reading pseudowords) and spelling, more negative outcomes in eighth grade were found for the reading disabled children with higher IQ scores. This unexpected result suggests that the brighter children with reading disabilities may have been at a disadvantage over the long term in developing their decoding/encoding skills, perhaps because their greater general aptitude allowed them to be more successful at using visual memory, contextual cues, and astute guessing when reading unfamiliar words in text. To my knowledge, however, this finding has not been noted previously, and it would be very unwise to place much weight on it until additional evidence for a such a relationship becomes available, if ever.

The finding of greatest interest and potential practical utility was that rapid serial naming speed was a consistently strong prognostic indicator for the children with RD, making a substantial contribution to the prediction of all aspects of their eighth grade reading and spelling skills except comprehension. Rapid naming was the only measure in this study that tapped children's speed of processing, and this may account for its success as a predictor of adolescent outcomes (e.g., Kail and Hall 1994). It has been widely observed that during the elementary school years, reading curricula typically make increasing demands for fluency and speed in reading and writing beyond the primary grades. If two children have mastered decoding to an equivalent extent, the one who can do so more rapidly will be at an advantage. This child will be able to accomplish more reading in a given amount of time, increasing print exposure and gaining practice that improves accuracy and fluency even more. How well the children with reading disabilities did on the Grade 8 reading tests presumably reflected such differences in prior learning experiences, even though the outcome measures were not themselves speeded tasks. Of course, naming speed could also reflect constitutional, as well as experiential, ability differences among children with reading disabilities.

Ordinarily, a great deal of caution would be called for in drawing conclusions from multivariate analyses conducted in a sample as small as this one. In this instance, however, the results gain credence because there is converging evidence from several sources regarding the particularly strong role of rapid serial naming speed in predicting the future progress of children with reading disabilities. First, similar results to those reported here recently have been reported by Meyer, Wood, Hart, and Felton (1998) for two different longitudinal samples, each evaluated at Grades 3, 5, and 8. In their first study, prediction of later outcomes from third grade measures was compared for 15 poor readers (bottom 10 percent) versus their classmates. For the poor readers only, rapid serial naming was highly correlated with future word identification ($r = .64–.68$) but not with future comprehension. Phonemic awareness and IQ were not effective predictors. Similarly, in a larger sample of 64 impaired readers, word identification (but again not comprehension) at the later grades was predicted by rapid naming but not by phonemic awareness or IQ, even when the analyses controlled for Grade 3 differences in word reading ability which, as in the present study, were not very strong correlates of later reading scores within the RD sample ($r = .24$). This independent replication of the current findings certainly adds a great deal to their credibility.

Two other studies provide converging evidence for the special importance of rapid naming speed in predicting the future achievement of children with reading disabilities. Korhonen (1991) used cluster analyses to identify subgroups among third graders with learning disabilities. One subgroup was characterized by slow naming speed, and when follow-up evaluations of the sample were made in sixth grade, it was found that this naming subgroup had shown the least progress in reading achievement, whereas more of the children with other cognitive profiles had improved over the three intervening years. In an intervention study, Lovett (1995) examined individual differences in naming speed as a predictor of response to remedial efforts. Based on pre-treatment diagnostic testing of children with severe reading disabilities (aged 7 to 13 years), three subgroups were identified according to whether their deficits were in phonological awareness only, in naming speed only, or in both domains. Compared to children in a control condition, all three subgroups made significant gains in word reading abilities following 35 hours of treatment (involving *phonological awareness and blending* or *word identification strategy training*). However, the phonological awareness deficit group made much more progress than the other two groups which did not differ. That is, both remedial programs were less effective at improving the word recognition skills of the children with rapid serial naming deficits, even though they had higher IQ and comprehension scores than the other groups.

Despite the convergence of findings from these various studies that differences among poor readers in their rapid naming skills are predictive of future gains in reading achievement, this prognostic relationship has not always been observed. Torgesen et al. (1997) conducted predictive analyses, from second to fourth and from third to fifth grade, in a subsample of 43 poor readers (bottom 20 percent) from a longitudinal study of 215 children who were followed from Kindergarten to Grade 5. With IQ controlled, rapid naming speed predicted reading, but phonemic awareness was an even stronger predictor. Notably, in the Torgesen et al. sample, the temporal stability of reading scores over the two-year interval was much higher ($r = .66$ from Grade 2 to Grade 4, and .85 from Grade 3 to Grade 5 for word identification) than in other samples of poor readers. This may explain why rapid naming made no unique contribution to prediction above and beyond that made by the prior reading score. The authors report, furthermore, that their sample was exceptionally heterogeneous with regard to SES and ethnicity; they suggest that the greater homogeneity in other samples may account for the weaker temporal stability and larger effects of cognitive differences. Moreover, Torgesen et al. noted that very few of the poor readers showed significant improvement in reading ability over time (relative to norms), and suggested that cognitive differences among them perhaps did not affect rates of progress as much as in other samples because effective instruction had not been received. In other words, the special prognostic value of rapid naming may only apply under circumstances in which future reading ability is not so heavily determined by previous achievement.

Taken together, the findings suggest that when children with reading disabilities show differential rates of progress in reading achievement over the elementary school years, those with slower naming abilities tend to show the least improvement. Rapid serial naming tasks may thus prove to be a useful means of identifying children who may need additional assistance, above and beyond the kinds of interventions that are effective for poor readers with unimpaired naming speeds. At present, however, the basis for the close association between rapid naming speed and future reading abilities is not entirely clear. Inefficient retrieval of lexical information, slow articulation of speech, difficulty in sustaining attention, poorly established phonological representations of names, and other weaknesses in poorer readers have been mentioned by various researchers as possibly underlying the observed relationship (Ackerman and Dykman 1993; Bowers and Swanson 1991; Kail and Hall 1994; Wagner and Torgesen 1987; Wolf 1991). Little research has been conducted, however, to evaluate the relative merits of these possibilities. Until this question is clarified, it is difficult to know precisely what kind of training would be most effective for children whose reading disabilities are accompanied by slow naming speed.

Address for correspondence: 309 Grove Road, South Orange, NJ 07079, (973) 762-3482, Hscarbor@email.gc.cuny.edu.

## ACKNOWLEDGMENTS

I am grateful to the families who participated in the study, to the many assistants over the years who assisted in collecting and analyzing the data, and to the March of Dimes Birth Defects Foundation for financial support for the research. Some of these results were previously reported to the Society for Research in Child Development (Scarborough 1995).

## References

Ackerman, P. T., and Dykman, R. A. 1993. Phonological processes, confrontation naming, and immediate memory in dyslexia. *Journal of Learning Disabilities* 26:597–609.

Ackerman, P. T., Dykman, R. A., and Gardner, M. 1990. Counting rate, naming rate, phonological sensitivity, and memory span: Major factors in dyslexia. *Journal of Learning Disabilities* 23:325–27.

Adams, M., and Bruck, M., 1995. Resolving the "great debate". *American Educator* 19:7–20.

Badian, N. A. 1988. The prediction of good and poor reading before kindergarten entry: A nine-year follow-up. *Journal of Learning Disabilities* 21:98–123.

Bloom, B. S. 1964. *Stability and Change in Human Characteristics*. New York: Wiley.

Bowers, P. G. 1993. Text reading and rereading: Determinants of fluency beyond word recognition. *Journal of Reading Behavior* 25:133–53.

Bowers, P. G. 1995. Tracing symbol naming speed's unique contributions to reading disabilities over time. *Reading and Writing* 7:189–216.

Bowers, P. G., and Swanson, L. B. 1991. Naming speed deficits in reading disability. *Journal of Experimental Child Psychology* 51:195–219.

Bowers, P. G., Steffy, R. A., and Tate, E. 1988. Comparison of the effects of IQ control methods on memory and naming speed predictors of reading disability. *Reading Research Quarterly* 23:304–19.

Bowers, P. G., and Wolf, M. 1993. A double-deficit hypothesis for developmental reading disorders. Paper presented to the Society for Research in Child Development, March, New Orleans.

Brady, S. A. 1991. The role of working memory in reading disability. In S. A. Brady and D. P. Shankweiler, eds., *Phonological Processes in Literacy*. Hillsdale, NJ: Lawrence Erlbaum Associates.

Brady, S. A., and Shankweiler, D. P. eds. 1991. *Phonological Processes in Literacy*. Hillsdale, NJ: Lawrence Erlbaum Associates.

Bruck, M. 1992. Persistence of dyslexics' phonological awareness deficits. *Developmental Psychology* 28:874–86.

Bruck, M. 1993. Component spelling skills of college students with childhood diagnoses of dyslexia. *Learning Disabilities Quarterly* 16:171–84.

Butler, S. R., Marsh, H. W., Sheppard, M. J., and Sheppard, J. L. 1985. Seven-year longitudinal study of the early prediction of reading achievement. *Journal of Educational Psychology* 77:349–61.

Byrne, B., and Fielding-Barnsley, R. 1989. Phonemic awareness and letter knowledge in the child's acquisition of the alphabetic principle. *Journal of Educational Psychology* 81:313–21.

Cornwall, A. 1992. The relationship of phonological awareness, rapid naming, and verbal memory to severe reading and spelling disabilities. *Journal of Learning Disabilities* 25:532–38.

Cunningham, A. E., and Stanovich, K. E. 1997. Early reading acquisition and its relation to reading experience. *Developmental Psychology* 33:934–45.

Denckla, M. B., and Rudel, R. G. 1976. Rapid "automatized" naming (R.A.N.): Dyslexia differentiated from other learning disabilities. *Neuropsychologia* 14:471–79.

Ehri , L., and Wilce, L. S. 1980. The influence of orthography on readers' conceptualization of the phonemic structure of words. *Applied Psycholinguistics* 1:371–84.

Fergusson, D. M., Horwood, L. J., Caspi, A., Moffitt, T. E., and Silva, P. A. 1996. The artefactual remission of reading disability: Psychometric lessons in the study of stability and change in behavioral development. *Developmental Psychology* 32:132–40.

Hansen, J., and Bowey, J. A. 1994. Phonological analysis skills, verbal working memory, and reading ability in second-grade children. *Child Development* 65:938–50.

Hollingshead, A. B., and Redlich, F. C. 1958. *Social Class and Mental Illness*. New York: Wiley.

Juel, C. 1988. Learning to read and write: A longitudinal study of 54 children from first through fourth grades. *Journal of Education Psychology* 80:437–47.

Kail, R. V., and Hall, L. K. 1994. Processing speed, naming speed, and reading. *Developmental Psychology* 30:949–54.

Korhonen, T. T. 1991. Neuropsychological stability and prognosis of subgroups of children with learning disabilities. *Journal of Learning Disabilities* 24:48–57.

Kyle, F., and Oakhill, J. 1998. The relation between phonological awareness and working memory. Paper presented to the Society for the Scientific Study of Reading, San Diego.

Liberman, I. Y., Shankweiler, D., Fischer, F. W., and Carter, B. 1974. Explicit syllable and phoneme segmentation in the young child. *Journal of Experimental Child Psychology* 18:201-12.

Lovett, M. W. 1995. Remediating word identification deficits: Are the core deficits of developmental dyslexia amenable to treatment? Paper presented to the Society for Research in Child Development, April, Indianapolis.

McBride-Chang, C., and Manis, F. R. 1996. Structural invariance in the associations of naming speed, phonological awareness, and verbal reasoning in good and poor readers: A test of the double deficit hypothesis. *Reading and Writing* 8:323–29.

McDougall, S., Hulme, C., Ellis, A., and Monk, A. 1994. Learning to read: The role of short-term memory and phonological skills. *Journal of Experimental Child Psychology* 58:112–33.

McGee, R., Williams, S., and Silva, P. A. 1988. Slow starters and long-term backward readers: A replication and extension. *British Journal of Educational Psychology* 58:330–37.

Meyer, M. M., Wood, F. B., Hart, L. A., and Felton, R. H. 1998. Selective predictive value of rapid automatized naming in poor readers. *Journal of Learning Disabilities* 31:106–17.

Perfetti, C.A. , Beck, L., Bell, L., and Hughes, C. 1987. Phonemic knowledge and learning to read are reciprocal: A longitudinal study of first grade children. *Merrill-Palmer Quarterly* 33:283–319.

Sattler, J. 1992. *Assessment of Children*. 3rd ed.. San Diego: Sattler.

Satz, P., Fletcher, J., Clark, W., and Morris, R. 1981. Lag, deficit, rate, and delay constructs in specific learning disabilities: A reexamination. In A. Ansara, N. Geschwind, A. Galaburda, M. Albert, and N. Gartrell, eds., *Sex Differences in Dyslexia*. Towson, MD: Orton Dyslexia Society.

Scarborough, H. S. 1989. Prediction of reading disability from familial and individual differences. *Journal of Educational Psychology* 81:101–8.

Scarborough, H. S. 1991. Antecedents to reading disability: Preschool language development and literacy experiences of children from dyslexic families. *Reading and Writing* 3:219–33.

Scarborough, H. S. 1995. Long-term prediction of reading skills: Grade 2 to grade 8. Paper presented to the Society for Research in Child Development, April, Indianapolis.

Shaywitz, S. E., Escobar, M. D., Shaywitz, B. A., Fletcher, J., and Makuch, B. 1992. Evidence that reading disability may represent the lower tail of a normal distribution of reading ability. *New England Journal of Medicine* 326:145–50.

Snyder, L. S., and Downey, D. M. 1995 Serial rapid naming skills in children with reading disabilities. *Annals of Dyslexia* 45:31–50.

Stanovich, K. E., Cunningham, A. E., and Cramer, B. R. 1984. Assessing phonological awareness in kindergarten children: Issues of task comparability. *Journal of Experimental Child Psychology* 38:175–90.

Stone, B., and Brady, S. 1995. Evidence for phonological processing deficits in less-skilled readers. *Annals of Dyslexia* 45: 51-78.

Torgesen, J. K., Wagner, R. K., Rashotte, C. A., Burgess, S., and Hecht, S. 1997. Contributions of phonological awareness and rapid automatic naming ability to the growth of word-reading skills in second- to fifth-grade children. *Scientific Studies of Reading* 1:161–85.

Treiman, R. 1984. Individual differences among children in spelling and reading styles. *Journal of Experimental Child Psychology* 37:463–77.

Wagner, R. K., and Torgesen, J. K. 1987. The nature of phonological processing and its causal role in the acquisition of reading skill. *Psychological Bulletin* 101:192–212.

Wagner, R. K., Torgesen, J. K., and Rashotte, C. A. 1994. Development of reading-related phonological processing abilities: New evidence of bidirectional causality from a latent variable longitudinal study. *Developmental Psychology* 30:73–87.

Wagner, R. K., Torgesen, J. K., Rashotte, C. A., Hecht, S. A., Barker, T. A., Burgess, S. R, Donahue, J., and Garon, T. 1997. Changing relations between phonological processing abilities and word-level reading as children develop from beginning to skilled readers: A 5-year longitudinal study. *Developmental Psychology* 33:468–79.

Waters, G. S., Bruck, M., and Malus-Abramowitz, M. 1988. The role of linguistic and visual information in spelling: A developmental study. *Journal of Experimental Child Psychology* 45:400–21.

Wechsler, D. 1989. *Wechsler Intelligence Scale for Children–Revised*. San Antonio: Psychological Corporation.

Wimmer, H. 1993. Characteristics of developmental dyslexia in a regular writing system. *Applied Psycholinguistics* 14:1–33.

Wolf, M. 1991. Naming speed and reading: The contribution of the cognitive neurosciences. *Reading Research Quarterly* 26:23–141.

Wolf, M. 1997. A provisional, integrative account of phonological and naming-speed deficits in dyslexia: Implications for diagnosis and intervention. In B. Blachman, ed., *Cognitive and Linguistic Foundations of Reading Acquisition: Implications for Intervention Research*. Hillsdale, NJ: Lawrence Erlbaum Associates.

Woodcock, R., and Johnson, M. B. 1978. *Woodcock-Johnson Psychoeducational Battery*. Allen Park, TX: DLM Teaching Resources.

# Dyslexia and Learning Musical Notation: A Pilot Study

B. S. Jaarsma

A. J. J. M. Ruijssenaars

W. Van den Broeck

Leiden University, the Netherlands

*Both the alphabet and our system of musical notation are largely based on arbitrary conventions and associations. Conforming to the Dyslexic Automatization Deficit Hypothesis, children suffering from dyslexia are supposed to have difficulty in automating these types of conventions and/or associations. Scientific research into the relation between dyslexia and learning musical notation is rare. Therefore, we developed a new intervention paradigm on learning musical notation. This program was followed by five dyslexic children and four children without dyslexia, in order to study and compare the learning processes of both groups. The program consisted of instruction, practice in the skills and knowledge related to musical notation, and test assignments. During each session, the problem-solving process of the individual child was observed and the amount of time required to complete each assignment in the program was recorded. In addition we analyzed the errors made by the two groups of children in each session. A pretest-posttest comparison revealed that dyslexic children needed more time to learn musical notation than did children without dyslexia. Dyslexic children also made more mistakes and produced more 'third transpositions'. The implications for teaching musical notation are outlined.*

Annals of Dyslexia, Vol. 48, 1998
ISSN 0736-9387

## INTRODUCTION

There is a growing body of evidence that children suffering from dyslexia might have a general deficit in automating a variety of cognitive and motor skills (Nicolson and Fawcett 1990, 1994a, 1994b, 1995; Yap and Van der Leij 1994; Fawcett, Nicolson, and Dean 1996). This Dyslexic Automatization Deficit (DAD) hypothesis may explain some behaviors not readily accounted for by the dominant explanation of dyslexia, the phonological deficit hypothesis (cf. Stanovich 1988; Brady and Shankweiler 1991). One of the intriguing elements of the DAD hypothesis is its prediction that people with dyslexia are likely to have problems in learning which does not involve reading per se. One such task, learning to read musical notes, is especially interesting because it is conceptually analogous to learning to read the alphabet. Both the alphabet and our system of musical notation are based largely on arbitrary conventions and associations. Moreover, there is empirical evidence that disabled readers have particular problems in learning the structural or rule-governed aspects of reading and language-related skills (Manis et al. 1987; Scarborough 1990). Manis et al. (1987) found that, in learning arbitrary paired associates, disabled readers performed at a level below that of nondisabled readers only when the associates conformed to specific underlying rules (see also Morrison 1993). Should the prediction that dyslexic children have difficulties in learning musical notation be confirmed, it will further support the DAD hypothesis, and from a practical point of view, it may improve techniques for teaching music to dyslexic children. In fact, scientific research into the relation between dyslexia and difficulty in learning musical notation is rare. This is surprising given that the problems that dyslexic persons have with the automatization of grapheme-phoneme association would seem a necessary obstacle to the process of associative learning, critical in musical instruction.

Research on the learning of musical notation by persons with dyslexia has been carried out by Atterbury (1983, 1984), Hubicki (1994), and Ganschow, Lloyd-Jones, and Miles (1994). In the article "Music teachers need your help," Atterbury (1984) describes the regrettable lack of communication between the resource teachers and the music educators of learning disabled children and their resulting lack of knowledge regarding each other's long- and short-term goals. Atterbury describes specific problems LD children may have with music notation because of their excessive visual material and confusing formats. Any child with a reading disability may have problems, not only in reading the music but also with the physical layout of the page. Although Atterbury's article was published several years ago, only a few studies have been done to document a relation between dyslexia and difficulty in learning musical notation, or to identify difficulties children with dyslexia experience when confronted with music in school.

Hubicki (1994) also describes some of the difficulties people with dyslexia experience when learning musical notation. She focusses on awareness of implied information,[1] that is, the gap dividing the abstract sound of music itself from both the facts of musical theory and its notation. She highlights the difficulties experienced by individuals with dyslexia in processing this information which includes words and names referring to the pitch or the lengths of notes, and symbols which represent pitch, lengths of note, phrase markers, and interpretation signs. She claims this notation poses particular difficulty to persons with dyslexia for whom words and symbols are problematic (Hubicki 1994). According to Hubicki, some of the music reading terms which can cause difficulty include "high", "low", "left", and "right". She describes some compensatory strategies that could heighten awareness. Based on research and on her own clinical experience, Hubicki proposes the use of colors for each pitch symbol, or of familiar object symbols (like fruits) to represent the corresponding notes. In our opinion, this type of mediation does not solve the problem because people with dyslexia would still have to automatize a system based on arbitrary associations. Even if easier, it is not a permanent solution. The exclusive learning of an alternative system would become limiting as a student's musical ability increased. To play Mozart or Chopin, a gifted musician with dyslexia would either have to recode the composition in the familiar system, memorize it, or ultimately learn to read the traditional musical notation after all.

Ganschow et al. (1994) investigated the difficulties dyslexic musicians face during the formalized study of music, particularly with musical notation. Through seven case studies based on self-reports, they present individual experiences with learning the musical notation system. In their article, Ganschow and her colleagues also discuss the possible correspondence between learning to read and learning to interpret musical notation. They see a similar pattern in the difficulties experienced with the no-

---

[1] This 'implied information' falls into two categories of symbols: those which represent time (time symbols follow one another across the page from left to right) and pitch (pitch symbols are placed one above or below another) (Hubicki 1994).

tation system of music and that of written language: problems
with the representation of time, rhythm, and sequencing might
be compared to the difficulties some dyslexics have with identifying and representing phonological units of language.

Both the paucity of research on the relation between
dyslexia and difficulty in learning musical notation, and the
need for empirical information on this topic, prompted us to
carry out this study. Our main goal was to gain more insight
into the possible difficulties children with dyslexia experience
when they learn musical notation. To this end, we developed a
music program which was followed by a group of children
with dyslexia ($n = 5$), as well as a group of children without
dyslexia ($n = 4$) in order to study and compare the learning
processes of both groups. This music program was structured
as an intensive individual training, where special attention was
given to a qualitative analysis of the learning process. The main
principles to structure the training program were comparable
to the adaptive strategies used in the tradition of dynamic assessment procedures: gradual structuring of item presentation
and modeling (Ruijssenaars and Hamers 1989; Lidz 1991;
Haywood and Tzuriel 1992).

Because of the intensity required to prepare and execute the
training program, we opted for a small-size intensive pilot
study to determine whether our approach was meaningful and
feasible. We sought answers to the following questions:

What specific difficulties do children with dyslexia have
when learning musical notation, and are these shared by
children without dyslexia?

What specific mistakes do children with and without
dyslexia make when learning musical notation?

How much learning gain in the naming of notes is evident
over time within groups? Is there a difference in learning
rate between children with and without dyslexia?

The results of the investigation pertain not only to differences in
learning gain between the two groups, but also within each
group. Even though our research is at a preliminary stage and
presently consists of only a small pilot study, we believe this
kind of research to be relevant to the debate on automaticity
versus exclusively phonological deficits in reading disability.
Looking at the acquisition of musical notes seems a very good
test of the DAD hypothesis. To meet these research goals we
compared—in a pretest-posttest design—a group of dyslexic

children with a group of nondyslexic children based on their progress in learning musical notes.

# METHOD

## DESCRIPTION OF THIS SAMPLE

Nine children participated in the investigation (seven boys and two girls, aged nine years, two months to nine years eleven months). Five of the participants were dyslexic and received special education at a school for children with learning disabilities (LD). The other four attended standard primary school and were confirmed by their teachers to have no reading problems. The children were enrolled in the study by the head teachers of two primary schools and three LD schools from the Middle Holland region, and were selected according to explicit criteria.

In order for the children from the LD schools to qualify for the study, the specific learning disorder of dyslexia had to have been diagnosed by an expert. In the Netherlands, the criteria outlined in the DSM-IV (APA 1996) are used for this diagnosis. Experimenters administered standardized didactic tests on word identification (AVI-test 1996) to reaffirm that the reading development of these children was at least two years below age level. The children from standard primary school scored above average and showed no reading difficulties on these tests. All participating children had to be at least nine years old (the average age at which children start formalized music education in the Netherlands). In addition, the children had to be of normal intelligence (IQ > 90) and free of visual and auditory handicaps. Finally, the children did not have any previous musical instruction, nor have been in special contact with musical notation in any other way. These selection criteria were strictly applied in an effort to ensure integrity of the data.

## PROCEDURE

For the collection of data in this pilot study, a chronological-age-match design was used. We chose this design both because it was appropriate for use with our selection criteria, and because many nine-year olds without previous musical training were available to participate. An acknowledged drawback of this design is that a posttest learning difference between the two groups can be interpreted as the result of the

initial differences in reading levels; a reading-level-match design should also be applied in future research. Both groups
were offered the music reading program in which measurements were taken before and after the assignments. The music
reading program consisted of individual sessions, each lasting
a maximum of forty-five minutes, which took place once a
week over a period of five weeks. The training consisted of instruction and practice in the skills and knowledge related to
musical notation (completed with assistance from the experimenter) and test assignments (completed without assistance).
During each session, the problem-solving process of the individual child was observed. In this way, it was possible to work
out how the child made a mistake. Afterwards, the mistakes
were discussed with the child in order to verify whether the
investigator's conclusions about their origins were correct. In
addition, at a later stage, we analyzed the errors made by the
two groups of children in each session. Using these two approaches (on-line and post hoc), we were able to gain more insight into the difficulties experienced by the children with
dyslexia in comparison with those experienced by the children
without dyslexia. By comparing the errors in the two samples,
it was possible to investigate whether the errors made by the
children with dyslexia were qualitatively unique.

In addition to observing errors made, the amount of time
required to complete each assignment in the program was
recorded. To this end, each of the first four training sessions
was followed by a test in which the children had to name, as
quickly as possible, the notes taught so far. These four
posttests were repeated in the final session, so each was presented twice. Next, we compared the difference between the
time to name the notes at initial and final posttest. If less time
was needed for the second note-naming exercise, this might
indicate that a learning or automatization process had taken
place. By carrying out further intergroup comparisons, we
were able to investigate whether dyslexic children had more
trouble automating musical notation than did children without dyslexia.

## THE INDIVIDUAL TRAINING PROGRAM FOR READING MUSIC

The program's assignments were specifically designed to cultivate the ability to "read music": to give the name of a particular
note. The program consisted of five series of notes, which the
child was taught over five sessions. As shown in figure 1, each

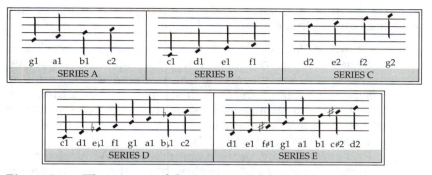

*Figure 1.* The content of the progam: the five series of notes.

series contained four different notes[2]. Series A contained g1, a1, b1, and c2; Series B contained c1, d1, e1, and f1; and Series C included d2, e2, f2, and g2. In Series D and E, the child learned flats (♭) and sharps (♯). In these series, the notes which were taught in series A through C were used, with the addition of b♭ and e♭, and f♯1 and c♯2, respectively. We chose to teach the flats and sharps because these symbols imply additional information which must be interpreted by the child. In the Dutch language, these symbols change not only the pitch of a previously learned note, but its name as well; for example, a "b" becomes a "bes" (b flat) and an "f" becomes a "fis" (f sharp). The phenomenon of a sound changing because of cumulative factors is also common in alphabetic orthographies; for example the letter "o" represents /a/ in hot and the letter "e" represents /ɛ/ in pet. But "oe" together represents /u/ (as in shoe). Dyslexic children often have difficulty understanding this concept when learning to read words. The addition of flats and sharps to certain series in our program was intended to test whether similar difficulty would arise when learning to read notes.

Each training session was based on one or more of these note series, and included a maximum of eight different exercises. The same exercises were repeated in the next session, but with a different series of notes in order to allow the children to familiarize themselves with the task. When carrying out the exercises, the children were allowed to make use of a learning aid, a chart showing

---

[2] The Western system of musical notation comprises 8 octaves. One octave contains,in this connection, the string c d e f g a b c. The numbers following the note names are a form of official musical notation and refer to the octave in question. A '1' following a note indicates the first string. A '2' following the note refers to a second string of notes which have the same names, but are in a different octave and hence are graphically represented in a different way, and sound at a different pitch.

all the notes with their names. The order of the assignments was always the same (with the exception of training sessions 4 and 5):

1. *Learning the new series* (week 1 = Series A, week 2 = Series B, and so forth). The four notes from a series were graphically presented and offered to the child on separate small cards, four times in a random order. The child received four small cards containing the names of the notes and was asked to place the name of the note with its corresponding picture.

2. *Recognizing notes within composition.* Within four different compositions consisting of eight notes divided in two bars, the child was asked each time to point to a different requested note.

3. *Reviewing the notes from a previous series.* The child was either asked to draw the requested notes on the staff or to complete a task as described in assignment 1. However, this time, the child had to identify a greater number of notes, in five different orders.

4. *Combining notes from previously learned series.* In each session, the child was shown a four-bar composition consisting of 16 notes, and was asked to point to notes named, to name notes, or to find errors in bars where notes had been named.

5. *Drawing notes whose names were under the staff, or were read out loud.*

6. *Naming notes shown on a large chart, or finding (from a collection of small cards laying on the table) the correct corresponding cards to the notes presented on the large chart.*

7. *Testing ready knowledge of note names with five flash cards.* The cards were presented in ascending order of difficulty. The first card contained two to five different notes (depending on the week), the second card contained three to six different notes, the third card four to seven, and so on.

8. *Evaluation of what the child considered difficult/easy or fun/boring.*

During all assignments except the seventh, extra help was given when needed. The assignments were designed to utilize different learning processes such as visual discrimination, recognizing associations, knowing associations, reproduction, and applying knowledge. In the study, no use was made of a clef sign at the beginning of a staff. This was a conscious choice, intended to ensure that any error made in the execution of assignments could be attributed to problems with the naming of the notes rather than with a possible failure in understanding the clef and the conventions associated with it.

## RESULTS

By analyzing the errors made by the children of both groups, and observing the problem-solving processes of each child, we tried to find an answer to our first research question: What specific difficulties do the children with dyslexia encounter in the formalized study of musical notation? By comparing errors and observations between the groups, we hoped to be able to discover whether there was a difference between the learning processes of children with and without dyslexia.

On one assignment in particular, the dyslexic children performed considerably below the level of the nondyslexic children. During this, the sixth assignment of the second session, children had to choose two to five cards whose graphic representation matched the notes pictured on a large chart (see individual training program). Although other assignments (in which the children had to compare two notes which were presented on different charts) demonstrated that the visual aspect of note matching did not cause any problems, the dyslexic children performed markedly worse on this assignment. During 70 trials, they made a total of 18 mistakes (26 percent), of which about 30 percent were third transpositions.[3] The nondyslexic children, on the other hand, did not make a single mistake and required far less time to complete the assignment.

As the study progressed, the dyslexic children gradually made fewer mistakes, corrected themselves more often, and experienced less difficulty in the naming of some notes. Over the course of the investigation, some children also made less use of the learning aid, a long chart divided into five series, showing all the notes and their names, which was always on the table. Those who continued to use it showed an increasingly more efficient routine, knowing exactly where to look for each note.

The goal of our second research question was to determine which specific mistakes are most likely to be made by children

---

[3] A third is a distance of two whole tones between notes. In the investigation we mainly used notes from the scale of c: c1 d1 e1 f1 g1 a1 b1 c2 (and d2 e2 f2 g2). A third transposition occurs when two notes separated by two whole tones are interchanged (for instance e1–g1).

with dyslexia when learning musical notation. Our error analysis, summarized in table I, showed that the dyslexic children not only made more mistakes, but also were particularly prone to making third transposition errors. That is, rather than confusing two notes next to each other (a1, g1), they confused notes that were either both on a line or on a space (a1, f1).

During the training and test sessions, the five dyslexic children made a total of 262 errors, out of which 160 (61 percent) were third transpositions. In comparison, the four nondyslexic children made a total of 146 errors, of which 56 were third transpositions (38 percent). On average, the dyslexic children made twice as many third transpositions as did the nondyslexic children ($t = 1.70$, $7df$, $p = 0.05$ by randomization test; cf. Edgington 1987), while making only equally as many other mistakes as the nondyslexic children. The most frequent mistake

| TABLE I. NUMBER OF THIRD TRANSPOSITIONS AND OTHER ERRORS MADE BY THE CHILDREN OF BOTH GROUPS. | | |
|---|---|---|
| | **Number of Errors** | |
| | **Third Transpositions** | **Other Errors** |
| **Children with Dyslexia** | | |
| 1. | 46 | 12 |
| 2.* | 9 | 5 |
| 3. | 40 | 24 |
| 4. | 16 | 26 |
| 5. | 49 | 35 |
| Average | 32 | 20.4 |
| Total | 160 (61%) | 102 (38%) |
| **Children without Dyslexia** | | |
| 1. | 5 | 21 |
| 2. | 12 | 25 |
| 3. | 31 | 25 |
| 4. | 8 | 19 |
| Average | 14 | 22.5 |
| Total | 56 (38%) | 90 (61%) |

*This child became ill during the test period and could therefore only finish the sessions 1 to 4. It seems that in general most of the mistakes were made in the fifth session, where they had to name the notes without any help. These figures will therefore be misleading, since this child hasn't done as many assignments as the other children.

made by the nondyslexic children was to identify the note in question with the name of a note just above or below it.

One of the nondyslexic children (No. 3) also made a relatively large number of third transpositions. Upon inquiry, we found that this child had difficulties with arithmetic, and was receiving remedial teaching in that subject. The nondyslexic children were also found to have more problems with b♭/e♭ and f♯/c♯.

Not all the thirds that were taught in the program were transposed with equal frequency. In the error analysis, we found that of the possible 20 third transpositions, only 13 were made by any of the children. Except for the transposition "a1 named as c2" (see figure 2), six transpositions were made to either side (that is upward as well as downward in the scale). The transpositions b1/d1,

| | Third Transposition | Note Names | Children with Dyslexia | Children without Dyslexia |
|---|---|---|---|---|
| 1. | 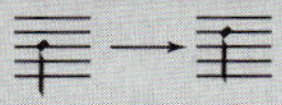 | b1 is named d1 | 37 | 14 |
| 2. | 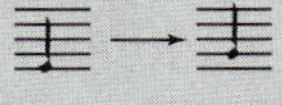 | e1 is named g1 | 21 | 2 |
| 3. | 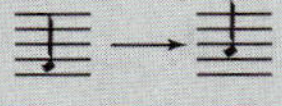 | f1 is named a1 | 19 | 10 |
| 4. | 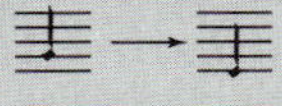 | g1 is named e1 | 19 | 5 |
| 5. | 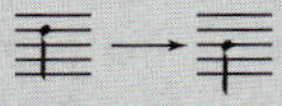 | d2 is named b1 | 13 | 4 |
| 6. | 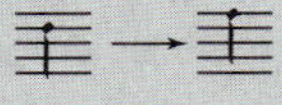 | d2 is named f2 | 12 | 1 |
| 7. | 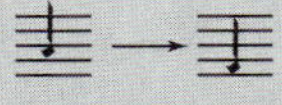 | a1 is named f1 | 11 | 4 |
| 8. | 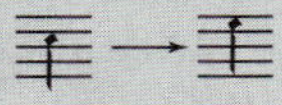 | c2 is named e2 | 8 | 9 |
| 9. | 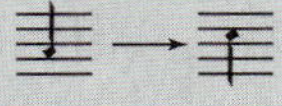 | a1 is named c2 | 5 | 1 |
| 10. | 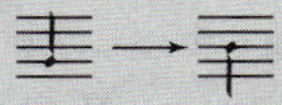 | g1 is named b1 | 5 | 1 (g is named b♭) |
| 11. | 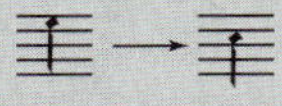 | e2 is named c2 | 4 | 0 |
| 12. | 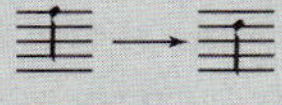 | f2 is named d2 | 3 | 1 |
| 13. | 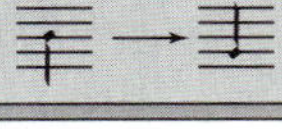 | b2 is named g1 | 3 | 2 |

*Figure 2.    Third transpositions made by the children of both groups.*

e1/g1, f1/a1, g1/e1, d2/b1, d2/f2, and a1/f1 were the most common made by the dyslexic children. The most frequent and intriguing transposition, in both groups of children, was b1/d1. In figure 2, the possible third transpositions, and the number of times these transpositions were made during the music program by the dyslexic and nondyslexic children, are shown.

Notably, transpositions of thirds did not occur in the naming of notes whose graphic representation was located above or below the five lines of the staff (c1/e1, d1/f1, e2/g2) (see figure 3).

*Figure 3.    Third transpositions that did not occur.*

The third research question asked how much time was required by the two groups of children for the naming of the notes. Each training session was followed by a test of the material learned at that session. This test consisted of five graded cards, based on one or more note series, presented in ascending order of difficulty. The first measurement took place at the end of the relevant practice session, and the second took place in the fifth and final session, when all cards were tested consecutively. The purpose of these two tests was to ascertain whether dyslexic children have more problems with this learning process than do nondyslexic children. First, we compared the average times for the dyslexic children (group I) and the nondyslexic children (group II) at the time of the first measurement. Figure 4 shows the results.

This chart shows that on all but five cards, the nondyslexic children needed less time to complete an assignment than the dyslexic children ($t = 3.13$, 24 $df$, $p = 0.0012$ by randomization test with 50,000 random permutations). For four of the cards (A2/A4/C4/D2), the time differences between groups were caused primarily by the long latencies of two children with dyslexia. Table II contains the average times scored on the cards by group I (dyslexic) and group II (nondyslexic). Times were scored without regard to errors in note naming.

Next, we compared the average times scored on the final posttest. By this time, the children had been taught all the notes. The less automated this knowledge, the more time a child would need in order to name the notes correctly. Figure 5 shows the average scores of group I and group II at the time of the final posttests.

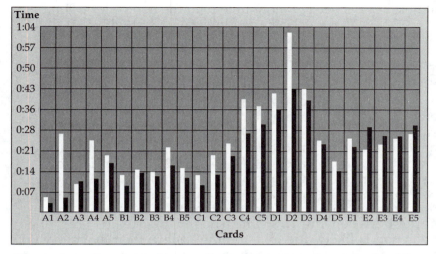

Figure 4.    Bar chart showing the average scores for group I (white bar: dyslexic) and group II (black bar: nondyslexic) on the first measurement.

Figure 5 shows that, at the final posttest, both groups generally needed less time for the assignments than in the initial posttests. The difference between the groups here was smaller compared with the first measurement, but the dyslexic children

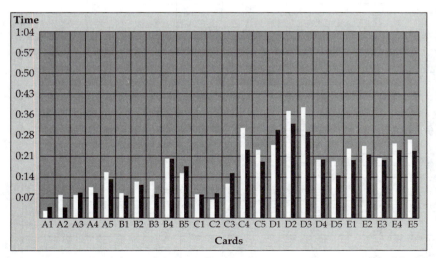

Figure 5.    Bar chart showing the average scores for group I (white bar: dyslexic) and group II (blackbar: nondyslexic) on the second measurement.

almost always needed more time than the nondyslexic children ($t$ = 2.37, 24 $df$, $p$ = 0.015 by randomization test with 50,000 random permutations).

Finally, we looked at the gain scores within each group. Table II contains the average times on both measurements and the learning gain scores in seconds. The figures show an average learning gain, for both groups, of 4.8 seconds. We considered an average learning gain of over 5 seconds per card to be substantial (shaded gray). For almost all cards, the children needed less time in the final posttest, with a pronounced learning gain on cards A2/A4 and C2 through D2 for the dyslexic children; their average gain in time is 7.1 seconds. If we compare the first and second measurements for the nondyslexic children, we notice that they made only modest gains between the first and second posttests. This phenomenon is likely due to a "ceiling" effect; their average gain in time is 3.4 seconds. The most noticeable gains were scored on the more difficult D and E series.

| Card | Group I (Dyslexic) | | | Group II (Nondyslexic) | | |
|------|-------------------|-------------------|------------------|-------------------|-------------------|------------------|
| | First Measurement | Second Measurement | Learning Gain | First Measurement | Second Measurement | Learning Gain |
| A1 | 05 | 03 | + 02 | 02 | 04 | − 02 |
| A2 | 27 | 08 | + 21 | 05 | 04 | + 01 |
| A3 | 10 | 08 | + 02 | 11 | 09 | + 02 |
| A4 | 25 | 11 | + 14 | 12 | 09 | + 03 |
| A5 | 20 | 16 | + 04 | 18 | 14 | + 04 |
| B1 | 13 | 09 | + 04 | 10 | 08 | + 02 |
| B2 | 15 | 13 | + 02 | 14 | 12 | + 02 |
| B3 | 14 | 13 | + 01 | 12 | 09 | + 03 |
| B4 | 23 | 21 | + 02 | 17 | 21 | − 04 |
| B5 | 15 | 16 | + 01 | 12 | 18 | − 06 |
| C1 | 13 | 08 | + 05 | 10 | 08 | + 02 |
| C2 | 20 | 07 | + 13 | 14 | 09 | + 05 |
| C3 | 24 | 12 | + 12 | 20 | 16 | + 04 |
| C4 | 39 | 31 | + 08 | 28 | 24 | + 04 |
| C5 | 37 | 24 | + 13 | 31 | 20 | + 11 |
| D1 | 41 | 25 | + 16 | 26 | 31 | + 05 |
| D2 | 63 | 37 | + 26 | 43 | 33 | + 10 |
| D3 | 43 | 38 | + 05 | 39 | 30 | + 09 |
| D4 | 25 | 20 | + 05 | 24 | 20 | + 04 |
| D5 | 18 | 19 | − 01 | 15 | 15 | 00 |
| E1 | 26 | 24 | + 02 | 23 | 20 | + 03 |
| E2 | 22 | 25 | − 03 | 30 | 22 | + 08 |
| E3 | 23 | 21 | + 02 | 27 | 20 | + 07 |
| E4 | 26 | 26 | 00 | 27 | 24 | + 03 |
| E5 | 28 | 27 | + 01 | 31 | 24 | + 07 |

TABLE II.   AVERAGE SCORES ON BOTH MEASUREMENTS, AND LEARNING GAIN SCORES FOR BOTH GROUPS IN SECONDS.

## DISCUSSION

As we mentioned in the introduction, we hypothesize that dyslexic children will have notable difficulty learning and automating the connection between a symbol and a label (and vice versa). One, therefore, expects these children to have more problems in a training program for musical notation than would nondyslexic children. This difficulty may be reflected in the number and type of mistakes dyslexic children make, and the time they need to complete the assignments. The results of the investigation described here bear out this hypothesis.

This study demonstrates that, during the entire learning process, the dyslexic children needed more time for the assignments, making almost twice as many mistakes as the nondyslexic children. In addition, they showed a specific error pattern which included frequent third transpositions, suggesting that the specific patterns of the lines and the labels connected to them had not yet been sufficiently internalized. Nondyslexic children made, in a manner of speaking, more precise errors by mistaking a note for the one directly above or below it (the so-called second). These findings suggest that dyslexic children are less sensitive to the crucial position of the notes on the lines. They preferentially give their attention to more superficial cues (whether a specific note is on the line or between lines).

There was one type of assignment with which the dyslexic children had noticeably more problems regarding both numbers of mistakes and time. In this assignment, the children were asked to match notes on a large chart to notes on separate small cards. As these cards were spread randomly over the table, the children had to be able to memorize the notation before starting to look for it. It was an advantage here to be able to name the note, but when this knowledge was less automated, the task became very difficult. The assignment at that point specifically drew on the ability to transfer the material learned.

Learning musical notation caused dyslexic children more trouble, even though learning benefits did occur. Given the time scores of the nondyslexic children on the first and second measurements, we may conclude that with them the automatization process is completed sooner.

All our conclusions, however, are conditional on the assumption the dyslexic-nondyslexic distinction was the only factor significant enough to account for the observed differences between groups. Although we suspect that neither differences in reading ability nor intellectual discrepancies between the two groups were sufficient to explain our data, the only way to rule out these possibilities is to replicate this study on a larger scale, using appropriate designs and controls. This pilot study was mainly intended to explore the feasibility of this newly developed paradigm for the study of learning processes in dyslexia.

## CONCLUSION

The results of our investigation show that dyslexic children are able to learn musical notation, but that they experience considerable difficulty with the automatization of this system of conventions. This conclusion paves the way for further research. The process of associative learning seems to be central to learning to read and spell. In particular, the automatization of arbitrary associations warrants further investigation. Associative learning is a time-consuming process for children with dyslexia in learning musical notation. It is imaginable that the lack of contextual support (top-down processing) is an extra handicap for them. The absence of compensatory procedures probably elicits a more structured weakness in this type of learning. For the musical learning process to succeed, it is important that music teachers take the effects of this laborious automatization into account. With music subjects in school, or with other types of musical education, dyslexic children will need more time not only to achieve automatization in music reading but also possibly for the automatization of the link between notation and playing techniques on an instrument.

Alternative musical notation systems such as color or picture codes (Hubicki 1994; Oglethorpe 1996) do not seem to be satisfactory aids for dyslexics, as the process of automating a system of arbitrary conventions is not the same as learning all the codes separately. When learning to read, dyslexic children often manage to learn the separate connections between graphemes and phonemes, but cannot automatically apply this knowledge in the reading process (Gough 1996). They do not progress beyond reading slowly, sound-by-sound. Put differently, explicit instruction in subskills does not automatically result in an integrated and partly unconscious (automated) final process.

A solution for this problem may, therefore, be found in putting less emphasis on explicit subskills. Instead, instruction should be structured in such a way that subskills are also acquired implicitly. At present, this approach is used in reading instruction by employing series of orthographically overlapping words. By the process of covariant learning these overlaps become, as it were, implicitly reinforced (cf. Van Orden and Goldinger 1994; Van den Broeck 1997).

Applying this carefully structured process of implicit learning in the musical instruction of dyslexic children would, for instance, mean that less attention would be given to the explicit naming of notes. Learning to read musical notation would then be integrated in its application to the playing of an instrument. Particular emphasis would have to be placed on becoming familiar with the constantly shifting patterns of musical notation. Knowledge of subpatterns and of separate notes would, in this way, be implicitly acquired and reinforced. Only when a reasonable proficiency is attained at this level should we implement an explicit phase to make the pupil aware of the more specific body of knowledge.

Whether or not such an approach is desirable, of course, depends on the purpose of the music instruction. This explicit phase would be a standard part of a professional course, but not of regular musical education in schools.

A follow-up study with a larger sample of children may afford more insight into specific automatization problems, and allow for more generalized conclusions about typical error patterns of dyslexic children.

Address correspondence to: Birgit Jaarsma, Leiden University/Faculty of Social and Behavioral Sciences, Pieter de la Court Building, Wassenaarseweg 52, P.O. Box 9555, 2300 RB Leiden, the Netherlands. Tel: +31-71-527-4072, Fax: +31-71-527-3619,E-mail: jaarsma@rulfsw.fsw.leidenuniv.nl

## References

American Psychiatric Association. *Diagnostic and statistical manual of mental disorders,* Fifth Edition. Washington, DC. American Psychiatric Association 1996.

Atterbury, B. W. 1983. A comparison of rhythm pattern perception and performance in normal and learning-disabled readers, age seven and eight. *Journal of Research in Music Education* 31(4):259–70.

Atterbury, B. W. 1984. Music teachers need your help. *Journal of Learning Disabilities* 17(2): 75–77.

Brady, S. A., and Shankweiler, D. P. (eds.) 1991. *Phonological Processes in Literacy.* Hillsdale, NJ: Lawrence Erlbaum Associates.

Edgington, E. S. 1987. *Randomization Tests (2nd Ed.).* New York: Marcel Dekker.

Fawcett, A. J., Nicolson, R. I., and Dean, P. 1996. Impaired Performance of Children with Dyslexia on a Range of Cerebellar Tasks. *Annals of Dyslexia* 46:259–83.

Ganschow, L., Lloyd-Jones, J., and Miles, T. R. 1994. Dyslexia and Musical Notation. *Annals of Dyslexia* 44:185–202.

Gough, P. 1996. How children learn to read and why they fail. *Annals of Dyslexia* 46:3–20.

Haywood, H. C., and Tzuriel, D. (eds.) 1992. *Interactive Assessment*. New York: Springer Verlag.

Hubicki, M. 1994. Musical problems? Reflections and suggestions. In G. Hales, ed., *Dyslexia Matters*. London: Whurr Publishers.

Lidz, C. S. 1991. *Practitioner's Guide to Dynamic Assessment*. New York: The Guilford Press.

Manis, F. R., Savage, P. L., Morrison, F. J., Horn, C. C., Howell, M. J., Szeszulski, P. A., and Holt, L. J. 1987. Paired associate learning in reading-disabled children: Evidence for a rule-learning deficiency. *Journal of Experimental Child Psychology* 43:25–43.

Morrison, F. J. 1993. Phonological processes in reading acquisition: Toward a unified conceptualization. *Developmental Review* 13:279–85.

Nicolson, R. I., and Fawcett, A. J. 1990. Automaticity: A new framework for dyslexia research? *Cognition* 35:159–82.

Nicolson, R. I., and Fawcett, A. J. 1994a. Comparisons of deficits in cognitive and motor skills among children with dyslexia. *Annals of Dyslexia* 44:147–64.

Nicolson, R. I., and Fawcett, A. J. 1994b. Reaction times and dyslexia. *Quarterly Journal of Experimental Psychology* 47A:29–48.

Nicolson, R. I., and Fawcett, A. J. 1995. Dyslexia is more than a phonological disability. *Dyslexia: An International Journal of Research and Practice* 1:19–37.

Oglethorpe, S. 1996. *Instrumental Music for Dyslexics: A Teaching Handbook*. London: Whurr Publishers.

Ruijssenaars, A. J. J. M. and Hamers, J. H. M. 1989. Assessment of Learning Ability. Learning Ability Tests and Analysis of Learning Processes. In H. Mandl, H. Bennet, E. De Corte, and A. F. Friedrich, eds., *Learning and Instruction*, Vol II. Oxford: Pergamon Press.

Scarborough, H. S. 1990. Very early language deficits in dyslexic children. *Child Development* 61:1728–43.

Stanovich, K. E. 1988. The right and wrong places to look for the cognitive locus of reading disability. *Annals of Dyslexia* 38:154–77.

Van den Broeck, W. 1997. Phonological Processes in Reading Development (Ph.D. diss.) University of Leiden.

Van Orden, G. C. and Goldinger, S. D. 1994. Interdependence of form and function in cognitive systems explains perception of printed words. *Journal of Experimental Psychology: Human Perception and Performance* 20:1269–91.

Visser, J., Laarhoven, A., and van Beek, A. 1996. *AVI-toetspakket. Handleiding*. 's-Hertogenbosch: KPC.

Yap, R., and Van der Leij. 1994. Automaticity deficits in word reading. In R. I. Nicolson and A. J. Fawcett, eds., *Dyslexia in Children: Multidisciplinary Perspectives*. New York: Harvester Wheatsheaf.

# Motion Detection, Letter Position Encoding, and Single Word Reading

*P. L. Cornelissen*

Psychology Department, Newcastle University, United Kingdom

*P. C. Hansen*

Physiology Department, Oxford, United Kingdom

*Recent research has shown that many people with dyslexia find it unusually difficult to detect flickering or moving visual stimuli, consistent with impaired processing in the magnocellular visual stream. Nonetheless, it remains controversial to suggest that reduced visual sensitivity of this kind might affect reading. We first show that the accuracy of letter position encoding may depend on input from the magnocellular pathway. We then suggest that when children read, impaired magnocellular function may degrade information about where letters are positioned with respect to each other, leading to reading errors which contain sounds not represented in the printed word. We call these orthographically inconsistent nonsense errors letter errors. In an unselected sample of primary school children, we show that the probability of children making "letter" errors in a single word reading task was best explained by independent contributions from motion detection (magnocellular function) and phonological awareness (assessed by a spoonerism task). This result held even when controlling for chronological age, reading ability, and IQ. Together, these findings suggest that impaired magnocellular visual function, as well as phonological deficits, may affect reading.*

Annals of Dyslexia, Vol. 48, 1998
Copyright© 1998 by The International Dyslexia Association
ISSN 0736-9387

## INTRODUCTION

Despite adequate educational opportunity and intellectual ability, somewhere between 3 and 15 percent of children fail to acquire competent reading skills (Rutter and Yule 1975). Such children are commonly described as having developmental dyslexia. Given that reading requires a rapid association of visual with linguistic information, it is natural to ask whether problems with either visual or language processing could cause these individuals' reading difficulties.

As far as language is concerned, two decades of research have firmly established that the poor reading of people with dyslexia is often correlated with phonological problems. Typically, their phonological difficulties are revealed by poor performance in a variety of phonological awareness tasks such as rhyme detection ("mat" is the odd man out in the sequence "mat", "had", "sad", "bad"), phoneme counting ("cat" has 3 phonemes: /k/, /æ/, and /t/), and phoneme deletion (saying "flin" without the /f/). This is thought to be due to "fuzzy" or underspecified phonological representations which lead to difficulties with mapping letters onto sounds (Bradley and Bryant 1983; Brady and Shankweiler 1991), and cause people with dyslexia to be extremely slow and inaccurate readers. Reading nonsense words aloud, where successful decoding depends on the use of letter-to-sound correspondence rules, is an extremely good demonstration of the weaknesses experienced by people with dyslexia (Snowling 1980).

Recent research has shown that many dyslexic individuals also may have specific and subtle visual problems. They find it unusually difficult to detect flickering or moving visual stimuli. This finding has been replicated in a variety of ways including psychophysical and electrophysiological techniques, as well as functional brain imaging (Martin and Lovegrove 1987; Brannan and Williams 1988; Mason, Cornelissen, Fowler, and Stein 1993; Waltherm, Iler 1995; Cornelissen, Richardson, Mason, and Stein 1995; Lehmkuhle, Garzia, Turner, Hash, and Baro 1993; Livingstone, Rosen, Drislane, and Galaburda 1991; Eden, VanMeter, Rumsey, Maisog, Woods, and Zeffiro 1996). To illustrate this phenomenon, figure 1 shows a diagrammatic representation of the kind of visual stimulus used to measure motion sensitivity. It is called a random dot kinematogram (RDK).

In this example, movement of the dots in the left-hand panel is random, similar to the snow storm on a "detuned" television screen. In the right-hand panel, half of the dots move randomly

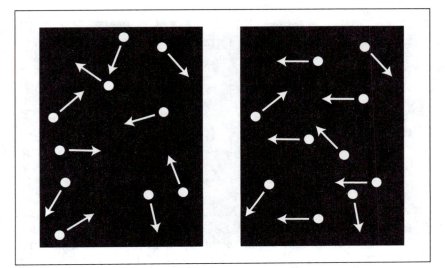

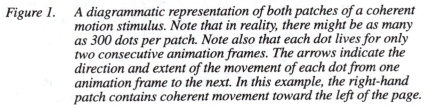

*Figure 1.*    *A diagrammatic representation of both patches of a coherent motion stimulus. Note that in reality, there might be as many as 300 dots per patch. Note also that each dot lives for only two consecutive animation frames. The arrows indicate the direction and extent of the movement of each dot from one animation frame to the next. In this example, the right-hand patch contains coherent movement toward the left of the page.*

and half move in one direction. The presence of these so-called "coherent" dots induces the perception of global movement to the left. An important feature of RDKs is that each dot only stays on the screen for a very short time. Consequently, the viewer cannot detect which patch contains global motion simply by concentrating on just one or two dots on the screen. Instead, the visual system must integrate the local motion vectors of a much larger number of dots over two or more animation frames before the perception of global motion emerges (Smith and Snowden 1994).

In a previous study (Cornelissen et al. 1995), we used RDKs to measure motion sensitivity, both in people with dyslexia and in a nondyslexic comparison group of the same age. In that study, percentage coherence was systematically varied over a large number of trials. The goal was to find the minimum coherence necessary for individuals to be able to detect the presence of global motion (a higher coherence "threshold" indicates worse motion detection). Figure 2 shows the distributions of coherent motion thresholds in the samples of

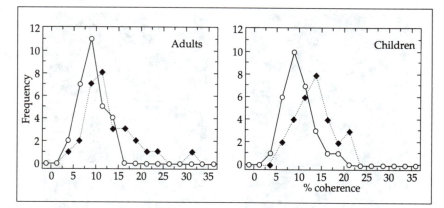

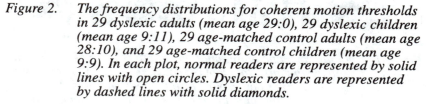

Figure 2.    *The frequency distributions for coherent motion thresholds in 29 dyslexic adults (mean age 29:0), 29 dyslexic children (mean age 9:11), 29 age-matched control adults (mean age 28:10), and 29 age-matched control children (mean age 9:9). In each plot, normal readers are represented by solid lines with open circles. Dyslexic readers are represented by dashed lines with solid diamonds.*

children and adults who have dyslexia together with the non-dyslexic comparison groups. In both samples, the dyslexic individuals found it significantly harder to detect motion than the nondyslexic individuals.

## A MAGNOCELLULAR VISUAL DEFICIT IN DEVELOPMENTAL DYSLEXIA?

One way to interpret results like these is to compare them with behavioral studies of macaque monkeys with specific lesions to the magno- or parvocellular visual pathways. The macaque brain has similar neuroanatomical structures and is thought to be sufficiently closely related to the human brain to justify applying anatomical and electrophysiological data from that species to human vision.

In both macaques and humans, the visual information contained in the output of the retina is derived from two kinds of ganglion cell: M cells and P cells. En route to the cortex, the axons of M and P cells target the magnocellular and parvocellular layers of the lateral geniculate nucleus (LGN) of the thalamus. At this subcortical stage of processing, information derived from M and P cells is strictly segregated. Livingstone and colleagues made histological comparisons of the LGN from five dyslexic and five normal brains (Livingstone et al. 1991). The study revealed that the ventral, magnocellular layers of the LGN (mLGN) from the dyslexic brains contained fewer, smaller cells than did the comparable layers in the normal brains. By contrast, no group differences were found in the cell sizes of the parvocellular layers of the LGN (pLGN). These findings suggested the existence of an anatomical abnormality of mLGN in people who have dyslexia. Further support is provided by the fact that lesions to mLGN (but not pLGN) cause motion-blindness in macaques (Schiller, Logothetis, and Charles 1990). When combined, these results suggest that the reduced motion sensitivity of people with dyslexia could be explained by a magnocellular system deficit which originates subcortically.

Whereas the anatomical segregation of magno- and parvo-streams from the LGN is maintained only as far as the input layers of the primary visual cortex (V1), the responses of cells beyond this point reflect the fact that information derived from M and P cells becomes increasingly mixed (see figure 3A). This

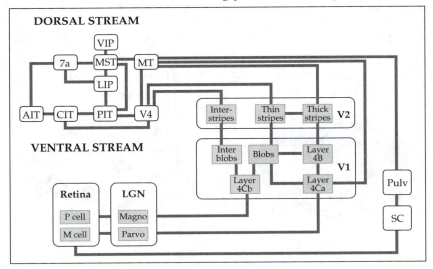

*Figure 3A. A schematic diagram of the two streams of visual processing in primate cerebral cortex. LGN: lateral geniculate nucleus; SC: superior colliculus; Pulv: pulvinar; PIT: posterior inferotemporal cortex; CIT: central inferotemporal cortex; AIT: anterior inferotemporal cortex; MT: middle temporal area; MST: middle superior temporal area; LIP: lateral intraparietal sulcus; and VIP: ventral intraparietal sulcus. (Adapted from Goodale and Milner 1995.)*

has been shown convincingly by inactivation of either pLGN or mLGN combined with simultaneous recordings in V1, middle temporal area (MT), and visual area 4 (V4). Magnocellular, rather than parvocellular blockade, was more detrimental to MT neuronal responses, reflecting a predominant input from M cells to the dorsal stream of visual processing. Blockade of both mLGN and pLGN, however, affected the responses of cells in V1 and V4 about equally, indicating mixed M and P cell input to the ventral stream of visual processing (Maunsell, Nealy, and DePriest 1990; see also Milner and Goodale 1995 for review). Figure 3B shows the approximate locations of V1, V4, and MT(V5) in the human brain, in addition to those of the dorsal (DS) and ventral (VS) visual streams.

Given the interaction between M and P information at the level of the cortex, how should we best interpret the reduced motion sensitivity shown by people with dyslexia? Lesions of human MT (sometimes referred to as V5) cause akinetopsia, an inability to see movement (Zihl, von Cramon, and Mai 1983). Recordings in macaque monkeys have shown that neuronal responses in MT can account for behavioral decisions during coherent motion detection tasks (Britten, Shalden, Newsome, and Movshon 1992; Shadlen, Britten, Newsome, and Movshon

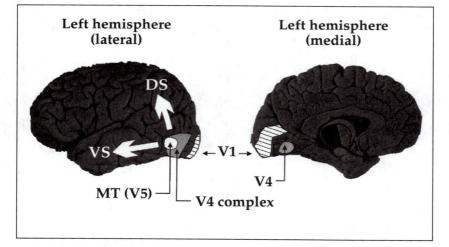

*Figure 3B.* The approximate locations of the human equivalents to V1, MT, V4, and V4 complex. The arrows marked DS and VS represent the dorsal stream (predominant magnocellular input) and ventral stream (mixed magno- and parvocellular input ) of visual processing, respectively. (Adapted from Kaas 1995.)

1996). Since the predominant input to area MT is from the magnocellular system, we argue that reduced motion sensitivity in dyslexic people is consistent with impaired magnocellular function. Nevertheless, it remains to be seen whether the source of the problem is subcortical (cf. Livingstone et al. 1991), cortical, or possibly both. In the face of such uncertainty, we use the term "magnocellular impairment" to refer to degraded information processing in regions of the brain known to receive information which is derived anatomically from M ganglion cells.

How should the nonspecialist reader interpret these admittedly complex data? We think three points should be emphasized. First, we use motion detection as an indirect measure of magnocellular dependent processes (as a "magno-meter"). Second, in the same way that the phrase phonological deficit is used as an umbrella to describe the phonological difficulties of dyslexic people, the term magnocellular deficit tends to be used by researchers as a convenient shorthand for reduced visual sensitivity to flicker and motion. Third, the reader should bear in mind that the hypothesis that impaired motion and flicker sensitivity in people with dyslexia is caused by magnocellular dysfunction is still under investigation. Despite these caveats, the reader's attention should not be diverted from the crucial issue. The very existence of an association between developmental dyslexia and reduced motion sensitivity raises a clinically important question: does abnormal visual processing, independent of phonological problems, affect some children's reading? It should be noted, however, that this question does *not* imply a conflict between visual and phonological processing problems because both could exist independently.

### THE PRESENT STUDY

Normally, information from the magnocellular system provides major input to those visual cortical areas responsible for analyzing object movement and location (Milner and Goodale 1995). It may be no coincidence that many poor readers complain that letters seem to "drift on the page" or "move over each other," as though their visual world becomes unstable when they read (Eden, Stein, Wood, and Wood 1994). Consequently, we propose that when some children read, impaired magnocellular function could lead to uncertainty about where letters and letter features are positioned with respect to each other, subsequently leading to predictable reading errors. This hypothesis, which we have tested in the two experiments reported here, is consistent both with recent models of word recognition (Grainger and Dijkstra 1995) and with the suggestion that magnocellular input is likely to be important for encoding spatial position (Mishkin, Ungerlieder, and Macko 1983; Milner and Goodale 1995).

## METHODOLOGICAL ISSUES

Figure 2 shows two trends commonly found in studies of visual processing and developmental dyslexia. First, the participants' performance on the motion detection task was quite variable within the comparison groups. Second, even though the differences between mean thresholds for the dyslexic and nondyslexic participants were statistically significant, the distributions overlap considerably and there seems to be a continuum of visual performance between persons with and without dyslexia. In light of such variability, how should one test whether reduced sensitivity of this kind might affect reading? One way is to avoid comparing groups of dyslexic and nondyslexic individuals altogether. Instead, we have investigated the relationship between motion detection and letter position encoding in the population at large, including some people conventionally regarded as having dyslexia. Similarly, we have looked at the correlation between motion detection and reading behavior in a sample of school children who were not preselected in any way. An advantage of this strategy is that it circumvents the difficult task of defining who is dyslexic, an issue that is sometimes difficult for researchers (Stanovich, Siegel, and Gottardo 1997), let alone clinicians.

# EXPERIMENT 1: DOES LETTER POSITION ENCODING REQUIRE INPUT FROM THE MAGNOCELLULAR SYSTEM?

## OBJECTIVE

In Experiment 1, we sought direct evidence linking motion detection with letter position encoding. We propose that people who are poor at motion detection should encode letter position less accurately than people who are good at motion detection. Therefore, poor motion detectors should be more likely to inadvertently unscramble briefly presented anagrams and respond to them as if they were words.

## PARTICIPANTS

A total of 48 undergraduate students from Newcastle University took part in this study. Each student carried out a coherent-motion detection task, two subtests (Similarities and Block Design), from the *Wechsler Adult Intelligence Scales–Revised* battery (Wechsler 1981), and two timed reading tests. The characteristics of the participants are described in table I. All of them had normal or corrected-to-normal visual acuity.

## PSYCHOLOGICAL TEST BATTERY

All participants were given the WAIS-R subtests, similarities and block design, to assess verbal and nonverbal reasoning, respectively. Each participant was asked to read aloud all the items from the Schonell reading accuracy test (Schonell 1950), as well as a list of 30 nonwords (Castles and Coltheart 1993). In each case, we recorded the number of errors that participants made and the time it took them to complete the list.

## COHERENT MOTION DETECTION

Participants sat 60 cm from a 17" computer monitor on which the random dot kinematograms were displayed. We used a two-alternative force-choice method (2AFC) to identify students' coherence thresholds. On each trial, which lasted 2300 msec, coherent motion appeared randomly in one of the two patches. The experimenter initiated each trial, and students

TABLE I. EXPERIMENT 1—PARTICIPANT CHARACTERISTICS.

$n = 48$

| Variable | M (SD) range |
|---|---|
| Coherence at threshold (percentage) | 21.3 (10.4) 8.5–45.8 |
| Chronological age (years: months) | 20:4 (1:4) 18:0–24:0 |
| WAIS-R Block Design (scaled score, max = 19) | 12.1 (2.3) 6–17 |
| WAIS-R Similarities (scaled score, max = 19) | 12.7 (1.5) 9–16 |
| Schonell single word reading list errors (max = 110) | 5.3 (3.7) 0–17 |
| Time taken to read Schonell (seconds) | 80.5 (19.7) 47–164 |
| Nonword reading errors (max = 30) | 2.2 (2.8) 0–14 |
| Time to read nonword list (seconds) | 24.6 (7.3) 14–52 |

were asked to indicate which panel contained coherent motion either by pointing or by naming the side (labeled 1 or 2) on which it appeared. Once the experimenter keyed in each response, the next trial started automatically one second later. Participants were encouraged to make sure that they had looked carefully at both panels before they made their decision. Coherence was varied according to a 1-up-1-down staircase procedure. The staircase procedure started well above threshold at 90 percent. Coherence was then adaptively decreased by a factor of 1.122 for every correct response, and increased by a factor of 1.412 for every incorrect response. These two factors are equivalent to changes of 1dB and 3dB respectively (dB = 10 . $\text{Log}_{10}(k)^2$, where: k = percent coherence). Every staircase procedure was run for a total of ten reversals. Threshold was estimated as the geometric mean of the coherence levels at which the last eight reversals occurred. The geometric, rather than the arithmetic, mean was calculated to minimize the skewing effect of outlying data points. We obtained a total of three thresholds for each subject. The first threshold was discarded as a learning period and the remaining two thresholds were averaged together.

In this study, the motion detection task used was improved relative to the one used in Cornelissen et al. (1995). The most significant change was to reduce the lifetime of coherently moving dots to only two animation frames. As described in the introduction, this maneuver ensures that subjects cannot solve the task by concentrating on only a few dots at a time.

## LEXICAL DECISION TASK

We used a lexical decision task in which participants were presented with five-letter words or five-letter anagrams with equal probability of occurrence. Anagrams were generated by swapping the positions of two of the internal letters contained in five-letter words:

a) left anagrams (L): letter positions 2 and 3 were swapped (OCEAN > OECAN).
b) right anagrams (R): letter positions 3 and 4 were swapped (OCEAN > OCAEN).
c) far anagrams (F): letter positions 2 and 4 were swapped (OCEAN > OAECN).

One half of the word and anagram stimuli were based on high frequency words, whereas the other half of the stimuli were based on low frequency words. (Mean Kucera-Francis word frequencies: 192.8, $SD = 315.7$, and 2.8, $SD = 2.0$, respectively).

## PROCEDURE

Using a counterbalanced design, participants were presented with a total of 144 five-letter stimuli for lexical decision (36 high frequency words, 36 anagrams based on a different set of high frequency words, 36 low frequency words, and 36 anagrams based on a different set of low frequency words). Each set of 36 anagrams was further divided into 12 L, 12 R, and 12 F anagrams such that the L, R, and F anagrams were based on different words.

Participants sat 60cm in front of a computer monitor. Upper case black letters and symbols were presented on a white background. Each trial comprised the following sequence of events which appeared in the middle of the monitor screen: fixation cross (300ms), blank screen (300ms), letter string target (43ms), pattern mask (100ms), and response prompt. At the end of each trial, participants were asked to respond as quickly as possible by pressing a "1" if they had seen a word and "0" if they had not. For example, if the stimulus OCAEN was presented, a *correct* response would have been to press "0" and an *incorrect* response to press "1" because "ocaen" is not a real word. However, if the stimulus had been OCEAN, a *correct* response would have been to press "1" and an *incorrect* response to press "0," because "ocean" is a real word. Participants' responses and reaction times were automatically recorded.

## RESULTS

Table II shows participants' mean reaction times in the lexical decision task for words and L, R, and F anagrams. Although there is wide variability, table II suggests that participants reacted more quickly to high frequency anagrams than to low frequency ones.

This impression was confirmed by a two-way repeated measures ANOVA of participants' reaction times which showed significant main effects of both stimulus (word, L, R, and F anagram) and word frequency (high or low), $F(3,141) = 5.7$, $p = 0.001$ and $F(1,47) = 13.7$, $p < 0.0005$, respectively. The two-way interaction of *stimulus x word frequency* was not significant at $p < 0.05$.

We used multiple regression analysis to investigate the relationship between reaction time in the lexical decision task, motion detection, and word frequency. We ran the following model once for each stimulus type (word, and L, R, or F anagram):

$y = b_1 x_1 + b_2 x_2 + e$ where: $y$ = reaction time, $x_1$ = motion detection
$x_2$ = word frequency (high or low)

Only the model for word stimuli was significant at $p < 0.05$ and only the main effect of word frequency in this model was

**TABLE II. EXPERIMENT 1—REACTION TIMES (MS) FOR THE LEXICAL DECISION TASK.**

| n = 48 | |
| --- | --- |
| Stimulus | M (SD) |
| **High frequency** | |
| Words | 512 (198) |
| L anagrams | 568 (221) |
| R anagrams | 592 (314) |
| F anagrams | 630 (249) |
| **Low frequency** | |
| Words | 623 (263) |
| L anagrams | 621 (251) |
| R anagrams | 661 (303) |
| F anagrams | 693 (364) |

significant $F(1,93) = 5.5$, $p < 0.05$. Motion detection was not significantly associated with reaction time for any of the four stimulus types.

Table III shows the mean percentage errors that participants made in the lexical decision task. Overall, participants made fewer errors to words than to anagrams, and made more errors to high frequency anagrams than to low frequency anagrams.

This was confirmed by a two-way repeated measures ANOVA of the arcsine transformed proportions of participants' errors. Both

**TABLE III. EXPERIMENT 1—PERCENTAGE ERRORS FOR THE LEXICAL DECISION TASK.**

| n = 48 | |
| --- | --- |
| Stimulus | M (SE) |
| **High frequency** | |
| Words | 11.4 (1.9) |
| L anagrams | 53.6 (3.1) |
| R anagrams | 62.4 (3.1) |
| F anagrams | 29.8 (2.8) |
| **Low frequency** | |
| Words | 30.3 (2.8) |
| L anagrams | 37.2 (2.5) |
| R anagrams | 36.0 (2.9) |
| F anagrams | 24.3 (2.6) |

main effects of word frequency (high or low) and stimulus (word and L, R, or F anagram) were significant, $F(1,47) = 19.3, p = 0.0001$ and $F(3,141) = 62.7, p = 0.0001$, respectively, as was the two-way interaction *frequency x stimulus*, $F(3,141) = 51.8, p = 0.0001$.

To investigate the relationship between motion detection and the kinds of errors made by participants, we carried out four multiple logistic regression analyses. For each of the four stimulus types (words and L, R, or F anagrams), we tested for an association between motion detection and the proportion of errors on the lexical decision task while controlling for any effects of word frequency, chronological age, WAIS-R Similarities, WAIS-R Block design, Nonword and Schonell reading errors, and time. We permitted differential effects of word frequency (coded 1 for high frequency or 0 for low frequency) by including the interaction term *motion detection x frequency*. This provides a convenient way of estimating separate regression lines and intercepts for high and low frequency stimuli in the same model, and means that we only had to run four models instead of eight. Because we were dealing with proportionate data with a binomial distribution, we applied the logit transform (log odds) to stabilize the variance in our multiple regression analyses (see Altman 1991). Regression coefficients are expressed as log odds ratios which can be converted to odds ratios $(p/1-p)$, also known as risk values. Odds ratios greater than one represent increased risk; values less than one represent reduced risk.

We explored a variety of different methods for rejecting or retaining explanatory variables including fitting of the complete model, backward elimination, forward selection, and stepwise selection. Note that the output from these methods does not depend on the order in which explanatory variables are entered in the model. They merely represent different algorithms for finding a minimum set of explanatory variables, each of which satisfies the significance criterion ($p < 0.05$) for inclusion in the model. All four fitting procedures gave the same outcomes with goodness of fit measures (using the -2 log likelihood statistic) which were significant at $p < 0.0005$. We have reported the output from the stepwise procedure in table IV.

Table IV shows that a significant association exists between motion detection and the proportion of errors made in the lexical decision task for high frequency L and R anagrams and low frequency R anagrams, but not for F anagrams or words. Figure 4 illustrates these regression models. It shows a series of plots for the predicted probability of an error in the lexical decision task (y-axis in each case) as a function of motion detection

**TABLE IV.  EXPERIMENT 1—OUTPUT FROM
LOGISTIC REGRESSION MODELS.**

| Stimulus | Explanatory Variable | Regression Coefficient (logit) | SE | Change in $\chi^2$ at 1 df | p value | Odds Ratio /unit |
|---|---|---|---|---|---|---|
| **L anagrams** | Intercept | −0.51 | 0.086 | 36.1 | p = 0.0001 | |
| | *Motion x Frequency* | 0.029 | 0.0085 | 11.7 | p = 0.0006 | 1.030 |
| | Nonword time | 0.027 | 0.0085 | 10.0 | p = 0.002 | 1.027 |
| | Word frequency | 0.67 | 0.12 | 30.8 | p = 0.0001 | 1.95 |
| **R anagrams** | Intercept | −0.57 | 0.087 | 44.0 | p = 0.0001 | |
| | *Motion detection* | 0.016 | 0.0061 | 6.6 | p = 0.01 | 1.016 |
| | Nonword time | 0.029 | 0.0088 | 11.3 | p = 0.0008 | 1.030 |
| | Word frequency | 1.10 | 0.12 | 80.8 | p = 0.0001 | 3.002 |
| **F anagrams** | Intercept | −1.20 | 0.099 | 146.3 | p = 0.0001 | |
| | Nonword errors | 0.062 | 0.022 | 7.5 | p = 0.006 | 1.064 |
| | Schonell time | 0.0099 | 0.0033 | 9.1 | p = 0.002 | 1.010 |
| | Chronological age | 0.036 | 0.017 | 4.3 | p = 0.04 | 0.037 |
| | Word frequency | 0.28 | 0.13 | 5.2 | p = 0.02 | 1.326 |
| **Words** | Intercept | −0.91 | 0.053 | 285.8 | p = 0.0001 | |
| | Schonell errors | 0.07 | 0.011 | 38.3 | p = 0.0001 | 1.073 |
| | Chronological age | 0.031 | 0.011 | 7.8 | p = 0.005 | 1.031 |
| | Word frequency | −1.23 | 0.092 | 180.0 | p = 0.0001 | 0.291 |

(x-axis in each case) for each stimulus type. In each case, the effects of age, IQ, and reading have been taken into account.

Figure 4 shows that the effect for high frequency L anagrams was equivalent to a 36 percent increase (4.3 out of 12 stimuli) in the errors made in the lexical decision task over the motion coherence range of 8 percent to 45 percent. Students with the highest motion detection thresholds made the most errors. The effect for R anagrams was present for both high and low frequency stimuli, but was generally weaker, evidenced by an 11 percent increase in errors over the same motion detection range.

One possibility to account for the lack of an effect of motion detection on the errors made to F anagrams might be that these five-letter strings contain more unusual bigrams (e.g.,QI, PZ, and XM) than do L and R anagrams. To test this possibility, we extracted all the position-dependent token frequencies of bigrams from the CELEX psycholinguistic database (Centre for Lexical Information, Nijmegen, the Netherlands). We calculated a position sensitive bigram frequency score for each anagram,

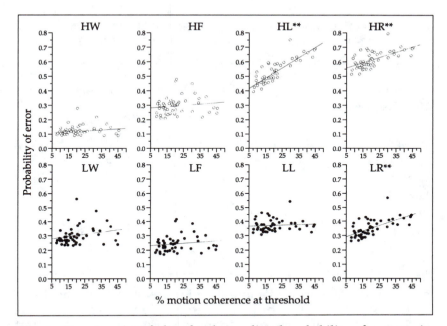

*Figure 4.* A series of plots for the predicted probability of an error in the lexical decision task (y-axis in each case) as a function of motion detection (x-axis in each case) for each stimulus type. HW: high frequency words; HF: high frequency F anagrams; HL: high frequency L anagrams; HR: high frequency R anagrams; LW: low frequency words; LF: low frequency F anagrams; LL: low frequency L anagrams; and LR: low frequency R anagrams. NB** = $p < 0.005$.

then compared these scores across the three kinds of anagrams. For example, the L anagram BRAON comprises four bigrams: BR, RA, AO, and ON, which have token frequency counts (in units of 10,000) of 4.8, 22.1, 1.8, and 22.3, respectively (total = 49.4). Since a one-factor ANOVA (anagram type L, R, or F) of the total bigram scores (L mean = 41.8, R mean = 39.6, F mean = 36.9) was not significant, $F(2,213) = 0.65$, $p = 0.5$, it is unlikely that bigram frequency can explain why there was no association between motion detection and errors made to F anagrams.

Finally, we wanted to exclude the possibility that participants may have traded speed of response for accuracy in the lexical decision task. Table V shows the correlations between reaction speed (1/reaction time) and percentage errors for the four stimulus types (words and L, R, and F anagrams) at high and low word frequency. None of the correlations was signifi-

TABLE V.  EXPERIMENT 1—PEARSON CORRELATIONS
BETWEEN REACTION TIME AND PERCENTAGE ERRORS IN THE
LEXICAL DECISION TASK.

| Stimulus | Correlation Coefficent ($r$) | $p$ value |
|---|---|---|
| **High Frequency** | | |
| Words | −0.37 | $p < 0.005$ |
| L anagrams | −0.08 | $p > 0.5$ |
| R anagrams | −0.19 | $p > 0.1$ |
| F anagrams | −0.12 | $p > 0.1$ |
| **Low Frequency** | | |
| Words | −0.25 | $p > 0.05$ |
| L anagrams | 0.005 | $p > 0.5$ |
| R anagrams | −0.25 | $p > 0.05$ |
| F anagrams | −0.14 | $p > 0.1$ |

cant at $p < 0.05$ except the one for high frequency words. Even
in this situation we could not find evidence for a speed-
accuracy trade off. Faster responses were always associated
with more accurate responses.

## DISCUSSION

The mean threshold coherence for the adults in this study (~21 percent) was considerably higher than that for the normal reading
adults in our previous study, shown in figure 2 (~10 percent)
(Cornelissen et al. 1995). This is due to the fact that the coherently
moving dots in our previous study had longer lifetimes, compared
to only two animation frames in the current stimuli. Thus the motion detection task in the present study was more difficult.

Reaction time is probably the most common outcome measure
to be analyzed in lexical decision experiments and the fact that we
found no association between it and motion detection requires
some explanation. We suggest two factors that may account for
this result. First, when the lexical decision task was being explained to participants, accuracy, rather than speed of response,
was emphasized. Second, and probably more significantly, succes-
sive trials automatically followed each response. Subjectively, this
gave the task a natural rhythm that was easy to fall into; this
would have strongly encouraged participants to focus on accuracy
rather than on speed of reaction.

In Experiment 1, participants were considerably quicker and
more accurate at responding to words than to anagrams. This is

likely to have been due to the word-pseudoword advantage; when viewing tachistoscopic displays, people can correctly report words at shorter exposure times than pseudowords (Carr 1986; Henderson 1982). The main finding from Experiment 1 which supports our hypothesis is that participants who were poor at motion detection were also more likely to make errors on high frequency L and R anagrams as well as low frequency R anagrams. Research suggests that during the early visual analysis of text, the positions of the first and last letters of a word are rigidly encoded (Hammon and Green 1982; Mason 1982). However, internal letter position encoding is more flexible, and consequently more fallible (Humphreys, Evett, and Quinlan 1990; Mozer 1983). Therefore, it is plausible that errors in the anagram task could reflect some uncertainty about the positions of adjacent letters. Specifically, a participant might encode the stimulus OCAEN as O + C + E + A + N, and as a result, respond to it as if it was a word instead of an anagram. The fact that there was no effect of motion detection on error rates for F anagrams may also be explained in terms of letter position encoding. In order to unscramble an F anagram, letter positions 2 and 4 would have to be swapped around. When, in a lexical decision task, such a briefly presented (40ms) letter string is encoded by the visual system, we suggest that positional uncertainty would be much less likely to cause the large jumps of letter position necessary to unscramble F anagrams, as compared to merely shifting adjacent letter positions as required by L and R anagrams.

The overall error rates for the low frequency anagrams were smaller than those for the high frequency anagrams. It is plausible that the word frequency effect (Monsell 1991) could account for this result. All participants made more errors to low frequency words than to high frequency words; that is, they were more likely to respond to low frequency words as if they were nonwords. Therefore, presenting participants with anagrams based on the kind of words that were already being treated as nonwords was unlikely to have elicited anything other than a nonword response (an appropriate response to anagram stimuli), and would account for the lower error rates for the low frequency anagrams.

In this study of young adults, we have found an association between coherent motion detection and performance in a task in which optimal responses explicitly depend on accurate information about letter position. Our analyses suggest that neither reading ability, IQ, nor a speed-accuracy trade off can adequately explain this association. Nevertheless, there are still at least two alternative explanations for it. The first we propose is a "bottom-up" process: variability in our motion detection task directly reflects abnormal magnocellular system function. Any process that requires input derived from the magnocellular system—such as position encoding and motion detection—would, therefore, be impaired. Alternatively, a "top-down" mechanism might affect performance in the motion detection tasks and the letter position tasks. A likely candidate for such a mechanism is attentional processing in which the magnocellular pathway has also been implicated (Steinman, Steinman, and Lehmkuhle 1997). Further research is required, either to rule out an attentional component, or to elucidate the nature of any interaction between attention, motion detection, and letter position coding.

In conclusion, the findings of Experiment 1 make an explicit, albeit tentative, link between motion detection and letter position encoding. (For further analysis and supportive experimental data see Cornelissen, Hansen, Gilchrist, Cormack, Essex, and Frankish 1998). In Experiment 2, we go on to explore whether motion detection predicts the pattern of children's reading errors.

## EXPERIMENT 2: DOES REDUCED MAGNOCELLULAR FUNCTION AFFECT READING?

Fluent reading involves a rapid, alternating pattern of fixation and saccadic (jumping) eye movements. When we read, it is during these brief periods of fixation that our visual systems sample the text image projected onto our retinae. Unlike images from the natural world, printed words represent a very unusual visual stimulus. Specifically, all the information available in a page of text is compressed into three discrete spatial scales: coarse, intermediate, and fine. These scales approximate the average size of a word, the average size of a letter, and the average thickness of the lines that make up each letter. There is no other useful information at intermediate spatial scales. This contrasts with natural images which contain a smooth continuum of information across all spatial scales. Figure 5 illustrates this situation for text, with the three discrete spatial scales represented by the three degrees of blur. (Although the three spatial scales are placed under each other in figure 5, in reality they would effectively be superimposed.)

We have printed the two words in figure 5 in a stylized font using simple, discrete features: long and short horizontal or ver-

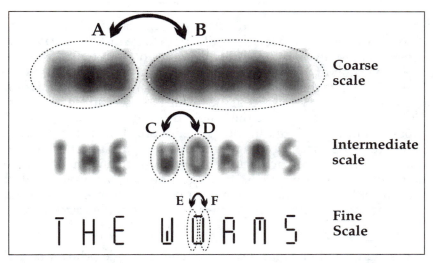

*Figure 5.* Information available in the phrase THE WORMS at three discrete spatial scales. The double-headed arrows represent examples of feature mislocations at each scale which could be caused by positional uncertainty. See text for details.

tical bars. This is meant to emphasize the fact that the identity of a particular letter is determined by the combination of *what* features are *where*. The visual system must reliably extract information about both *shape* and *position* of features.

Our brains are thought to process visual information by using a coarse-to-fine strategy. First, large objects (A and B in figure 5) and their relative positions are detected at the coarsest spatial scales. Coarse scale information not only confirms that object A is to the left of object B but also constrains the location of objects at the next, finer scale. For example, the two objects C and D in figure 5 are associated with object B at the coarsest scale, but not with object A. Position information at the intermediate scale also shows that object C is to the left of object D. At the finest scale, a similar argument applies. The two vertical features (marked E and F in figure 5) belong to the "O" in "Worms" and are associated with object C at the intermediate scale. In addition, position information at this scale determines where horizontal and vertical features are located with respect to one another.

We suggest that poor magnocellular function—revealed by high motion detection thresholds—is associated with poor position coding. In terms of figure 5, we argue that this positional uncertainty acts both within and between the three spatial scales.

Consequently, positional uncertainty could cause letter clusters, individual letters, or even parts of letters to be lost, duplicated, or even incorrectly bound together, leading to a scrambled or nonsense version of what is actually printed on the page. This is especially likely when two or more fixations are required per word. When children try to read aloud what they see under these circumstances, we predict that their utterances should contain sounds not represented in the printed word. It is as if they literally translate visual garbage into spoken garbage. For convenience, we refer to such orthographically inconsistent nonsense responses as letter errors. In Experiment 2, we investigated whether the probability of children making letter errors during reading was predictable from their motion detection thresholds.

## PARTICIPANTS

Fifty-eight children were chosen from a Newcastle primary school to take part in this study. They represented all of the 33 boys and 25 girls in the two most senior classes of the school (mean age 10:5). All children had normal or corrected-to-normal visual acuity. The characteristics of the sample are described in table VI.

TABLE VI. EXPERIMENT 2—PARTICIPANT CHARACTERISTICS.

| Variable (units) | M range | (SD) |
|---|---|---|
| Chronological Age (years: months) | 10:5 9:4–11:5 | (0:6) |
| Reading Age (years: months) | 9:11 6:5–14:5 | (2:1) |
| Nonverbal IQ (number correct / 48) | 27.9 11–42 | (7.6) |
| Verbal IQ (quotient: 70–130) | 96.8 83–118 | (8.9) |
| Rhyme Detection (PhAB) (number correct / 21) | 17.1 8–21 | (3.2) |
| Spoonerism (PhAB) (number correct / 40) | 23.3 2–39 | (9.7) |
| Motion Detection (percent coherence at threshold) | 17.2 7.1–42.8 | (8.4) |
| Letter Errors in Experimental Word lists (max = 45) | 6.2 0–16 | (4.3) |
| Total Errors in Experimental Word lists (max = 45) | 19.2 8–34.5 | (6.5) |

*n* = 58

**PSYCHOLOGICAL TEST BATTERY.**

*Nonverbal IQ.* AH1 X and Y Group Tests of Perceptual Reasoning (Heim, Watts, and Simmonds 1977).

*Verbal IQ.* Non-Reading Intelligence Tests (NRIT), level 3, (Young 1996).

*Reading Age.* Children's reading ages were assessed using the British Ability Scales (BAS) single word reading accuracy test.

*Phonological Awareness.* We administered two subtests of the Phonological Awareness Battery (1995) including rhyme detection and a set of three spoonerism tasks. In part 1 of the spoonerism test the child is asked to replace the first sound of a word with a new sound ("cot" with a /g/ results in "got"). Part 2 also involves semispoonerisms, but here the child replaces the first sound of the first word with the first sound of the second word ("die" with "pack" results in "pie"). Part 3 is a full spoonerism measure in which the child is asked to exchange initial sounds in two words ("sad cat" becomes "cad sat").

**EXPERIMENTAL WORD LISTS AND ADMINISTRATION**

At the beginning of each assessment, children were given the BAS single word reading test. Next, they were asked to read 45 regularly spelled words selected on the basis of their BAS reading age. The task difficulty was adjusted individually so that all children made 30 to 50 percent errors. (Details of the experimental word lists can be obtained from Cornelissen, Bradley, Fowler, and Stein 1991; Cornelissen 1992). All children's responses were tape recorded for later analysis. The scorer listened for the *first complete utterance* in response to a target word; partial responses were ignored. Errors were subsequently classified as real words, orthographically consistent nonsense errors, or orthographically inconsistent nonsense errors (equivalent to the letter errors defined above). Examples of children's errors are shown in table VII. Finally, the proportion of letter errors that each child made was calculated, where $p = $ total number of letter errors/total number of errors.

**COHERENT MOTION THRESHOLDS**

We used the same method described earlier to obtain four motion detection thresholds from each participant. The first was discarded as a learning period; the remaining three thresholds were averaged together for further analysis.

### TABLE VII. EXPERIMENT 2—EXAMPLES OF CHILDREN'S READING ERRORS.

| Error Category | Target Word | Error |
|---|---|---|
| **Real Word** | fool | floor |
| | banker | blanket |
| | feeling | flooding |
| | contents | constant |
| | seduction | suggestion |
| **Orthographically Consistent Nonsense Error** | leap | lep |
| | perish | purrish |
| | fever | fevver |
| | wither | whyther |
| | prosper | pro-spur |
| **Orthographically Inonsistent Nonsense Letter Error** | victim | vikim |
| | garden | grandeen |
| | suspect | subpact |
| | temper | templay |

## STATISTICAL MODELING OF THE DATA

We used multiple logistic regression to examine the relationship between the proportion of letter errors that children made and their motion detection thresholds, while controlling for any effect due to IQ, chronological age, reading ability, and phonological awareness.

We carried out multiple regression analyses in two phases. In the first phase, we included all explanatory variables in the linear model below to elucidate only those factors which had a significant effect on the proportion of letter errors that children made. The phase one model was as follows:

$$\text{Model: } \log_e(p/[1-p]) = b_1 x_1 + b_2 x_2 + b_3 x_3 + b_4 x_4 + b_5 x_5 + b_6 x_6 + b_7 x_7$$

where: $p$ = (letter errors)/(total error)     $x_5$ = rhyme detection
$x_1$ = chronological age     $x_6$ = spoonerism task
$x_2$ = reading age     $x_7$ = motion detection
$x_3$ = non-verbal IQ
$x_4$ = verbal IQ

In the second phase, we explored a variety of methods to optimize a model which was built from the significant explanatory variables identified in phase one.

## RESULTS

*Univariate Statistics.* Table VIII shows the matrix of Pearson correlations between the psychological measures. Motion detection is also included. As would be expected, we found significant positive correlations among reading ability, both IQ measures, and both phonological awareness tasks. Motion detection did not correlate with any measure except for verbal IQ. We suggest that brighter children obtained lower coherent motion thresholds, either because they learned the task more quickly, or because they were better able to discover optimal viewing strategies during the task.

*First phase of logistic regression modeling.* Table IX shows the output of the first regression model, predicting letter errors as described above. It is clear that the only factors accounting for significant changes in $\chi^2$ were reading ability, phonological awareness measured by the spoonerism task, and motion detection. The fact that there was no effect of rhyme detection when both phonological tasks were included in the same model is probably because of the high correlation between rhyme detection and the spoonerism task (see table VIII). Henceforth, chronological age, rhyme detection, and both IQ measures are excluded from the analyses.

*Second phase of logistic regression modeling.* Figures 6A, 6B, and 6C show plots of the proportion of letter errors that the children made as a function of motion detection, reading age, and the spoonerism task, respectively.

---

**TABLE VIII. EXPERIMENT 2—PEARSON CORRELATIONS BETWEEN PSYCHOLOGICAL MEASURES, INCLUDING MOTION DETECTION.**
$*p < 0.05$, $**p < 0.005$, $***p < 0.0005$

|  | 1 | 2 | 3 | 4 | 5 | 6 | 7 |
|---|---|---|---|---|---|---|---|
| 1. Age |  |  |  |  |  |  |  |
| 2. Reading Ability | −0.018 |  |  |  |  |  |  |
| 3. Nonverbal IQ | 0.20 | 0.41** |  |  |  |  |  |
| 4. Verbal IQ | −0.23 | 0.36** | 0.51*** |  |  |  |  |
| 5. Rhyme Detection | −0.12 | 0.40** | 0.51*** | 0.44* |  |  |  |
| 6. Spoonerism Task | −0.0098 | 0.57*** | 0.47*** | 0.42** | 0.58*** |  |  |
| 7. Motion Detection | 0.018 | −0.19 | −0.093 | −0.28* | −0.064 | −0.053 |  |

**TABLE IX. EXPERIMENT 2—OUTPUT FROM PHASE ONE LOGISTIC REGRESSION MODEL.**

| Explanatory Variable units | Regression Coefficient (logit) | SE | Change in $\chi^2$ at 1 df | p value | Odds Ratio /unit |
|---|---|---|---|---|---|
| Intercept | 1.69 | 2.35 | 0.52 | $p > 0.1$ | |
| Chronological Age months | −0.0057 | 0.015 | 0.15 | $p > 0.5$ | 1.06 |
| Reading Age months | −0.01 | 0.0039 | 6.38 | $p < 0.05$ | 0.99 |
| Nonverbal IQ number correct / 48 | 0.056 | 0.11 | 0.24 | $p > 0.5$ | 1.058 |
| Verbal IQ quotient | −0.0087 | 0.012 | 0.53 | $p > 0.1$ | 0.991 |
| Rhyme Detection number correct / 21 | 0.0048 | 0.033 | 0.021 | $p > 0.5$ | 1.005 |
| Spoonerism Task number correct / 40 | 0.019 | 0.011 | 4.13 | $p < 0.05$ | 1.02 |
| Motion Detection percent coherence | 0.024 | 0.0093 | 6.89 | $p < 0.005$ | 1.025 |

In support of our hypothesis, figure 6A shows that children who perform well on the motion detection task (low percent coherence at threshold) made appropriately less letter errors than those who performed poorly at this task (high percent coherence at threshold). However, this relationship is nonlinear in that the proportion of letter errors asymptotes above 20 percent coherence. Figure 6B also reveals a nonlinear relationship between the proportion of letter errors and level of phonological awareness. These results can be explained by data from a small number of participants who obtained either very low or very high scores on the spoonerism task, causing the proportion of letter errors to alternately rise and fall as values along the x-axis increase.

In view of figures 6A and 6B, we felt we should take these nonlinearities into account when optimizing the final model. However, there are many functions which could, in principle, be used to achieve this. Since our analysis was post hoc and exploratory, we chose to use the simplest approach possible by including second order terms (see Altman 1991). We included the three explanatory variables which survived the first phase: reading ability, the spoonerism task, and coherent motion detection. To account for the nonlinearities shown in figure 6, we

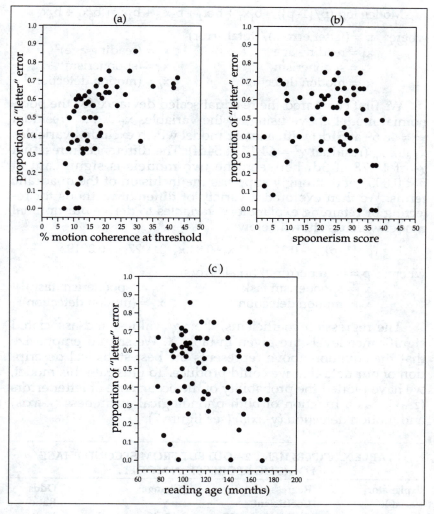

*Figure 6.* Scatter plots of the relationship between the proportion of letter errors and (A) motion detection (percent coherence at threshold), (B) phonological awareness (spoonerism task), and (C) reading age.

then added the squared terms: (reading ability)$^2$, (spoonerism task)$^2$, and (motion detection)$^2$. There appears to be little justification in the physiological or psychological literature for fitting a more complex function. The second phase regression model is shown below:

Model: $\log_e(p/[1-p]) = b_1x_1 + b_2x_2 + b_3x_3 + b_4x_4 + b_5x_5 + b_6x_6$

where:  $p$ = (letter errors)/(total error)

$x_1$ = reading age          $x_4$ = (reading age)$^2$

$x_2$ = spoonerism          $x_5$ = (spoonerism)$^2$

$x_3$ = motion detection     $x_6$ = (motion detection)$^2$

We first compared the residual scaled deviance for the polynomial model above using all the variables $x_1 \ldots x_6$ (residual $\chi^2$ = 46.69 at 51df) with a linear model which excluded variables $x_4 \ldots x_6$ (residual $\chi^2$ = 64.47 at 54df). The difference in residual $\chi^2$ of 17.78 at 3df between the two models is significant at $p < 0.0005$ and strongly supports the inclusion of the quadratic terms. We then explored a variety of different methods for rejecting or retaining explanatory variables to derive our optimal model which is shown below:

$$\log_e(p/[1-p]) = -0.37 + 0.11.x_1 + 0.04.x_2 - 0.0027.x_3 - 0.0019.x_4$$

where:  $p$ = (letter errors)/(total errors)

$x_1$ = spoonerism task       $x_3$ = (spoonerism task)$^2$

$x_2$ = motion detection      $x_4$ = (motion detection)$^2$

The regression coefficients, their $\chi^2$ values, and associated significance levels are given in table X. We should emphasize that the equation above represents the best statistical description of our data that we could produce. To illustrate this model, we have plotted the probability of the occurrence of letter errors (z-axis) as a function of both phonological awareness (x-axis) and motion detection (y-axis) (see figure 7).

### TABLE X. EXPERIMENT 2—OUTPUT FROM SECOND PHASE LOGISTIC REGRESSION MODEL.

| Explanatory Variable *units* | Regression Coefficient (logit) | SE | Change in $\chi^2$ at 1 $df$ | $p$ value | Odds Ratio /unit |
|---|---|---|---|---|---|
| Intercept | −0.37 | 0.37 | 0.99 | $p > 0.1$ | |
| **Spoonerism Task** *number correct/40* | 0.11 | 0.036 | 9.21 | $p < 0.005$ | 1.12 |
| **Motion Detection** *percent coherence* | 0.041 | 0.0090 | 20.26 | $p < 0.0005$ | 1.042 |
| **(Spoonerism Task)$^2$** *number correct/40* | −0.0027 | 0.00095 | 7.97 | $p < 0.005$ | 0.997 |
| **(Motion Detection)$^2$** *percent coherence* | −0.0019 | 0.00088 | 4.50 | $p < 0.05$ | 0.998 |

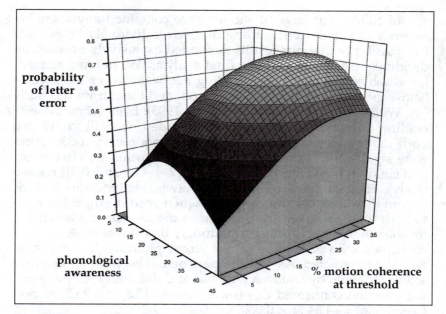

*Figure 7.* A 3-dimensional surface plot in which the probability of the occurrence of letter errors (z-axis) is shown as a function of both phonological awareness (x-axis) and motion detection (y-axis).

Probability values are calculated from logits such that if $l$ = $logit(p)$, then $p = e^l/(1+e^l)$. Figure 7 shows that the likelihood of letter errors increases sharply with poorer performance on the motion task, but that the rate of increase tails off above 20 percent coherence. The effect of phonological awareness (spoonerism task) is clearly nonlinear; the children most likely to make letter errors are those with *intermediate* phonological skills, whereas children with either very poor or very good phonological skills have a much lower incidence of letter error. It should be emphasized, however, that the nonlinear relationship between letter errors and phonological skills is caused in our data by a small number of children who obtained extreme scores on the spoonerism task. Therefore, further samples of children would be required to confirm this finding.

**Exclusion of reading disabled participants.** In the current study, we tested an unselected sample of primary school children on the grounds that our previous study (Cornelissen et al. 1995) suggested a continuum of performance at coherent motion detection. Therefore, if our sample was representative of school children at large, it should have contained anywhere between 5 and 15 percent reading disabled individuals. To exclude the possibility that our results depended exclusively on such individuals, we carried out one final analysis. We defined as reading disabled anyone whose reading age was two or more years below their chronological age and excluded them from the study ( cf. Williams, May, Solman, and Zhou 1995). Even when these 17 reading disabled individuals were excluded, we still found that both motion detection thresholds and spoonerism task scores were significantly correlated with the proportion of letter errors that children made ($r = 0.56$, $p < 0.0005$; $r = -0.36$, $p = 0.01$, respectively). The fact that the correlation between letter errors and the spoonerism task became negative when reading disabled individuals were excluded (as opposed to the nonlinear relationship for the whole sample) suggests strongly that it was these very individuals who had some of the worst phonological skills, as would be predicted. A $t$-test comparison between the spoonerism scores obtained by children who did and did not qualify as reading disabled confirmed this (mean scores: 15.8 and 26.5, respectively; $t(56) = -4.34$, $p < 0.0005$).

## DISCUSSION

We found a positive relationship, albeit a nonlinear one, between children's motion detection thresholds and the likelihood of them making letter errors. This result held when chronological age, IQ, reading age, and phonological awareness were taken into account. This result supports the hypothesis that poor motion sensitivity (reflecting poor magnocellular function) leads to greater uncertainty about letter position and consequently, an increase in the chances of children making letter errors. It should be noted (table VIII) that children's motion detection thresholds were not correlated with their reading abilities, as assessed by an untimed single word reading task (the BAS word reading accuracy test). This suggests that when children are reading single words in the absence of time constraints—as in Experiment 2—magnocellular function appears to predict only the pattern of errors that they make rather than the overall number of errors. However, in a recent functional imaging (fMRI) study, Demb, Boynton, and Heeger (1997) showed that participants' reading rate for prose was correlated with a measure of magnocellular function calculated from the fMR signals. Therefore, time pressure may be needed in single word reading tasks before motion detection is observed to correlate not only with the pattern of reading errors but also with the total number of errors that children make. Future research is necessary to clarify this important issue.

In Experiment 2, we found that phonological factors also played an important part in explaining children's letter errors. Those individuals with intermediate phonological skills (assessed by the spoonerism task) were much more likely to make letter errors than children who had either very poor or very good phonological skills. Since there was very little correlation between children's motion detection thresholds and their performance on the phonological tasks (see table VIII), this effect must have been independent of motion detection and requires a separate explanation.

Gough and Walsh (1991) and Baldwin (1990) have described how children can make nonsense errors for phonological reasons alone. This is easily predicted if we consider children who misapply letter-sound conversion rules. For example, if asked to read the word PERISH, they may accurately identify two graphemic units (PER- and -ISH). But they might incorrectly translate the first unit as PURR, leading to the nonsense error PURRISH. This kind of error is consistent with the printed orthography and was deliberately excluded from our analysis. However, children who apply letter-sound conversion rules imperfectly, and who would arguably be the same children who had intermediate scores in the spoonerism task, may also make letter errors for phonological reasons. For example, when such children see PERISH, they may associate at least one letter/letter cluster with an incorrect sound/sound cluster, thereby mistaking /p/ for /b/ and resulting in BERRISH; or /ı/ for /ɛ/, resulting in PERESH. According to our definition, since either response would constitute a letter error, such a mechanism could certainly account for children making some letter errors for phonological reasons. By contrast, children with the highest scores on the spoonerism task may have such good phonological skills that they can apply letter-sound correspondences faultlessly and not make this kind of mistake. At the opposite extreme, children who score particularly poorly on the spoonerism task may not yet have developed the kind of fine-grained, analytical strategy which, when applied incorrectly, could lead to phonologically based letter errors. In this respect, their reading strategy may be comparable to Frith's logographic stage of reading development (Frith 1985).

At this point in the discussion, we have accounted for children's letter errors in terms of motion detection. We also have suggested that children can make letter errors for phonological reasons. So have we created a dilemma? We propose an explanation which reconciles these two possibilities in a complementary way.

*Multiple-level models of reading.* The visual analysis of print makes available orthographic information at a variety of scales from single letters to syllables (Prinzmetal, Trieman, and Rho 1986; Treiman and Zukowszki 1988). In order that words can be read aloud, however, this multiscale orthographic activity must be associated with appropriate phonological output. Shallice, Warrington, and McCarthy (1983) proposed a solution to this problem in which multiple parallel correspondences are allowed between orthographic and phonological units of varying sizes. Their scheme comprised seven levels: initial consonant clusters, vowels, syllable-final consonant clusters, initial cluster plus vowel, rimes, syllables, and morphemes. Recently, this multiple-levels approach has been successfully implemented in artificial neural network models of reading aloud (Norris 1994; Brown 1987). Since orthographic units are directly connected to phonological units in parallel, it is plausible that distortion at either the orthographic or the phonological ends of these connections could have similar effects. Thus, while the presence of magnocellular impairment need not necessarily be associated with a phonological deficit in the same individual (the two can be independent of each other), the effects of damage in either domain could produce the same errors in letter/letter cluster to sound/sound cluster mapping; both could result in letter errors. Ideas like these are consistent with the present findings, but further experiments are clearly required to test them. In particular, it would be interesting to try to dissociate phonological from visual effects, perhaps by manipulating the spelling-sound consistency of target words, as well as the physical appearance of text. In addition, we need to control explicitly for visual attentional factors.

*Developmental dyslexia and the magnocellular deficit hypothesis.* The correlational design of the experiments described here, and the nature of the participant samples, make it difficult to relate our findings directly to the comparison between children who have dyslexia and those who do not. Nevertheless, it is possible to offer some speculations. A key observation is the continuum of visual performance between the dyslexic and nondyslexic comparison groups shown in figure 2. This finding is reminiscent of Seymour's (1986) serial case studies of reading disabled individuals which suggested that many of the component skills in reading are distributed continuously in the population. If we accept this idea, children's reading problems can be considered within the following information processing framework. Let us assume, for the sake of simplicity, that reading can be described by a multi-channel model in which, for example, visual processing, phonological processing, and short-term memory are all necessary components. The amount of information which can flow through each channel can vary continuously between a minimum and maximum value. Since reading requires several channels, the net flow of information through the model can be described by some function of these channels (linear or otherwise). If an individual's information processing capacity falls below some critical value, then they may experience difficulty with reading. In this view, a critical reduction in information flow could be caused either by a restriction within a single channel, or by a variable combination of restrictions across two or more channels. Clearly, this model avoids the problem of forcing a division between phonological and visual impairments when trying to explain children's reading problems. It allows variable contributions from several factors in different individuals and is consistent with the interrelationships we found between motion detection and phonological awareness in primary-school children.

In conclusion, we have identified a novel association which suggests that motion sensitivity statistically predicts the pattern of children's reading errors when they read regularly spelled words. We argue that this is caused by positional uncertainty. We have also shown that while the magnitude of this effect depends on children's phonological skills, these two factors seem to be independent from one another—at least in this sample of children. The framework we have used to interpret our results is open to further experimental testing, but our results do suggest that both visual and phonological problems may contribute to children's reading problems.

Address correspondence to: P. L.Cornelissen, email: p.l.cornelissen@ncl.ac.uk.

## ACKNOWLEDGMENTS

This work was supported by funds awarded by the Royal Society, the Orton Dyslexia Society and the Research Committee of Newcastle University.

## References

Altman, D. G. 1991. *Practical Statistics for Medical Research*. London: Chapman and Hall.

Baldwin, S. 1990. Reading skills and special needs: Survey of recent research. In N. Jones, ed., *Special Educational Needs Review: Vol. 3, Part IV, Integration and Pupil Skills*. Chapter 14, 202–14.

Bradley, L., and Bryant, P. E. 1983. Categorising sounds and learning to read - a causal connection. *Nature* 301, 419–21.

Brady, S. A., and Shankweiler, D. P., eds. 1991. *Phonological Processes in Literacy*. Hillsdale, NJ: Lawrence Erlbaum Associates.

Brannan, J., and Williams, M. C. 1988. The effects of age and reading ability on flicker threshold. *Clinical Vision Science* 32, 137–42.

Britten, K. H., Shalden, M. N., Newsome, W. T., and Movshon, J. A. 1992. The analysis of visual motion: A comparison of neuronal and psychophysical performance. *Journal of Neuroscience* 12, 4745–65.

Brown, G. D. A. 1987. Resolving inconsistency. A computational model of word naming. *Journal of Memory and Language* 26, 1–23.

Carr, T .H. 1986. Perceiving visual language. In K. R. Boff and L. Kauffman, ed., *Handbook of Perception and Human Performance*. New York: Wiley.

Castles, A., and Coltheart, M. 1993. Varieties of developmental dyslexia. *Cognition* 47, 149–80.

Cornelissen, P. L., Hansen, P. C., Gilchrist, I.D., Cormack, F., and Essex, J. 1998. Magnocellular visual function and letter position encoding. *Vision Research* (in press).

Cornelissen, P. L., Hansen, P. C., Hutton, J. L., Evangelinou, V., and Stein, J. F. 1998. Magnocellular visual function and children's single word reading. *Vision Research* 383, 471–82.

Cornelissen, P .L., Richardson, A. J., Mason, A. J., and Stein J. F. 1995. Contrast sensitivity and coherent motion detection measured at photopic luminance levels in dyslexics and controls. *Vision Research* 3510: 1483–94.

Cornelissen, P. L., Bradley, L., Fowler, M. S., and Stein, J. F. 1991. What children see affects how they read. *Developmental Medicine and Child Neurology* 33:755–62.

Cornelissen, P. L., 1992. What children see affects how they read. D. Phil. Thesis, University of Oxford, U.K.

Demb, J. B., Boynton, G. M., and Heeger, D. J. 1997. Brain activity in visual cortex predicts individual differences in reading performance. *Proceedings of the National Academy of Sciences* 94(24):13363–66.

Eden, G. F., VanMeter, J. W., Rumsey, J. M., Maisog, J. M., Woods, R. P., and Zeffiro, T. A. 1996. Abnormal processing of visual motion in dyslexia revealed by functional brain imaging. *Nature* 382:66-70.

Eden, G. F., Stein, J. F., Wood, H. M., and Wood, F. B. 1994. Differences in eye-movements and reading problems in dyslexic and normal-children. *Vision Research* 3410:1345–58.

Educational Psychology Publishing. 1995. *Phonological Awareness Battery*. UCL: Educational Psychology Publishing.

Frith, U. 1985. Beneath the surface of developmental dyslexia. In K. Patterson, J. Marshall, and J. Coltheart, eds., *Surface Dyslexia*. London: Routledge and Kegan Paul.

Gough, P. B., and Walsh, M. A. 1991. Chinese, Phoenician and the orthographic cipher of English. In S. Brady and D. Shankweiler, eds., *Phonological Processes in Literacy*. Hillsdale, NJ: Lawrence Erlbaum.

Grainger, J., and Dijkstra, T. 1995. Visual word recognition. In A. Dijkstra and K. Smedt, eds., Computational *Psycholinguistics: Symbolic and Subsymbolic Models of Language Processing.* UK, Harvester Wheatsheaf.

Hammon, E. J., and Green , D. W. 1982. Detecting targets in letter and in non-letter arrays. *Canadian Journal of Psychology* 36:67–82.

Heim, A. W., Watts, K. P., and Simmonds, V. 1977. *The AH1 X and Y Group Tests of Perceptual Reasoning.* NFER-NELSON.

Henderson, L. 1982. *Orthography and Word Recognition in Reading.* London: Academic Press.

Humphreys, G. W., Evett, L. J., and Quinlan, P. T. 1990. Orthographic processing in visual word identification. *Cognitive Psychology* 22:517–60.

Kaas, J. H. 1995. Human Visual Cortex: Progress and Puzzles. *Current Biology* 5(10): 1126–28.

Lehmkuhle, S., Garzia, R. P., Turner, L., Hash, T., and Baro, J. A. 1993. A defective visual pathway in children with reading-disability. *New England Journal of Medicine* 32814:989–96.

Livingstone, M. S., Rosen, G. D., Drislane, F. W., and Galaburda, A. 1991. Physiological and anatomical evidence for a magnocellular deficit in developmental dyslexia. *Proceedings of the National Academy of Science* 88:7943–47.

Martin, F., and Lovegrove, W. 1987. Flicker contrast sensitivity in normal and specifically disabled readers. *Perception* 16:215–21.

Mason, A. J., Cornelissen, P. L., Fowler, M. S., and Stein, J. F. 1993. Static and flicker contrast sensitivity in children with unstable visual direction sense. *Clinical Vision Science* 84:345–53.

Mason, M. 1982. Recognition time for letters and non-letters: Effects of serial position, array size and processing order. *Journal of Experimental Psychology: Human Perception and Performance* 8:724–38.

Maunsell, J. H. R., Nealey, T. A., and DePriest, D. D. 1990. Magnocellular and parvocellular contributions to responses in the Middle Temporal Visual Area MT. of the macaque monkey. *Journal of Neuroscience* 1010:3323–34.

Milner, D. A., and Goodale, M. A. 1995. *The visual brain in action.* Oxford: Oxford University Press.

Mishkin, M., Ungerlieder, L. G., and Macko, K. A. 1983. Object vision and spatial vision: Two cortical pathways. *Trends in Neuroscience* October:414–17.

Monsell, S. 1991. The nature and locus of word frequency effects in reading. In D. Besner and G. Humphreys, eds., *Basic processes in Reading: Visual Word Recognition.* Hillsdale NJ: Lawrence Erlbaum Associates.

Mozer, M. C. 1983. Letter migration in word perception. *Journal of Experimental Psychology: Human Perception and Performance* 9:531–46

Norris, D. 1994. A quantitative multiple levels model of reading aloud. *Journal of Experimental Psychology: Human Perception and Performance* 20:1212–32.

Prinzmetal, W., Treiman, R., and Rho, S. H. 1986. How to see a reading unit. *Journal of Memory and Language* 25:461–75.

Rutter, M., and Yule, W. 1975. The concept of specific reading retardation. *Journal of Child Psychology and Psychiatry* 16:181–97.

Schiller, P. H., Logothetis, N. K., and Charles, E. R. 1990. Role of the colour-opponent and broad-band channels in vision. *Visual Neuroscience* 5:321–46.

Schonell, F. J. 1950. *Diagnostic and Attainment Testing.* London: Oliver and Boyd.

Seymour, P. H. K. 1986. *Cognitive Analysis of Dyslexia.* London: Routledge and Kegan Paul.

Shadlen, M. N., Britten, K. H., Newsome, W. T. and Movshon, J. A. 1996. A computational analysis of the relationship between neuronal and behavioral-responses to visual-motion. *Journal Of Neuroscience* 16:1486–1510.

Shallice, T., Warrington, K. E., and McCarthy, R. 1983. Reading without semantics. *Quarterly Journal of Experimental Psychology* 35A:111–38.

Smith, A. T., and Snowden, R. J. 1994. *Visual Detection of Motion*. London: Academic Press.

Snowling, M. J. 1980. The development of grapheme-phoneme correspondences in normal and dyslexic readers. *Journal of Experimental Child Psychology* 29:294–305.

Stanovich, K. E., Siegel, L. S., and Gottardo, A. 1997. Progress in the search for dyslexia sub-types. In C. Hulme and M. Snowling, eds., *Dyslexia: Biology, Cognition and Intervention*. London: Whurr Publishers.

Steinman, B. A., Steinman, S. B., and Lehmkuhle, S. 1997. Transient visual attention is dominated by the magnocellular stream. *Vision Research* 37(1):17-23.

Treiman, R., and Zukowski, A. 1988. Units in reading and spelling. *Journal of Memory and Language* 27:466–77.

Waltherm, ller, P. U. 1995. Is there a deficit of early vision in dyslexia? *Perception* 248:919–36.

Williams, M. C., May, J. G., Solman, R. ,and Zhou, H. 1995. The effects of spatial filtering and contrast reduction on visual search times in good and poor readers. *Vision Research*, 35(2):285-291.

Young, D. 1996. *Non-Reading Intelligence Tests*. Hodder and Stoughton.

Zihl, J., von Cramon, D., and Mai, N. 1983. Selective disturbance of movement vision after bilateral brain damage. *Brain* 106:313–40.

# PART III
## Intervention Programs for Students with Reading Disabilities

Numerous studies over the years have documented gains in reading when students receive systematic, sequential instruction in the alphabetic code that makes explicit links between spoken and written language. The intervention studies in the present volume incorporate some or all of the components of these previously successful studies, but were designed to enhance progress in three areas not directly targeted in code emphasis intervention programs.

Chapter 8, by Westervelt and his colleagues, describes efforts to enhance self-esteem in youngsters receiving intensive reading intervention in a summer camp setting. The goal of that study was to incorporate esteem-building activities to accompany the reading instruction; the hypothesis was that students would make progress in both areas and that each would aid the other (i.e., that reading gains would enhance self-esteem and that self-esteem gains would enhance reading performance). The paper offers a detailed account of an intervention that was successful with many students, yields some interesting results worth investigating in future work (e.g., students with attentional deficits did not make self-esteem gains), and introduces measures of self-esteem useful for further study on this topic.

The intervention study described by Joanna Williams in chapter 9 focuses on comprehension, but borrows from code emphasis approaches the insight that students with LD often require explicit, highly structured instruction. The students in her study clearly did not extract thematic structure on their own, but did learn to identify explicitly taught story themes. The study is important as a model for the kind of instruction that may assist students in interpreting texts, but even more so as a demonstration of the tremendous challenge in providing the kind of scaffolding that is effective for improving the comprehension skills of low-achieving students.

The final intervention study in this volume, by Sparks and his colleagues (chapter 10), applies multisensory instructional techniques to foreign language instruction for high school students with learning disabilities. The gains in native and foreign language skill obtained via multisensory-based instruction are impressive, both in absolute terms, and relative to gains obtained by LD students receiving traditional foreign language instruction. My concern about this study is its dependence on a single instructor who has accomplished impressive gains among her students for year after year. It will be important, therefore, to replicate this teaching strategy among many teachers and make it accessible to schools who otherwise might be inclined to give up trying to teach foreign language to students who could benefit greatly.

# Changes in Self-Concept and Academic Skills During a Multimodal Summer Camp Program

*Van D. Westervelt*

University of Virginia Children's Medical Center

*Daniel C. Johnson*

University of Virginia

*Mark D. Westervelt and Scott Murrill*

Camp Glencoe, Jemicy School, Baltimore, Maryland

*The impact of a six-week multimodal summer camp program on the self-concept and reading/writing skills of a group of dyslexic students (n = 42) was assessed. Campers ranged in age from 9 to 14 years (mean = 11 years, 5 months) and came from public, private, and specialized private schools serving students with learning disability (LD). Twenty-six percent of the sample had a comorbid diagnoses of attention deficit disorder (ADD) and 11 percent had attention deficit hyperactivity disorder (ADHD). Campers improved significantly in phonetic reading and spelling skills, but not in sight word vocabulary or reading speed. Campers also exhibited significant improvements in self-concept, both on a general level and in the specific areas of reading and overall academic competence. The kinds of changes observed on the more general measures of self-concept, however, were not the same for the various groups of campers. Campers from regular private*

Annals of Dyslexia, Vol. 48, 1998
Copyright© 1998 by The International Dyslexia Association
ISSN 0736-9387

*schools and from public schools typically experienced greater gains in general self-concept than did campers from LD private schools. Campers with diagnosed comorbid disorders typically realized little or no gains, whereas campers without ADD or ADHD displayed significant improvement in general self-concept.*

# INTRODUCTION

Many educators endorse using the summer months to enhance children's basic academic skills which are deficient relative to age and/or cognitive ability (Conderman, Snider, and Crawford 1997). One of the early camp programs for dyslexic students was established in 1946 by Helene C. Durbrow in the foothills of Vermont's Green Mountains through the encouragement of her colleagues and mentors, Samuel Orton and Anna Gillingham. After a few summers of the eight-week sessions, it was clear not only that the camp improved deficient reading, spelling, and writing skills, but also that positive social-emotional changes occurred along with the acquisition of academic and physical skills. These were informally observed by staff and were noticeable to parents in the fall. The camp's guiding theme soon became "a strong mind in a strong body."

Many states now offer sleep-away camps for children to address academic, social-emotional, and physical skill development. Some camps are more comprehensive in their mission than others. One comprehensive camp is Camp Glencoe outside of Baltimore which runs a six-week summer session (five days a week boarding) for children with specific reading disabilities (dyslexia). The camp offers many features not experienced by most children during the school year. These include a chance to meet other capable students with specific academic weaknesses, a structured and balanced day where they can receive one-on-one instruction targeted to their needs at a time of day when they are the freshest, recreational activities that range from challenging to purely fun, creative arts, and group living with peers and young adult counselors. Exposure to radio and television is minimized to encourage pleasure reading, contact with nature, and more interpersonal involvement.

Children with specific learning disabilities have been shown to experience a lack of confidence in approaching academic tasks (Harter 1990). The presence of a negative self-concept in regard to a certain academic skill area can be a factor in the future development of that skill. Using math as an example,

Marsh (1990) has reviewed findings (Meece et al. 1982; Relich 1983; Marsh, Smith, and Barnes 1985) that indicate that, relative to boys, fifth- and sixth-grade girls have higher math achievement levels but lower math self-concepts. Interestingly, by high school, girls' math achievement is significantly lower than boys, thereby falling in line with their previously evident lower self-concepts in math. Although a multitude of factors may be at play, such a pattern suggests that a socialization process, as reflected by self-concept, may precede and influence later achievement differences. Such a process could further impair learning disabled children who do not feel they have the potential to improve deficit skills.

In order to determine the multidomain impact of a summer camp program, both academic and self-concept measures need to be employed. In this program, academic measures focused on growth in phonological awareness. The efficacy of intensive programs focusing on phonological awareness skills in students, kindergarten through elementary school, has been documented (Wagner, Torgesen, and Rashotte 1993). Torgesen and Davis (1996) note the substantial evidence linking early development of phonological awareness and subsequent acquisition of reading skills. When phonological awareness is explicitly taught and related to beginning reading activities, significant growth in reading skills occurs. This process is at the core of many phonetics-based instructional curriculums. Camp Glencoe's language program is based on the Orton-Gillingham approach of teaching phonetic concepts, progressing from the simple to the complex, learned and reinforced through all the senses (Gillingham and Stillman 1997). The multisensory emphasis of this program meets the needs of students with poor visual and/or auditory memories. Every student learns the language from single sounds and letters to syllables, words, phrases, and sentences. This approach develops skills in oral language, reading, writing, and spelling. The efficacy of individualized and systematically sequenced phonetics-based interventions for reading deficits in elementary through high school aged students has been substantially documented (Ball and Blachman 1988; Felton 1993; Greene 1993, 1996; Lyon 1995).

The measurement of self-concept in children is derived mainly through two theoretical perspectives (Harter 1990). One model ( Rosenberg 1979) emphasizes a person's general sense of self-esteem or self-worth, and the other (Shavelson, Hubner, and Stanton 1976; Harter 1986) postulates that self-concept is multidimensional and made up of a person's perceived competence in multiple specific domains. Harter (1986) has delineated five specific domains—scholastic competence, athletic competence, physical appearance, peer social acceptance, and behavioral conduct—which children can distinguish and reliably rate themselves on by eight years of age. Based on the Shavelson, Hubner, and Stanton (1976) theory of a multifaceted, hierarchical model of self-concept, Marsh et al. (1984) developed the *Self-Description Questionnaire-I* (SDQ-I) (see Figure 1), which incorporates academic and nonacademic facets of self-concept, and also has a "general self" scale designed to capture Rosenberg's more global sense of self-esteem. Marsh's measure provides a helpful degree of specificity of subdomains that appeared to be relevant to our camp intervention.

The purpose of this study was to document the changes in children's self-concept and select academic skills during a comprehensive six-week camp program for dyslexic students involving multiple modes of intervention: tutorial instruction, interpersonal, and physical skill development. We hypothesized that campers would make gains in reading and spelling skills. In addition, we expected concurrent improvements in specific areas of self-concept pertaining to confidence in reading, general school abilities, physical abilities, and peer relations.

## METHOD

### PARTICIPANTS

The 48 students participating in the camp program had been previously diagnosed with reading and/or written language disabilities and were referred by parents, educators, and psychologists

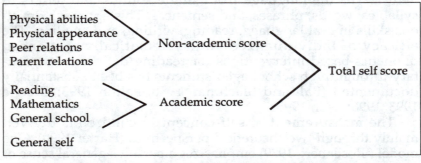

*Figure 1.    Scale components from Herbert W. Marsh's Self-Description Questionnaire I (SDQ–I).*

from the Baltimore-Washington area. Thirty percent were from specialized private schools for learning disabled students, 45 percent attended regular private schools, and 25 percent were from public school settings. The campers were generally from middle- to upper-middle-class families. Nine children received tuition waivers: one full and eight partial. The age of the campers ranged from 9 years, 3 months to 14 years, 3 months, with a mean age of 11 years, 5 months. Other characteristics were gender (64 percent boys, 36 percent girls), race (85 percent white, 15 percent black), and comorbidity (26 percent ADD, 11 percent ADHD). Forty-two campers had received an intellectual evaluation with the *Wechsler Intelligence Scale for Children* - Third Edition (WISC-III) within the past three years, and the remainder had been tested with the WISC-III ($n = 4$) or WISC-R ($n = 2$) within the past six years. For the whole sample, the standard score means and standard deviations were Verbal IQ 112 (13), Performance IQ 108 (17), and Full Scale IQ 111 (15).

Because of family vacations and one broken ankle, six of the 48 students were not present for the standardized academic posttests; complete academic data was available for the remaining 88 percent of the campers. Due to logistical problems in implementing the self-concept testing as a new procedure in the camp program, only 32/48 (67 percent) of the campers received both the pre- and posttests on that measure. The characteristics of this subset were not significantly different from the whole camper group except the percentage of boys went from 65 percent to 54 percent.

**PROCEDURES**

All of the campers with comorbid ADHD or ADD were on their morning dose of stimulant medication during the camp program. The campers received the following academic measures, individually administered, at testing sessions one to three weeks before camp and again immediately at the end of camp: *Woodcock Johnson-Revised* Word Attack subtest (Woodcock 1989); *Diagnostic Potential Spelling Test* (DP) (Arena 1982); and the *Gray Oral Reading Test* - Third Edition (Wiederholt and Bryant 1992). For the spelling test (DP) and the Gray Oral (GORT-3), alternate forms were used for the pre- and posttests.

To measure self-concept, the campers received the 76-item SDQ-I which yields subscales in four nonacademic areas, three academic areas, and a separate General Self scale (shown in figure 1). Sample items from each subscale are presented in

## TABLE I. ITEMS FROM SUBSCALES OF THE SDQ-I*

**Physical Abilities Scale**
3.         I can run fast.
56.       I am a good athelete.

**Physical Appearance Scale**
1.         I am good looking.
54.       I am better looking than most of my friends.

**Peer Relations Scale**
7.         I have lots of friends.
28.       I get along with kids easily.

**Parental Relations Scale**
5.         My parents understand me.
50.       My parents are easy to talk to.

**Reading Scale**
11.       I like READING.
49.       Work in READING is easy for me.

**Mathematics Scale**
13.       Work in MATHEMATICS is easy for me.
50.       I like MATHEMATICS.

**General School Scale**
2.         I am good at all SCHOOL SUBJECTS.
55.       I look forward to all SCHOOL SUBJECTS.

**General Self Scale**
45.       In general, I like being the way I am.
53.       Overall I have a lot to be proud of.

*Copyright H. Marsh

table I. The subscales, in turn, sum into nonacademic, academic, and total self scores (separate from the General Self scale). Test items were read to the campers individually or in small groups, and campers circled one of the five responses in a grid labeled False, Mostly False, Sometimes False/ Sometimes True, Mostly True, and True. The internal consistency reliability estimates for the various scales and total scores are in the .80s or .90s whereas the average correlation among the individual self-concept scales is relatively low, with a mean of $r = .17$ (Marsh 1990). The stability of fourth to sixth graders' self-concepts over a six month interval was high for both individual scales (mean $r = .61$) and total score (mean $r = .65$) (Marsh 1990). Although the instrument is normed on school-aged children from Australia, a sample of American students taking the SDQ revealed only slight differences compared to Australian children (Marsh 1994).

## INTERVENTION

The setting for the camp was a girl's boarding school in the rolling hills of Greenspring Valley outside of Baltimore, Maryland, which was leased for the summer.

*Staff.* Assembling a capable staff is an essential part of producing a successful outcome for the camp session. The camp model tends to attract energetic individuals with idealistic interests in counseling and educational intervention. Some counselors and tutors identify with the camper population from previous experience with learning disabilities in family members or in themselves. Training sessions for both counselors and tutors involved a rigorous schedule covering theoretical viewpoints and practical application of intervention techniques during a precamp week. The sessions were both didactic and experiential, which enabled the camp staff to develop a high degree of cohesion and open communication. The academic staff of sixteen tutors was composed mainly of teachers who had varying degrees of background experience in Orton-Gillingham type approaches, and who worked during the school year with LD students in private or public school settings. Each tutor was assigned to work individually with three to five students. In addition, four tutor interns worked under supervision with two students each. Tutors received a review of Orton-Gillingham instruction (Gillingham and Stillman 1997) and other phonetic approaches (Wilson 1988), and shared complementary techniques with each other.

The counselors were mainly college students with interests in education, psychology, or health care. The counselor training followed a handbook covering communication, conflict management, creative problem-solving, camper incentives, and general camp procedures.

During the precamp week, full staff meetings were held to develop individual profiles on each camper based on application materials and prior contact with the student. Strengths and weaknesses in academic and interpersonal skills, along with activity interests outlined in the profile, heightened the staff's awareness of how to engage campers and be of help from the outset.

*Academic.* Grouped by age, the campers moved through a daily individualized schedule. The morning hours were used for tutorials employing the multisensory and phonetics-based methods of language instruction. The core curriculum was Orton-Gillingham. Depending on the student's skill level, elements of sound/symbol relationships were taught, including how sounds are made in the mouth and throat, and how letters are written. The sequence of phonetic concepts progressed in the following order: single letters, digraphs, diphthongs, syllable types, syllable division patterns, roots, and affixes. The multisensory method included the presentation of information through the tactile/kinesthetic pathway, as well as through the auditory and visual pathways. Techniques such as tracing letters in the sand, skywriting, writing with eyes closed, identifying a letter written on one's back, and feeling the mouth/tongue positions when producing a sound engage the tactile/kinesthetic pathways. When students see a word, then say it and write it simultaneously, all three pathways are activated, increasing the likelihood that the word, with practice, will be committed to memory. Work with written language was guided by Diana King's (1989) curriculum for writing and keyboarding.

Each camper's hour of tutoring was complemented by an hour of supervised study hall and at least one half hour of oral reading. Daily oral reading was important to help the student make progress toward the goal of reading fluently, with understanding, and for enjoyment. The oral reading sessions allowed the tutor and student to know which skills had become internalized and automatic and which skills needed continued attention and reinforcement in isolation. Selection of books was geared to the student's reading skill level, vocabulary, and interests. On a weekly basis, the staff documented camper progress (or regress) on cards, which were submitted at staff meetings. On these cards, tutors noted progression: decoding/encoding skills, organization, pace, and study habits. Tutors acknowledged campers' achievement by placing their names on the roster of the Write Stuff Club, which was published in the weekly newsletter, *The Homing Pigeon*. Individually based criteria regarding progress and effort made it possible for each camper to achieve academic recognition, possibly for the first time ever. The tutor-camper relationship became one of trust and revelation. Campers realized in a short time that they could learn ways of doing "school stuff" that previously had not been available to them. In recognition of the close relationship attained, tutors presented a lavishly wrapped book to each of their campers at the banquet finale.

*Psychosocial.* For many of the children, the scars of struggling unsuccessfully in academic settings were quite apparent. Children would withdraw, avoid, subtly or overtly disrupt tutorials, and exhibit sarcasm, which could progress to frustration or anger when they were confronted with tasks that exposed their academic weaknesses. The counselors and tutors were committed to providing an experience that would interrupt this process of self-esteem deflation, by using dialogue, interactions, and sequenced learning opportunities. The staff saw themselves as "bricklayers" of positive esteem, building a more solid foundation of confidence and skills with which campers could engage their school tasks in the fall.

Three general themes governed staff practices:
1. Take every opportunity to praise a child.
2. Confidence comes through successful performance—create an environment where a child can succeed.
3. Prompt campers to be esteem builders among themselves.

With regard to the first theme, "taking every opportunity to praise a child," counselors worked to transform themselves into observant people who were on the "hunt" for times that they could inject uplifting statements about campers. Counselors were guided by the belief that if they were not sincere, the campers would pick up on that right away and kind words would turn into a joke. Counselors also realized that they needed to gain the campers' respect, as any statement that came from a person the campers valued would go a long way.

The staff also built in opportunities to praise campers. Breakfast was a time of general announcements, and was also used as a time for individual recognition of as many campers as possible. Recognition was in the form of verbal praises accompanied by awards of food. A person would win the "golden banana" if they had an outstanding night. The "orange you cool" was given to someone who had shown a bright spirit that morning. The "buddy bagel" recognized two friends who had treated each other well. As time went on, counselors focussed more on specific attributes they wished to highlight. At lunch, counselors gave the "sunshine" award, to praise someone who had done an act of kindness that brightened someone else's day. In the evenings they would comfort a child who was feeling down by doing the "dead lift." The unhappy child was lifted over the heads of other campers, while validations were voiced, in an attempt to raise the child's spirits. As the summer progressed and counselors became better acquainted with the students, the awards and praise time became opportunities to deepen relationships.

Camp staff held the conviction that children feel confidence through success, so they set out to create environments where campers could succeed. At breakfast, a place where all the campers were together, campers were taught the importance of clapping and cheering for each other. Many announcements and activities that had initially been run by adults in the morning were turned over to the campers. Children were chosen to stand up and tell a joke, give the weather, outline the day, or share any other news that had to be given. Afterwards, they were bathed in applause. Some children who had never previously talked in school learned, through these little exercises, that they could stand up in front of people and do well.

Both athletic and academic performance were always recognized through medals, certificates, and creative trophies. However, counselors also wished to recognize the campers who did not excel in these areas. As they got to know the campers better, the counselors began to design tournaments and activities to highlight the talents of the children who were not quite as capable in sports or academics. One example was a staring contest that the staff held for a withdrawn child. Over the course of several meals, this boy out-stared everyone at his table, then the winners of other tables, until he was in the final stare-down with a girl. With their eyes locked and faces frozen, he began to minutely wiggle his ears which caused the girl to break into a smile and his fellow campers to cheer loudly. This victory was a turning point for this boy who subsequently became more involved with the other campers and camp activities.

At sunset, staff and campers ate snacks while each child was encouraged to share with the others, his or her thoughts about the day. It was truly encouraging to watch campers be supported and take risks.

The camp was run on the principle that to be able to build esteem in others, one must have a fair appreciation of one's own self-worth. Conversely, to maintain self-esteem, one must be able to build it in others. Counselors were committed to teaching the campers how to become esteem builders of others. During the last three weeks of camp, the staff used several tools to encourage positive affirmation among the campers. In one activity, students gave each other pennies, saying something they appreciated about the next child as they handed over the penny. Another activity around the campfire involved one person leaving while the group came up with uplifting statements which were related by the group, one at a time, when the person returned. The session concluded with a candle-lighting ceremony in which campers stood up and acknowledged one person who had "lit a fire under them" over the summer.

# RESULTS

## GAINS ON SELF-CONCEPT

It is to be expected that children entering camp programs such as the one studied here will generally have self-concept profiles that differ somewhat from those of the reference group norms. Means are based on scale scores that have been standardized to the reference group norms with a mean of zero and a standard deviation of one. As can be seen in table II, the initial mean self-concept scores for the total sample of Camp Glencoe children are in keeping with this expectation. The children entered camp with an average reading self-concept score that was well below the norm, and were generally below the norm regarding their overall confidence to perform in school. They also tended to have lower self-concepts where physical ability was concerned, although to a slightly lesser degree. On the other hand, campers generally came in with significantly greater than average self-concept scores about their physical appearance.

Gain scores on the "total self" score generated from the SDQ-I confirmed our personal sense that the camp experience had a positive impact on overall self-concept. The mean total self-concept score for campers, which was 29.61 prior to camp, rose to 31.20 by the session's end. A simple repeated measures ANOVA indicates that this increase was significant at $p = .002$, $F(1,31) = 11.416$.

Our interest, however, was in pinpointing where subjects experienced the most substantial changes in self-concept. The "nesting" of more specific scales within the total scale allows

### TABLE II. INITIAL SELF-CONCEPT SCORES[1]

|  | Mean | Percentile |
| --- | --- | --- |
| Reading | −.46** | 32 |
| Math | .06 | 52 |
| Overall school | −.53** | 30 |
| Physical abilities | −.28* | 39 |
| Appearance | .50** | 69 |
| Peer relations | .19 | 57 |
| Parental relations | .03 | 51 |
| General self | .23 | 59 |

\* Difference from national mean significant at $p < .05$
\*\* Difference from national mean significant at $p < .01$
[1] Based on scale scores with a mean of 0 and an $SD$ of 1.

just that. By including each distinct set of variables in a doubly multivariate repeated measures design, we tested whether significant increases occurred in connection with the set as a whole, while simultaneously checking to see in which specific area(s) such improvement has occurred.

When the total scale was divided into academic and nonacademic components, the overall change observed across the two scales was statistically significant, $F(2,30) = 5.597$, $p = .009$. When each scale is considered separately, we find that increases are also statistically significant, $F(1,31) = 8.260$, $p = .007$ for the academic scale; $F(1,31) = 5.827$, $p = .022$ for the nonacademic scale. The mean academic self-concept score increased more than two points (from 27.10 to 29.27) whereas the corresponding value for the nonacademic scale increased about half as much (from 32.12 to 33.14).

Breaking these composite scales down still further affords more of an opportunity to do the sort of pinpointing discussed above, as the SDQ-I provides the national normative data needed to standardize the raw scores generated by the basic scales. This allows us to identify the specific areas wherein significant changes occurred, and to make direct comparisons across scales.

We turn first to the campers' scores on the SDQ-I's three academic scales which, when combined, yield a significant multivariate $F$-ratio, $p = .023$ $F(3,30) = 3.672$. This justifies a separate look at the changes in each of the three scales. As depicted in figure 2, the increases observed in connection with self-assessments of reading skills and of general school skills were roughly equivalent (from -.41 to -.08 on the reading scale; from -.52 to -.18 on the general school scale). In both cases, moreover, the increases were statistically significant, $F(1,32) = 6.913$, $p = .013$ for the reading scale; $F(1,32) = 7.278$, $p = .011$ for the general school scale. In sum, the increase in overall academic self-concept can be rather neatly characterized as a joint increase in campers' assessments of their specific capacities to read, and of their more general capacities to perform in school.

Unfortunately, we cannot be so precise regarding where changes occurred in connection with nonacademic factors. When the four nonacademic scales were entered into a repeated measures ANOVA, the overall change across this whole set of scales was not great enough to give us much confidence in our ability to isolate singly significant changes, $F(4,29) = 1.542$, $p = .216$. Although the composite nonacademic measure (formed by adding the four scales) does indicate significant

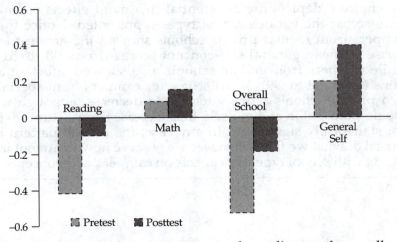

Figure 2.      Pre- and posttest means on the reading, math, overall
               school, and General Self scales from the SDQ-1.

gain as mentioned earlier, there is little that we can say to identify more specific areas of gain. Accordingly, figure 2 does not
depict the changes observed in campers' mean scores on the
four nonacademic scales.

The final change depicted in figure 2 involves the General
Self scale, the one basic SDQ-I scale not included in any of the
academic or nonacademic composite measures. Here, as with
the reading and general school scales, the mean standardized
score increased substantially from pretest to posttest (from .21
to .39), and this increase was statistically significant
$F(1,32) = 5.213, p = .029$.

In addition to testing for basic treatment effects, we also explored the possibility that the treatment might interact significantly with certain between-subject factors. The type of school
regularly attended and any prior diagnosis of comorbid disorders were the two most promising factors to consider along
these lines. The consistent informal observation was that treatment seemed to have the greatest effects on the self-esteem of
those students who were enrolled in regular private schools,
modest effects for those who attended public school, and the
smallest effects for students from specialized private schools for
the learning disabled. This was confirmed by a significant correlation between treatment and school type on the General Self
scale, $F(2,28) = 8.132, p = .002$.[1]

---

[1] There is no joint interaction of school type and comorbid diagnosis with
treatment.

Figure 3 depicts the differential treatment effects on this scale across the various school types represented. Notice that campers from regular private schools showed the greatest increase in mean general self-concept scores (from .08 to .51), while campers from public schools also showed substantial gains (from .30 to .49). Mean scores for campers from specialized private schools actually tended to decrease, although we should note that in and of itself, this decrease (from .31 to .18) is not statistically significant. In any case, the overall pattern is typical of what we find whenever we observe how treatment interacts with school type in its effects on campers' self-concepts.

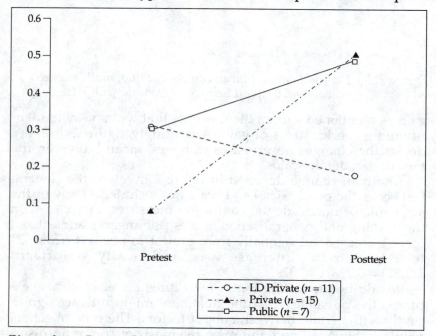

*Figure 3.*    *Pre- and posttest means on the General Self scale from the SDQ-1, for campers drawn from three kinds of schools.*

In addition, campers who were diagnosed with ADD or ADHD generally manifested much smaller increases in self-concept than campers without such disorders, as evident in a significant interaction between treatment diagnosed comorbid disorder on general self-concept $F(2,28) = 3.567, p = .042$.

Figure 4 illustrates the typical pattern for the interaction of treatment with comorbid diagnoses. Campers with no diagnosed comorbid disorders showed a marked increase in

General Self scores (from .10 to .39), while those campers diagnosed ADD or ADHD showed almost no change (from .50 to .51 and from .04 to .03, respectively).

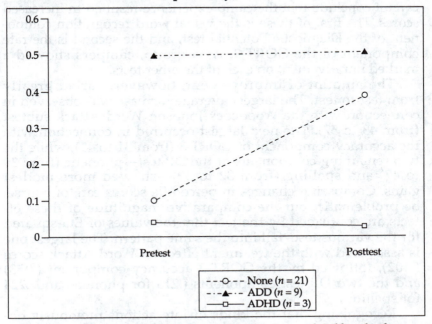

*Figure 4.*    *Pre- and posttest means on the General Self scale, for campers with and without comorbid diagnoses.*

## ACADEMIC GAINS

The second series of analyses dealt with the effects of the camp experience on participants' reading abilities as measured by a battery of standardized tests. All raw scores from the tests were converted to percentiles for the purposes of analysis. The investigation followed much the same course as that above, with doubly multivariate repeated-measures analyses of variance generating the relevant test statistics.[2]

The changes observed in reading from pretest to posttest are presented in table III. The multivariate statistics assessing overall changes across the full complement of tests, $F(6,35) = 8.777$,

---

[2] The fact that the GORT-3 generates a total score as well as separate component scores moved us to carry on with the full logic of the previous analyses, conducting initial tests using the total GORT-3 score and then exploring what happens when that score is broken down into its constituent elements. The observations made during these preliminary passes over the data add little to the overall analysis, so they have been dropped here.

$p <. 001$, suggest that we can proceed with confidence in identifying the specific tests where subjects' scores improved or declined. It so happens that there are only two tests for which we cannot conclude that the camp experience resulted in increased scores. The first of these is the visual word recognition component of the Diagnostic Potential test, and the second is the rate component of the GORT-3. As a group, campers showed a marked improvement on each of the other tests.

The amount of improvement, however, varied greatly from test to test. The largest average increase was observed in connection with the Woodcock-Johnson Word Attack subtest (from 43 to 57). The next largest occurred in connection with the accuracy component of GORT-3 (from 31 to 41), while the two remaining components of the DP test—phonetic (from 39 to 47) and spelling (from 32 to 39)—showed more modest gains. Comparing changes in percentile scores can, of course, be problematic, but the comparative magnitude of these effects are confirmed by the fact that the values of Eta-squared for the various tests fall into the same pattern. The largest one is associated with the treatment effect on Word Attack scores (.402), followed by the GORT-3 accuracy component (.253) and the two DP test components (.215 for phonetic and .224 for spelling).

Recognizing that the kinds of interactions previously observed between treatment and school type or comorbid diagnosis might might also apply to academic gains, we conducted a final analysis incorporating the two between-subject factors. However, these interactions were not significant: $F(12,64) = 1.442$, $p = .171$ for treatment x school type; $F(12,64) = 1.302$,

**TABLE III. CHANGES IN ACADEMIC SCORES FROM PRETEST TO POSTTEST.**

|  | Pretest mean | Posttest mean | F-ratio | Significance |
|---|---|---|---|---|
| *Word Attack* | 42.29 | 57.39 | 26.875 | <.001 |
| *Diagnostic Potential Test:* |  |  |  |  |
| Word recognition, sight | 30.93 | 33.37 | 1.029 | .316 |
| Word recognition, phonetic | 38.68 | 46.76 | 10.949 | .002 |
| Spelling | 32.20 | 38.63 | 11.536 | .002 |
| *GORT-3:* |  |  |  |  |
| Rate | 24.34 | 26.39 | 1.285 | .264 |
| Accuracy | 30.69 | 41.41 | 13.527 | .001 |

* For all tests of significance, $df_1 = 1$ and $df_2 = 29$.

$p = .240$, for treatment x comorbid diagnosis.[3] The increase in reading abilities associated with the camp program was equally distributed across the various groups of campers.

## DISCUSSION

This study was designed to assess the effectiveness of a summer camp program for dyslexic students on two different fronts. The conventional evaluative focus for such programs is on their success in improving objective reading skills. Beyond this, however, this study also sought to evaluate how much such programs contribute to a subjective sense of competency in reading, and perhaps in other areas as well. Several observations made over the course of the study suggest that, for most campers, the camp program was effective on both fronts.

First, the children in the study exhibited clear improvements in phonetic reading and spelling skills, but not in sight word knowledge or in rate of reading skills. This finding parallels results of an intensive eight-week tutorial program for third, fourth, and fifth graders involving systematic, explicit instruction in phonics (Torgesen, Rashotte, and Wagner 1997). Very large gains in phonetic reading skills were evident over a relatively short period, but deficient skills remained for fluency of both phonetic decoding and sight-word reading. Other intervention studies have produced similar results (McGuinness, McGuinness, and McGuinness 1996; Alexander et al. 1991). At least in a six-week summer program, acquisition of decoding skills do not move the student into the automatic and fluent reading that is characteristic of skillful readers. Fluency is receiving increased attention from researchers as a potential key to understanding and improving the reading levels of deficient readers (Foorman, Francis, and Fletcher 1997; Torgesen, Rashotte, and Wagner 1997).

Second, the observed academic improvements were closely linked to the specific interventions employed, with little indication that they were any more or less pronounced in the various subgroups of the camp population. Campers who had been diagnosed with ADD or ADHD were not significantly more or less responsive to the interventions than were campers who had no such diagnoses. Nor could we conclude that the type of school in which campers were regularly enrolled had any im-

---

[3] The $F$ statistic used here is Pillai's Trace.

pact on how much their academic skills improved as a result of the program. Therefore, the educational intervention seemed to be equally effective across the entire range of students at camp.

Third, along with these objective improvements in reading and spelling skills, the academic self-concepts of children were apparently enhanced as a consequence of the camp experience. On a purely subjective level, campers felt more capable of performing academically at the end of camp than they had felt at the outset. The specific areas where this increased sense of academic competence took hold corresponded with what we would expect given the nature of the educational intervention. We would not expect to find that campers felt themselves better equipped in the area of mathematics, for example, and indeed, we observed no such change. Campers did, however, come to think of themselves as better readers by the time the camp let out. Moreover, we found that they were also able to extend this new self-confidence somewhat, regarding themselves as better able to handle the more general challenges associated with school life. To the extent that such feelings of academic competence can be shown to affect one's performance in school, it seems the camp program is helpful for those students who face specific learning challenges.

Fourth, the camp program apparently helped to promote an even more generalized sense of competence and self-worth than is narrowly associated with specific skills such as reading. The sources of this heightened self-concept were probably numerous. In part, campers' confidence may have arisen as an "overflow" of their newfound sense of academic competence. It is also likely that it evolved out of the overall atmosphere of acceptance and affirmation that the camp staff worked to cultivate. Whatever the source, campers clearly embraced a more positive view of themselves as camp progressed.

Fifth, when it comes to these kinds of changes in overall self-concept, the effects of the camp intervention did seem to differ for different types of campers. The differences in the observed effect patterns proved to be significant for only the most general self-concept scales, but the patterns themselves were quite similar for all of the dimensions of self-concept we explored. For the most part, campers who were diagnosed ADD or ADHD did not experience significant gains in self-concept despite academic gains similar to the other campers. Although the numbers are too small to make comparisons between campers with ADD ($n = 9$) and those with ADHD ($n = 3$), inspection of the mean scores in figure 4 suggests that the campers with ADD show pre-camp general self concepts that are relatively high compared to campers with ADHD. Perhaps the behavioral-social difficulties associated with ADHD made these three youngsters less frequent recipients of affirmation and positive feedback from staff and peers. Alternatively or in addition, the same difficulties that children with ADHD have with internalizing rules to guide their behavior could interfere with the internalization of positive feedback or other information to change their self-concepts (Barkley 1997).

Regarding the relationship of school type to self-concept, the most positive changes in self-concept were found among campers who attended regular private schools, with campers from public schools enjoying the next most positive changes. Campers from specialized LD private schools typically experienced no significant changes in self-concept. For those students who are accustomed to an individualized, tutorial (or small group) format with supportive teachers during the regular school year, the camp environment may be "business as usual."

A factor that may partially explain why campers from private and public school settings experienced significant increases in positive self-concept may be the effect of their reference group on self-concept. Marsh (1990) has termed this the "Big Fish Little Pond Effect" where equally able students have lower academic self-concepts when they compare themselves to more able students, and higher academic self-concepts when they compare themselves to less able students. Therefore, the private school students may have entered camp with an academic self-concept referenced against a more competitive academic peer group. The same may be true for the public school campers but to a more moderate degree because of the wider academic ability range of their public school peers. Along with the other ingredients in the camp environment, the private and public school campers may have been more primed by the reference group shift to appreciate the camp setting where they were not in the minority as students with specific learning difficulties. This suggests that some homogenous grouping of dyslexic students may be more helpful for self-esteem development than the prevailing practice of universal inclusion.

The major limitation of this program-evaluation study is the lack of a control group to control for threats to internal validity. It could be argued that the campers showed positive changes because it was summer and the Baltimore Orioles were having a good season! However, the specificity of changes in self-concept and academic skills support the argument that the changes were mediated by the interventions in the camp program.

A second limitation is that there were not enough campers to statistically analyze in a more thorough manner the relationship between changes in academic scores and changes in self-concept scores. Little can be said about the causal direction of the relationship of these variables, but Marsh (1990) provides support for a reciprocal causal effects relationship between academic self-concept and academic achievement, where changes in one facilitate changes in the other. It may not be important to establish causal priority, but rather to determine whether an intervention designed to focus on both factors has a greater impact on dependent variables of interest compared to an intervention focusing on only academic skills or self-concept (Marsh 1990).

A final limitation is the lack of follow-up after the campers returned to school. A follow-up would yield information about the durability of the effects observed at the end of camp and also about the relative influence on self-concept of the peer reference group in the various school settings to which campers return. On the latter point, if the reference group effect is a dominant factor, then we would expect private and public school students' self-concept scores to decrease while LD private school students' self-concepts would stay the same. As a source of information on durability of effects, we have only unsolicited reports and letters from parents. These have been encouraging, at least for some campers. One parent of a camper who returned to public school wrote after several months into the fall, "There has been a tremendous change in Will both academically and personally. He began middle school this year with very little anxiety and difficulty. Historically, Will has been very timid, shy, and frightened when attempting something new. We were extremely concerned about his not being able to adjust to 6th grade in a new school. . . . To make a long story short, he is doing extremely well. Academically, he is performing much better than we ever hoped, he seems content and well-adjusted, and most miraculously, is able to work INDEPENDENTLY."

In conclusion, the study provides support that a multimodal camp program of six weeks' duration has a positive impact on the self-concept and select academic skills of dyslexic students. Future studies are needed to more rigorously control for the validity of and to determine the durability of these effects. An intensive camp program may offer some students a real turn-around platform to begin a trend of more fruitful academic and interpersonal growth; for others, it may at least prevent regression in skills and/or provide continuity for services during the school year in addressing more persistent academic and social difficulties.

Address correspondence to: Van D. Westervelt, Ph.D., Learning Assistance Center, Wake Forest University, P.O. Box 7283, Reynolda Station, Winston-Salem, NC 27109    email: westervd@wfu.edu

## REFERENCES

Alexander, A. W., Anderson, H. G., Heilman, P. C., Voeller, K. K., and Torgesen, J. K. 1991. Phonological awareness training and remediation of analytic decoding deficits in a group of severe dylexics. *Annals of Dyslexia* 41:193–206.

Arena, J. 1982. *Diagnostic Potential Spelling Test.* Novato, CA: Academic Therapy.

Ball, E. W., and Blachman, B. A. 1988. Phoneme segmentation training: Effect on reading readiness. *Annals of Dyslexia* 38:208–25.

Barkley, R. A. 1997. Behavioral inhibition, sustained attention and executive functions: Constructing a unifying theory of ADHD. *Psychological Bulletin* 121:65–94.

Conderman, G., Snider, V. E., and Crawford, D. 1997. Establishing high expectations through the LEAP clinic. *Intervention in School and Clinic* 33(2):98–102.

Felton, R. H. 1993. Effects of instruction on the decoding skills of children with phonological-processing problems. *Journal of Learning Disabilities* 26:575–82.

Foorman, B. R., Francis, D. J., and Fletcher, J. M. 1997. NICHD early interventions project. *Perspectives, International Dyslexia Association* 23(4):4–5.

Gillingham, A., and Stillman, B. W. 1997. Gillingham Manual: *Remedial Training for Students with Specific Disabilities in Reading, Spelling and Penmanship.* Cambridge, MA: Educators Publishing Service.

Greene, J. F. 1993. Systematic phonology: Critical element in teaching, reading and language to dyslexics. In S. F. Wright and R. Groner, ed., *Facets of Dyslexia and Its Remediation.* Amsterdam: Elsevier Science Publishers.

Greene, J. F. 1996. Language!: Effects of an individualized structured language curriculum for middle and high school students. *Annals of Dyslexia* 46:97–121.

Harter, S. 1986. Processes underlying the construct, maintenance, and enhancement of self-concept in children. In J. Suls and A. Greenwald, eds., *Psychological Perspectives on the Self.* Hilldale, NJ: Lawrence Earlbaum Associates, 137–81.

Harter, S. 1990. Issues in the assessment of the self-concept of children and adolescents. In A. M. LaGreca, ed., *Through the Eyes of the Child.* Boston: Allyn and Bacon, 292–325.

King, D. H. 1989. *Writing Skills 1 and 2.* Cambridge, MA: Educators Publishing Service.

Lyon, G. R. 1995. Research initiatives in learning disabilities. *Journal of Child Neurology* 10(1):120–26.

Marsh, H. W. 1990. *Self Description Questionnaire-I Manual.* MacArthur, Australia: University of Western Sydney.

Marsh, H. W. 1994. Using the National Longitudinal Study of 1988 to evaluate theoretical models of self-concept: The Self Description Questionnaire. *Journal of Educational Psychology* 86:439–56.

Marsh, H. W., Barnes, J., Cairns, L., and Tidman, M. 1984. The Self Description Questionnaire (SDQ): Age effects in the structure and level of self-concept for preadolescent children. *Journal of Educational Psychology* 76:940–56.

Marsh, H. W., Smith, I. D., and Barnes, J. 1985. Multidimensional self-concepts: Relationships with sex and academic achievement. *Journal of Educational Psychology* 77:581–96.

McGuinness, C., McGuinness, D., and McGuinness, G. 1996. Phono-graphix: A new method for remediating reading difficulties. *Annals of Dyslexia* 46:73–96.

Meece, J. L., Parsons, J. E., Kaczala, C. M., Golf, S. B., and Futterman, R. 1982. Sex differences in math achievement: Toward a model of academic choice. *Psychological Bulletin* 91:324–48.

Relich, J. D. 1983. Attribution, affective variables, and arithmetic achievement. Ph.D. class. University of Sydney, Australia.

Rosenberg, M. 1979. *Conceiving the Self.* New York: Basic Books.

Shavelson, R. J., Hubner, J. J., and Stanton, G. C. 1976. Validation of construct interpretations. *Review of Educational Research* 46:407–41.

Torgesen, J. K., and Davis, C. 1996. Individual difference variables that predict response to training in phonological awareness. *Journal of Experimental Child Psychology* 63:1–21.

Torgesen, J. K., Rashotte, C. A., and Wagner, R. K. 1997. Research on instructional interventions for children with reading disabilities. Paper read at Annual Meeting of the International Dyslexia Association, November 1997, Minneapolis.

Wagner, R. K., Torgensen, J. K., and Rashotte, C. 1993. The efficacy of phonological awareness training for early reading achievement: A meta analysis. Symposium presentation at annual meeting of American Education Research Association, April 1993, Atlanta.

Wiederholt, J. L., and Bryant, B. R. 1992. *Gray Oral Reading Tests.* (3rd Ed.). Austin, Texas: PRO-ED.

Wilson, B. 1988. *The Wilson Reading System.* Hopedale, MA: Educomp Publications.

Woodcock, R. W. 1989. *Woodcock Johnson-Revised, Tests of Achievement.* Banning, CA: Riverside Publishing Company.

# Improving the Comprehension
# of Disabled Readers

*Joanna P. Williams*

Teachers College, Columbia University

*Students with learning disabilities (LD) often have difficulty compre-
hending what they read. Although reading comprehension problems
frequently are associated with inadequate word recognition, students
also have difficulties related to comprehension itself—a passive approach to the reading task, insensitivity to text structure, and poor
metacognitive skills. The reading and language arts curricula that
have emerged from today's constructivist paradigm can pose problems
for these students. Whereas the new curricula emphasize personal interpretations of text and relatively unstructured teaching strategies,
students with LD do well with explicit, highly structured instruction.
This paper introduces an instructional program designed to teach students with serious learning disabilities how to identify a story theme,
and how to relate it to their own real-life experiences. The program focused on understanding a text as a whole, and integrating text meaning with concepts and experiences that are personally meaningful,
goals shared by a constructivist approach. At the same time, the program incorporates the explicit, structured instruction that these students also need. A study to evaluate the program's effectiveness is
described, as are current efforts to refine the program to promote
transfer of comprehension strategies.*

Annals of Dyslexia, Vol. 48, 1998
ISSN 0736-9387

# INTRODUCTION

Over the last few years, research in beginning reading has led to substantial progress in our understanding of how children acquire word recognition skills. The increasing enthusiasm in many quarters for instruction in decoding acknowledges what we have learned from research about reading processes. This orientation to reading instruction fits well with the general consensus that students with learning disabilities need structured and explicit instruction. However, even when fluent in word recognition, many students with learning disabilities fail to comprehend what they read. Just as they need explicit instruction in decoding, so do they require specific instruction in comprehension (Swanson and McMahon 1996; Gersten and Carnine 1986).

The research base in comprehension is not as well developed as the research base in beginning reading, although there have been some notable advances (Anderson and Pearson 1984). Our current conception of reading comprehension focuses on the process by which people incorporate new information from what they are reading into their already existing knowledge base. Meaning is constructed from this integration of information; this is the heart of what has been labeled the constructivist approach.

Many empirical studies in cognitive psychology have demonstrated the importance of the knowledge base in the comprehension process. For example, one study showed that children who knew a great deal about spiders understood a new text about spiders better than other children did, and were especially good at making inferences that involved information not explicitly presented in the text (Pearson and Fielding 1991). These empirical studies also emphasized the notion that as one's knowledge base of a particular concept (called a schema, as in "restaurant schema") becomes better organized with general experience and with schooling, it becomes more easily accessible in encounters with texts, and comprehension is improved. To extend the analogy, given a well-developed restaurant schema, information that is presented in a new text about restaurants will be more easily integrated.

A similar constructivist approach underlies reader-response theory. This theory derives from the field of literary criticism (Tompkins 1980) and has greatly influenced the new orientation to comprehension instruction (Beach 1993). An important idea here is that since each person has a unique history of cognitive development, each person's knowledge base is unique.

Therefore, each person's integration of the new information in a text with what is already known will yield a unique meaning. Reader-response theory underscores the complex, dynamic, and ultimately individualistic nature of comprehension.

The instructional strategies emerging from this approach emphasize the multidimensional nature of comprehension and the importance of the reader's self-generated interpretations (Beach 1993; Au and Carroll 1997). Most constructivist instruction holds that teachers should serve as guides and facilitators in instruction, and should not impose their own interpretations of texts on their students. Rather, both teachers and fellow students are important resources in the classroom because they contribute their own interpretations in discussion, and this provides opportunities for students to enlarge and refine their own meaning construction. Such peer-oriented, sometimes even peer-led, classroom discussion is prevalent in classes taught using the constructivist approach. Like most constructivist teaching, the use of such discussion is a relatively unstructured teaching strategy.

Such strategies have often proved to be a distinct improvement over earlier types of comprehension instruction (Allington and McGill-Franzen 1989), which focused excessively on short pieces of text and the identification of details, sequences of events, and other particular features in those fragments, rather than on the whole text and its overall meaning (Dole, Williams, Osborn, Bourassa, Bartisias, Greene, and Terry 1998). However, these unstructured strategies present a real challenge to special educators. Specifically, many students with learning disabilities are not prepared to take advantage of such instruction. These students often suffer from poor comprehension monitoring, a passive approach to tasks, inefficient text-scanning strategies, and insensitivity to text structure (Cain 1996; Oakhill and Yuill 1996; Wolman, van den Broek, and Lorch 1997). Without such foundational skills in place, the new constructivist curricula are not likely to be effective. A student's interpretation of a text might well be enhanced by hearing discussion of the interpretations of their peers, but only if the student has a stable interpretation of his or her own. Some students do not, and they need help on this more basic level. Moreover, students with learning disabilities respond well to explicit and well-structured instruction (Wixson and Lipson 1991), and this type of instruction is quite antithetical to the constructivist teaching paradigm.

One can hold constructivist goals and yet not endorse constructivist teaching techniques. Consider beginning reading instruction. According to the proponents of whole language, the ultimate goal of the reader is getting meaning from written language. One can fully subscribe to this goal and still endorse a synthetic phonics approach to instruction.

The same thing holds true in comprehension instruction. My students and I have been involved in developing instruction that fits the new constructivist goals in a way that will work for students with serious learning disabilities. We emphasize the holistic nature of the comprehension process and the importance of integrating text meaning with concepts and experiences that are personally meaningful, but we also acknowledge the demonstrated value of structured, direct instruction for this group of learners. We have developed an instructional program for students with serious learning disabilities that teaches them to go beyond plot-level comprehension of a story, that is, beyond the sequence of specific events of a story. We teach them to identify a theme that is exemplified by the story as a whole, and to abstract that theme so that it can be understood in relation to the students' personal experiences as well as to other stories.

Surprisingly little research has been done, either theoretical or instructional, that addresses the question of the abstract, holistic meaning of a story. The large amount of research on narrative text that was jump-started by the introduction of schema theory (Anderson and Pearson 1984) focused primarily on a story's plot level. But a story's general holistic meaning, as expressed in a theme, is essential for complete comprehension, as well as for understanding how a story relates to other stories and to real-life experiences. This more extended comprehension is a primary goal of the new constructivist curricula, and indeed of any study of literature (Beach 1987, 1993; Singer and Donlan 1982), and should be addressed in research, in part in order to devise ways of improving instruction.

What is a theme? Lukens (1988) defined theme as "the idea that holds the story together, such as a comment about either society, human nature, or the human condition." Lehr (1991) classified children's stories as exemplifying concepts such as "friendship" or "courage," and she called these the themes.

Our own definition of theme acknowledges the centrality of a concept (Williams, Brown, Silverstein, and deCani 1994, Williams, Leung, Wilder and deCani 1997); however, we believe that theme involves not only a concept but something more. We follow Dorfman and Brewer (1994; Dorfman 1989), who addressed one specific type of story—the fable—in which the theme is the didactic lesson embodied in the text. They proposed that the value-valence accorded to the plot components (main story event and story outcome) was an essential aspect of the knowledge necessary to understand the theme of the fable. That is, one evaluates the event and outcome in terms of one's moral understanding; this evaluation embodies a moral judgment. The combination of the plot pattern (concept) and the moral judgment results in the theme. For example, if the event is an immoral action (such as lying) and the outcome is negative, the story communicates a theme such as "we should not lie."

Dorfman and Brewer's (1994) analysis was geared to young children; the authors focused on fables because they are traditionally used by parents to socialize young children. We felt that fables would be readily grasped by students with learning disabilities so we formulated the themes we used in our instruction in a fable-like "We should/should not. . ." format.

Of course, it is also important to show that Dorfman and Brewer's model could be expanded to make it relevant to other types of stories and theme, and in our full definition of theme we do make this expansion. A theme expresses a pattern among story components in a form that is abstracted from the specific story context and also comments on that pattern in some way. The comment need not be evaluative; therefore, we define a theme as involving a commentary attached to a core concept (Williams et al. 1997). The commentary can take the form of a lesson with a value judgment as in "we should not lie," or it can consist simply of an observation with no value judgment attached (some people lie). This commentary operates at the concept level, not the plot level; that is, the lesson or the observation is generalized beyond the specifics of the particular story plot.

In our first foray into this topic (Brown and Williams 1991), we studied children in the fourth, sixth, and eighth grades, and identified two aspects of knowledge as essential to the understanding of theme: identifying the plot components (main character, main story event or problem, and final outcome or resolution) and understanding the motivation of the story characters (cf. Beach 1987, 1993). Identifying the characters' motivation is important because it helps in interpreting the sequence of events. This information is often not explicitly stated. It must be inferred, and the inference depends on general social knowledge. We found that awareness of plot components and character motivation develop with age, as does comprehension of the overall story theme. Williams et al. (1997) replicated these findings and found that patterns of performance were similar for students both with and without learning disabilities. Performance levels on all three tasks decreased as the stories became more abstract and as more general world knowledge was required.

Of course, one need not always be able to identify every important plot component and the underlying motivation of each main character of a story in order to identify the theme. Although, in such situations, it could be tempting to characterize the requisite information-processing as completely bottom-up, we know such characterization to be inaccurate. Rather, the process is interactive. Experience in the real world or knowledge of other stories may provide the basis for top-down inferences, and sometimes an identification of theme may be made prior to the completion of the reading of a story (Leung and Williams 1997). For example, someone might start to read a story about a boy who always helps himself to his brother's belongings and who, at school, takes the lion's share of everything. Even before getting the main story event, the reader might think, "This boy is greedy; I wonder if he'll get punished, because one should not be greedy."

## THE THEMES INSTRUCTION PROGRAM

Our program consists of a series of twelve forty-minute lessons. Each is organized around a single story and comprises five parts:

1. prereading discussion of the purpose of the lesson and the topic of the story to be read;
2. reading of the story;
3. discussion of the important story information using organizing (schema) questions as guides;
4. identification of a theme for the story, stating it in general terms so that it is relevant to a variety of stories and situations; and
5. practice in applying the generalized theme to real-life experience.

### THE STORIES

The twelve stories were taken from basal readers (four different series). In most cases, the stories originally appeared in trade books (see Appendix I). Each story is under seven pages long and contains a clear theme, as judged by a consensus of three adult readers.

Five of the stories exemplify a single theme, "We should persevere." Each of the other seven stories exemplifies a different theme—cooperation, responsibility, and respect for others—all expressed in the theme format (We should . . .), described above.

**LESSON PARTS**

1. *Prereading discussion about lesson purpose and story topic.* In the first part of each lesson, theme is defined (a lesson that you can learn from a story), the value of understanding themes is discussed, and background for the specific story for that lesson is introduced, including its relevance to personal experiences. This instruction is heavily scaffolded, with teachers initially modeling each step and students taking on progressively more responsibility (Brown and Palincsar 1989). In the first three lessons, teachers define theme and lead the discussion on the importance of theme and the story topic, making associations between the story and personal experiences. Starting in Lesson 4, the students offer definitions of theme and lead the discussions themselves. As is the case throughout the lessons, only a general outline is given to the teachers who are expected to use their own expertise in developing discussions and guiding the instruction.

2. *Reading the story.* Next, the teacher reads the story aloud while students follow along with their texts so that decoding difficulties do not interfere with comprehension. At various points during the reading, the teacher interposes questions. These questions are designed to encourage students to process the text actively (to make associations between their own knowledge and the text information and to clarify the text information). The teacher asks the students to make predictions about what would happen next in the story and to explain major story events. Student responses are discussed, and students are encouraged to ask their own questions.

   After reading the story, the class discusses the main points and reads a summary (which we wrote) highlighting the main events and outcome. This is done because students with learning disabilities are particularly likely to have trouble identifying the important story components (Wong 1984), and their story comprehension is often idiosyncratic (Williams 1993).

3. *Discussion of important story information using organizing (schema) questions.* Teacher and students discuss five questions designed to help organize the important

story components and derive the thematic material. The teacher encourages students to internalize these generic questions over the course of the lesson series.

The first three organizing questions focus on the important story components from which a theme concept will be derived: main character, central event, and outcome. The questions are:

• Who is the main character?
• What did he or she do?
• What happened?

These questions direct students to focus on the important information and enable them to develop and internalize questions to help extract and organize important story components independently. Again, instruction is scaffolded.

The final two organizing questions are designed to encourage the students to make the judgments that, when combined with the theme concept, lead to theme identification. These questions are:

• Was this good or bad?
• Why was this good or bad?

Although teachers modeled their responses to the first four questions for four lessons, the final question— why was this good or bad—required teacher modeling through Lesson 7. Also through Lesson 7, teachers modeled the way in which their answers to the five questions led to a theme, and they state the theme. After Lesson 7, responsibility for identifying and stating the theme was gradually transferred to the students. Teachers provided feedback to help the students in this process.

4. *Identification of the theme in standard format.* Students next learned to state the theme in a standard format defined as a "should" statement. Teachers modeled two generic statement frames:

(Main character) should have (should not have)

_____.

We should (should not)

_____.

The first frame puts the theme into the *should* format. The second frame applies the theme to situations and people in general rather than just to those in the story. Following teacher modeling, students gradually learned to state the theme in this format.

5. *Application of theme to real-life experiences*. Teachers then taught the students to ask two questions to help extend the theme to specific and often personal real-life scenarios:

- To whom would this theme apply?
- When would it apply? In what situation?

In this step, too, instruction proceeded by means of scaffolding. For each story, more explicit forms of the questions were also included, elaborating on "who" and "in what situation", to be used as prompts when necessary.

The main purpose of the present study was to compare the Themes Instruction program to more traditional instruction.

## PRELIMINARY EVALUATION

Prior to conducting the study reported here, we evaluated our instructional program using fifth- and sixth-grade students who were either typically achieving or mainstreamed with mild disabilities. We wanted to assess the effectiveness of the program initially with children who were making satisfactory progress. The assumption with these children was that any difficulties with the program would not be attributable to their own learning problems. In this initial study, students were taught by their own teachers, in classrooms that had been randomly assigned to either receive the instructional program or to serve in a control condition receiving no special instruction.

As reported in Williams et al. 1994, this initial study provided positive evidence for the effectiveness of our instructional program. Students who went through our program performed significantly better than the control group on posttest measures tapping what they had been taught explicitly, as well as on measures of transfer. These measures were comparable to those in the present study, described below in more detail. Importantly, both the students with mild disabilities and the nondisabled students performed at similar levels, indicating that the methods were successful across a range of abilities.

Encouraged by these preliminary results, we turn now to assess the efficacy of our comprehension instruction for students with more severe learning disabilities (Williams et al. 1994). It was for those students, who do not respond well to normal classroom instruction, that our program was initially designed.

# METHOD

## PARTICIPANTS

Ninety-three students from seventh- and eight-grade special education classrooms of three junior high schools in a small city about twenty miles from New York City were the participants. Eighty percent of the student population qualified for free or reduced rate lunches. The participating students received all their instruction in their own classrooms; they were not mainstreamed.

Twelve intact classes were used. All students in these classes had been certified by the school as having learning disabilities, indicating that every child exhibited a discrepancy of 50 percent or more between expected achievement and actual achievement. Although some of the students in our sample (whose IQ scores were below 85) may not be technically classifiable as students with learning disabilities, all of them qualify for at-risk status. All were performing at a very low level of reading (see table I).

We did not impose any further criteria on this school-identified group because we feel that instructional studies are most useful if conducted in ecologically valid settings; that is, in actual classroom situations as they exist in schools. While our prime focus is on learning disabilities, we believe that adhering to a strict definition of learning disability is inappropriate for this type of research. Well-structured instruction should be effective with all students who are functioning at a low level, regardless of how they have been classified. This point of view is reflected in many schools' current grouping policies, written in terms of

TABLE I.   CHARACTERISTICS OF THE PARTICIPANTS.

| Instructional Treatment | Groups n | Students[†] M | F | Age(yrs.) Mean | SD | Verbal IQ[*] Mean | SD | Reading Level[**] Mean | SD | Grade Eq. |
|---|---|---|---|---|---|---|---|---|---|---|
| Themes | 6 | 35 | 18 | 14.2 | (.86) | 78.5 | (3.3) | 612.9 | (15.0) | 4-1 |
| Traditional | 6 | 22 | 18 | 14.1 | (.73) | 75.8 | (3.8) | 610.5 | (12.3) | 4-2 |

* This is an estimated Verbal IQ, based on four WISC-R subtests (Information, Similarities, Vocabulary, and Digit Span).

** Metropolitan Achievement Test, Reading Comprehension subtest, scaled scores.

† The sample was composed of equal proportions of Hispanics, Blacks, and Caucasians.

level of functioning and not of classification status (New York City Board of Education 1991).

## TEACHERS

All twelve participating teachers (volunteers) held master's degrees and were certified in special education. Each had at least 15 years of teaching experience. A 90-minute inservice session was scheduled to familiarize the teachers with the program. We worked with teachers in small groups or individually; we gave them the "Theme Scheme" (the organizing questions, the theme-statement frames, and the generalization questions), and discussed general guidelines concerning strategic instruction. However, we asked teachers to formulate the actual discussions according to their own style and preference. A similar inservice session was provided for the teachers involved in the comparison "traditional-instruction" program. As in the Themes Instruction, the outlined lessons were presented to the teachers as general guidelines; the teachers were encouraged to tailor their instruction according to their own professional judgment. Teachers were invited to discuss their work further, request help, and so forth, at any time during the study.

## PROCEDURE

The twelve classrooms were randomly assigned to either of the two programs—Themes Instruction or Traditional Instruction— with the restriction that the same number of classrooms in each school and grade be assigned to each program. Both programs were administered in twelve 40-minute instructional sessions, spread out over four weeks.

The pretest and the posttest consisted of audiotaped individual interviews. On the pretest, we first asked students to define *theme*, and then explained that "a theme is a lesson that you can learn from a story." A story was then read by the interviewer (students followed along with their own copies of the text). The theme of the story was "We should always be ourselves." After listening to the story, students answered a series of comprehension questions about the story, stated a theme of the story ("If you were going to use this story to teach a lesson to someone, what would that lesson be?"), and told a story of their own to which the same theme was applicable. The interview allowed a natural interchange between student and interviewer. Pretest interviews lasted about 20 minutes.

All posttests were administered within three days of the final instructional session. The posttest was similar to the pretest. A story whose theme was not represented in any of the instruction ("We should be considerate of others") was used. In addition, students listened to a second story that exemplified the theme on which much of the instruction had focused ("We should persevere"). Students provided a theme statement, told a story of their own, and defined perseverance. Posttest interviews lasted approximately 30 minutes.

We observed each classroom twice in the course of the instruction, but no formal observational measures were used. These teachers were all experienced and we did not want to intrude excessively. Although we felt that all teachers followed our guidelines closely, they displayed a wide variety of teaching styles (in terms of personal warmth, for example).

## THE COMPARISON PROGRAM: TRADITIONAL INSTRUCTION

Students in the comparison classrooms received instruction similar to that currently found in basal readers, using the same twelve stories as were used for the Themes Instruction. Traditional instruction was derived from the basal teachers' manuals, with modifications and additions where necessary to conform to the structure just described. Each of the twelve lessons consisted of four parts:

1. *Prereading discussion.* Teachers began each lesson by reading a short paragraph that told briefly what the story was about. Then, students were asked questions to help them think of any previous experiences they had had with the story topic.
2. *Vocabulary development.* A short list of words, along with their definitions, was presented on the chalkboard. Teacher and students together generated sentences that included the vocabulary items.
3. *Story reading.* The teacher read the story aloud to circumvent decoding difficulties while students followed with their own copies. At various points, the teacher stopped to ask questions. These questions were the same as those used in the Themes Instruction.
4. *Postreading questions.* The teacher asked several questions about the story. These questions related both to factual details of the story and to inferences derived from it, and provided the basis for further discussion of the story.

## MEASURES

The dependent measures derived from the interviews ranged from measures of content explicitly taught in the program to measures of both "near" and "far transfer" (Brown and Palincsar 1989). The terms near and far transfer indicate the degree to which the performance assessed during the interview differed from the performance required during the instruction itself. It is notoriously difficult to achieve any transfer (generalization), near or far, as a consequence of instructing low-functioning students (Brown and Palincsar, 1989).

The interview items that evaluated explicitly taught content included definition of the concepts of theme and of perseverance, and application of the perseverance theme, generating a story with that theme. The item that evaluated near transfer was identification of the theme of a previously unheard perseverance story; to evaluate far transfer we asked children to identify the theme of a story and to generate a story about that theme which had not been represented in any of the instructional stories. We also included comprehension questions dealing with information of two types: (a) specific details explicitly stated in the story; and (b) major story components such as main character, main action, and outcome. These questions were included as a check to ensure that students understood the stories on the plot level.

## SCORING

To develop the scoring system for each measure, two scorers read the protocols and sorted responses into categories based on accuracy and completeness. The two scorers were aided by a third in arriving at a consensus in rating acceptability of the responses (See Appendix III for examples of acceptable and unacceptable answers for these measures). As seen in the appendix, for some measures, response categories were ordered from best answers to worst answers, and corresponding numerical scores were assigned to each category.[1]

The actual scoring was done by individuals blind to status of student and condition. Interrater reliability for the scoring of each measure (percent agreement between two independent

---

[1] I have included the scoring guides for both the preliminary study and the study that is described here in full so that the difference in quality of response between the two populations is clear. Because this difference was so great, the entire scoring system had to be developed separately for each study.

scorers, who scored about 15 percent of the data on each measure) was 90 percent or better.

## RESULTS

Table I presents descriptive information about the participants. At pretest, children in the two treatment conditions did not differ in mean age, $t(10) = 0.04$; mean WISC-R prorated verbal IQ score, $t(10) = 1.29$; or mean score on the Reading Comprehension subtest of the Metropolitan Achievement Test, $t(10) = 0.30$. Because there were no significant differences on any of the pretest measures, there was no need to covary on these factors on the posttest.

A direct comparison between pretest and posttest was possible for one measure, Concept of Theme. A repeated-measures analysis of variance with two factors (*treatment*, themes-instructed versus traditional-instructed and *test*, pre- and post-), was performed. Only one of the main effects, treatment, was significant (see table II). There was also a significant interaction, indicating that, as expected, only the themes-instructed group improved as a function of instruction.

Table II presents means and standard deviations of the posttest scores and results of the statistical tests. As expected, there was a significant difference between the themes-instructed and the traditional-instructed groups when the first four measures (evaluating explicitly taught content and near transfer) were analyzed as a set, Hotelling's $T^2 = 55.39$, $F(4,7) = 9.69$, $p < .01$. In order to determine which of the four measures contributed to this difference, simple $t$-tests were performed. A Bonferroni-adjusted alpha level of .0125 was used. The themes-instructed students outperformed the others on Measure #1, Concept of Theme; Measure #2, Concept of Perseverance; and Measure #3, Theme Identification (Perseverance). However, they did not excel on Measure #4, Theme Application (Perseverance).

The result on Measure #3 was not because of a response bias; only two students responded with a perseverance theme to the novel story which had been presented earlier in the same session. Moreover, the results on Measure #4 strongly suggested a trend in the expected direction. Overall, these results indicated clearly that the Themes Instruction program aided students in their comprehension. They also suggest that these students, with their severe learning disabilities, need a great deal of practice when they are learning higher-order comprehension skills.

TABLE II.   POSTTEST PERFORMANCE—
MEANS AND STANDARD DEVIATIONS.

| Measure | Instructional Treatment | | |
| --- | --- | --- | --- |
| | Themes | Traditional | |
| *1. Concept of Theme | 1.61 | .31 | $t(10) = 4.37$, |
| (scored 0–3, 3 high) | (.68) | (.27) | $p < .001$ |
| **Perseverance Story** | | | |
| *2. Concept of Perseverance | .72 | 0 | exact $p < .001$ |
| (scored 0–2, 2 high) | (.43) | | |
| *3. Theme Identification | .59 | .17 | $t(10) = 4.96$, |
| (proportion of acceptable responses) | (.12) | (.17) | $p < .001$ |
| 4. Theme Application | .68 | .49 | $t(10) = 1.53$ |
| (proportion of acceptable responses) | (.28) | (.16) | |
| **Novel Theme Story** | | | |
| *5. Story Details | 4.69 | 4.17 | $t(10) = 2.10$, |
| (maximum score = 6) | (.45) | (.40) | $p < .05$ |
| 6. Story Components | 2.52 | 2.16 | $t(10) = 1.52$ |
| (maximum score = 3) | (.38) | (.43) | |
| 7. Theme Identification | .08 | .04 | $t(10) = .74$ |
| (proportion of acceptable responses) | (.09) | (.06) | |
| 7a. Theme Gist | .65 | .59 | $t(10) = .45$ |
| (proportion of acceptable responses) | (.16) | (.29) | |
| 8. Theme Application | .31 | .27 | $t(10) - .43$ |
| (proportion of acceptable responses) | (.09) | (.20) | |

* The difference between Themes Instruction and Traditional Instruction was significant.

Across both groups, performance was high on the two measures of plot-level comprehension (Measures #5 and #6), indicating that the students had understood the story on the plot level and that performance on the other measures was not effected by a lack of comprehension. On Measure #6, Story Components (Novel Theme), there was no difference between the themes-instructed and the traditional-instructed groups. On Measure #5, Story Details (Novel Theme), the themes-instructed group scored significantly higher than the traditional-instructed group. This suggests that instruction geared to achieving an overall abstract meaning of the story (the story theme) had an organizing effect and facilitated lower level comprehension. *Theme* in narrative, although a more abstract concept, may perform a function similar to that of *main idea* in expository text (Williams, Taylor, and deCani 1984).

Three measures assessed far transfer. Very few students were able to provide an acceptable theme statement, as assessed by Measure #7, Theme Identification (Novel Theme). This is not surprising, given the expressive language difficulties and other problems typically seen in students with learning disabilities. In order to arrive at a more liberal scoring of theme identification, we included another measure, #7a, Theme Gist (Novel Theme). Scorers reviewed students' entire protocol, searching for terms and phrases indicating that they had an incipient understanding of the theme, even though they were unable to give an adequate theme statement. According to this measure, many students had some awareness of the theme. However, there was no difference as a function of instructional treatment on either measure of theme identification. In addition, there was no significant difference on Measure #8, Theme Application (Novel Theme).

## DISCUSSION

The Themes Instruction Program helped teach students the fundamental aspects of theme comprehension: the concept of theme and the identification of an instructed theme in a previously unheard story. The program also helped in related areas. It taught content, (the concept of perseverance), and improved lower level comprehension as evidenced by the fact that students in the Themes Instruction were better able to reproduce details about the story. In addition, the themes-instructed students demonstrated near transfer.

One of the biggest challenges in designing instruction for students with learning disabilities is to develop techniques that will foster generalization (Simmons, Fuchs, Fuchs, Mathis, and Hodge 1995). Indeed, educational goals are rarely couched simply in terms of mastery of what is actually taught; we conceive of education as helping students to transfer their knowledge and skills to new situations. While it might seem that we achieved only a modest degree of generalization, the results of the program actually demonstrate a level of transfer that represents substantial achievement for students with severe learning disabilities (Pressley and McCormick 1995). Overall, our results indicate that these students are able to respond positively to an integrated approach to comprehension when it is well structured.

We asked both teachers and students, informally, to tell us what they thought of the program. Both groups indicated that they liked it; in fact, the response was enthusiastic. Positive aspects of the program specifically mentioned by the teachers included its structure, explicitness, and the levels of interest and challenge.

Our results, however, suggest that the benefits of the instruction did not readily transfer to stories with novel themes. There had been considerably more transfer in our earlier study with nondisabled and mildly disabled students. While these findings are not at all atypical (Pressley and McCormick 1995), the value of the instructional program would certainly be further enhanced if it enabled students with severe learning disabilities to generalize what they had learned to an even greater extent than was demonstrated in the present study.

This is the focus of our current work. Alice Wilder and I (Wilder and Williams 1997) have designed a refined version of the program that focuses specifically on the achievement of transfer. In this redesign, three themes are given equal instructional time. Four lessons are devoted to the following three themes: one should persevere; one should be oneself; and one should not prejudge. We expect, following classic principles of learning, that this more extended exposure to several different examples (themes) during instruction will pave the way for the identification of novel themes; what we are calling far transfer.

There is also a second important design element in this new version of the program. We included a variety of instructional activities that, we hope, students will find particularly engaging. A different group activity was incorporated into each of the four lessons devoted to each theme. The first lesson on each theme concentrated on discussion, in order to ensure that the students understood the theme. Then, each of the following lessons on that theme included one of three activities. Students drew pictures, wrote rap songs, or role-played. In all cases, the content of the pictures, songs, and scenarios focused on exemplifying the theme of the lesson, not on representing the particular story plot. The teachers were given suggestions to prompt students to generate ideas.

The redesign also incorporates other refinements such as an expansion of the types of stories used. Some stories have been taken directly from trade books, some are quite long, and several genres (realistic fiction, fables, and fairy tales) are included.

## CONCLUSION

In summary, our Themes Instruction Program improved performance on an important higher level comprehension task. Our results suggest that explicit teaching of this neglected aspect of comprehension is helpful to students with severe learning disabilities. We hope that the work in which we are currently engaged will extend the effectiveness of the program by promoting even greater transfer than was achieved by the original program.

It should be noted that we are not endorsing this type of highly structured and explicit instruction for higher-functioning, mainstreamed students with learning disabilities. For them, our program would be slow paced and redundant. Other approaches might be more appropriate, such as those which incorporate features of the recently developed, literature-based language arts curricula, for example, using complex stories that have multiple themes and emphasizing unstructured classroom discussion (Rogers 1990; Allington et al. 1996).

However, students with severe learning disabilities enter instruction at a different point. They need to develop a basic concept of theme and an understanding of how narratives embody themes. To acquire these skills, they need clear, simple stories and explicit, structured instruction. Our work demonstrates that with such appropriate materials and methods, these low-functioning students can achieve competence in higher-order comprehension skills.

## References

Allington, R. L., and McGill-Franzen, A. 1989. School response to reading failure: Chapter I and special education students in grades 2, 4, and 8. *Elementary School Journal* 89:529–42.

Anderson, R. C., and Pearson, P. D. 1984. A schema-theoretic view of basic processes in reading comprehension. In P. D. Pearson, R. Barr, M. L. Kamil, and P. Mosenthal, eds., *Handbook of Reading Research*, Vol. I. White Plains, NY: Longman.

Au, K. H., and Carroll, J. H. 1997. Improving literacy achievement through a constructivist approach: The KEEP Demonstration Classroom Project. *Elementary School Journal* 97:203–21.

Beach, R. 1993. *A Teachers' Introduction to Reader Response Theories*. Urbana, IL: National Council of Teachers of English.

Brown, L. G., and Williams, J. P. 1991. A developmental study of theme comprehension. Paper read at the 41st Annual Meeting of the National Reading Conference, December 1991, Palm Springs.

Brown, A. L., and Palincsar, A. M. 1989. Guided, cooperative learning and individual knowledge acquisition. In L.B. Resnick, ed., *Knowing and Learning: Essays in Honor of Robert Glaser*. Hillsdale, NJ: Lawrence Erlbaum Associates.

Cain, K. 1996. Story knowledge and comprehension skill. In C. Cornoldi and J. Oakhill, eds., Reading Comprehension *Difficulties: Processes and Intervention*. Hillsdale, NJ: Lawrence Erlbaum Associates.

Dole, J. A., Williams, J. P., Osborn, J., Bourassa, J., Bartisias, K., Greene, S. and Terry, D. 1998. *Reading Comprehension Instruction*. Washington, DC: American Federation of Teachers.

Dorfman, M. H. 1989. Understanding the Points of Fables: A Developmental Study. Unpublished manuscript.

Dorfman, M. H., and Brewer, W .F. 1994. Understanding the Points of Fables. *Discourse Procedures* 17:105–29.

Dyer, M. G. 1983. *In-depth Understanding: A Computer Model of Integrated Processing for Narrative Comprehension*. Cambridge, MA: MIT Press.

Gersten, R., and Carnine, D. 1986. Direct instruction in reading comprehension. *Educational Leadership* 43:70–78.

Lehr, S. 1991. *The Child's Developing Sense of Theme*. New York: Teachers College.

Leung, C. C., and Williams, J. P. 1997. Aspects of Moral Theme Comprehension. In J. P. Williams, ed., *Interpretation of Theme in Narrative*. Final Report to U.S. Department of Education.

Lukens, R. 1988. A Critical Handbook of Children's Literature. Glenview, IL: Scott, Foresman.

New York City Board of Education. 1991. *Educational Services for Students with Handicapping Conditions*. Joseph A. Fernandez, Chancellor.

Oakhill, J., and Yuill, N. 1996. Higher order factors in comprehension disability: Processes and remediation. In C. Cornoldi and J. Oakhill, eds., *Reading Comprehension Difficulties: Processes and Intervention*. Hillsdale, NJ: Lawrence Erlbaum Associates.

Pearson, P. D., and Fielding, L. 1991. Comprehension instruction. In R. Barr, M. L. Kamil, P. Mosenthal, and P. D. Pearson, eds., *Handbook of Reading Research*, Vol. II. White Plains, NY: Longman.

Pressley, M., and McCormick, C. 1995. *Advanced Educational Psychology*. New York: Harcourt Brace.

Rogers, T. 1990. A point, counterpoint response strategy for complex short stories. *Journal of Reading* 34:278–82.

Seifert, C. M., Dyer, M. G., and Black, J. B. 1986. Thematic knowledge in story understanding. *Text* 6:393–425.

Simmons, D. C., Fuchs, L. S., Fuchs, D., Mathes, P. G., and Hodge, J. P. 1995. Effects of explicit teaching and peer tutoring on the reading achievement of learning-disabled and low-performing students in regular classrooms. *The Elementary School Journal* 95:387–408.

Singer, H., and Donlan, D. 1982. Active comprehension: Problem-solving schema with question generation for comprehension of complex short stories. *Reading Research Quarterly* 17:166–86.

Swanson, H. L., and McMahon, C. M. 1996. Synthesis of intervention research for students with learning disabilities. Preliminary Report, U.S. Department of Education Grant H023E40014.

Tompkins, J. P. (Ed.). 1980. *Reader-response Criticism*. Baltimore, MD: The Johns Hopkins University Press.

Wilder, A. A., and Williams, J. P. 1997. Promoting transfer in an instructional program in the comprehension of narrative themes. In J. P. Williams, ed., *Interpretation of Theme in Narrative*. Final report to U.S. Department of Education.

Williams, J. P. 1993. Comprehension of students with and without learning disabilities: Identification of narrative themes and idiosyncratic text representations. *Journal of Educational Psychology* 85:631–41.

Williams, J. P., Taylor, M. B., and deCani, J. S. 1984. Constructing macrostructure for expository text. *Journal of Educational Psychology* 76:1065–75.

Williams, J. P., Brown, L. G., Silverstein, A. K., and deCani, J. S. 1994. An instructional program for adolescents with learning disabilities in the comprehension of narrative themes. *Learning Disability Quarterly* 17:205–21.

Williams, J. P., Leung, C. C., Wilder, A. A., and deCani, J. S. 1997. Comprehension profiles of adolescents as a function of age and learning-disability status. In J. P. Williams, ed., *Interpretation of Theme in Narrative*. Final Report to U.S. Department of Education.

Wixson, K. K., and Lipson, M. Y. 1991. Perspectives on reading disability research. In R. Barr, M. L. Kamil, P. Mosenthal, and P. D. Pearson, eds., *Handbook of Reading Research*, Vol. II. White Plains, NY: Longman.

Wolman, C., van den Broek, P., and Lorch, R. F. 1997. Effects of causal structure on immediate and delayed story recall by children with mild mental retardation, children with learning disabilities, and children without disabilities. *Journal of Special Education* 30:439–55.

Wong, B. Y. L. 1984. Metacognition and learning disabilities. In T. Waller, D. Forrest, and E. MacKinnon, eds., *Metacognition, Cognition, and Human Performance*. New York: Academic Press.

# APPENDIX I

## References for Stories

Bealer, A. 1985. Sequoyah and the talking leaves. In Z. Sutherland, ed., Close to the Sun (pp. 160–64). LaSalle, IL: Open Court Publishing Company. Reprinted from A. Bealer. 1972. Sequoyah and the Talking Leaves. *Only the Names Remain*. Boston: Little, Brown and Company. (LESSON 5)

Bunting, E. 1985. A fish for Finn. In Z. Sutherland, ed., *Close to the Sun* (pp. 255–62). LaSalle, IL: Open Court Publishing Co. (PRETEST)

Clyne, P. E. 1985. Well done, Sybil Ludington. In Z. Sutherland, ed., *Close to the Sun* (pp. 107–12). LaSalle, IL: Open Court Publishing Company. Reprinted from P. E. Clyne. 1976. Well Done, Sybil Ludington. *Patriots in Petticoats*. New York: Dodd, Mead and Co. (LESSON 2)

Freedman, F. B. 1985. Two tickets to freedom. In Z. Sutherland, ed., *Close to the Sun* (pp. 113–21). LaSalle, IL: Open Court Publishing Co. Adapted by F.B. Freedman. 1971. *Two Tickets to Freedom*. New York: Simon and Schuster. (LESSON 11)

Grail, G. 1985. The second voyage of Sinbad. In Z. Sutherland, ed., *Close to the Sun* (pp. 429–32). LaSalle, IL: Open Court Publishing Co. (LESSON 8)

Hurwitz, L. 1989. Ali Baba Bernstein. In P. D. Pearson, D. D. Johnson, T. Clymer, et al., eds., *On the Horizon* (pp. 42–54). Needham, MA: Silver Burdett and Ginn. Reprinted from L. Hurwitz, *The Adventures of Ali Baba Bernstein*. (LESSON 9)

LeGrand, H. 1986. How baseball began in Brooklyn. In Z. Sutherland, ed., *Close to the Sun* (pp. 381–88). LaSalle, IL: Open Court Publishing Co. Reprinted from H. LeGrand. 1958. *How Baseball Began in Brooklyn*. New York: McIntosh and Otis. (LESSON 7)

Pinkwater, D. M. 1989. The big orange splot. In P. D. Pearson, D. D. Johnson, T. Clymer, et al., eds., *On the Horizon* (pp. 14–19). Needham, MA: Silver Burdett and Ginn. (LESSON 4)

Rosenbaum, J. 1989. King Midas and the gold touch. In P. D. Pearson, D. D. Johnson, T. Clymer, et al., eds., *On the Horizon* (pp. 130–36). Needham, MA: Silver, Burdett and Ginn. (LESSON 1)

Semyonov, S. T. 1979. The servant. In C. G. Spiegler and R. B. Goodman, eds., *A Matter of Judgment* (pp. 80–85). New York: Globe Book Co. Reprinted from Seltzer (ed.), *Best Russian Short Stories*. New York: Random House. (POSTTEST)

Wagner, E. 1970. The night a sitter stood tall. In W. J. Halliburton, D. Minor, and M. E. Pelkonia, eds., *New Worlds of Literature* (pp. 92–94). New York: Harcourt, Brace and World, Inc. (LESSON 10)

Waters, J. 1985. Kate Shelley and the Midnight Limited. In Z. Sutherland, ed., *Close to the Sun* (pp. 396–401). LaSalle, IL: Open Court Publishing Co. Reprinted from J. Waters. 1978. Kate Shelley and the Midnight Limited. *Cricket Magazine*. (LESSON 3)

Webb, B. O. 1978. Jump for center. In I. E. Aaron, G. W. Gray, A. Johns et al., eds., *Batter Up!* (pp. 224–28). Glenview, IL: Scott, Foresman and Co. Reprinted from B. O. Webb. 1976. *Jump for Center. Instructor*. (LESSON 12)

Wiesner, W. 1985. The tower of Babel. In Z. Sutherland, ed., *Close to the Sun* (pp. 170–73). LaSalle, IL: Open Court Publishing Co. Reprinted from W. Wiesner. 1968. *The Tower of Babel*. New York: Viking, Penguin, Inc. (LESSON 6)

# APPENDIX II

### A Lesson Outline

I. Lesson Purpose and Prereading Discussion

II. Reading the Story: "Kate Shelley and the Midnight Limited"

*Summary of the Story*:

One night in 1991, a young girl named Kate Shelly saw a railroad bridge collapse during a heavy storm. She knew that a passenger train, The Midnight Limited, was scheduled to cross the bridge, and that if she did not get to the station with a warning, everyone aboard the train would be killed. Kate ran over a mile through the darkness. Despite extremely dangerous conditions, she pushed on until she reached the station in time to save the train.

*Interposed Questions*:

"What do you think will happen next?"

"Do you think Kate was brave? Why?"

III. Organizing Questions (and acceptable answers)

Who is the main character? (Kate Shelly)

What did she do? (She ran more than a mile in dangerous conditions during a terrible storm to give a warning about a collapsed railroad bridge; she persevered.)

What happened? (She reached the station in time to save the lives of the people on the train.)

Was this good or bad? (Good.)

Why was it good? (It was good that Kate persevered because she was able to save people's lives.)

IV. Statement of the Theme in Standard Format

Kate should have persevered.

We should persevere.

V.   Generalization to Real-Life Experiences

*Specific Questions*:

How might this theme apply to parents?
Could it apply to your parents when they get a hard job to do at work?

# APPENDIX III

| Examples of Responses and Their Scores (Preliminary Study) |

*Concept of Theme:*
"What is a theme?"                                                    Score

| | |
|---|---|
| What it's really about—sometimes it's like a lesson | 3 |
| Something that tells you about the story. | 2 |
| It's like a part of the story—the main part of the story. | 1 |
| Main character—is it good or bad, and how is it good or bad. | 0 |

*Posttest Perseverance Story*:

Iris was 14 years old. She had a beautiful voice and she loved to sing and write music. She wanted more than anything else to go to a special high school for talented teenagers where she could learn to be a professional singer and songwriter.

Iris knew that she needed to study with an excellent piano teacher if she wanted to pass the special high school audition, but her mother could not afford it. So Iris earned money after school walking her neighbor's dogs. On Saturdays she worked, too, babysitting and doing odd jobs. It was tiring, but she made enough money to pay for her piano lessons. She practiced piano two hours every day. Good grades are required in the special high school, so Iris stayed up late to study and do her homework.

Last week, Iris had her audition at the special high school. Yesterday, the director notified her that she had been accepted.

*Concept of Perseverance:*
"What does perseverance mean?"                                      Score

| | |
|---|---|
| To keep on going—keep trying—no matter what. | 2 |
| Try your best. | 1 |
| It means to check everything out—see what's going on. | 0 |

*Theme Identification: "What is a theme or a lesson of this story?"*

**Acceptable**

Even if people say "no way," or "can't," there's still a possibility if you work hard and use your brain.

That you should never give up. You should work hard; do your best; and work up to your potential.

**Unacceptable**

The girl was talented, and she went to a school that she could do.

She wanted to go to a nice college or high school to learn how to be a better singer and song writer.

*Theme Application: "Can you give me an example of when it is important to persevere in life?"*

**Acceptable**

There's a family. One of the people gets sick. The father has to go all across the city to get medicine for the child. It took days, but he made it and sent the medicine back. And they lived happily ever after.

You're a rescue worker, and there's three hundred pounds of rocks buried on a bunch of people. You really have to persevere because the quicker you get them out, the better chance they have.

**Unacceptable**

When your parents can't afford something, and you really need it.

My family is important.

*Posttest Novel Story*

**Synopsis:**

A young man named Gerasim had left his job and could not find a new one. He was cold and hungry. He desperately wanted a job. He met an old friend who offered him a job and a place to stay. Gerasim was overjoyed, and accepted the job gratefully. When he went the next day to work for his new master, he discovered that he was replacing two elderly workers who were being thrown out on the street because Gerasim was taking their job. Gerasim decided to refuse the job, and felt much the better for it.

**Comprehension Questions** (and acceptable answers);

1. Why was Gerasim out of work? (He quit his old job.)
2. In addition to a job, what did the master offer Gerasim? (a room)

3. Who was Gerasim going to replace? (two older servants)
4. How did Gerasim find out about the old people's problem? (He snuck underneath their window and listened to their conversation.)
5. What was the master going to do with the old people when he hired Gerasim? (fire them)
6. What did Gerasim think about when he found the old people crying? (his parents)

**Story Component Questions** (and acceptable answers):
1. Who was the main character of the story? (Gerasim)
2. What did he do? (He was trying to find a job with the help of a friend.)
3. What happened? (He refused a job he was offered, because if he took it, two elderly people would be out of work.)

*Theme Identification:* "*If you were going to use the story you just heard to teach a lesson to someone, what would it be?*"

**Acceptable**
You should care for others.
If someone offers you something, and you think it's wrong to take it—if it's going to hurt someone else's feelings—do the right thing.

**Unacceptable**
Try to look for a job on your own. You'd be better off doing things for yourself than by people doing things for you.
Never to leave your own job. It's better to leave the job to old people.

*Theme Application:* "*Can you give me an example of a time that this lesson came up, or could come up in real life?*"

**Acceptable**
You could be rich, and you wanted to buy a house, and a couple of people who are poor are living there; and they can't pay their taxes. You don't have to take it (the house).
A person that's very good at sports, but there's another person that's not as good as him, and the other person needs to be on a team more (cause the person that's better is on a team already), so the person that's on a team already lets the other person get on the team.

**Unacceptable**

> If there was a real king, and the servant thought he
> might hurt the old people, then he might think it
> over and not go back.
> Someone that's not exactly a steady worker—it's prob-
> ably not going to come up anyways—he shouldn't
> take a job with someone he hasn't met, cause that
> person might make a rule that he doesn't like.

---

| Examples of Responses and Their Scores (Main Study) | |
|---|---|
| *Concept of Theme: "What is a theme?"* | Score |
| You learn something from it. | 3 |
| It tells about the story. | 2 |
| Something from the story. | 1 |
| Don't know. | 0 |

### The Perseverance Story

*Concept of Perseverance: "What does 'perseverance' mean?"*

| | |
|---|---|
| To never stop; keep on giving your best. | 2 |
| To try hard. | 1 |
| Don't know. | 0 |

*Theme Identification: "What is a theme or a lesson of this story?"*

**Acceptable**

> Persevere; I like that word.
> Keep on trying.

**Unacceptable**

> When you're 14 years old—she wanted to be a singer.
> Her mother said she couldn't.
> She didn't have money. She tried to get money, walk-
> ing dogs and babysitting.

*Theme Application: "Can you give me an example of when it is im-
portant to persevere in life?"*

**Acceptable**

> There's a kid in my class. He was failing. Now he's
> going up in his grades. He's been studying hard.
> Like if you're not good in math, you should try to
> pass it, even if you think you're not good.

**Unacceptable**

> When somebody's robbing someone else's things—
> breaking into things—to let them know not to steal,
> you can call the police.

If the old guy sees the young guy who's working and wants to change, the old guy will quit.

### Posttest Novel Story

*Comprehension Questions*: See Preliminary Study.

*Story Component Questions*: See Preliminary Study.

*Theme Identification*: "If you were going to use the story you just heard to teach a lesson to someone, what would that lesson be?"

### Acceptable

Like don't take advantage or hurt someone for gain.

Do unto others as you would have them do unto you.

### Unacceptable

To try to help people.

To try to find your own job; don't grub off everyone else.

*Theme Application: "Can you give me an example of a time that this lesson came up, or could come up in real life?"*

### Acceptable

A little girl who wanted to play jump rope with older girls. They didn't want her to play—too young. One of the other girls said, "I won't play if you don't let her play."

Two boys working—needed the job—caddy mates. They're no good. They want to keep it. I just come in and take their place. I wouldn't do that. They just started. They need to learn more, even though I needed the job.

### Unacceptable

This kid wanted a job. His friend, he was working at a store. He asked the boss to give him a job doing what he's doing.

If older lady needs help crossing the street—you could help.

# Benefits of Multisensory Structured Language Instruction for At-Risk Foreign Language Learners: A Comparison Study of High School Spanish Students

*Richard L. Sparks*

College of Mount St. Joseph

*Marjorie Artzer*

Northern Kentucky University

*Jon Patton and Leonore Ganschow*

Miami University

*Karen Miller*

St. Paul's School for Girls

*Dorothy J. Hordubay*

Oldfields School

*Geri Walsh*

St. Ursula Academy

*In this study, the benefits of multisensory structured language (MSL) instruction in Spanish were examined. Participants were students in high-school-level Spanish attending girls' preparatory schools. Of the 55 participants, 39 qualified as at-risk for foreign language learning*

Annals of Dyslexia, Vol. 48, 1998

*difficulties and 16 were deemed not-at-risk. The at-risk students were assigned to one of three conditions: (1) MSL—multisensory Spanish instruction in self-contained classrooms (n = 14); (2) SC—traditional Spanish instruction provided in self-contained classrooms (n = 11); and (3) NSC—traditional Spanish instruction in regular (not self-contained) Spanish classes (n = 14). Not-at-risk students (n = 16) received traditional Spanish instruction in regular classes similar to the instruction provided to the NSC group.*

*All three at-risk groups made significant gains over time on some native language skills regardless of teaching method. The MSL group also made significant gains on a foreign language aptitude measure. The MSL group and the not-at-risk group made greater gains than the two other at-risk groups on foreign language aptitude and native language measures of reading comprehension, word recognition, and pseudoword reading.*

*Although most at-risk learners achieved an "expected" level of foreign language proficiency after two years of instruction, significant group differences were found. On measures of oral and written foreign language proficiency, the MSL and not-at-risk groups scored significantly higher than the at-risk groups instructed using traditional methods. After two years of Spanish instruction, no differences in foreign language proficiency were found between the MSL group and the not-at-risk group.*

There is extensive evidence that students who have difficulty learning a foreign language are likely to have weaker native language skills than students who have few or no difficulties learning a foreign language in traditional classroom settings. Anecdotal evidence in the foreign language and learning disabilities (LD) literature suggests that students classified as LD or as at-risk for foreign language learning problems require instructional accommodations or modified teaching techniques to pass foreign language courses (e.g., Barr 1993; Mabbott 1994; Ganschow and Sparks 1986). Some students classified as LD receive course substitutions/waivers for the college foreign language requirement (e.g., Freed 1987; Ganschow, Myer, and Roeger 1989). There is an ongoing debate about whether students classified as LD should receive course substitutions for, or waivers from, the foreign language requirement (Moore 1995; Sparks and Javorsky in press; Sparks, Philips, and Ganschow 1996).

Sparks, Ganschow, and their colleagues have hypothesized that students have difficulty with foreign language learning because of the same overt or subtle difficulties encountered with their native language (Sparks and Ganschow 1991; Sparks,

Ganschow, and Pohlman 1989). Specifically, they and other researchers have found that students with foreign language learning problems have weaker phonological/orthographic skills than students without foreign language learning problems (Ganschow, Sparks, Javorsky, Pohlman, and Bishop-Marbury 1991; Service 1992; Sparks, Ganschow, Javorsky, Pohlman, and Patton 1992a, 1992b). Sparks, Ganschow, and colleagues have conducted considerable research on what they term the Linguistic Coding Differences Hypothesis (LCDH), a theoretical position they derived from research by Vellutino and Scanlon (1986) on native language reading (Sparks 1995; Sparks and Ganschow 1991, 1993a, 1993b, 1995a). The LCDH posits that native language skills—phonological/orthographic (sound and sound-symbol), syntactic (grammar), and semantic (meaning)—serve as the foundation for successful foreign language learning. The LCDH further posits that both foreign language and native language learning depend on basic language skill and that problems with one language component (for example, phonological/orthographic processing) will have a negative effect on other components (for example, vocabulary or syntax) of both native language and foreign language acquisition.

Considerable empirical evidence has been generated in support of the LCDH. Studies demonstrate that at-risk foreign language learners have significantly poorer phonological/ortho-graphic and syntactic native language skills (as measured by standardized tests of decoding, phonemic awareness, and grammar) and significantly poorer foreign language aptitude, as measured by the Modern Language Aptitude Test (MLAT) (Carroll and Sapon 1959). Carroll describes foreign language aptitude as "a fairly specialized talent (or group of talents), relatively independent of those traits ordinarily included under intelligence." (1962, p.89) To assess foreign language aptitude, the MLAT is a simulated learning task which measures the phonetic, grammatical, semantic, and rote memory aspects of language learning. It has been employed in numerous studies (Ganschow and Sparks, 1995, 1996; Ganschow, et al. 1991; Ganschow, Sparks, Anderson, Javorsky, and Skinner 1994; Sparks and Ganschow 1993c, 1995b, 1996; Sparks, Ganschow, Artzer, and Patton 1997; Sparks, et al. 1992a, 1992b; Sparks, Ganschow, Pohlman, Skinner, and Artzer 1992; Sparks, Ganschow, Artzer, Siebenhar, and Plagemen 1997, 1998; and Sparks, Ganschow, and Pohlman 1989). In general, these studies suggest that students with foreign language learning difficulties are comparable to not-at-risk learners in the semantic aspects of language, and achieve comparable IQ scores.

Sparks, Ganschow, and their colleagues have suggested that approaches to foreign language education that provide direct instruction in the phonological/orthographic and grammatical systems of that language would be beneficial to students with weaknesses in native language learning. An MSL approach to teaching a foreign language emphasizes the direct and explicit teaching of the phonology/orthography (spelling-sound relations), grammar (syntax), and morphology (meaning units) systems of a foreign language. This approach also encourages the simultaneous use of students' visual, auditory, and kinesthetic (motor) skills. Lessons are taught in both English and Spanish. At a secondary level of education, motor skills are engaged by means of writing on paper or the blackboard, and by pronouncing sounds and syllables.

In an MSL approach, the teacher initially introduces letters (graphemes) that represent sounds (phonemes) of a new language and combines the phonemes to form words. As students learn the phonemes and graphemes of the new language, they participate in daily review lessons of previously introduced sounds and letters. Grammatical rules are presented one at a time in structured exercises. To aid morphological awareness, students are taught how to build words (prefixes, suffixes, roots). Lessons are carefully sequenced from those with simple to increasingly more complex rule systems. Generally, a daily lesson plan using an MSL approach includes: (1) blackboard (or otherwise written) drills of phonology/orthography and grammar; (2) oral-sound drills of new and previously taught phonemes; (3) teaching of grammatical concepts; (4) teaching of vocabulary; and (5) reading/communicative activities in the foreign language using the previously learned concepts. The teacher coordinates the MSL approach with a regular Spanish-language curriculum. (See Sparks, et al. 1991 for a comprehensive description of the MSL approach to teaching a foreign language.)

The same MSL approaches used in teaching students with weaknesses in native language learning may benefit students who have problems with learning a foreign language. Descriptive and empirical studies on the efficacy of using MSL approaches have been reported for several languages, including Spanish (Ganschow and Sparks 1995; Sparks, Ganschow, Pohlman, et al. 1992, Sparks and Ganschow 1993c; Sparks, Ganschow, Artzer, and Patton 1997), Latin (Sparks, Ganschow, Fluharty, and Little 1996), German (Ganschow, Sparks, and

Schneider 1995; Schneider in press), and French (Gordon 1994). Studies using an MSL approach also have been reported for at-risk foreign language learners who are learning English as a second language (Roffman and Teitelbaum 1993, 1996).

In our first MSL study with Spanish (Sparks et al. 1992c) we examined the pre- and posttest scores on native language and foreign language aptitude measures for three groups of at-risk high school students enrolled in special, self-contained sections of first-year Spanish. Two groups were instructed using an MSL approach, and the third group was instructed using traditional foreign language teaching methods. One of the MSL groups was taught Spanish using both Spanish and English; the other was taught using only Spanish. After one year, the Spanish/English group had made significant gains on the foreign language aptitude test as well as on general measures of native language phonology/orthography (spelling, phonemic awareness, word recognition, and pseudoword reading), receptive vocabulary, and verbal memory. The MSL group taught only in Spanish made significant gains over one year on the MLAT, but not on native language measures. The at-risk group taught using traditional foreign language methodologies made no significant gains over the year on any of the native language measures or the foreign language aptitude test. The authors speculated that what the MSL program offered—structured, direct teaching of the phonological/orthographic and syntactic aspects of the foreign language—was lacking in traditional teaching methods.

In a replication and follow-up study (Sparks and Ganschow 1993c), we followed, for a second year of Spanish instruction, those students from the Sparks et al. (1992c) study who had received MSL instruction in both Spanish and English. This group maintained its initial gains on all native language measures and the foreign language aptitude test. In the same study, we also compared pre- and posttest scores of a second cohort of first year, at-risk foreign language learners receiving MSL instruction in both Spanish and English. That group also made significant gains on native language phonological/orthographic measures (phonemic awareness and pseudoword reading) and the MLAT.

In a third study (Ganschow and Sparks 1995), we compared the foreign language aptitude and native language skills of high school Spanish students classified as at-risk and not-at-risk for foreign language learning difficulties. The at-risk group received MSL instruction in Spanish; the not-at-risk group received traditional foreign language instruction. On the foreign language aptitude test, both groups improved significantly after one year of instruction, but the MLAT scores of the at-risk group still lagged significantly behind those of the not-at-risk group. Only the at-risk group made significant gains over the year on native language measures of phonology/orthography, including word recognition, pseudoword reading, phonemic awareness, and spelling.

In a pilot study, Sparks, Ganschow, Artzer, and Patton (1997) examined the foreign language *proficiency*—the ability to read, write, speak, and listen to a foreign language—of a small sub-group of the at-risk and not-at-risk foreign language learners after a second year of foreign language instruction. Although the at-risk group made significant gains on three native language phonological/orthographic measures (phonemic awareness, word recognition, and pseudoword reading) and the MLAT, they had not "caught up" with the not-at-risk group. Moreover, informal results of the foreign language proficiency measures favored the not-at-risk group. On "speaking/listening" to a foreign language, six of the eight not-at-risk, but only three of seven at-risk learners, met or exceeded their range of expected performance. In "writing" a foreign language, all of the not-at-risk and five of the seven at-risk foreign language learners met or exceeded their level of expected performance.

The present study differs from the four aforementioned studies in several respects. First, none of the participants was included in any previously published studies. Second, the present study compares three different at-risk groups on native language, foreign language aptitude, and foreign language proficiency measures; previous studies did not compare multiple at-risk groups. Third, the at-risk groups varied in the type of foreign language classroom (self-contained versus not self-contained) and in the type of foreign language instruction (for example, MSL versus traditional with instructional accommodations). Previous studies did not compare MSL directly with traditional instruction. Fourth, the present study includes a not-at-risk group whose performance on all native language, foreign language aptitude, and foreign language proficiency measures can be compared to the three at-risk groups. Previous studies compared the not-at-risk group only to at-risk students receiving MSL instruction. Fifth, the present study measured the four groups' oral and written proficiency in a foreign language using proficiency guidelines from the American Council on the Teaching of Foreign Languages (ACTFL). This is the first study to quantify differences in foreign language proficiency of at-risk and not-at-risk foreign language learners and to compare the effects of different instructional methodologies on proficiency.

## PURPOSES OF STUDY

Our study has two purposes. The first is to compare the effects of MSL instruction in Spanish with the effects of traditional, textbook-based (non-MSL) instruction on the native language skills and foreign language aptitude of at-risk and not-at-risk foreign language learners. The second is to compare MSL and traditional, textbook-based instruction on the oral and written foreign language proficiency of at-risk and not-at-risk foreign language learners.

## METHOD

### PARTICIPANTS

The participants were 55 high school females attending private, selective, single-sex college preparatory high schools. All participants had completed two years of high school Spanish. The three groups of students classified as at-risk for foreign language learning difficulties came from three different high schools. Students were classified as at-risk using the same criteria as our previous studies. Such students had (1) failed or exhibited inordinate struggle in a previous foreign language course, (2) been recommended for a separate section of a foreign language course based on a history of native language learning problems, or (3) been previously classified as learning disabled. To be classified as at-risk, students had to meet at least one of the three criteria. The participants also included a group of not-at-risk students who had completed two years of high school Spanish.

The three at-risk groups included:

*MSL Group.* The 14 students in the MSL group received multisensory instruction in a special, self-contained section of Spanish. Each had met at least one of the at-risk criteria stipulated above. Six of the MSL participants had been classified as learning disabled (LD) by the private school, a local school district, or a private diagnostician. All students began Spanish instruction as ninth graders with a mean age of 14 years, 7 months (range: 13 years, 9 months to 15 years, 8 months). The MSL group had received instruction in Spanish using an MSL approach in the special class for two years. Class size was approximately 12–15 students. Some students in the MSL class did not participate in the study because, although all class members were considered by school officials to be at some risk for foreign language learning difficulty, not all met one of the three specific study criteria. The Spanish teacher for the MSL group in the present study had participated as the MSL instructor in our previous studies (Ganschow and Sparks 1995; Sparks and Ganschow 1993c; Sparks, Ganschow, Pohlman, et al. 1992; Sparks, Ganschow, Artzer, and Patton 1997).

*SC Group.* The 11 students in the SC group also were enrolled in a special, self-contained section of Spanish, but received traditional, textbook-based instruction. All members of the SC group had met the same criteria as those students in the MSL group. Six students had been previously identified and classified as LD by a local school district or a private diagnostician. All students began Spanish instruction as ninth graders with a mean age of 14 years, 8 months (range: 14 years, 2 months to 15 years, 1 month). The SC group received classroom instruction in Spanish for two years, using traditional, textbook-based foreign language teaching methodologies. Class size was approximately 8–10 students. Again, not all students in the special self-contained class were eligible to participate in the study.[1]

*NSC Group.* The 14 students in the NSC group were enrolled in regular classes of Spanish (with not-at-risk students) and received instructional accommodations in Spanish from the school's LD program. Accommoda-tions included allowances for extended time, reading and taping of tests and quizzes, assistance with spelling and homework, and availability of a Spanish wordbank for vocabulary tests. All NSC students participating in the study had been classified previously as LD by their local school district or a private diagnostician. Twelve students began the study (and Spanish instruction) as tenth graders and two students began as ninth graders; mean age at this time was 15 years, 5 months (range: 14 years, 6 months to 16 years, 0 months). The NSC group received classroom instruction in Spanish for two years using traditional, textbook-based foreign language teaching methodologies. The size of the regular foreign language classes in which the NSC students were enrolled was approximately 20 students.

*NAR Group.* The 16 students in the NAR group were enrolled in regular sections of Spanish. Potential NAR participants

[1] Special thanks are extended to Chuck Jewitt who provided invaluable assistance with the SC group in the completion of the study.

were chosen on a random basis from class lists of students enrolled in first-year Spanish courses. The first 16 students to return signed permission slips from their parents were included in the study. None of the NAR students had a history of native language or foreign language learning problems and none had been classified as LD. Thirteen students began the study (and Spanish instruction) as ninth graders and three students began as tenth graders, with a mean age of 14 years, 8 months (range: 14 years, 1 month to 15 years, 8 months). The NAR group received classroom instruction in Spanish using traditional, textbook-based foreign language teaching methodologies for two years. Class sizes were approximately 20 students.

All participants were assessed on cognitive ability using the Woodcock-Johnson Psychoeducational Battery: Brief Cognitive Ability Cluster during the first phase of testing (Pretest) at the beginning of their first year of foreign language study. The mean scores and standard deviations (*SD*) of the four groups on the IQ measure were:

MSL: $M = 100.0$, $SD = 7.6$;
SC:   $M = 94.8$, $SD = 6.7$;
NSC: $M = 101.6$, $SD = 5.9$; and
NAR: $M = 110.0$, $SD = 5.2$.

Results of an ANOVA showed significant differences on the cognitive ability measure among the four groups, $F(3,51) = 13.69$; $p = .0001$. Between-group analyses using a Scheffe' correction showed significantly higher cognitive ability in the NAR group than in the three at-risk groups. No differences on the cognitive ability measure were found among the three at-risk groups.

## INSTRUMENTS

The native language battery and foreign language aptitude test were chosen to maintain consistency with the instruments used in our previous studies involving students receiving MSL instruction (Ganschow and Sparks 1995; Sparks and Ganschow 1993c; Sparks, Ganschow, Pohlman, et al. 1992; Sparks, Ganschow, Fluharty, et al. 1996; Sparks, Ganschow, Artzer, and Patton 1997). Foreign language proficiency measures were developed for this study.

*Native Language*.   To assess phonological/orthographic skill, we included measures of spelling, phonemic awareness, word recognition, and pseudoword reading. To assess comprehension, we included a measure of reading comprehension and of receptive vocabulary. To assess verbal memory, we relied on the Woodcock-Johnson Psychoeducational Battery: Memory Cluster.

*Foreign Language Aptitude.* The foreign language aptitude measure used in this study was the Modern Language Aptitude Test: Long Form (MLAT). This test measures foreign language aptitude by the administration of subtests found to predict subsequent foreign language learning skill through phonetic coding, grammatical sensitivity, inductive language learning ability, and rote memory (Carroll 1962). These subtests are described in figure 1.

*Foreign Language Proficiency.* The proficiency measures used in this study were developed by the second author—a professor of Spanish who has extensive experience working with high school students and beginning and intermediate university students, and who was trained to administer proficiency tests in Spanish.[2] Proficiency is defined as "what an individual can and cannot do [with a foreign language], regardless of where, when, or how the language has been learned or acquired" (ACTFL Proficiency Guidelines 1989). In

| INSTRUMENT | DESCRIPTION |
| --- | --- |
| **NATIVE LANGUAGE** | |
| *Lindamood Auditory Concept-ualization Test* (LAC), Forms A and B (Lindamood and Lindamood 1979). | Manipulate wooden blocks to show number and order of phonemes in syllables. |
| *Nelson-Denny Reading Test,* Forms E and F (NELSON) (Brown, Bennett, and Hanna 1981). | Silently read eight paragraphs and answer multiple-choice, comprehension questions. Timed. |
| *Peabody Picture Vocabulary Test-Revised* (PPVT-R), Forms L and M (Dunn and Dunn 1981). | Select which of four pictures best depicts word spoken by tester. |
| *Wide Range Achievement Test-Revised* (WRAT SPELL) Spelling subtest (Jastak and Wilkinson 1984). | Write single words to dictation. |
| *Woodcock Reading Mastery Test-Revised* (WRMT), Forms G and H | Basic Skills Cluster combining Word Identification, and Word Attack scores. |
| *WJ Psychoeducational Battery* (WJ MEM) (Woodcock and Johnson 1978). | Memory Cluster combining Memory for Sentences presented aloud, and Numbers Reversed (a backwards digit span). |

*continued. . .*

[2] David Siebenhar, Ph.D. and Mark Plageman, Ph.D. worked with the second author in the development of the proficiency measures.

## FOREIGN LANGUAGE APTITUDE SUBTESTS

**Modern Language Aptitude**
**Test (MLAT) Long Form**
**(Carroll and Sapon 1959)**

| INSTRUMENT | DESCRIPTION |
|---|---|
| Number Learning: | Learn numbers of a made-up language, then transcribe spoken numbers into written digits. Timed. |
| Phonetic Script: | Listen to sequence of syllables while looking at their graphemic transcriptions. Must learn how the sounds correspond to the letters. |
| Spelling Clues: | Read English words presented as abbreviated spellings and choose the one word out of five that corresponds most closely in meaning. |
| Words in Sentences: | Read a "key" sentence in which a word is underlined, and then choose which word or phrase in a second sentence has the same grammatical function as the originally marked word or phrase. |
| Paired Associates: | Learn to pair nonsense words to their assigned English meanings. |

*Figure 1     Test instruments.*

the late 1970s, experts in foreign language education realized the need for a common measure of language ability. In order to meet this need, the ACTFL Provisional Proficiency Guidelines were published in 1983 and revised in 1986 and 1989. These guidelines contain generic and language-specific descriptors in the areas of speaking, listening, reading, and writing. It is important to note that the proficiency guidelines are not achievement tests, nor are they tests with standardized norms. The rating that individuals receive in each skill area is based on their ability to perform various language functions (tasks) regarding topics appropriate to a given level with a specified degree of accuracy. The rating scales of the ACTFL Proficiency Guidelines are widely used and are generally accepted by foreign language professionals as the best method currently available to measure an individual's performance level in a foreign language.

All of the proficiency tests in this study were designed and scored according to ACTFL Guidelines. The proficiency tests were designed to measure the four skills of listening, speaking, reading, and writing in a foreign language and were based on the tasks at the novice and intermediate levels of the ACTFL Proficiency Guidelines (1989). We estimated that a second-year high-school student with a strong aptitude for language learning would not be able to perform beyond the intermediate/high level.

Two measures were used to assess a student's proficiency in reading a foreign language. The first was a fictitious letter written in Spanish from Claudia Rivera, a high school student in Argentina, to a family in the United States. Claudia was planning to spend a year as an exchange student with the family to whom she was writing. The letter contained information about her, her family in Argentina, and a series of five questions that she wished to have answered prior to her arrival in the United States. The student was given 15 minutes to read the letter and answer ten multiple-choice questions in English about the contents of the letter. The second measure of reading proficiency was a slightly more difficult passage. The student was given 15 minutes to read a brief article from *Selecciones* (*Readers Digest* in Spanish) entitled "Los Palos de Punta" and answer ten multiple-choice questions in English about the passage. The student could achieve a combined maximum score of 20 on this reading comprehension measure (FL READ COMP).

To assess writing in a foreign language, the student was given 15 minutes to write a response to Claudia's letter, incorporating the answers to her five questions. ACTFL Guidelines were used in assigning a holistic proficiency level (one score based on all the criterion statements in a specific level of the ACTFL Guidelines) on the writing test. After the holistic score was determined, the student's performance was further defined by assigning a score of 0–5 for each of the following writing skills: vocabulary, cultural appropriateness, structures, comprehensibility, and spelling (0 = no production, 1 = Novice/Low, 2 = Novice/Mid, 3 = Novice/High, 4 = Intermediate/Low, 5 = Intermediate/High). A score of 0 was included in the scoring because some students at this level of education may have been unable to produce any response in Spanish. A student could achieve a maximum score of 25 on the writing measure (FL WRITING).

To measure the student's ability to listen to and speak a foreign language, a 10–15 minute oral interview was conducted individually with each student, incorporating the four phases prescribed in the ACTFL Guidelines: warm-up, level-check, probes, and wind-up (Omaggio 1986). The entire interview was audiotaped for later scoring. Prior to the beginning of the oral interview, the tester explained to the student in English that, after she had had an opportunity to chat for a few moments in Spanish, she would be given a conversation card in English to help her begin the conversation (Spinelli 1988). The interview proceeded as a friendly conversation in Spanish about topics which naturally emerged as the interviewer guided the conversation through the phases listed above. The ACTFL Proficiency Guidelines for determining proficiency levels were used in assigning a holistic score on the oral interview. The student's performance was further defined by assigning a score of 0–5 on each of the following skills: pronunciation, vocabulary, grammar, comprehensibility, and listening comprehension. The scoring procedure for the listening/speaking test was the same as for the foreign language writing test. The student could achieve a maximum score of 25 on the listening/speaking measure (FL LISTEN/SPEAK).

The student's total test score (FL TOTAL) was the combination of scores on the reading comprehension, writing, and listening/speaking tests. The student could achieve a maximum score of 70 on FL TOTAL.

The reliability of the three proficiency subtests (FL READ COMP, FL WRITING, and FL LISTEN/SPEAK) and the total proficiency test (FL TOTAL) were checked by a Cronbach's Alpha calculation. For FL READ COMP, the Cronbach's Alpha was .73; for FL WRITING, .76; for FL LISTEN/SPEAK, .97; and for FL TOTAL, .87.

To assess word recognition, students also were asked to read a list of 20 words in Spanish, some of which they had never seen before. This served to assess directly phonological/orthographic skills in Spanish, and indirectly, pronunciation ability. Each word was chosen because it contained a letter or letter combination with a phonetic sound (for example, the /a/ sound in the Spanish word *casa* is different from the /a/ sound in the English word *cat*) or a phonetic element that is different in Spanish than in English (for example, in the Spanish word *teléfono*, the diacritical mark changes the syllable that is stressed). The vowel sounds in Spanish, diphthongs, words with diacritical marks, and multisyllabic words were included within the target words.

## PROCEDURE

All participants were pretested with the native language and foreign language aptitude measures during their first month of first-year Spanish (Pretest). They were posttested during the last month of first-year Spanish (Posttest 1), and again in the last month of second-year Spanish (Posttest 2). All 55 participants completed the Pretest, Posttest 1, and Posttest 2 testing. Native language tests were administered individually to students over a one-hour time period. The foreign language aptitude test, the MLAT, took one hour to complete; it was administered to the total MSL group at one time, and in small groups of five to six students to the SC, NSC, and NAR groups. Tests were administered by the first three authors of this study as well as by special education majors trained by the authors prior to the study.[3]

The oral and written foreign language proficiency measures were administered by the second author to students during the last four weeks of second-year Spanish (Posttest 2). The foreign language reading and writing tests were administered in one session and lasted 40 minutes. The reading and writing tests were administered to the NSC and NAR groups in small groups of five to six students, and to the total MSL and SC groups at one time. The foreign language listening/speaking test, an oral interview that lasted 10 to 15 minutes, and the foreign language word recognition test, which lasted 5 minutes, were administered individually.

## ANALYSIS OF DATA

Because there were significant differences on the cognitive ability (IQ) measure among the four groups, we relied on a multivariate repeated measures ANCOVA with IQ as the covariate to determine whether there were overall main effects of time and group on each of the native language and foreign language aptitude measures. Where significant main effects were found, post hoc analyses were conducted, using paired $t$-tests to analyze differences between Pretest and Posttest 1, Posttest 1 and Posttest 2, and Pretest and Posttest 2.

To assess overall group differences on the three foreign language proficiency measures, we conducted a separate Multiple Analysis of Covariance (MANCOVA) with IQ as covariate. In the event that the MANCOVA was significant, follow-up ANCOVAs were used to determine where the differences occurred. A separate ANCOVA procedure with IQ as covariate also was used to determine if there were significant differences

---

[3] The authors wish to thank Loreli Albus, Carolyn Fehr, Vicki Gunn, Shannon Ritter, Janie Roots, and Andrea Saurber for their time and effort in administering the tests.

on the foreign language WORD REC test. A level of .05 was used as the criterion for significance in all of the analyses.

# RESULTS

Table I presents Pretest, Posttest 1, and Posttest 2 means and standard deviations of the four groups on the native language and foreign language aptitude measures, as well as a summary of gain comparisons within groups.

## DID OVERALL GAINS VARY AS A FUNCTION OF GROUP?

The MANCOVA with IQ as a covariate showed no main effects of group, Wilks' Lambda = .551, $F(18,128) = 1.67$; $p = .054$, or time, Wilks' Lambda = .779, $F(12,39) = .923$; $p = .53$, in the amount of gains made on the six native language testing measures. However, there was a significant time and group interaction effect, Wilks' Lambda = .259, $F(36,116) = 1.86$; $p = .007$. Follow-up ANCOVAs indicated significant interactions between time and group on the reading comprehension measure, NELSON, Wilks' Lambda = 7.48, $F(6,98) = 2.55$; $p = .03$; and on the word reading test, WRMT Wilks' Lambda = 7.49, $F(6,98) = 2.53$; $p = .03$. On the NELSON, results favored the MSL group over the SC and NSC groups, and the NAR group over the NSC group. On the WRMT, results favored the MSL group over the NAR group, and the NAR group over the NSC group. On none of the aforementioned measures was there a significant difference between the SC and NSC at-risk groups.

Figure 2 shows that there were also significant time and group interaction effects on the MLAT, Wilks' Lambda = .630, $F(6,98) = 4.25$, $p = .0008$. Results favored the MSL group over the SC and NSC groups, and the NAR group over the SC and NSC groups. There also were significant time and group interaction effects on one MLAT subtest, Phonetic Script, Wilks Lambda = .749, $F(6,98) = 2.54$; $p = .03$. Both the MSL and NAR groups improved more than the SC and NSC groups, with no significant differences between the MSL and NAR groups or between the SC and NSC groups.

## DID GROUPS MAKE DIFFERENTIAL GAINS AS A FUNCTION OF TIME OF TEST?

Follow-up tests indicated that the MSL group made significant gains between Pretest and Posttest 1 on two native language measures, LAC ($t = 2.12$, $df = 13$, $p = .05$), and WJ MEM

TABLE I. GROUP MEANS AND STANDARD DEVIATIONS ON PRETEST, POSTTEST 1, AND POSTTEST 2 ON THE NATIVE LANGUAGE AND FOREIGN LANGUAGE APTITUDE MEASURES.

| | Multisensory Structured Language (MSL) | | | | | | Self-Contained (SC) | | | | | |
| | Pretest | | Posttest 1 | | Posttest 2 | | Pretest | | Posttest 1 | | Posttest 2 | |
| | M | SD | M | SD | M | SD | M | SD | M | SD | M | SD |
|---|---|---|---|---|---|---|---|---|---|---|---|---|
| **NATIVE LANGUAGE** | | | | | | | | | | | | |
| LAC[a] | 87.4 | 10.8 | 91.4[c] | 7.9 | 90.6 | 9.6 | 81.1 | 11.1 | 87.0[c] | 8.6 | 88.5[e] | 8.7 |
| NELSON | 102.3 | 13.0 | 106.2 | 11.0 | 100.0 | 13.5 | 88.9 | 10.6 | 86.8 | 10.0 | 93.7[d] | 10.3 |
| PPVT-R | 100.5 | 11.5 | 101.6 | 10.7 | 99.6 | 12.2 | 92.8 | 12.3 | 95.8 | 11.0 | 95.5 | 10.3 |
| WJ MEM | 102.0 | 14.0 | 109.1[c] | 14.2 | 113.6[d,e] | 13.7 | 95.6 | 12.5 | 101.8 | 11.0 | 103.3 | 15.3 |
| WRAT SPELL | 95.5 | 9.3 | 98.3 | 10.4 | 98.5 | 10.5 | 87.1 | 12.7 | 92.6[c] | 11.2 | 90.8[e] | 13.6 |
| WRMT BSC | 95.8 | 8.1 | 97.3 | 7.6 | 99.0[e] | 6.9 | 90.1 | 8.1 | 90.4 | 8.6 | 90.2 | 9.2 |
| **FL APTITUDE** | | | | | | | | | | | | |
| MLAT[b] | 88.9 | 11.7 | 106.7[c] | 10.5 | 103.0[e] | 8.6 | 81.0 | 8.5 | 86.5[c] | 8.3 | 86.0 | 8.7 |
| Number Learning | 95.4 | 17.7 | 113.1[c] | 15.3 | 115.4[e] | 10.1 | 85.2 | 15.9 | 93.0[c] | 18.4 | 95.3 | 19.0 |
| Phonetic Script | 92.6 | 12.3 | 111.0[c] | 26.8 | 109.2[e] | 12.3 | 84.5 | 15.8 | 89.9 | 12.3 | 89.1 | 6.8 |
| Spelling Clues[a] | 7.6 | 4.9 | 11.6[c] | 6.0 | 12.1[e] | 7.5 | 6.3 | 6.1 | 7.7 | 4.6 | 9.5 | 6.0 |
| Words in Sentences | 85.9 | 7.5 | 80.6[c] | 6.1 | 84.8[e] | 6.8 | 79.8 | 7.4 | 72.8 | 6.4 | 77.3 | 7.4 |
| Paired Associate | 94.0 | 13.6 | 104.9[c] | 17.0 | 101.8[e] | 11.1 | 82.0 | 6.6 | 84.0 | 12.8 | 89.0 | 7.5 |

[a]Raw Scores. [b]MLAT is the Total Test score; includes all five subtests. [c]Indicates significant gains between Pretest and Posttest 1. [d]Indicates significant gains between Posttest 1 and Posttest 2. [e]Indicates significant gains between Pretest and Posttest 2.

TABLE I.  continued

| | Not Self-Contained (NSC) | | | | | | Not-At-Risk | | | | | |
| | Pretest | | Posttest 1 | | Posttest 2 | | Pretest | | Posttest 1 | | Posttest 2 | |
| | M | SD | M | SD | M | SD | M | SD | M | SD | M | SD |
|---|---|---|---|---|---|---|---|---|---|---|---|---|
| **NATIVE LANGUAGE** | | | | | | | | | | | | |
| LAC[a] | 84.5 | 10.4 | 87.1 | 6.6 | 91.0 | 7.7 | 91.4 | 8.3 | 92.9 | 9.9 | 95.1[e] | 6.7 |
| NELSON | 99.4 | 12.3 | 94.8 | 9.6 | 101.6 | 14.5 | 110.8 | 8.9 | 113.8 | 8.9 | 115.2 | 10.5 |
| PPVT-R | 103.3 | 6.7 | 105.0 | 7.9 | 103.6 | 9.1 | 107.4 | 8.8 | 116.3 | 12.3 | 116.3[e] | 9.8 |
| WJ MEM | 101.7 | 13.1 | 108.1 | 15.9 | 109.9[e] | 13.6 | 110.6 | 12.3 | 119.3[c] | 8.7 | 116.2[e] | 9.6 |
| WRAT SPELL | 97.6 | 8.6 | 99.1 | 6.6 | 101.2 | 6.0 | 110.6 | 7.2 | 113.8 | 8.0 | 111.7 | 6.3 |
| WRMT BSC | 95.8 | 6.3 | 93.9[d] | 4.7 | 98.1 | 6.1 | 103.3 | 6.1 | 102.6 | 7.6 | 102.9 | 6.5 |
| **FL APTITUDE** | | | | | | | | | | | | |
| MLAT[b] | 94.1 | 9.5 | 96.8 | 8.1 | 98.1 | 14.3 | 104.8 | 10.0 | 120.5[c] | 10.3 | 118.9[e] | 10.1 |
| Number Learning | 95.6 | 13.9 | 103.4 | 11.3 | 106.7 | 18.8 | 106.6 | 15.6 | 119.2[c] | 11.1 | 120.4[e] | 11.9 |
| Phonetic Script | 94.2 | 12.3 | 96.5 | 9.9 | 98.1 | 12.3 | 99.6 | 13.7 | 111.4[c] | 11.7 | 114.1[e] | 12.2 |
| Spelling Clues[a] | 10.2 | 4.5 | 13.7 | 5.3 | 13.4 | 5.7 | 12.6 | 5.2 | 18.7[c] | 3.7 | 19.9[e] | 6.7 |
| Words in Sentences | 81.3 | 10.2 | 84.2 | 5.7 | 87.4 | 9.2 | 96.4 | 12.6 | 99.3 | 11.1 | 104.4[e] | 9.1 |
| Paired Associates | 93.7 | 14.5 | 95.8 | 13.7 | 97.6 | 14.2 | 104.7 | 16.4 | 106.4 | 16.9 | 105.2[e] | 13.6 |

[a]Raw Scores. [b]MLAT is the Total Test score; includes all five subtests. [c]Indicates significant gains between Pretest and Posttest 1.
[d]Indicates significant gains between Posttest 1 and Posttest 2. [e]Indicates significant gains between Pretest and Posttest 2.

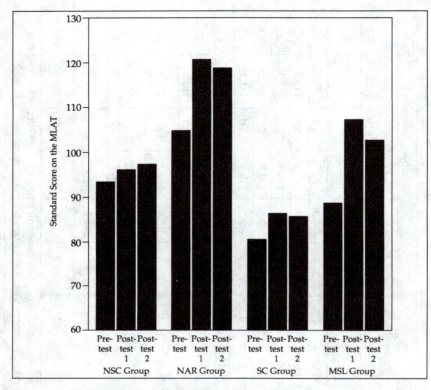

*Figure 2.* Histogram of MLAT scores on Pretest, Posttest 1, and Posttest 2 for the NSC, NAR, SC, and MSL groups.

($t$ = 2.29, $df$ = 13, $p$ = .04), between Posttest 1 and Posttest 2 on one native language measure, WJ MEM ($t$ = 2.24, $df$ = 13, $p$ = .04), and significant gains between Pretest and Posttest 2 on two native language measures, WJ MEM ($t$ = 4.38, $df$ = 13, $p$ = .0008) and WRMT BSC, ($t$ = 2.37, $df$ = 13, $p$ = .03). Regarding the foreign language aptitude measure, the MLAT, the MSL group also made significant gains overall between Pretest and Posttest 1, $t$ = 6.55, $df$ = 13, $p$ = .0001, and between Pretest and Posttest 2, $t$ = 6.84, $df$ = 13, $p$ = .0001. The MSL group made significant gains between Pretest and Posttest 1 on four of the five MLAT subtests: Number Learning, $t$ = 4.16, $df$ = 13, p = .008; Phonetic Script, $t$ = 2.90, $df$ = 13, $p$ = .01; Spelling Clues, $t$ = 3.08, $df$ = 13, $p$ = .008; and Paired Associates, $t$ = 3.10, $df$ = 13, $p$ = .007. Gains also were recorded between Posttest 1 and Posttest 2 on one subtest: Words in Sentences, $t$ = 2.25, $df$ = 13, $p$ = .04; and between Pretest and Posttest 2 on four subtests:

Number Learning, $t$ = 4.75, $df$ = 13, $p$ = .0004; Phonetic Script, $t$ = 6.81, $df$ = 13, $p$ = .0001; Spelling Clues, $t$ = 3.99, $df$ = 13, $p$ = .002; and Paired Associates, $t$ = 3.81, $df$ = 13, $p$ = .002.

The SC group made significant gains between Pretest and Posttest 1 on two native language measures: WRAT SPELL, $t$ = 3.69, $df$ = 10, $p$ = .004; and LAC, $t$ = 2.96, $df$ = 10, $p$ = .01, and between Posttest 1 and Posttest 2 on one measure: NELSON, $t$ = 2.28, $df$ = 10, $p$ = .05. Significant gains between Pretest and Posttest 2 were found on two measures: WRAT SPELL, $t$ = 2.65, $df$ = 10, $p$ = .03; and LAC, $t$ = 3.61, $df$ = 10, $p$ = .005. The SC group also made significant gains on the foreign language aptitude measure between Pretest and Posttest 1, $t$ = 2.45, $df$ = 10, $p$ = .03, but made no significant gains on any of the five MLAT subtests.

The NSC group made no significant gains between Pretest and Posttest 1 on either the six native language measures or the MLAT. The only significant gains observed were between Posttest 1 and Posttest 2 on the WRMT reading test, $t$ = 3.95, $df$ = 13, $p$ = .002; and between Pretest and Posttest 2 on the WJ MEM, $t$ = 2.88, $df$ = 10, $p$ = .01.

The NAR group made significant gains between Pretest and Posttest 1 on two native language measures: WJ MEM, $t$ = 3.15, $df$ = 15, $p$ = .007; and WRAT SPELL, $t$ = 3.21, $df$ = 15, $p$ = .006, but made no significant native language gains between Posttest 1 and Posttest 2. Significant gains between Pretest and Posttest 2 were obtained for: WJ MEM, $t$ = 2.15, $df$ = 15, $p$ = .05; LAC, $t$ = 2.73, $df$ = 15, $p$ = .02; and PPVT, $t$ = 4.73, $df$ = 15, $p$ = .0003. On the foreign language aptitude measure, the NAR group made significant gains between Pretest and Posttest 1, $t$ = 7.33, $df$ = 15, $p$ = .0001; and between Pretest and Posttest 2, $t$ = 4.87, $df$ = 15, $p$ = .0002. Of the five MLAT subtests, the NAR group made significant gains between Pretest and Posttest 1 on three subtests: Number Learning, $t$ = 3.62, $df$ = 15, $p$ = .003; Phonetic Script, $t$ = 4.02, $df$ = 15, $p$ = .001; and Spelling Clues, $t$ = 3.72, $df$ = 15, $p$ = .002. Gains were recorded between Pretest and Posttest 2 on four subtests: Number Learning, $t$ = 3.61, $df$ = 15, $p$ = .003; Phonetic Script, $t$ = 6.03, $df$ = 15, $p$ = .0001; Spelling Clues, $t$ = 3.54, $df$ = 15, $p$ = .003; and Words in Sentences, $t$ = 2.60, $df$ = 15, $p$ = .02.

## DID OUTCOME SCORES ON FOREIGN LANGUAGE PROFICIENCY MEASURES VARY AS A FUNCTION OF GROUP?

Table II presents means and standard deviations of the four groups on the foreign language proficiency measures. Results of

**TABLE II.   GROUP MEANS AND STANDARD DEVIATIONS
ON THE FOREIGN LANGUAGE PROFICIENCY MEASURES
IN FOUR INSTRUCTIONAL CONDITIONS.**

| INSTRUCTIONAL CONDITIONS | MSL | | SC | | NSC | | NAR | |
|---|---|---|---|---|---|---|---|---|
| FOREIGN LANGUAGE MEASURE | M | SD | M | SD | M | SD | M | SD |
| FL READING COMPREHENSION (Maximum Score = 20) | 11.2[a] | 2.1 | 7.1[b] | 1.6 | 8.9[b] | 3.6 | 11.9[a] | 2.6 |
| FL WRITING (Maximum Score = 25) | 16.9[a] | 3.1 | 12.0[b] | 4.5 | 16.5[a] | 3.3 | 19.5[a] | 3.0 |
| FL LISTENING/SPEAKING (Maximum Score = 25) | 17.6[a] | 5.0 | 10.0[b] | 7.2 | 14.6[b] | 3.6 | 17.7[a] | 3.3 |
| FL TOTAL TEST (Maximum Score = 70) | 45.7[a] | 8.5 | 28.4[b] | 10.0 | 40.1[b] | 7.0 | 49.1[a] | 4.4 |
| FL WORD RECOGNITION (Maximum Score = 20) | 12.8[a] | 3.0 | 6.8[b] | 3.3 | 8.4[b] | 3.2 | 11.9[a] | 3.2 |

[a,b]Mean scores with different superscripts were significantly different in group comparisons; e.g., on FL READING COMPREHENSION, MSL group was significantly different from the SC and NSC groups but not from the NAR group.

the MANCOVA procedure with IQ as covariate showed a significant main effect of group on the reading, writing, and listening/speaking measures, Wilks' Lambda = .557; $F(9,117) = 3.54$, $p = .0007$.

Individual ANCOVAs with IQ as covariate showed significant differences among the groups on each of the three foreign language proficiency tests: reading comprehension, $F(4,50) = 7.37$; $p = .0001$; writing, $F(4,50) = 8.35$; $p = .0001$; and listening/speaking, $F(4,50) = 6.04$; $p = .0005$. Results of post hoc analyses are marked on table II. Where significant between-group differences were found, results favored MSL over SC and NSC, NSC and NAR over SC, and NAR over NSC. There were no significant differences between the MSL and NAR groups on any of the three proficiency measures.

Results of a separate ANCOVA procedure with IQ as covariate showed significant overall differences among the four groups on foreign language word recognition, $F(4,50) = 8.34$; $p = .0001$. Post hoc comparisons are summarized in table II. Where there were significant between-group differences, results favored MSL and NAR over SC and NSC. There were no significant differences between the MSL and NAR groups or between the SC and NSC groups.

## FOLLOW-UP RESULTS

To further study the foreign language proficiency of the at-risk groups, we conducted a qualitative analysis of scores on the foreign language writing and foreign language listening/speaking tests. As noted earlier, in addition to quantitative scores presented in table II, each student also received a holistic proficiency level score (Novice/Low through Superior on these two measures, based on ACTFL Guidelines). Using these overall proficiency ratings, we assigned students to one of five levels on the foreign language writing task and one of five levels on the foreign language listening/speaking measures. The five levels were:

1.  *No Production;*
2.  *Novice*—Novice/Low and Novice/Mid;
3.  *Expected*—Novice/High and Intermediate/Low;
4.  *Intermediate*—Intermediate/Mid and Intermediate/High; and
5.  *Advanced*—Advanced.

The Expected category was formed to reflect the fact that after two years of foreign language study in high school, students should be at the Novice/High or the Intermediate/Low level of proficiency. As evident in table III, no student scored in the No Production or Advanced levels of foreign language proficiency. Whereas the at-risk students in the SC group tended to perform at the Novice level in both writing and listening/speaking to a foreign language, the large majority of at-risk students in the MSL and NSC groups achieved the expected level of proficiency in both writing and listening/speaking after two years of foreign language study. In the NAR group, all students achieved at least at the Expected level and some achieved at the Intermediate level in both writing and listening/speaking to a foreign language.

To determine whether there were differences among the four groups who scored at each proficiency level on the foreign language writing and listening/speaking measures, a Chi-square test was performed on each of the three proficiency levels for both the writing and listening/speaking measures. Statistical significance was set at the .05 level. Results indicated that there were reliable differences among the four groups at the following proficiency levels: Writing-Novice, $\chi^2(3, n = 55) = 20.12$, $p = .0002$; Writing-Expected, $\chi^2(3, n = 55) = 14.32$, $p = .003$; Writing-Intermediate, $\chi^2(3, n = 55) = 10.51$, $p = .02$; Listening/Speaking-Novice, $\chi^2(3, n = 55) = 15.61$, $p = .001$; and Listening/Speaking-Expected, $\chi^2(3, n = 55) = 8.20$, $p = .04$.

Additional Chi-square tests were performed to determine which of the four groups scored differently on each of the levels

TABLE III.  DISTRIBUTION OF PROFICIENCY LEVELS ON FOREIGN LANGUAGE WRITING AND FOREIGN LANGUAGE LISTENING/SPEAKING MEASURES.[a]

| Proficiency Skill | Multisensory Structured Language (MSL) (n = 14) | | | | | | Self-Contained (SC) (n = 11) | | | | | |
|---|---|---|---|---|---|---|---|---|---|---|---|---|
| | Novice | % | Expected | % | Intermediate | % | Novice | % | Expected | % | Intermediate | % |
| FL Writing | 1 | 7% | 13 | 93% | 0 | 0% | 7 | 64% | 4 | 36% | 0 | 0% |
| FL Listening/ Speaking | 2 | 14% | 10 | 72% | 2 | 14% | 7 | 64% | 4 | 36% | 0 | 0% |

| Proficiency Skill | Not Self-Contained (NSC) (n = 16) | | | | | | Not-At-Risk (NAR) (n = 14) | | | | | |
|---|---|---|---|---|---|---|---|---|---|---|---|---|
| | Novice | % | Expected | % | Intermediate | % | Novice | % | Expected | % | Intermediate | % |
| FL Writing | 2 | 14% | 12 | 86% | 0 | 0% | 0 | 0% | 12 | 75% | 4 | 25% |
| FL Listening/ Speaking | 5 | 36% | 8 | 57% | 1 | 7% | 0 | 0% | 14 | 87% | 2 | 13% |

[a]Shaded areas represent percentages of students who reached expected proficiency for students completing two years of high school FL courses.

on the proficiency measures. On the writing measures, the MSL, NSC, and NAR groups outperformed the SC group at the Novice and Expected levels and the NAR group performed better than all other groups at the Intermediate level. On both the Novice and Intermediate levels of listening/speaking, the MSL group outperformed the SC group, and the NAR group scored higher than the SC and NSC groups.

## DISCUSSION

In this study we assessed the native language skills, foreign language aptitude, and foreign language proficiency scores of a group of students who were classified as at risk for foreign language learning difficulty, and who received MSL instruction in Spanish over two years, in comparison with the scores of two other groups of at-risk students and one group of not-at-risk students, all of whom had received two years of traditional, textbook-based Spanish instruction. Whereas the at-risk group receiving MSL instruction made significant gains in foreign language aptitude (on the MLAT), at-risk groups receiving traditional instruction did not. This finding is consistent with the results of previous studies, which also found that MSL instruction led to significant increases in the foreign language aptitude of students classified as at risk for foreign language learning difficulty, whereas traditional, textbook-based instruction led to no significant gains in foreign language aptitude in other at-risk students (Sparks, Ganschow, Pohlman, et al. 1992; Sparks, Ganschow, Fluharty, et al. 1996). These findings suggest that MSL instruction may be more helpful than non-MSL instruction to at-risk foreign language learners.

In the present study, the NAR group began with much higher foreign language aptitude and also made significant gains on the MLAT over the two years. Even after two years of MSL instruction in Spanish, the mean MLAT score of the MSL group was still not as high as the Pretest score of the NAR group. After two years of instruction, the NAR group was scoring 16 standard score points above the MSL group on the MLAT. These findings are consistent with the results of the authors' previous studies, which showed that students classified as at-risk for foreign language learning do not "catch up" with their not-at-risk peers in foreign language aptitude (Ganschow and Sparks 1995; Sparks, Ganschow, Fluharty, et al. 1996, Sparks, Ganschow, Artzer, and Patton 1997). On the other hand, those students receiving MSL instruction improved 17.8 standard score points in foreign language aptitude after one year, which left them better prepared for foreign language instruction.

An important finding from the present study was that the MSL group made greater gains than the other at-risk groups, not only on the MLAT total score, but also on the Phonetic Script subtest in particular, which measures a student's ability to learn a new sound and sound-symbol system quickly. On this measure, MSL students gained as much—and ultimately performed as well—as the NAR students. MSL students also made significant gains between Pretest and Posttest I and Pretest and Posttest 2 on the Spelling Clues subtest, which measures, at least in part, phonological/orthographic skill. These findings suggest that MSL instruction, by focusing directly on the phonology/orthography of the foreign language, may be particularly beneficial for students classified as at-risk for difficulty in foreign language learning (Sparks 1995; Sparks and Ganschow 1995a). The positive effects on foreign language aptitude, and on oral and written proficiency in the foreign language, support the linguistic coding differences hypothesis (LCDH), which suggests that immediate and direct instruction in the phonological/orthographic system of the foreign language will be beneficial to at-risk learners.

All four groups made significant gains over two years in some native language skills. For example, all but the SC at-risk group made significant gains in verbal memory (WJ MEM) and both the SC and NAR groups made significant gains on the LAC, a phonemic awareness measure. However, different groups made significant gains on other native language measures: word recognition and pseudoword reading (MSL); spelling (SC), and vocabulary (NAR). These findings are generally consistent with prior foreign language studies, in which both at-risk students receiving MSL instruction and not-at-risk students taught using traditional methods made significant gains on measures of native language phonology/orthography, verbal memory, and vocabulary (Sparks and Ganschow 1993c; Sparks, Ganschow, Pohlman, et al. 1992; Sparks, Ganschow, Fluharty, et al. 1996). However, the scores of at-risk foreign language learners on these measures usually continued to lag behind those of not-at-risk students after one and two years of foreign language instruction (Ganschow and Sparks 1995; Sparks, Ganschow, Artzer, and Patton 1997). A new finding of the present study is that students classified as at risk for foreign language learning who did not receive MSL instruction also made significant, albeit small, gains on three native language measures (spelling, phonemic awareness, verbal memory). This suggests that foreign language learning may have a positive effect on the phonological/orthographic and verbal memory skills of at-risk learners.

In the present study, after controlling for cognitive (IQ) differences, no significant differences were found among the four groups in their gain scores on the native language and foreign language aptitude measures. For example, the groups made equal progress from Pretest to Posttest 1 to Posttest 2. However, there were significant interaction effects between time and group on three testing measures: MLAT, NELSON, and WRMT BSC. This finding suggests that on these three testing measures, there may have been significant differences in gain scores among the groups at one time point (Posttest 1) but not another (Posttest 2). Because there were no significant differences in overall gain scores among the four groups, the improvements on the MLAT, NELSON, and WRMT BSC were likely due to time rather than group. That is, over two years, all four groups made some overall gains on these three testing measures.

On the three measures with significant time and group interaction effects (the MLAT, NELSON, and WRMT), the MSL and NAR groups made significantly greater gains than the SC and NSC groups. These findings suggest that the MSL curriculum may have specific and significant benefits for at-risk students in foreign language aptitude, reading comprehension, and native language phonological/orthographic skill relative to traditional, textbook-based classroom teaching methodologies and instructional accommodations. The findings also suggest that placement in a self-contained classroom alone did not account for the MSL group's gains. Importantly, the MSL group benefited just as much from the MSL methodology over the two years as the NAR group benefited from the traditional, textbook-based foreign language teaching methodology employed in their classrooms.

Perhaps the most beneficial aspects of MSL instruction were with regard to foreign language proficiency. At-risk students receiving MSL instruction achieved higher scores in reading, writing, speaking, and listening to Spanish than at-risk students who received traditional instruction. It is also important that there were no significant differences between the MSL and NAR groups on any of the three foreign language proficiency measures that comprised the foreign language total test. Follow-up analyses on the proficiency levels (Novice, Intermediate) of the foreign language writing and listening/speaking measures showed that there were differences between the MSL and NAR groups at only one level (writing-Intermediate), whereas there were differences between the SC and NAR groups and the NSC and NAR groups at several levels of proficiency on both the writing and listening/speaking measures. These findings suggest that, when learning a foreign language, the at-risk students benefited from the MSL methodology as much as not-at-risk students from a traditional, textbook-based foreign language teaching methodology.

There are a number of ways to explain the striking success of the MSL group. Service (1992) finds that the learning of foreign language vocabulary is due to phonological working memory, which MSL instruction appears to enhance. Ehri (1987) hypothesizes that written language development positively enhances oral language development because written language serves as a "visual-spatial model for speech" (p. 361). She suggests that when "children learn to read and spell, this model and its symbols are internalized as a representational system in memory" (p. 361). We ourselves have speculated that the immediate introduction of the sound and sound-symbol system (reading and the phonological/orthographic aspects of a foreign language) of a new language using MSL methodology positively enhances the MSL group's skills in both the written *and* oral aspects of Spanish (Sparks, Ganschow, and Patton 1995). We interpret the present findings to indicate that students in the MSL group were able to rely on the written (reading and writing) aspects of the foreign language to help them with the oral (listening and speaking) aspects of Spanish. Strong evidence of the efficacy of MSL instruction for teaching a foreign language to students classified as at risk derives from the finding that the MSL and NAR groups exhibited no significant differences on three of the four foreign language proficiency measures. These two groups differed in only one level of proficiency (writing-Intermediate).

Findings showed that there were significant group differences on the foreign language word recognition measure (FL word recognition). Results showed that the MSL and NAR groups scored significantly higher on this measure than either the SC or NSC groups, and that there were no significant differences between the MSL and NAR groups. These findings suggest that the MSL group may have received greater benefit from the MSL methodology in dealing with the sound and sound-symbol system of a new language than the NSC and SC groups did from foreign language teaching methodologies that

did not explicitly teach the new sound and sound-symbol system of a foreign language. Support for the aforementioned
speculation also comes from the finding that the MSL group
made significantly greater gains than the SC and NSC groups
on the Phonetic Script subtest of the MLAT. This finding is consistent with results of a recent study showing skill in decoding
words in a foreign language to be a good predictor of overall
proficiency in reading, writing, speaking, and listening to a foreign language (Sparks, Ganschow, Patton, Artzer, Siebenhar,
and Plageman 1997).

An important finding of the present study is that students
classified as at-risk for foreign language learning (many diagnosed with LD) passed foreign language courses without the use
of the MSL teaching methodology. For example, the NSC group,
all of whom were diagnosed as LD and who received instructional accommodations from the school's LD program, successfully completed two years of foreign language courses in a
highly competitive high school program. The final grades of the
NSC group showed that when provided with instructional accommodations, all students in this group achieved grades of C or
better in first-year Spanish and all but two, who achieved final
grades of D+, achieved grades of C or better in second-year
Spanish. In other studies, many students classified as LD had
passed both high school and college foreign language courses
without tutoring and/or instructional accommodations (Sparks
and Javorsky in press; Sparks, Philips, and Ganschow 1996;
Sparks, Philips, Ganschow, and Javorsky in press).

In the present study, students classified as at risk and as
LD not only met their teachers' standards for passing, but
also demonstrated proficiency on an objective and independent outcome measure. At-risk students achieved at least
a Novice level of foreign language proficiency in both
oral and written Spanish; most at-risk students in the MSL
and NSC groups achieved the proficiency level expected after
two years of foreign language study for both writing and
listening/speaking. These findings suggest that at-risk foreign language learners and others classified as LD can
achieve levels of foreign language proficiency after two years
of foreign language study. Importantly, however, these studies suggest that the use of the MSL techniques may prove especially helpful to students classified as at risk for foreign
language learning, enabling them to attain levels of foreign
language proficiency above "expected" levels and closer to
those achieved by their not-at-risk peers.

## LIMITATIONS

The MSL instructor in this study had participated in all of Sparks, et al.'s previous research studies with at-risk foreign language learners (Ganschow and Sparks 1995; Sparks and Ganschow 1993c; Sparks, Ganschow, Pohlman, et al. 1992; Sparks, Ganschow, Artzer, and Patton 1997). Although the claim could be made that results showing an advantage for MSL instruction result from a singularly talented instructor, none of the aforementioned studies has compared at-risk students receiving MSL foreign language instruction with at-risk students receiving traditional foreign language instruction; nor have these studies used outcome measures assessing oral and written foreign language proficiency. To the authors' knowledge, this is the first study which demonstrates that at-risk foreign language learners who receive MSL instruction become more proficient in a foreign language than do at-risk foreign language learners who receive foreign language instruction using traditional, textbook-based foreign language teaching methodologies. Further replication with other MSL instructors is necessary to solidify the claim that gains can be attributed to instruction, per se.

## IMPLICATIONS

There are a number of implications that can be drawn from this study. First, a methodology that explicitly teaches the sound and sound-symbol (phonology/orthography), grammar (syntax), and morphology (word meanings) of a foreign language may be more effective for foreign language learners classified as at risk than one which uses only traditional, textbook-based foreign language instruction. Without explicit teaching of these systems, students with weaker native language skills and foreign language aptitude are unlikely to learn the phonological, orthographic, syntactic, and morphological systems of a new foreign language as easily as will students with stronger native language and foreign language aptitude.

Second, more consideration by foreign language researchers and educators should be given to Ehri's hypothesis that oral language skills are enhanced by exposure to written language. Immediate and frequent exposure to print (reading, spelling, writing) in a foreign language combined with listening to and speaking a foreign language is likely to be very helpful for students classified as at risk for foreign language learning difficulty because such exposure provides multisensory input, reinforcing both the written and spoken forms of the new and unfamiliar language.

Third, the present study is one of several which have shown that teaching a foreign language with the MSL approach produces greater gains in foreign language aptitude than does teaching with non-MSL methods in students classified as at risk for foreign language learning (Sparks and Ganschow 1993c; Sparks, Ganschow, Pohlman, et al. 1992; Sparks, Ganschow, Fluharty, et al. 1996).

Fourth, the study should be replicated with larger numbers of students, with coeducational groups in both public and private school settings, and with different MSL foreign language teachers.

Fifth, in order to provide the direct instruction that seems critical for successful foreign language instruction of at-risk learners, teachers themselves must have mastered the phonology/orthography (sound and sound/symbol), grammatical (syntactic), and morphological (word meanings) systems of the foreign language. Colleges and universities should consider training preservice teachers in these systems so that new foreign language instructors are themselves cognizant of these components of the foreign language they will be teaching.

Sixth, it is likely that students who are classified as LD (or as at risk for difficulty in learning a foreign language) can become proficient in a foreign language at some level. In the present study, at-risk students in all three groups acquired a level of foreign language proficiency that allowed them to pass foreign language courses and to meet their teachers' expectations. In other studies, students classified as LD passed high school and college foreign language courses without the aid of specialized teaching methodologies, placement in a self-contained classroom for at-risk learners, tutoring, and/or instructional accommodations. On the basis of these and other results, we suggest that students classified as LD or as at-risk for difficulty in learning a foreign language should enroll in foreign language courses and make use of appropriate instructional accommodations (increased time on tests) or specialized services (tutoring) to assist them as necessary. Additional studies should be conducted at the secondary and postsecondary levels of education to determine what level of proficiency at-risk foreign language learners can reach in regular foreign language classrooms, with and without instructional accommodations.

Correspondence should be directed to: R. Sparks, College of Mount St. Joseph, Cincinnati, Ohio email: richard_sparks@mail.msj.edu

## References

*ACTFL Proficiency Guidelines*. 1989. Yonkers, NY: ACTFL Materials Center.

Barr, V. 1993. *Foreign Language Requirement and Students with Learning Disabilities*. (Report No. EDO-FL-93-04). Washington, DC: Center for Applied Linguistics.

Brown, J., Bennett, J., and Hanna, G. 1981. *Nelson-Denny Reading Test*. Chicago, IL: Riverside.

Carroll, J. 1962. The prediction of success in intensive foreign language training. In R. Glaser, ed., *Training and Research in Education*. Pittsburgh, PA: University of Pittsburgh Press.

Carroll, J. 1973. Implications of aptitude test research and psycholinguistic theory for foreign language teaching. *International Journal of Psycholinguistics* 2:5–14.

Carroll, J., and Sapon, S. 1959. *Modern Language Aptitude Test*. San Antonio, TX: Psychological Corp.

Dunn, L., and Dunn, L. 1981. *Peabody Picture Vocabulary Test-Revised*. Circle Pines, MN: American Guidance.

Ehri, L. 1987. Effects of printed language acquisition on speech. In D. Olson, N. Torrence, and A. Hildyard, eds., *Literacy, Language and Learning*. Cambridge, MA: Cambridge University Press.

Freed, B. 1987. Exemptions from the foreign language requirement: A review of recent literature, problems, and policy. *ADFL Bulletin* 18:13–17.

Ganschow, L., Myer, B., and Roeger, K. 1989. Foreign language policies and procedures for students with specific learning disabilities. *Learning Disabilities Focus* 5:50–58.

Ganschow, L., and Sparks, R. 1986. Learning disabilities and foreign language difficulties: Deficit in listening skills? *Journal of Reading, Writing, and Learning Disabilities International* 2:306–19.

Ganschow, L., and Sparks, R. 1995. Effects of direct instruction in Spanish phonology on the native language skills and foreign language aptitude of at-risk foreign language learners. *Journal of Learning Disabilities* 28:107–20.

Ganschow, L., and Sparks, R. 1996. Foreign language anxiety among high school women. *Modern Language Journal* 80:199–212.

Ganschow, L., Sparks, R., Anderson, R., Javorsky, J., and Skinner, S. 1994. Differences in language performance among high and low anxious college foreign language learners. *Modern Language Journal* 78:41-55.

Ganschow, L., Sparks, R., Javorsky, J., Pohlman, J., and Bishop-Marbury, A. 1991. Identifying native language learning difficulties among foreign language learners in college: A 'foreign' language learning disability? *Journal of Learning Disabilities* 24:530–41.

Ganschow, L., Sparks, R., and Schneider, E. 1995. Learning a foreign language: Challenges for students with language learning difficulties. *Dyslexia* 1:75–95.

Gordon, S. 1994. Oral, motor, feel, and sound blending. Paper presented at the 67th Annual Conference of the American Association of Teachers of French, Quebec, Canada.

Jastak, S. and Wilkinson, G. 1984. *Wide Range Achievement Test-Revised*. Wilmington, DE: Jastak Associates.

Lindamood, P., and Lindamood, C. 1979. *Lindamood Auditory Conceptualization Test.* Austin, TX: PRO-ED.

O'Maggio, A. 1986. *Teaching Language in Context.* Boston, MA: Heinle and Heinle.

Mabbott, A. 1994. Students labeled learning disabled and the foreign language requirement: Background and suggestions for teachers. In C. Klee, ed., *The Individual Learner in Multisection Courses.* Boston, MA: Heinle and Heinle.

Moore, F. 1995. Section 504 and the Americans with Disabilities Act: Accommodating the learning disabled student in the foreign language curriculum. *ADFL Bulletin* 260:59–62.

Roffman, N., and Teitelbaum, T. 1993. Teaching English as a foreign language to learning disabled pupils in Israel. *Australian Journal of Remedial Education* 25:11–13.

Roffman, N., and Teitelbaum, T. 1996. Reflections of five years of teaching English as a foreign language to learning disabled students in Israel. *Australian Journal of Learning Disabilities* 2:23-24.

Schneider, E. in press. Multisensory structural metacognitive instruction: An approach to teaching a foreign language to at-risk students at an American college. Hamburg, Germany: Peter Lang.

Service, E. 1992. Phonology, working memory, and foreign language learning. *Quarterly Journal of Experimental Psychology* 45A:21–50.

Skehan, P. 1986. The role of foreign language aptitude in a model of school learning. *Language Testing* 3:188–221.

Sparks, R. 1995. Examining the Linguistic Coding Differences Hypothesis to explain individual differences in foreign language learning. *Annals of Dyslexia* 45:187–214.

Sparks, R., and Ganschow, L. 1991. Foreign language learning difficulties: Affective or native language aptitude differences? *Modern Language Journal* 75:3–16.

Sparks, R., and Ganschow, L. 1993a. Searching for the cognitive locus of foreign language learning difficulties: Linking first and second language learning. *Modern Language Journal* 77:289–302.

Sparks, R., and Ganschow, L. 1993b. The impact of native language learning problems on foreign language learning: Case study illustrations of the Linguistic Coding Deficit Hypothesis. *Modern Language Journal* 77:58–74.

Sparks, R., and Ganschow, L. 1993c. The effects of a multisensory structured language approach on the native language and foreign language aptitude skills of at-risk learners: A follow-up and replication study. *Annals of Dyslexia* 43:194–216.

Sparks, R., and Ganschow, L. 1995a. A strong inference approach to causal factors in foreign language learning: A response to MacIntyre. *Modern Language Journal* 79:235–44.

Sparks, R., and Ganschow, L. 1995b. Parent perceptions in the screening for performance in foreign language courses. *Foreign Language Annals* 28:371–91.

Sparks, R., and Ganschow, L. 1996. Teachers' perceptions of students' foreign language academic skills and affective characteristics. *Journal of Educational Research* 89:172–85.

Sparks, R., Ganschow, L., Artzer, M., and Patton, J. 1997. Foreign language proficiency of at-risk and not-at-risk foreign language learners over two years of foreign language instruction. *Journal of Learning Disabilities* 30:92–98.

Sparks, R., Ganschow, L., Artzer, M., Siebenhar, D., and Plageman, M. 1997. Anxiety and proficiency in a foreign language. *Perceptual and Motor Skills* 85:559–62.

Sparks, R., Ganschow, L., Artzer, M., Siebenhar, D., and Plageman, N. 1998. Differences in native language skills, foreign language aptitude, and foreign language grades among high, average, and low proficiency foreign language learners: Two studies. *Language Testing* 15:181–216.

Sparks, R., Ganschow, L., Fluharty, K., and Little, S. 1996. An exploratory study on the effects of Latin on the native language skills and foreign language aptitude of students with and without learning disabilities. *Classical Journal* 91:165–84.

Sparks, R., Ganschow, L., Javorsky, J., Pohlman, J., and Patton, J. 1992a. Identifying native language deficits in high- and low-risk foreign language learners in high school. *Foreign Language Annals* 25:403–18.

Sparks, R., Ganschow, L., Javorsky, J., Pohlman, J., and Patton, J. 1992b. Test comparisons among students identified as high-risk, low-risk, and learning disabled in high school foreign language courses. *Modern Language Journal* 76:142–59.

Sparks, R., Ganschow, L., Kenneweg, S., and Miller, K. 1991. Use of an Orton-Gillingham method to teach a foreign language to dyslexic/learning disabled students: Explicit teaching of phonology in a second language. *Annals of Dyslexia* 41:96–118.

Sparks, R., Ganschow, L., and Patton, J. 1995. Prediction of performance in first-year foreign language courses: Connections between native and foreign language learning. *Journal of Educational Psychology* 87:638–55.

Sparks, R., Ganschow, L., Patton, J., Artzer, M., Siebenhar, D., and Plageman, M. 1997. Prediction of foreign language proficiency. *Journal of Educational Psychology* 89:549–61.

Sparks, R., Ganschow, L., Pohlman, J., Skinner, S., and Artzer, M. 1992. The effects of a multisensory, structured language approach on the native and foreign language aptitude skills of at-risk foreign language learners. *Annals of Dyslexia* 42:25–53.

Sparks, R., Ganschow, L., and Pohlman, J. 1989. Linguistic coding deficits in foreign language learners. *Annals of Dyslexia* 39:179–95.

Sparks, R., and Javorsky, J. in press. Students classified as learning disabled and the college foreign language requirement: Replication and comparison studies. *Journal of Learning Disabilities*.

Sparks, R., Philips, L., and Ganschow L. 1996. Students classified as learning disabled and the college foreign language requirement. In: J. Liskin-Gasparro, ed., Patterns and Policies: *The Changing Demographics of Foreign Language Instruction*. Boston, MA: Heinle and Heinle.

Sparks, R., Philips, L., Ganschow, L., and Javorsky, J. in press. Comparison of students classified as learning disabled who petitioned for or fulfilled the college foreign language requirement. *Journal of Learning Disabilities*.

Spinelli, E. 1988. *Situation Cards for Oral Evaluation: First Year French, German, and Spanish*. New York: Holt, Rinehart and Winston.

Vellutino, F., and Scanlon, D. 1986. Linguistic coding deficits and metalinguistic awareness: Their relationship to verbal and code acquisition in poor and normal readers. In D. Yaden and S. Templeton, eds., *Metalinguistic Awareness and Beginning Literacy*. Portsmouth, NH: Heineman.

Woodcock, R. 1987. Woodcock Reading Mastery Test-Revised. Circle Pines, MN: American Guidance.

Woodcock, R., and Johnson, M.S. 1978. *Woodcock-Johnson Psycho-Educational Battery*. Allen Park, TX: DLM Teaching Resources.

# PART IV
## Adults with Dyslexia: Issues and Outcomes

For many years now, issues concerning adults with dyslexia have generated heated debate and the questions addressed in this volume are no exception. Chapter 11, by Keim, Ryan, and Nolan emphasizes the need to formulate a consistent policy regarding students with LD that can be shared by the diverse set of professionals who support them on a college campus. The results of their survey of support professionals trained in education and counseling do reveal differences in opinion, but it is reassuring that there is more overlap than disagreement. These results suggest a growing awareness of learning disabilities on college campuses.

Although professionals may be more aware of the need to support and provide allowances for college students with learning disabilities, there remain many controversies to be settled. In particular, Wertheim, Vogel, and Brulle (chapter 12) consider the complex legal, ethical, and educational issues surrounding college students with dyslexia who wish to become teachers. Although their potential students will benefit from the empathy and concern of teachers who themselves struggled with academic subjects, youngsters also need excellent informed instruction. Given the need for teachers to have explicit knowledge of language structure, and recent evidence that few new teachers possess that knowledge, it is widely believed we should be imposing higher professional standards. Should we be encouraging students who struggle with reading to become teachers of reading? How do we balance the rights of would-be teachers with the needs of their future students? And most importantly, how can we best prepare future teachers (with and without LD) for the challenging job they seek to undertake?

Equating "adults" with high school and college students can be misleading. As long as persons with dyslexia are in school, their difficulties with reading and testing loom large.

However, as documented in the chapter by R. Fink, persons with dyslexia can and do rise above their early schooling difficulties to achieve a level of success shared by few in society. Participants in her study agreed to be identified by name to further inspire others with dyslexia for whom "success" is still only an abstract concept. Comprehensive testing conducted by Fink supports what other studies have told us before—the difficulties that render a person vulnerable to reading difficulties do not just "go away", even in these successful doctors, lawyers, educators, and scientists. One novel feature of this study is the argument that interest (or passion) in a content area motivates the young person to read voraciously and thereby obtain the necessary practice in reading now deemed so essential to reading success.

As a group, these three papers on adults send an important message: the challenges of assisting talented young adults with LD forge a professional life are daunting and complex, but not insurmountable. The success stories shared by Fink not only offer useful insights regarding one important pathway to success (pursuing one's passion through reading), they make clear that the battles along the way are well worth fighting.

# Dilemmas Faced
# when Working with Learning Disabilities
# in Post-Secondary Education

Jeanmarie Keim

University of Memphis

Ann G. Ryan

University of St. Thomas

Burton F. Nolan

University of St. Thomas

*To explore principles that guide post-secondary professionals who work with students with learning disabilities, vignettes describing typical ethical dilemmas were presented to counselors and other educational professionals. The vignettes addressed issues such as consent, boundaries of competency, accommodation, and release of information. Respondents indicated whether they believed the behavior presented in the vignette was ethical or appropriate. Analyses of variance indicated overall significant differences of opinions between professionals trained in counseling and those trained in education. Chi-square analyses examining responses to individual dilemmas revealed much overlap in opinion, with significant differences of opinion on three of eight dilemmas. Those dilemmas distinguishing the two groups involved issues of confidentiality when providing references, dual relationships between provider and student and release of records.*

Annals of Dyslexia, Vol. 48, 1998
Copyright© 1998 by The International Dyslexia Association
ISSN 0736-9387

# INTRODUCTION

In this paper, we examine dilemmas faced by educators and counselors working with students who have learning disabilities. Although this topic has received little prior emphasis, professionals often are required to make complex choices. Within postsecondary settings, professionals from two types of educational training are likely to work with students with learning disabilities. The first group comprises professionals with educational training in the field of learning disabilities; the second includes professionals with training in counseling and/or psychology. Additionally, both students and educational specialists must interact with faculty members in various departments to arrange accommodation, testing, and so forth. Whereas the professional behavior of counselors is typically governed by the *Code of Ethics and Standards of Practice* (ACA 1995), with potential sanctions by State Boards of Psychology and Counseling, no such entities currently yield similar authority for individuals with training in education. Finally, there may be no specific professional ethical code to assist university professors in making decisions concerning students with learning disabilities. Inconsistent ethical standards and varying professional behaviors across disciplines may impede the consistent provision of service to students with learning disabilities.

The following vignette presents one scenario where professionals may have different opinions regarding ethical or appropriate behavior: A learning disabilities specialist from the university asks her brother-in-law to hire some of the students in the support program to work part-time in the family business. If the specialist's credentials are in education, is this unethical? If the specialist's credentials are in counseling, is this unethical?

# RELEVANT LITERATURE

An array of services has been identified as necessary in meeting the social, emotional, and academic needs of students with learning disabilities in postsecondary settings (Blalock and Dixon 1982; Gajar 1992; Keim, McWhirter, and Bernstein 1996; Nelson and Lignugaris/Kraft 1989; Ostertag, Pearson, and Baker 1986; Strichart and Mangrum 1986; and Wren, Williams, and Kovack 1987). These services include: tutoring, readers, reduced course loads, computer laboratories, study skills, academic advisement, counseling, and test accommodation. Because of the array of skills required to meet these demands, colleges and universities have sought the expertise of a variety of personnel from both counseling and education. These professionals have various kinds of training and requirements that influence their professional and ethical behavior.

Both counselors and educators may assess or counsel students in postsecondary settings, but depending on professional affiliations and licensure laws, ethical boundaries for the two groups differ. Additionally, there is no universal standard that guides the various professional groups in regard to students with learning disabilities.

For example, Cobb and Horn (1989) surveyed 1,000 members of the Council for Exceptional Children (CEC), the nation's largest organization for educators in special education. They found that only 51 of 381 respondents relied on CEC Standards. The remaining 330 either did not have a copy of the standards or did not actively use them. Most participants in Cobb and Horn's survey (71 percent) reported not using the standards because they were unaware of their existence. According to Heller (1983), these standards were developed by the CEC Professional Standards Committee for distribution in 1983.

In a recent survey of organizations participating in the National Joint Committee on Learning Disabilities (NJCLD), it was determined that standards for professional conduct were available on an irregular basis. Some organizations have documents specific to their profession (American Speech and Hearing Association and International Reading Association), but others currently have no documents (International Dyslexia Association) or have deferred to parent organizations such as the American Counseling Association (ACA), American Psychological Association (APA), and the Council for Exceptional Children (CEC). Two professional organizations in special education, however, have shown current interest in the development of ethical standards. The Association for Higher Education and Disabilities (AHEAD) has published "Standards of Professional Practice" (Shaw and Madaus 1997), and the Council for Learning Disabilities (CLD) recently adopted its own "Principles of Ethics" (1995).

Some have questioned the applicability of current education standards to postsecondary service providers in learning disabilities. Brinkerhoff, Shaw, and McGuire (1993) recognized the need for policies and procedures specific to personnel working in colleges, universities, vocational schools, and the like, asserting "Such a well-defined code of ethics is a critical component in daily service delivery by postsecondary practitioners" (p. 165).

Despite current discrepancies among organizations regarding standards for professional conduct, public law has provided protection for people with disabilities and procedural guidelines for those who work with them. Most notably, the Individuals with Disabilities Education Act (IDEA) has delineated many of the safeguards for both students and evaluators in such areas of assessment as assuring consent, establishing reasonable timelines, and requiring both assessment and feedback in appropriate language formats. Section 504 of the Rehabilitation Act of 1973 established guidelines for providing physical and programmatic accessibility for people with identified or "perceived" disabilities. "Thus, only private postsecondary institutions that do not receive government funds are not covered by broader 504 or ADA Title II requirements" (Leuchovius 1995, p. 13).

Whereas a number of ethical and legal standards for postsecondary service providers may be combined from various sources, the difficulty is that professional ethical guidelines are generally developed for the professional focus of the association's members rather than for all professionals working with a specific population. That is, counseling associations develop guidelines for counselors, and educational associations develop guidelines for education professionals. Therefore, professionals working across disciplines (academic counseling or learning disabilities) must assume individual responsibility for either piecing together these standards or for relying on their own integrity, skills, and intuition (Brinkerhoff, Shaw, and McGuire 1993).

For more than a decade, leaders in special education have urged the development and broad dissemination of a concise set of ethical guidelines (Bateman 1982; Dobson and Dobson 1983). Although the issues inherent in the establishment of enforceable standards are many, they remain important enough to warrant continued attention. Both Heller (1983) and Turnbull and Barber (1984) point to the importance of special education professional organizations addressing ethical issues.

The purpose of the present study was to construct a set of dilemmas typically faced by professionals who work with students who have learning disabilities, and to clarify where differences of opinion exist between individuals trained primarily in education versus individuals trained in counseling. To determine whether differences existed, we sent a set of vignettes to 500 members of the American Counseling Association and to 500 members of AHEAD. Although we worked with experts in establishing "appropriate" responses to aid in discussion and data analysis, we were more interested in investigating whether differences of opinion existed than in arriving at an indisputable, ultimate, correct answer to each of the dilemmas. Clarification of these differences should be helpful as future guidelines are developed.

## METHOD

### INSTRUMENTS

As a result of numerous discussions with professionals who work with students who have learning disabilities, a survey including various vignettes and dilemmas faced by these professionals was written. This group of professionals included individuals who had worked in collegiate settings within the learning disabilities area as either educational specialists, counselors, or psychologists for a minimum of ten years.

The vignettes consisted of various dilemmas involving university staff or faculty and students with learning disabilities. For each vignette, the participants were asked whether they felt the person's behavior was ethical or appropriate. Additionally, they were asked to indicate the primary issue involved. Vignettes are contained in Figure I with what we believe are appropriate answers to these "grey areas" based on the consensus arrived at by our consultants (Keim, Nolan, an Ryan 1994; Ryan, Keim, and Nolan 1995).

In addition to the vignettes, the respondents were asked demographic questions about their gender, educational training area, highest degree earned, and professional license or credential. The primary occupational area question had four alternatives: learning disabilities, counseling, professor, and other. Respondents also were asked to indicate whether their school was public or private, a college or a university, and to indicate the number of undergraduate and graduate students enrolled.

Another part of our survey focused on attitudes about ethical guidelines. Respondents answered questions using a Likert-type scale ranging from 1 to 4 (from not important to very important).

1. *Transfer of information between universities.*
   A student with a learning disability transfers from the state university where you work to another state university in the same state. Your colleague at the other university's support service center calls to request information about the student. You refuse since the student has not contacted you regarding this information. Do you consider refusing this request ethical or appropriate behavior? (Correct to refuse, psychological report ownership.)

2. *Providing information to faculty for accommodation.*
   A learning disabilities specialist feels caught in the middle. A college student with a learning disability desires and qualifies for accommodations. The student refuses to allow thelearningdisabilities specialist to discuss any aspect of her assessment with her professors. One professor refuses to provide accommodations without some understanding of what the specific disability is in order to determine what accommodations are appropriate. Do you consider the professor's behavior ethical or appropriate? (Correct behavior by the professor, academic integrity.)

3. *Record maintenance following termination of service.*
   Tom, a college student with a learning disability, decides that he no longer desires services, nor does he want his file kept at the support center for students with disabilities. Do you consider it ethical or appropriate to refuse to give the student the file? (Correct to refuse to give the student the file, record maintenance.)

4. *Appropriate test accommodation.*
   A history professor refuses to allow an open book accommodation for an essay exam. The student has a mathematics disability with no memory problems documented. Do you consider this ethical or appropriate? (Correct behavior by the professor, academic integrity.)

5. *Providing references.*
   Amanda is in the process of completing her BA degree in Accounting. Her faculty advisor in Accounting is providing job recommendations for her. The faculty advisor mentions Amanda has a learning disability to a company to which she has applied. The faculty member adds that this disability does not impact Amanda's performance. The professor further states that, while she will fulfill a "disability quota" for the company, the learning disability should not impair her performance. Do you consider this ethical or appropriate behavior? (Incorrect behavior by the professor, privacy rights.)

6. *Providing psychotherapy.*
   A student with a learning disability has deep-seated self-esteem issues regarding the diagnosis. The learning disabilities specialist has a master's degree in education and feels the student would benefit from counseling, but refuses to engage in psychotherapy with the student. Do you consider this ethical or appropriate be

*continued*

havior? (Correct behavior by the learning disabilities specialist, competency issues.)

7. *Release of assessment information.*
A private practice psychologist conducts a psychoeducational assessment of John, a local community college student. John is diagnosed with a learning disability and the psychologist forwards the report to the college's learning disabilities support center. One of the learning disabilities specialists releases portions of the report, without the student's knowledge, to the student's professors so they may better assist the student. Do you consider this ethical or appropriate behavior by the LD specialist? (Incorrect behavior by the learning disabilities specialist, informed consent.)

8. *Hiring students.*
A learning disabilities specialist from a private university asks her brother-in-law to hire one of the students in the support program to work part-time in the family business. Do you consider this ethical or appropriate behavior by the LD specialist? (Incorrect behavior by the learning disabilities specialist, dual relationship.)

*Figure 1.*     *Post-Secondary Vignettes Presented to Respondents (Expert decision and rationale presented in parenthesis)*

Questions included:
1. How important do you consider having a set of ethical guidelines for your professional interactions with students who have learning disabilities? and
2. How important do you consider having one set of ethical guidelines that guide the work of both education specialists and psychologists for working with students who have learning disabilities?

## PARTICIPANTS

Potential participants included members of AHEAD and those members of ACA who belonged to the American College Counselors Division and indicated their work setting was at a college or university as a counselor. In total, surveys were sent to 1,000 professionals nationwide (500 from each organization) who work with students who have learning disabilities. Surveys were completed by 422 respondents. We included only those individuals whose training was either primarily education or counseling in the final analysis and excluded those with training in both areas or in different areas altogether. This resulted in 245 participants. Demographic information for these individuals with primary training in education and counseling is presented in table I.

TABLE I. DEMOGRAPHIC INFORMATION ON PROFESSIONALS
WITH PRIMARY TRAINING IN EDUCATION OR COUNSELING.

| | Primary Training | |
| --- | --- | --- |
| | Education | Counseling |
| **Information on Respondent** | | |
| Gender (percent) | | |
| Male | 19.7 | 33.7 |
| Female | 80.3 | 66.3 |
| Occupational Focus (percent) | | |
| LD Service Provider | 36.1 | 8.4 |
| Psychologist/Counselor | 8.2 | 56.1 |
| Professor | 4.8 | 7.1 |
| LD Service Provider/Psychologist | 2.0 | 1.0 |
| Professor/Psychologist | 0.7 | 4.1 |
| Professor/LD Service Provider | 6.8 | 0.0 |
| Other | 41.5 | 13.3 |
| Highest Earned Degree (percent) | | |
| Bachelors | 8.2 | 6.1 |
| Masters | 71.4 | 61.2 |
| Doctorate | 20.4 | 32.7 |
| **Information on University** | | |
| Students, Mean (SD) | | |
| Undergraduate (in thousands) | 8.16 (8.12) | 6.94 (6.68) |
| | (range 0–4.40) | (range .6–35.00) |
| Graduate (in thousands) | 2.00 (3.10) | 1.81 (2.40) |
| | (range 0–15.00) | (range 0–12.00) |
| College/University (percent) | | |
| Public | 66.0 | 65.3 |
| Private | 33.3 | 34.7 |
| Missing data | 0.7 | |

## PROCEDURES

Each vignette was developed and field-tested (Keim, Nolan, and Ryan 1994). The vignettes were subsequently modified in accordance with suggestions from a number of professionals involved in graduate training in education and counseling related areas. These experts taught courses in ethics, served on professional licensing boards, provided services to students with learning disabilities, and supervised graduate student training in education and counseling. Following extensive discussion, these experts arrived at a general consensus as to the most appropriate responses to each vignette. As previously stated, our concern was not whether respondents necessarily agreed with the experts, but whether and how their opinions differed from one another. The expert opinions provided an excellent starting point for examining the vignettes, and the issues surrounding them.

Each potential participant was mailed a packet containing a letter covering informed consent, demographic questions, the survey, and a ticket for a drawing. In order to increase return of surveys, our letter stated that anyone who returned the survey, blank or completed, could fill out the drawing ticket and be eligible for a $25 gift certificate to a restaurant. Although the drawing tickets were marked with participants' names and addresses, the tickets were immediately separated from the survey to assure anonymity of survey responses. The two items were not connected in any way when returned to the researchers and tickets were shredded following the drawing.

## ANALYSIS

Prior to examining the eight vignettes individually, we looked for overall differences in response to the vignettes as a function of group. Scores on the combined eight items were tallied based on agreement or disagreement with the experts on each of the eight items and submitted to ANOVA. Following significant ANOVA results, chi-square analyses were used to compare individuals with education backgrounds to those with counseling-related backgrounds for each of the vignettes. A protected $F$ approach, as suggested by Kirk (1982), was utilized for the Chi-square comparisons. This resulted in eight comparisons. Percentages also were calculated for those who had a set of ethical principles. Finally, a mean was calculated based on a Likert-type scale to indicate whether the respondent valued ethical guidelines.

## RESULTS

The ANOVA results examining overall response to vignette revealed a significant effect of group, $F(1, 243) = 4.83$, $MSE = .02$, $p < .05$. Given the significance in overall opinions between the two groups, chi-square analyses on each of the eight vignettes were conducted. Results of analyses are presented in table II, demonstrating significant group effects for vignettes number 3, 5, and 8.

T-tests were calculated to determine whether the two groups differed in how much they value ethical guidelines. On a four-point Likert-type scale, with four being highly valued, both groups valued a separate set of ethics for their own profession at approximately 3.75. Each of the groups also valued a com-

**TABLE II.   RESPONSE TO VIGNETTES AS A FUNCTION OF TRAINING.**

| | Consistent w/Expert | | |
| | Education | Counseling | |
| | % (n) | % (n) | Chi-square** |
|---|---|---|---|
| 1. Appropriate to refuse to provide information without consent | 98 (143) | 94 (91) | (1, n = 243, 2.79) |
| 2. Appropriate to refuse to provide accommodation without knowledge of disability | 44 ( 63) | 46 (44) | (1, n = 240, 0.10) |
| 3. Ethical to refuse to give the file to the student | 46 ( 67) | 61 (58) | (1, n = 240, 5.07)*** |
| 4. Ethical to refuse accommodation for a certain exam | 94 (133) | 89 (85) | (1, n = 236, 1.90) |
| 5. Ethical to state a student has a learning disability | 98 (144) | 93 (89) | (1, n = 243, 4.06)*** |
| 6. Ethical to refuse to provide counseling to a student | 96 (140) | 97 (95) | (1, n = 244, 0.18) |
| 7. Appropriate to release psycheducational assessment results without consent | 99 (146) | 97 (95) | (1, n = 245, 2.08) |
| 8. Ethical to have a relative hire students from one's support-service program | 51 (71) | 79 (77) | (1, n = 236, 19.57)*** |

** Note some respondents did not answer each question.
*** $p < .05$.

bined separate set of ethical guidelines, with a rank score of approximately 3.5. The groups were not significantly different in valuing ethical guidelines for their own profession, $t$ (242) =.94, $p > 0.05$, and they were not different regarding how they valued a combined set of ethical guidelines, with a rank score of approximately 3.5 for working with students with learning disabilities, $t$ (239) = −.04, $p > 0.05$.

## DISCUSSION

The findings indicate similarity of opinions between professionals trained in education and counseling on most of the situations presented. Each of the eight vignettes illustrated basic educational situations with ethical concerns as opposed to complex ethical dilemmas requiring more detailed knowledge of professional guidelines and legal rulings. In regard to ethical guidelines, the data suggest that those trained in both fields expressed valued ethical guidelines in general, and specifically valued ethical guidelines for working with students who have learning disabilities.

Data from the first vignette indicated no significant differences between individuals trained in counseling and those trained in education with regard to appropriate responses. The experts reviewing the question indicated that it was ethical to refuse to release requested information without appropriate student/client authorization, including information between two universities within the same state system. Both educational and counseling professionals seemed aware of confidentiality, privacy, and ownership issues relating to this vignette. In particular, the professionals were concerned with the importance of a student's informed consent. Historically, ethical guidelines of the American Association for Counseling and Development (AACD 1988) have addressed the confidential retention and disposal of records and stress that client information be released only with client consent. The current ethical code of the American Counseling Association (ACA; formerly AACD) requires written client permission to provide information or transfer records to outside parties (ACA 1995). The Americans with Disabilities Act (ADA) describes information provided by students as voluntary and confidential (34 C.F.R. 104.42 [c][2][1994]). There is, however, no specific ADA or Section 504 requirement for the university to have written policies regarding students with learning disabilities. Therefore, verbal transmission of information and policies may occur and potentially increase inconsistency and inappropriate release (Tucker and Goldstein 1996).

The second vignette involved an issue relating to academic honesty and fairness to all students. The experts who were consulted considered it acceptable for a professor to refuse to provide accommodations without some understanding of the specific disability and the accommodation required. Ethical behavior in this context is based on principles of academic integrity and fairness to all students. While responses to this vignette did not vary significantly as a function of group, professionals were divided on whether the situation was ethical. Overall, 55.4 percent considered it unethical to refuse accommodation, and 44.6 percent felt it was ethical. Apparently, professionals dealing with this type of situation hold contradictory opinions regardless of training. At issue is whether a professor has the right to know the type of disability and what has been historically viewed as appropriate accommodation prior to granting a student's request. This situation concerns who is responsible—the professor or the disability specialist—for maintaining academic integrity/expectations of the course and who decides whether accommodation is reasonable without creating undue advantage. In this vignette, the professor does not appear to trust that the disability specialist will recommend the appropriate accommodation, and seems to fear that overaccommodation will occur. ACA ethical guidelines (1995) require counselors to "avoid illegal and unwarranted disclosure of confidential information" (Section B.1) in order to protect their clients' privacy. At the same time, the code states that accepting employment represents an agreement to abide by the policies of the hiring institution (ACA 1995, Section D.1). Kitchener's (1984) Critical-Evaluation Model for ethical decisions is helpful when making these difficult decisions. The four-level model includes the following moral principles: autonomy, beneficence, nonmaleficence, and justice (fairness). Justice or fairness is defined as equal treatment for all. This portion of the model perhaps best applies to this scenario and the balancing of equal academic opportunity through accommodation with equal treatment or academic expectations. The ADA (1990) is clearer on this matter and states that while an agent of the university (for example, the disability coordinator) must be notified of the disability, disclosure need not be made to every university employee. In vignette number two, it appears that full disclosure of the disability to determine eligibility was made to an appropriate university employee. Clearly, opinions vary in regard to this vignette and continued discussions are warranted.

Vignette number three raised questions about a student's right to obtain his file from the support center on completion of service. This vignette examined issues relating to record maintenance and student rights concerning access to records. The experts consulted viewed the appropriate ethical response as refusal to give the student the file based on the need to maintain records for a specific time. This vignette yielded a significant difference between professionals with education backgrounds and those with counseling backgrounds. Although the respondents within both groups were somewhat divided in their opinions, those trained in education were more likely to give the student his file whereas those trained in counseling were more likely to refuse.

This difference may stem from ethical guidelines for counselors and psychologists regarding record maintenance, and from analogous medical records guidelines which require service providers to maintain the records while allowing the client to review records. The American Psychological Association's Ethical Principles (1992) cover the creation of files and releasing of information, as well as record storage and disposal. The ACA code (1995, Section B.4) centers on the fact that records are maintained for the benefit of clients, and therefore, clients should have access to review their records. However, the code cautions that client access should occur only when the client is competent and the information will not be harmful or misleading.

Individuals with training in education may view this ethical dilemma more from a consumer rights perspective. That is, students have the right to their files because the file is about them and they are the "customer" at the university. The Family Education Rights and Privacy Act (FERPA, Buckley Amendment) states that information provided to the university becomes property of the university and students may view their file but not remove it. An appropriate university employee may need to review the file prior to giving it to the student to remove letters of recommendation or other documents to which the student waived his or her viewing rights.

The fourth vignette focused on the professor's behavior regarding appropriate accommodation for a student's learning disability. The experts considered it appropriate for the faculty member to refuse to accommodate a student with an open book exam. They viewed this as ethical because the student's mathematics disability with no memory problems should not influence performance on a history examination. The experts did not, however, take issue with providing a distraction-free, private room, or extended test time for the student. The issues of academic integrity and fairness were the basis for this ethical decision. Both participants with training in education and counseling agreed that the accommodation requested would create unfair advantage because neither the test material nor method of examination was related to the disability. Within ACA (1995, Section A.1) guidelines, this appears most congruent with the prohibition against inappropriate disclosure of confidential information, with counselors called on to protect both the dignity and welfare of their clients. However, counselors are also expected to provide unbiased information to third parties who receive their reports (ACA 1995). Therefore, it would be unethical to suggest accommodations that are not warranted by the documented disability.

Previous AACD (1988) codes reminded counselors that their responsibilities rested not only with their client but also with educators, and that both parties deserved the highest professional service. This would concur with current ACA guidelines. In regard to the Americans with Disabilities Act (1990), the question is not whether accommodation be provided, as the disability is documented, but rather that accommodation be both reasonable and appropriate. Issues to be addressed in this vignette include whether the area of mathematics is a documented function of the disability, and whether altering the exam constitutes a substantial modification of the program, provides preferential treatment, or undermines the purpose of the exam.

Another issue arising in postsecondary settings concerns the writing of references for students with disabilities. The fifth vignette portrayed a professor who revealed the student's learning disability to a potential employer. The experts consulted believed that the ethical, professional behavior would be for the professor not to reveal information regarding the student's disability without specific consent to do so by the student. This vignette yielded significant differences between individuals trained in education and those trained in counseling. Professionals with education backgrounds viewed the release of information regarding the student's disability as unethical to a greater degree than did professionals trained in counseling, although the majority of both groups felt it was unethical. The difference between education and counseling professionals may be related to knowledge regarding the spirit of ADA and the rights of privacy concerning student information in employment hiring practices. Professionals trained in counseling may be more concerned about the integrity of the recommendation versus the rights of the student. ACA (1995, Section B.1, ) requires counselors to respect client's privacy; however, it does not state some or all aspects of client information, nor does it address the integrity of a recommendation containing limited information.

Perhaps the answer lies in whether the disclosure was warranted, and whether full disclosure of all known information is necessary. If the professor does not believe the disability will have an impact, then one might ask what the purpose was in disclosing the information. Additionally, given mixed opinions regarding whether disclosure affects employment success regardless of whether accommodation is utilized, one might be cautious in disclosing the disability. Anecdotal reports from support service workers in response to this vignette cite numerous instances of graduates who choose not to disclose the disability, in an effort to avoid stereotype judgments and subsequent lower performance evaluations based on the assumed impact of a disability regardless of any actual impact. Additionally, if examined only from an ethical point of view, professionals trained in counseling may view professors who are not in counseling or psychology as outside of the same ethical guidelines and not needing to comply with the more restrictive guidelines. The professionals in counseling may not have viewed confidential and privacy rights as extending to privacy in regard to having a disability. The ADA (1990, 45 CFR 84.14) clearly prohibits prospective employers from inquiring about an applicant's possible disability. Both the Equal Opportunity for Employment and Affirmative Action guidelines also bear on this vignette and employer questions.

The sixth vignette focuses on specific competency to provide service to students with learning disabilities. This vignette describes a learning disability specialist with a master's degree in education refusing to engage in psychotherapy with the student. The experts consulted prior to the study viewed this refusal to provide services outside of the professional's areas of expertise as ethical behavior. The education and counseling professionals in this study agreed uniformly with this decision, with no significant differences between groups. According to the ACA (1995, Section C.2) code, it is unethical to practice in areas in which one does not have competence resulting from education or training. Additionally, counselors are cautioned to avoid dual relationships and those which exploit clients' trust or dependence (ACA 1995, Section A.6).

The seventh vignette involved a learning disability specialist who released portions of a student's psychoeducational assessment without the student's knowledge. The experts consulted during the development of this item viewed the release of information by the learning disabilities specialist without student consent as unethical. The primary reason supporting this decision was that the issue of informed consent had not been adequately addressed. Other issues such as report ownership, record maintenance, and competency were mentioned as ethical concerns. Participants in both groups were in agreement in their response to this item. The ACA (1995, Section B.4) code requires counselors to maintain records while providing services. It requires that the records be in compliance with local statutes and employer requirements, and that records be kept secure and properly destroyed when appropriate.

The final vignette portrayed a learning disability specialist who requested that her relative hire one of the students in the support program where she works. The experts consulted in the development of this item viewed this behavior as unethical based on dual relationships, potential social problems, potential work problems, and appropriate boundaries. The survey found a significant difference between those trained in education in comparison with those trained in counseling. Those with degrees in education were less likely than those trained in counseling to view the hiring of a student by a relative as unethical. In recent years, counselors have become very aware of boundary and dual relationship issues due to malpractice litigations (Corey, Corey, and Callanan 1993). The recent sensitivity to ethical concerns relating to dual relationships may be the explanation for the differences found in vignette number eight. Counselors were likely concerned about how the employee and student roles would overlap, clouding the roles of business owner and advisor with employee and student. The ACA (1995, Section A.6) cautions against dual relationships that might affect professional service and objectivity, and business relationships are specifically mentioned. While the ADA does not address hiring a student with a disability, there is potentially an issue if the student does not receive appropriate accommodation or if the student is fired and believes it was based on discrimination because of the disability.

Our survey also explored the value of a set of ethical guidelines for an individual's profession, and combined ethical guidelines for the fields of counseling and education in relation to students with disabilities. The results suggest that both groups valued this information to a similar extent. While the professionals with different kinds of training viewed many situations in a similar manner, a combined set of guidelines would serve to further clarify these ambiguous situations and provide a common frame of reference for other situations that this survey did not explore.

# IMPLICATIONS

As professionals serving students with learning disabilities examine the ethical problems relating to interdisciplinary action, the need for common understanding and professional standards emerges. "Practice guidelines and ethics are developed in response to practical concerns of people who work in a profession and people who use the services provided by the profession" (Bennett, Bryant, VandenBos, and Greenwood 1995, p. 17). In the recent *Journal of Postsecondary Education and Disability* (Vol. 12, No. 3), a number of education professionals called for further development of professional standards for service personnel working with students who have disabilities. Because of the interdisciplinary approaches to such service provision, the development of professional standards is slow and complex. Currently, these professional standards are, at best, in the early stage of development with general broad statements providing the basic framework to guide service providers. However, these standards must evolve and be based on interdisciplinary contributions from professionals in each of the areas impacted.

In psychology and medicine, the legal doctrine of informed consent has influenced the manner in which professionals practice. Moreover, service providers have developed materials to assist consumers in making crucial health care decisions. Service providers working with clients who have learning disabilities should consider utilizing modified informed consent procedures to proactively address potential ethical and legal problems. In medicine, informed consent requires disclosure of treatment risks, appropriate alternatives, a voluntary patient decision, and patient competency to make the decisions. Medical and psychological personnel have extended the informed consent process to include educating the consumer concerning the services provided. Such information as credentials, degrees, areas of competence, consumer rights, service limitations, confidentiality, releases of information, requirements to receive service, fee policies, appointment scheduling information, emergency services, office arrangements when referring to other providers, and guidelines for service provision may become part of the information to the consumer prior to the provision of service. This procedure of educating consumers could reduce future ethical problems. Consumer education, in addition to collaborative guidelines, appears to be the next logical step in refining professional services.

This research presents an opportunity for professionals with different educational backgrounds to respond to realistic situations encountered during the delivery of services to college students with learning disabilities. The ethical dimensions of each vignette allowed for meaningful comparison of ethical behavior as viewed through different professional lenses. Hopefully, this material will encourage further dialogue between educators, counselors, psychologists, and other university personnel concerning collaborative efforts to provide quality services to consumers. The time is right to work cooperatively to develop ethical guidelines for work with students who have learning disabilities.

Correspondence should be directed to:
Jeanmarie Keim, Ph.D.,Counseling, Educational Psychology and Research, 100 Ball Education Building, University of Memphis, Memphis, TN 38152 email: keim.jean@coe.memphis.edu

## References

American Association for Counseling and Development. 1988. Ethical standards of the American Association for Counseling and Development (3rd rev.) *Journal of Counseling and Development* 67:4–8.

American Counseling Association. 1995. *Code of Ethics and Standards of Practice.* Washington, DC: American Counseling Association.

American Psychological Association. 1992. Ethical principles of psychologists and code of conduct. *American Psychologist* 47(12):1597–1611.

Americans with Disabilities Act of 1990, 42 U.S.C. 12101 et seq.

Bateman, B. 1982. The special educator as a professional person. *Exceptional Education Quarterly* 2(4):57–69.

Bennett, B., Bryant, B., VandenBos, G., and Greenwood, A. 1995. *Professional liability and risk management.* Washington, DC: American Psychological Association.

Blalock, G., and Dixon, N. 1982. Improving prospects for the college-bound learning disabled. *Topics in Learning and Learning Disabilities* 2(3):69–78.

Brinkerhoff, L. C., Shaw, S. F., and McGuire, J. M. 1993. *Promoting Postsecondary Education for Students with Learning Disabilities: A Handbook for Practitioners.* Austin, TX: PRO-ED.

Cobb, H. B., and Horn, C. J. 1989. *Implementation of professional standards in special education: A national study.* ERIC Document Reproduction Service No. ED 344–79.

Corey, G., Corey, M., and Callanan, P. 1993. *Issues and Ethics in the Helping Profession* (4th ed.). CA: Brooks-Cole Co.

Council for Learning Disabilities. 1995. *Principles of ethics* (3rd ed.). Washington, DC: Council for Learning Disabilities.

Dobson, R., and Dobson, J. 1983. Teacher beliefs - practice congruency. *Viewpoints in Teaching and Learning* 59(1):20–27.

Gajar, A. H. 1992. University based models for students with learning disabilities: The Pennsylvania State University Model. In F. R. Rusch, L. DeStefano, J. Chadsey-Rusch, A. L. Phelps, and E. Szymanski, eds., *Transition from School to Adult Life: Models, Linkages, and Policy.* Sycamore, IL: Sycamore.

Heller, H. W. 1983. Special education professional standards: Need, value, and use. *Exceptional Children* 50:199–204.

Keim, J., McWhirter, J. J., and Bernstein, B. 1996. Academic success and university accommodation for learning disabilities: Is there a relationship? *Journal of College Student Development* 37(5):502–9.

Keim, J., Nolan, B. F., and Ryan, A. G. November, 1994. *Ethical dilemmas: Serving yet protecting university students with learning disabilities.* Paper read at the International Conference on Learning Disabilities, San Diego, California.

Kirk, R. E. 1982. *Experimental Design: Procedures for the Behavioral Sciences.* California: Brooks/Cole.

Kitchener, K. S. 1984. Intuition, critical evaluation and ethical principles: The foundation for ethical decisions in counseling psychology. *The Counseling Psychologist* 12(3):43-55.

Leuchovius, D. February, 1995. ADA question & answer: The ADA and postsecondary education. *The Pacesetter*: 12–13.

Nelson, R., and Lignugaris/Kraft, B. 1989. Postsecondary education for students with learning disabilities. *Exceptional Children* 56(3):246–65.

Ostertag, B. A., Pearson, M. J., and Baker, R. E. 1986. Programs for the learning disabled in California community colleges. *Reading, Writing, and Learning Disabilities* 2:331–47.

Rehabilitation Act of 1973, 29 U.S.C. 701 et seq.

Rehabilitation Act Amendments of 1992, P. L. No 102-569, 106 Stat. 4344.

Ryan, A. G., Keim, J., & Nolan, B. F. October, 1995. *Post-secondary professionals' perceptions of ethical dilemmas.* Paper read at the 17th International Conference on Learning Disabilities, Chicago, Illinois.

Shaw, S. F., and Madaus, J. W. 1997. *Journal of Postsecondary Education and Disability* 12(3):27–34.

Strichart, S. S., and Mangrum, C. T., II. 1986. College for the learning-disabled student: A new opportunity. *Reading, Writing, and Learning Disabilities* 2:251–66.

Tucker, B. P., and Goldstein, B. A. 1996. *Legal rights of persons with disabilities: An analysis of federal law.* LRP: Horsham, Pennsylvania.

Turnbull, R. N., and Barber, P. 1984. Perspectives on public policy. In E. L. Meyen, ed., *Mental retardation: Topics of today-issues of tomorrow* (1 Serial No. 1). Division of Mental Retardation of the Council for Exceptional Children.

Wren, C., Williams, N., and Kovitz, V. 1987. Organizational problems at the college level. *Academic Therapy* 23(2):157–65.

# Students with Learning Disabilities in Teacher Education Programs

*Cheruta Wertheim*

Beit Berl College

*Susan A. Vogel*

Northern Illinois University

*Andrew R. Brulle*

Wheaton College

*Education faculty are dedicated to preparing competent teachers. At the same time, they must provide reasonable accommodations in the teaching and evaluation of qualified students with disabilities, in compliance with the mandates of Section 504 of the Rehabilitation Act of 1973. This article describes some of the reasons that students with learning disabilities[1] (LD) choose teaching as a profession, and the difficulties that some students with LD have in teacher preparation programs. It discusses the underlying legal and ethical issues encountered when working with students with LD in teacher education programs, as well as some ways to enhance success.*

---

[1] The term learning disabilities is used since not all teacher candidates will have a language-based reading, spelling, and written expression disorder or dyslexia. It is assumed, however, that approximately 80 percent or more will have dyslexia.

Annals of Dyslexia, Vol. 48, 1998
Copyright© 1998 by The International Dyslexia Association
ISSN 0736-9387

## INTRODUCTION

Students with LD are no longer a rare phenomenon in higher education. One of the major factors leading to the increase in enrollment of students with LD is the enactment of Section 504 of the Rehabilitation Act of 1973 (P.L. 93-112). This act mandates that institutions of higher education that receive federal funds cannot discriminate on the basis of a disability, and stipulates that qualified students with disabilities receive reasonable accommodations so that programs are accessible. In 1985, 1.1 percent of all first-time, full-time freshmen indicated that they had a learning disability in self-reports. By 1989, service providers reported a significant increase in the numbers of students with LD on their campuses, resulting in difficulty fulfilling requests for examination accommodations because of space and staff constraints (Hayeslip, Hermanson, and Scales 1989). In 1995, Henderson confirmed these observations and reported that the number of students with LD among first-time full-time freshmen across the nation had increased threefold (to approximately 3 percent) and comprised approximately one-third of all first-year full-time students with disabilities. To date, no large-scale, systematic research has investigated the major areas of study among students with LD in higher education. However, Vogel and Adelman (1997) reported that 24 percent of the students with LD who were receiving support services at a small, private, competitive Midwestern college had chosen a major in education. Moreover, approximately half of these students chose to certify in special education. Similar data were found in a large, doctoral degree granting university; there, 25 percent of the undergraduate and graduate students with documented learning disabilities were in teacher preparation programs (Wyland 1996).

Consequently, faculty involved in teacher preparation must frequently face ethical dilemmas resulting from the conflict between increasing pressure to make accommodations for students with LD (following Section 504) and the demand for well-prepared teachers. While faculty strive to comply with Section 504, they also must ensure that their graduates possess a strong knowledge of the structure of spoken and written language, as well as effective strategies for teaching reading, literacy, and subject matter. The public demand for well-prepared teachers is reflected in the fact that all but seven states now mandate that teachers pass at least one type of competency examination (for example, basic skills or subject matter) in order to be licensed (NASDEC 1996). Additionally, a recent publication titled *What Matters Most: Teaching for America's Future* (National Commission on Teaching and America's Future 1996) has emphasized the importance of ensuring that all teachers be well-prepared, competent, and resourceful, and know how to teach all children to read based on the most recent research in reading funded by the National Institute of Child Health and Human Development (Brady and Moats 1997).

During our informal discussions with faculty, perusal of written reports, and interactions with teacher educators, some faculty members wondered whether providing instructional modifications and nonstandard administration of examinations might result in a lowering of standards. Others expressed concern regarding a conflict between accommodations and changing the objectives of the program, even though legal mandates clearly imply that accommodations should not result in a modification of the essential elements of the program (Rothstein 1993, 1998). To address these issues, Brulle (1996) recommended that faculty carefully scrutinize their programs to determine which competencies are essential to the program and what accommodations can be provided without altering critical aspects of these competency requirements. Even the designation of these necessary competencies, however, can be controversial. For example, some faculty might argue that all abilities assessed on a basic skills test are essential competencies, and that all students must receive a passing score on every section of the examination regardless of their teacher certification area. Such a decision could logically be upheld if the faculty feel that, for example, the mathematics skills tested are minimal in nature and should be demonstrated by all certification candidates. Different cases involving different skills and/or faculty, however, might result in varying decisions.

Teacher educators are also concerned about how students with learning disabilities will fare once they have classrooms of their own. For example, although many prospective teachers with LD use assistive technology extensively (e.g., previously prepared and spell-checked overheads in place of a chalkboard), their ability to recognize errors and to correct their students' written work are areas of concern. On this topic, the courts have provided some guidance. In Gurmankin v. Costanzo (1977), the court found that blindness in itself was not sufficient to disqualify a person from receiving a teaching certificate. The court felt that the district could make adaptations, such as providing a teacher's aide to handle such duties as checking written work. Logically, this decision also should apply to teachers with other disabilities.

Faculty have also expressed conflicting opinions regarding the impact of early school experiences on students with LD. Some faculty believe that past experiences related to their learning disabilities could help these candidates become more understanding and empathetic teachers, whereas other faculty are concerned that the students' empathy could result in lower expectations and lower achievement for students in their classes. Other faculty members have raised the question as to whether the candidates might inadvertently overgeneralize from their understanding of their own specific type of LD and misperceive the needs of students with a different type of learning disability.

In order to address the above concerns, data-based empirical studies are needed regarding students with LD in teacher preparation programs. In general, very little is known about adults with learning disabilities who are already employed in the teaching profession (Anderson, Keller, and Karp 1998; Gerber 1992, 1994, 1998; Gerber, Ginsberg, and Reiff 1992). Even less is known about students with LD in colleges and universities who are preparing to become teachers. Relying on clinical observation, our purposes in this paper are to describe the various reasons that students with LD choose teaching as a profession; to examine the legal and ethical issues involved concerning students with LD in teacher education programs; to describe the difficulties of students with LD in teacher preparation programs; and to suggest ways to enhance success for students with LD in teacher preparation programs.

## THE DECISION TO ENTER THE FIELD OF EDUCATION

Career decision-making is a very complex process for all young people, but for students with LD the decision to become a teacher may be even more complex, as it involves additional factors. These factors include, among others, how their disability will affect their performance in different teaching situations. The learning disability should have different consequences depending on the age of the students, the subject matter to be taught, and the level at which they will teach (elementary or secondary education). Regrettably, students with LD facing complex decisions in considering a future career in education are not likely to find much support in the typical career counseling center. Most colleges and universities have career counseling centers, but as reported by deBettencourt and Bonaro (1995), there has been very little communication between staff in the career counseling centers and staff providing services for students with disabilities. Most career counselors had little knowledge about LD and, consequently, did not modify their services to meet the needs of students with LD. Career counselors did not, for example, offer assistance with writing resumes or filling out job applications to students with written language disorders. Nonetheless, despite the complexity of the decision and the lack of support in career counseling centers, many students with LD do choose to become teachers, often in special education. Why did they decide to become teachers, and why is special education sometimes more attractive to students with LD than other areas of education?

Some insight into the decision-making process may derive from a case study reported by Gerber (1992, 1994, 1998) involving a beginning teacher with LD. The first reason for choosing teaching as a career was familiarity. Students with LD, as all other students, are familiar with individual teachers and teaching, and this familiarity is considered to be one of the main reasons for choosing education as a profession (Gerber 1992; Gerber, Ginsberg, and Reiff 1992). During their years in school, students with LD were exposed to a variety of teachers with different teaching styles and had the opportunity to learn about schools as a work environment. They have clear, often highly emotional recollections of the teachers who facilitated their learning and those who did not.

Another account of a teacher with LD expresses anger and frustration at childhood teachers who were ill-prepared to teach children with dyslexia to read, and simply passed them along from one grade to the next (Corcoran and Carlson 1994). According to Corcoran, negative experiences in school can have a major impact on the career choices of individuals with LD. Corcoran described many painful memories, and a host of misunderstandings, confusion, and decreased self-esteem. His personal history motivated him to become a teacher and later a national advocate for adult literacy opportunities.

Not all dyslexics remain angry and embittered by their early school experiences, however. Among students studied by Vogel and Adelman (1992), some dyslexic students cited positive experiences. They remembered teachers who helped them along the way, had confidence in their abilities, gave them encouragement in the face of disappointments, and had a significant impact on their development and success. These teachers often became role models for the students who then wanted to follow in their footsteps. Many of these students with LD reported having chosen special education because they felt they had unique knowledge in the area of learning disabilities. They had acquired valuable knowledge about special strategies that they developed and/or learned along the way (knowledge from the perspective of a student with LD about the educational system) and knowledge regarding how to effectively use help that is offered by the system. They felt that this personal knowledge was valuable and important to pass on to others like themselves, especially younger individuals with LD.

Gerber (1992) and Gerber, Ginsburg, and Reiff (1992) refer to the emotional process that students with LD experience as they grow up and cope with their disabilities as a process of reframing. Reframing is based on self-understanding and self-knowledge which serve as the foundation for the acceptance of one's learning disability. This process involves perceiving, not just the deficit but also special talents and strengths. Reframing helps an individual to identify educational goals and make career decisions. Choosing teaching as a profession can serve as part of the reframing process. It is possible that teaching students with special needs provides persons with LD with an empowering opportunity to help and support others, often after years of needing help themselves. Working in this type of a reversed role may become a healing process for those with disabilities (Gerber 1992).

Motivation to know more about one's own disability may be another reason that some students with LD choose to become special education teachers. Studying special education can provide students with increased knowledge about the causes and nature of learning disabilities, and help them to better understand themselves and others. Furthermore, these students may anticipate that, among special education faculty, they might find mentors who have a supportive attitude, are knowledgeable about their difficulties, and can appreciate their efforts. Working with professors who are anticipated to have this specific sensitivity certainly would seem a less threatening prospect than blindly enrolling in courses with faculty whose knowledge of, and support for, students with disabilities are unknown

Results of a survey sent to faculty in a Midwestern public university with a large teacher preparation program were recently reported by Brulle, Leyser, Vogel, and Wyland (1998). One of the goals of that survey was to examine the attitudes of education faculty toward students with LD enrolled in teacher certification programs, and their willingness to provide needed accommodations. Although the faculty surveyed were generally supportive of accommodations such as providing assignments early and allowing students to use assistive technology in clinical experiences, almost 90 percent of respondents were unwilling to alter examination formats (for example, change from multiple choice exams to short answer or essay exams). The majority also felt that the minimum grade point average (in this case, 2.50) should not be altered for students with LD provided that the students had received other, appropriate accommodations. However, despite their willingness to provide accommodations, about one-third of the respondents expressed the view that it would be appropriate to counsel students with LD to enter fields other than teaching. Some of these faculty may have been unaware that Section 504 mandates that it is discriminatory to restrict the range of career options for students with disabilities (Vogel 1997). On the other hand, one might interpret this finding to suggest that these respondents felt students with LD had sufficient capabilities to enter any field of their choosing. Further research is needed to clarify faculty attitudes, but the data suggest that there is a need for more faculty education about the mandates of Section 504. Comparisons of the survey responses from faculty in the College of Education (CoE) with responses from faculty in other departments within the university revealed that the CoE faculty had significantly more knowledge and skills for teaching individuals with disabilities, spent more time with students with disabilities, were more familiar with Section 504, were more willing to allow students to complete alternative assignments, and were more willing to provide tests in alternative formats (Vogel, Leyser, Brulle, and Wyland 1997).

In regard to career choice, some authors (Felton 1986; Gerber 1992; Silver and Hagin 1985) have pointed out that individuals with LD often choose a career in their perceived area of strength. Consistent with this, Vogel (1997) noted that students with LD who have strengths in oral expressive language and deficits in written expressive language, sometimes choose to teach young children because they feel that, for the curricula involved, they would be less dependent on their writing skills than in teaching older children.

The reasons that so many students with LD choose teaching as a career, and special education as a major, should be further explored in future research. In a large-scale interview project, it would be of interest to compare students with and without LD regarding individual reasons for entering the teaching profession. Until a project of this sort is completed, however, we can only speculate the relationship of these reasons to LD. Motivation notwithstanding, we must address the fact that about one-fourth of students with LD do choose to major in education and to enter the teaching profession (Adelman and Vogel 1993; Vogel and Adelman 1997; Wyland 1996).

## STUDENTS WITH LEARNING DISABILITIES IN TEACHER EDUCATION PROGRAMS AND THE LAW

In addressing the growing population of aspiring teachers with LD, there are a number of legal mandates that give teacher educators some guidelines. Section 504 is recognized as the primary statute guaranteeing that qualified students with disabilities, including those with LD, have the legal right to participate fully in the educational programs at all colleges and universities that receive federal funds. When creating standards for entering a professional school, especially to train for those professions that directly affect the lives of others (e.g., teaching, medicine), the goal is to preserve student rights without compromising the public interest (Brulle 1996). The law is clear about admission to higher education, but the courts have generally yielded to the expertise of faculty regarding requirements for graduation. If questions about graduation requirements are raised, courts will usually uphold these requirements when the faculty can show that they are essential for success in the profession. In the past, however, it has been difficult to reach a consensus within the education community concerning what functions are essential to the teaching profession. Hence, requirements often differed from program to program, and some students with learning disabilities may have been able to succeed in one program but not another. Recently, however, many colleges and universities have begun to use the ten principles promulgated by the Interstate New Teacher Assessment and Support Consortium (INTASC) as a basis for defining what new teachers should know and be able to do. These ten principles have gained general acceptance in higher education, and teacher educators may now be able to assist candidates with LD in devising whatever adaptations are necessary to allow them to meet these minimum requirements. Interesting legal challenges may occur in the future when some students with LD demonstrate that they can meet these minimum expectations for teaching but are still unable to pass some academic classes.

There have been several court decisions related to higher education, accommodations for individuals with disabilities, and the essential functions of the job. In the case of Southeastern Community College v. Davis (1979), the court denied a student with a serious hearing disability admission to a nursing program. The court noted that "nothing in the language of the history of Section 504 reflects an intention to limit the freedom of an educational institution to require reasonable physical qualifications for admission to a clinical training program" (p. 414). Brulle (1996) noted that the ruling on this case may be applicable to teacher education programs as well since teacher preparation programs are primarily clinical in nature. Faculty can and should set reasonable qualifications for entry to, and graduation from, their programs providing that the requirements are related to the individual's future professional responsibilities.

Another case (Lipsett v. University of Puerto Rico 1986), dealt with the criteria evaluating students' qualifications and appropriateness (referred to as "fitness") for completion of programs. In this case, the court did not limit the academic freedom of the university to decide how to define academic fitness for the medical profession. The plaintiff was dismissed from a program because of her abrasive manner. Although she alleged sexual discrimination, the court supported the dismissal, ruling that "there may be situations where academic fitness requires evaluation of subjective character traits since these may also be valid components of the characteristics of a certain trade or profession" (p. 808). Brulle (1996) proposed that the precedent set by this case might be extended to all cases of doubt regarding fitness for the teaching profession, whether or not students with disabilities are involved.

In addition, in order to determine when a student should be accepted to, or dismissed from, teacher education, the essential requirements of the program should be clearly delineated and defined in the interest of all students, including students with LD. Although students with LD may precipitate the necessity to clarify and define requirements and essential functions, it is important for all students to know the guidelines for acceptance or dismissal, and whether these requirements are essential for the teaching profession. Requirements should be discussed by education faculty members in each college of education so that they can provide acceptable explanations and demonstrate clearly how completion of the requirements is assessed and why these competencies are necessary for success in teaching. Even formal demands, such as getting a grade of "C" or above in certain classes, must be defensible. Coming to an agreement on such issues is not an easy task, as opinions on the issues are typically deeply rooted in faculty members' viewpoints on education. An example is the requirement for early childhood certification that a student teacher be able to read a story from a book to preschoolers. For a student with LD, this task could plausibly be altered by having the children listen to the story on tape while the teacher holds the book up for easy viewing of the illustrations. Some educators, however, may argue that it is important to see the reader's facial expression while reading the story and may not consider playing a tape-recorded story to be an acceptable substitute, especially for young children. Others may be willing to consider this alternative as a valid fulfillment of the requirement.

Brulle (1996) suggested that institutions, when dealing with individual cases, should have clearly written documentation describing the expectations of the student with LD, the accommodations that have been made, and the feedback that has been provided to the student, in order to avoid the risk of inadvertently discriminating on the basis of a disability. He also recommended that the documentation procedure be applied to every student, not just to students with LD, to monitor progress.

Yanok (1987) provides recommendations regarding dismissal procedures in order to protect students with disabilities as well as to avoid litigation for the teacher education faculty and the university. His recommendations are solidly grounded in the principles of due process. Yanok begins by noting the obligation of every teacher education program to have clearly written dismissal policies and procedures which are readily available to students. In addition, a student whose performance has not met academic standards must receive fair and reasonable treatment. Such treatment includes being fully informed, orally and in writing, at every stage in the deliberations, receiving written notification regarding performance evaluations, and being invited to participate in all meetings convened for the purpose of reviewing his or her performance in the teacher preparation program (Long 1984). In the case of disagreement regarding the student's performance, an independent evaluation should be undertaken by a qualified, impartial, third party (McGrath, Moody, and Olsen 1987). Once specific deficiencies have been identified, the student should be notified of them promptly, both orally and in writing. In some instances, the faculty may decide to give the student the opportunity to repeat the experience/course in order to improve performance. Yanok recommended that during this time period the student be given an interim grade of incomplete. If the student's performance does not improve sufficiently to warrant continuation in the program, then action should be taken to dismiss the student following the due process format of notification, participation, and written documentation.

## SPECIFIC DIFFICULTIES EXPERIENCED BY STUDENTS WITH LD IN TEACHER EDUCATION PROGRAMS

### TESTING AND ACADEMIC REQUIREMENTS

Students are usually admitted to teacher preparation programs during their second year of undergraduate studies. Requirements for admission vary, but most institutions demand proficiency in basic skills as indicated by competency examinations in reading, written expression, and mathematics. In addition, they require mastery of academic subject matter, demonstrated by a minimum grade point average, typically 2.50 on a 4.00 scale. Since nondiscriminatory practices are mandated, instructional and testing accommodations have been used widely in institutions of higher education for students with LD (Vogel 1997). In the aforementioned survey of faculty in a large Midwestern university, we found that faculty were most willing to allow students with LD to tape-record lectures; they were also willing to review assignments in progress, such as in commenting on preliminary drafts of written assignments. With regard to accommodations for testing, the faculty were most willing to allow students to take the examinations elsewhere, have extended time, or use assistive technology such as a word processor or calculator (Vogel et al. 1997 ). In addition to the accommodations described above, some faculty members may also consider allowing students to demonstrate mastery of course objectives using alternative methods such as a class demonstration, oral presentation, or independent study project in lieu of a written examination (Vogel 1997).

### CLINICAL EXPERIENCES

Additional accommodations may be needed to help students with LD succeed in clinical experiences and student teaching. During their years of schooling, students presumably studied in classroom settings and were likely evaluated on their knowledge of subject matter primarily by paper and pencil tests. Clinical practice, however, is a new experience for all preservice teachers; different skills have to be demonstrated and different methods of instruction and evaluation are employed. Clinical experience also provides an opportunity for students to test whatever hypotheses may have influenced their career choice. As a result, early clinical teaching experiences can initially cause great emotional tension.

Additional variables make this experience even more stressful for students with LD. Does the cooperating teacher realize that the student has a learning disability? If not, should the student let the teacher know? What about the children? Should student teachers disclose to their class that they have a learning disability? These questions have no easy resolution. Teacher educators must work closely with students to address these and other issues, on an individual basis, during the clinical experience. We recommend that teacher educators discuss such questions in a manner that communicates both respect for the student with LD and concern for the children in the classroom.

## WAYS TO ENHANCE SUCCESS

What we have learned from our experience thus far is that the usual procedures and preparation for certification may not be sufficient for students with LD. Three areas should be reexamined in light of reported failures in clinical settings. These include:

1. the demands of the specific clinical setting and the nature and severity of students' LD;
2. the preparation and attitude of the cooperating teacher; and
3. the preparation of the student teacher.

*The Setting.* The nature and severity of a student's LD has to be taken into consideration when placing a student teacher in the field. In matching students to appropriate sites, the clinical placement personnel should work closely with students and carefully assess their needs. While students should not be sheltered from the realistic demands of teaching, it is not appropriate to ignore a student's LD (for example, it would be ill-advised to place a student with a severe writing disability with a fifth grade teacher responsible solely for language arts). Obviously, the goal should be to match students' strengths to classroom demands. A successful clinical placement can also serve as a model to students in their future search for a permanent teaching position.

*Cooperating Teachers.* Sudzina and Knowles (1993) emphasized the importance of matching students (without LD) with appropriate cooperating teachers. They found that many students who failed student teaching were placed with teachers with whom they could not work comfortably. Making the right match can be even more difficult for student teachers with LD because their mentors have to be especially flexible and able to alter strategies which may previously have been successful with non-LD student teachers. It should be the students' responsibility to disclose the existence of their LD to the cooperating teacher, describe how the LD may affect performance in the classroom, articulate successful compensatory strategies they have used in the past, and describe any accommodations needed (Vogel 1997). The cooperating teachers, on the other hand, have to enjoy being challenged, must have a positive attitude toward adults with LD, and be willing to recognize and value the unique strengths and determination of any student assigned to them. A mismatch between students and cooperating teachers, or between students and settings can be devastating to the success of the students.

We saw evidence of this fact when one of our most highly motivated, capable students with LD almost failed his practicum during the final semester of his undergraduate career. As a special education major in the LD program, he had a very successful elementary student teaching experience. For his second experience, he was placed with a high school LD teacher who taught five different subjects. Because of the student's slow reading rate, he was unable to keep up with the demands of the curriculum in spite of his efforts to complete all of the assigned readings each night. He decided to disclose his LD to the cooperating teacher and requested a modification in his assignment. The cooperating teacher was unwilling to modify the demands of the setting, and insisted the student teach all five subject areas. Rather than delay his graduation in order to have a third student teaching assignment, the student agreed to receive a passing grade (rather than the usual "A") and credit for the experience in order to graduate with his class. During a long-term substitute teaching assignment in the same school, he was observed by the building principal on several occasions and ultimately offered a full-time position as a special education teacher in a self-contained setting.

*The Student.*   Former students with LD have taught us quite a bit about what it takes to succeed in teacher education programs. First, successful students need to be comfortable with themselves, have an in-depth understanding of their own learning disability, recognize their weaknesses and know how to compensate for them, and recognize their individual strengths and special talents (Vogel and Adelman 1992). Students with LD must also be able to articulate this information to their professors and cooperating teachers, and be able to discuss with them any needed accommodations. Students should describe any accommodations they may need early in the semester by scheduling a short meeting with their instructor or supervising teacher. Through friends, support groups, and networking, students with LD can often find out in advance which instructors are most attuned to the needs of students with LD in clinical settings. They should make special efforts to work with those teachers through priority registration, which is available on most campuses as part of the response to Section 504. If students have difficulty listening and taking notes simultaneously, they should request permission to tape-record meetings. Also, tape-recording feedback sessions and student-teaching seminars will enable students with LD to concentrate on content and suggestions rather than on taking notes and wondering if they have missed something important.

In addition to their regular preparation for clinical experiences, students with LD might benefit from an opportunity to meet in small groups with other students with LD who are in various stages of their clinical experiences. Students who have already completed some of the early clinical experiences may be able to provide emotional and practical support to the beginners. Students in the later stages of their programs might also benefit from the support of their peers, and by mentoring students in the earlier stages, should increase their own self-confidence and reinforce the use of successful strategies. During their clinical experiences, students also should have easy access to professionals who can offer teaching suggestions and feedback. Although it often becomes more difficult to meet on campus once students enter student teaching, e-mail communication and "chat" (discussion) groups can be orchestrated by university faculty. By means of e-mail, student teachers can receive answers to specific questions as they arise instead of having to wait until the next student teaching seminar or support group meeting.

Finally, the concept of a formal support group for first year teachers, sometimes called an induction program, is becoming popular in many school districts (Huling-Austin, Odell, Ishler, Kay, and Edefelt 1989), and is particularly helpful to new teachers with LD. Almost all new teachers feel overwhelmed and isolated (Veenman 1984). For the new teacher with LD, these feelings are often compounded. Thies-Sprinthall and Gerler (1990) provide suggestions to guide faculty members in assisting students to establish support groups, in working with beginning teachers, and in determining the outcomes of group work.

# CONCLUSION

Meeting the special needs of students with learning disabilities in teacher preparation programs needs further deliberation based on empirical data. As more students with LD enter universities and enroll in teacher preparation programs, a balance must be reached between satisfying the public demand for competent teachers and fulfilling the legal and moral obligations of people with LD. The fear of discrimination suits should not, on the one hand, discourage faculty from dismissing students who fail to meet requirements for admissions, certification, or graduation. On the other hand, institutions should neither arbitrarily reject nor dismiss students with LD; nor should they refuse to consider modifications of programs or provide reasonable accommodations. When and if faculty have doubts about the qualifications and/or performance of a specific student, they should conduct a thorough and careful evaluation leading to explicit and constructive recommendations. Students with LD have many reasons for choosing teaching as their profession. Some of the reasons are directly related to their disabilities or to their desire to pave the way for other students with LD. Their self-awareness, understanding, and empathy may help them to function very well as student teachers and to later become exemplary teachers if they are provided with a supportive, accommodating, responsive, and challenging teacher preparation program.

*References*

Adelman, P. B., and Vogel, S. A. 1990. College graduates with learning disabilities: Employment attainment and career patterns. *Learning Disability Quarterly* 13:154–65.

Adelman, P. B., and Vogel, S. A. 1993. Issues in employment of adults with learning disabilities. *Learning Disability Quarterly* 16(3):219–32.

Anderson, R., Keller, C., and Karp, J. 1998. *Enhancing Diversity: Educators with Disabilities in the Educational Enterprise*. Washington, DC: Gallaudet University Press.

Biller, E. F. 1988. Career decision-making attitudes of college students with learning disabilities. *Journal of Postsecondary Education and Disabilities* 6(4):14–20.

Brady, S., and Moats, L. 1997. *Informed Instruction for Reading Success: Foundations for Teacher Preparation*. A Position Paper of the Orton Dyslexia Association. Baltimore: International Dyslexia Association.

Brulle, A. R. 1996. Students with learning disabilities and teacher preparation. *Critical Issues in Teacher Education* 5:13–25.

Brulle, A. R., Leyser, Y., Vogel, S. A. , and Wyland, S. 1998. Faculty attitudes toward students with learning disabilities in teacher preparation. *Critical Issues in Teacher Education* VII: 24–32.

Corcoran, J., and Carlson, C. 1994. *The Teacher Who Couldn't Read*. Colorado Springs, CO: Focus on the Family.

deBettencourt, L. U., and Bonaro, D. A. 1995. Career development services offered to postsecondary students with learning disabilities. *Learning Disabilities Research and Practice* 10(2):102–7.

Felton, R. November, 1986. Bowman-Gray follow-up study. Paper presented at the Orton Dyslexia National Conference. Philadelphia.

Gerber, P. J. 1992a. Being learning disabled and a beginning teacher and teaching a class of students with learning disabilities. *Exceptionality* 3:213–31.

Gerber, P. J. 1992b. Reflections on being learning disabled and a beginning teacher and teaching a class of students with learning disabilities. *Exceptionality* 3:259–63.

Gerber, P. J. 1994. Case study 3: T. J: Starting all over again. In Foucar-Szicki, ed., *Case Studies for Teacher Training and Educational Leadership*. Harrisonburg, VA: The Commonwealth Center for the Education of Teachers.

Gerber, P. J. 1998. Trials and tribulations of a teacher with learning disabilities through his first two years of employment. In R. Anderson, C. Keller, and J. Karp, eds., *Enhancing Diversity: Educators with Disabilities*. Washington, DC: Gallaudet University Press, 41–59.

Gerber, P. J., Ginsberg, R., and Reiff, H. B. 1992. Identifying alterable patterns in employment success for highly successful adults with learning disabilities. *Journal of Learning Disabilities* 25(8):475–87.

Gurmankin vs. Costanzo. 1977. 556 F2d 184 (3d Cir. 1977).

Hayeslip, P., Hermanson, J., and Scales, W. 1989. Personal communication .

Henderson, C. 1995. College Freshmen with Disabilities: A Triennial Statistical Profile. Washington, DC: American Council on Education, HEATH Resource Center.

Huling-Austin, L., Odell, S. J., Ishler, P., Kay, R. S., and Edefelt, R. A. Eds. 1989. *Assisting the Beginning Teacher*. Reston, VA: Association of Teacher Educators.

Interstate New Teacher Assessment Support Consortium, 1991. Model Standards for Beginning Teacher Licensing and Development: A Resource for State Dialogue (Working Draft). Washington, DC: Council of Chief State School Officers.

Kearns, J. M. 1984. State competency testing for teacher certification. *Journal of Teacher Education* 35(2):58–59.

Leyser, Y. 1989. A survey of faculty attitudes and accommodations for students with disabilities. *Journal of Postsecondary Education and Disabilities* 7:97–108.

Leyser, Y., Vogel, S. A., Brulle, A., and Wyland, S. In press. Faculty attitudes and practices regarding students with disabilities: Two decades after implementation of Section 504. *Journal of Postsecondary Education and Disability*.

Lipsett vs. University of Puerto Rico. 637 F. Supp. 798(D.P.R. 1986).

Long, B. E. 1984. Ensuring due process in clinical education experiences. *Teacher Education* 19:29–33.

McGrath, M., Moody, D., and Olsen, H. C. 1987. Due process and avoidance of litigation in teacher education. *Association of Teacher Education Newsletter* 6:3–6.

National Commission on Teaching and America's Future. 1996. *What Matters Most: Teaching for America's Future.* Washington, DC: National Commission Teaching and America's Future.

NASDEC. 1996. *Manual on Certification and Preparation of Educational Personnel in the United States and Canada.* Dubuque, IA: Kendall/Hunt.

Rothstein, L. 1998. The Americans with Disabilities Act (ADA), Section 504, and adults with LD and ADHD in adult education, postsecondary education, and employment. In S .A. Vogel and S. Reder, eds., *Learning Disabilities, Adult Education, and Literacy.* Baltimore, MD: Paul H. Brookes, 29–41.

Rothstein, L. 1993. Legal issues. In S. A. Vogel and P. B. Adelman, eds., *Success for College Students With Learning Disabilities.* New York: Springer-Verlag, 21-35.

Silver, A. A., and Hagin, R. A. 1985. Outcomes of learning disabilities in adolescence. In M. Suger, A. Esman, J. Loony, A. Schwartzberg, and A. Sorosky, eds., *Adolescent Psychiatry Developmental and Clinical Studies.* Chicago: The University of Chicago.

Southeastern Community College vs. Davis. 1979. 442 U. S. 397.

Sudzina, M., and Knowles, J. G. 1993. Personal, professional and contextual circumstances of student teachers who "fail": Setting a course for understanding failure in teacher education. *Journal of Teacher Education* 44(4 ):254–62.

Thies-Sprinthall, L. M., and Gerler, E. R. 1990. Support groups for novice teachers. *Journal of Staff Development* 11(4):18–22.

Veenman, S. 1984. Perceived problems of beginning teachers. *Review of Educational Research* 54(2):143–78.

Vogel, S. A. 1997. *College Students with Learning Disabilities: A Handbook* (6th ed.). Pittsburgh, PA: Learning Disabilities Association of America.

Vogel, S. A., and Adelman, P. B. 1992. The success of college students with learning disabilities: Factors related to educational attainment. *Journal of Learning Disabilities* 25(7):430–41.

Vogel, S. A., and Adelman, P. B. (eds.). 1993. *Success for College Students with Learning Disabilities.* New York: Springer-Verlag.

Vogel, S. A., and Adelman, P. B. November, 1997. Adults with Learning Disabilities: A Fifteen-year Follow-up Study. Paper presented at the International Dyslexia Association International Conference, Minneapolis.

Vogel, S. A., Leyser, Y., Brulle, A. R., and Wyland, S. February, 1997. University Students with Learning Disabilities: Faculty Knowledge, Attitudes, and Practices. Paper presented at The International Learning Disabilities Association of America Conference, Chicago.

Willingham, W. W. 1988. Admissions decisions. In W. W. Willingham, M. Ragosta, R. E. Bennett, H. Braun, D. A. Rock, and D. E. Powers, eds., *Testing Handicapped People.* Needham Heights, MA: Allyn and Bacon, Inc., 71–81.

Wyland, S. 1996. Majors of Undergraduate and Graduate Students with Learning Disabilities Attending Northern Illinois University. Unpublished document. Northern Illinois University, DeKalb.

Yanok, J. 1987. Equal opportunity in teacher education programs for the learning disabled. *Journal of Teacher Education*, January-February 48–51.

# Literacy Development in Successful Men and Women with Dyslexia

*Rosalie P. Fink*

Lesley College

*To investigate how, when, and under what conditions individuals with dyslexia manage to develop high literacy levels, an interview and literacy assessment study was conducted with 60 highly successful men and women with dyslexia and 10 peers without dyslexia. The sample with dyslexia included a Nobel laureate, a member of the National Academy of Sciences, and leaders in a variety of fields requiring extensive reading (i.e., medicine, law, business, and the arts and sciences).*

*For both males and females with dyslexia, interest-driven reading was key to the development of high literacy levels. Results showed distinct groups of successful professionals with dyslexia: a compensated group and two partially compensated groups. In each group, literacy development was augmented by avid reading in a content area of passionate personal interest, along with systematic phonics instruction. Through avid reading on a specific topic, the individuals with dyslexia developed knowledge of the specialized vocabulary, typical text structures, concepts, themes, and issues of a particular field. Extensive reading about a favorite subject enhanced the background knowledge of these individuals and enabled them to gain reading practice, which in turn, fostered the development of reading fluency and increasingly sophisticated skills. Although topics and genres of personal interest varied, fascination with a subject area was a common theme among those interviewed.*

*In the literacy assessment, the 60 men and women with dyslexia demonstrated most of the salient characteristics of Chall's (1983)*

Annals of Dyslexia, Vol. 48, 1998
Copyright© 1998 by The International Dyslexia Association
ISSN 0736-9387

*Stage 5, the highest level of reading development. All participants comprehended sophisticated text, but some, with partially compensated dyslexia, showed continuing lags in basic, lower level "print" skills. Individuals with partially compensated dyslexia fell into two groups: one group showed specific deficits only in spelling, whereas the other group had difficulty in spelling, word recognition, and oral reading. Many, but not all, of the participants with dyslexia showed ongoing lags in reading rate. Gender differences were most apparent in topics of personal interest reading and in mentoring patterns.*

*The study explores how adults with dyslexia, who may continue to lack strong integration of lower level "print" skills, succeed in constructing higher order "meaning" skills. This analysis underscores the need for a balanced approach to literacy instruction that includes both "print" and "meaning" aspects. It emphasizes the need to integrate solid interest-based approaches as a centerpiece of instruction.*

## INTRODUCTION

How, when, and under what conditions do individuals with dyslexia develop high level literacy skills? This question prompted me to conduct a study comparing 60 highly successful adults with dyslexia with equally successful adults without dyslexia. Participants with dyslexia included a Nobel laureate, a member of the National Academy of Sciences, a member of the National Academy of Education, and others in a range of fields that require extensive reading (i.e., medicine, law, business, biology, chemistry, education, psychology, anthropology, theater, art, interior design, and literature). My rationale for studying literacy development in highly successful men and women with dyslexia lay in the hypothesis that these individuals may have devised novel strategies potentially useful in the education of others at risk for reading failure. This study included equal numbers of males and females in an effort to move away from the historical tendency of dyslexia research to focus disproportionately on males.

Previously, researchers and practitioners believed that dyslexia predominantly affected males, in a 3 or 4 to 1 male to female ratio. However, in recent years, this gender disparity has been questioned in a growing number of studies (Finucci and Childs 1981; Flynn and Rahbar 1994; Mellard and Byrne 1993; Naiden 1976; Nass 1993; Scarborough 1989; Shaywitz et al. 1990; Vogel 1990; Vogel and Walsh 1990). Converging evidence from recent studies suggests that dyslexia may affect boys and girls in equal proportions (Anderson 1997; Leinhardt et al. 1982; Wadsworth et al. 1992). The higher ratio of males to females in the reported dyslexic population is attributed (in part) to teacher reporting bias—teachers refer boys for diagnosis more frequently than girls because boys "act out" more (Anderson 1997; Shaywitz et al. 1990). In a comprehensive review of the literature, Vogel found that girls who were referred for diagnosis and remediation generally had more severe cognitive deficits than boys (Vogel 1990). Apparently, for a girl with dyslexia to receive attention, she had to have more serious learning problems than boys. It seems that females with dyslexia have been largely overlooked as a focus of inquiry in much the same way that females in general were omitted from studies of moral development prior to Gilligan's (1982) groundbreaking work. The present research was designed to address this gap in the dyslexia literature.

Historically, instructional research on dyslexia has focused primarily on the effectiveness of highly structured skills-based teaching approaches (Cox 1983; Gillingham and Stillman 1966; Orton 1937; Griesbach 1993). Such approaches, used at all levels of instruction, include systematic phonics instruction (Chall 1983) and multisensory methods such as simultaneous instruction in the use and association of the three sensory channels (visual, auditory, and kinesthetic). In addition, bypass approaches, such as the use of audio- or videotapes and other devices that circumvent and/or support reading, have served as integral components of dyslexia instruction, especially at middle school, secondary, and postsecondary levels (Knight 1986; Morris 1983; Vogel 1987). In recent years, computer assisted programs have been used at various developmental levels with increasing frequency (Anderson-Inman and Horney 1996/1997; Meyer et al. 1991; Rose and Meyer 1994; Rose and Meyer 1996).

There has been a growing interest in research on adults with learning disabilities (Blalock 1981; Bruck 1990; Blalock 1981; Felton et al. 1990; Fink 1992, 1993, 1995/1996; Finucci et al. 1985; Fowler and Scarborough 1993; Gerber et al. 1992; Gerber and Reiff 1992; Rawson 1968; Scarborough 1984). Studies overall have reported both successful adult outcomes and specific continuing difficulties. Fowler and Scarborough found that, while the reading disability persists in adulthood, "there is considerable variability in the severity of the ultimate deficit and its impact on overall functioning" (Fowler and Scarborough 1993, p. 62). In 1992, Gerber and his colleagues analyzed 71 case histories of successful adults with learning disabilities and devised a social/ecological framework that emphasizes locus of control and interpersonal relationships as key factors for understanding life success. Blalock (1981) reported that adults with dyslexia were "amazingly adept" at using context clues to enhance their reading ability; similarly, Bruck (1990) found that the use of context clues by adults with dyslexia simultaneously improved both the speed and accuracy of their reading. Lefly and Pennington (1991) found that a group of 25 adults with dyslexia decoded unfamiliar words nearly as accurately as did nondyslexic controls, albeit more slowly, confirming and extending results from research on learning disabled children (Meyer et al. 1997; Wolf 1997; Wolf and Bowers in review). Few studies have investigated the adult reading abilities, habits, attitudes, and experiences of highly successful adults with dyslexia (Feldman et al. 1993; Rawson 1968). The current study focused on these often neglected areas of research.

# METHOD

## PARTICIPANT RECRUITMENT, SELECTION, AND ASSESSMENT

The goal of recruitment was to find individuals who would inspire and motivate others currently struggling with dyslexia. All but one of the 60 participants with dyslexia agreed to be identified by name, education, and profession (see Appendix I).

*Successful professionals.* Recruitment methods were designed to identify participants with dyslexia who had achieved high levels of success in various professions that require reading and demand extensive training, skill, and responsibility. Therefore, the sample was not random or representative, but rather was selected on the basis of level of educational and career achievement, field of professional expertise, gender, age, and socioeconomic level. Participants were considered "successful" if they demonstrated professional competence recognized by peers in an area of expertise, and they supported themselves financially (unless currently enrolled in graduate school).

*Individuals with dyslexia.* The choice of selection criteria was guided by the International Dyslexia Association (IDA) research definition of dyslexia. Despite ongoing controversies (Aaron 1997; Stanovich 1991), this definition maintains the classic notion of an "unexpected" reading problem or discrepancy between the person's potential (often measured by the Full

Scale IQ) and his or her actual reading achievement (often measured by standardized diagnostic reading tests). The IDA definition conceptualizes dyslexia as:

> a specific language-based disorder of constitutional origin characterized by difficulties in single word decoding, usually reflecting insufficient phonological processing abilities. These difficulties . . . are often unexpected in relation to age and other cognitive and academic abilities. . . . Dyslexia is manifest by variable difficulty with different forms of language, often including, in addition to problems reading, a conspicuous problem with acquiring proficiency in writing and spelling (Orton Dyslexia Society Research Committee 1994, p. 4).

In the present study, participants were included and considered to have dyslexia if they reported having had difficulties learning to decode single words and/or acquiring adequate reading and spelling skills. This difficulty had to be evident by first grade and continue at least until third grade. Participants between the ages of 26 and 50 had been diagnosed with dyslexia by learning disabilities professionals using established assessment instruments. For those over 50 years of age (educated when documentation was less common), a case history of early and continuing difficulties in reading unfamiliar words, spelling, and writing constituted the "diagnostic signature" of dyslexia (Shaywitz et al. 1994, p. 7).

Participants were initially located by means of professional referrals, word of mouth, and notices distributed at professional conferences. In preliminary telephone interviews, I screened prospective participants for exclusionary criteria such as a history of inadequate schooling or poor vision. I recorded and analyzed profiles of participants' language-based difficulties based on retrospective face-to-face interviews that I conducted individually with each participant. A case history was conducted, and included a family history of reading disabilities, a personal history of diagnosis/remedial assistance for reading difficulties, and early and/or persistent difficulties with letter identification, word recognition, spelling, writing, slow speed of reading and writing, memory (e.g., difficulty memorizing multiplication tables), laterality (i.e., difficulty making left-right distinctions in speech or action), fine motor control, or second language learning. Males and females were matched for types of problems and severity of dyslexia (see table I).

*Academic degrees.* Of the 60 men and women with dyslexia, 30 had either repeated a grade in elementary school as

**TABLE I. MALES (n = 30) AND FEMALES (n = 30) WITH DYSLEXIA INCLUDING SPECIFIC PROBLEM AREAS IN SELF-REPORT.**

| Problem areas** | # Males | # Females | Total |
|---|---|---|---|
| Single word decoding | 29 | 30 | 59 |
| Spelling | 30 | 29 | 59 |
| Discrepancy | 26 | 27 | 53 |
| Diagnosis/Remediation | 25 | 25 | 50 |
| Letter identification | 23 | 23 | 46 |
| Writing | 25 | 24 | 49 |
| Slow reading and/or writing | 28 | 26 | 54 |
| Memory | 26 | 26 | 52 |
| Laterality (left-right distinction) | 16 | 22 | 38 |
| Second language acquisition | 27 | 28 | 55 |
| Fine motor skills (i.e., illegible handwriting) | 19 | 17 | 36 |
| Familial dyslexia | 22 | 26 | 48 |
| **Mean Number of Problems per Participant:** | | | |
| Mean # of Problems (SD) | 9.9 (1.3) | 10.0 (1.3) | |
| Range | 6-12 | 8-12 | |

**There were no significant differences between males and females ($t = 0.30$, $p = .767$).

a result of academic failure (not illness), or stated that their parents and teachers had seriously considered grade retention. Despite personal histories of serious reading problems, 59 of the 60 individuals with dyslexia had graduated from four-year colleges or universities. Furthermore, the majority had earned masters and/or doctorate degrees. Academic degrees earned by the 60 men and women with dyslexia included six MDs, seventeen PhDs, four JDs, nineteen Masters Degrees, and twelve Bachelors Degrees. One individual with dyslexia had attended but did not complete college.

The comparison group was matched on all criteria except dyslexia, and included individuals without dyslexia whose high professional and educational achievements were comparable to the study participants with dyslexia. The comparison group, which included one MD, five PhDs, one JD, and three individuals with masters degrees, was limited to 10 participants due to the study's limited resources. Like those with dyslexia, all participants without dyslexia were active professionals in fields that demand extensive reading. On average, both subjects with dyslexia and the control group in this study exceeded Gerber and Reiff's definition of "high success" (Paul Gerber personal communication; Gerber and Reiff 1991, p. 34). Many members of both groups were outstanding professionals in the top echelons of their fields (see Appendix I).

*Attempt to represent diversity of region, SES, and race.* The majority of participants were white, middle-class United States citizens who came from all regions of the country, including 18 states and the District of Columbia. Most had been raised in middle- to upper-middle-class families, although a few came from working class origins. (In one case, the participant's father had been a carpenter and the mother washed laundry for a living). A small number of African-Americans and Hispanics participated, but their numbers were not proportionately representative of minorities in the American population. Although more members of minorities were sought, finding them proved difficult, presumably because minorities are still not proportionately successful in our society because of ongoing discrimination (Gadsden 1991; Ladson-Billings 1994). At the time of the study, participants earned salaries that placed them in middle to high socioeconomic categories.

*Self-report better in successful middle-aged participants.* Recent literature indicates that self-report of childhood reading difficulties by learning disabled adults is valid and reliable (Decker, Vogler, and DeFries 1989; Finucci, Whitehouse, Isaacs, and Childs 1984; Gilger 1992; Lefly 1997; Lefly and Pennington in review). Apparently, accuracy and reliability of self-reported reading difficulties are especially high for middle-aged, normally achieving, or high-achieving individuals (Gilger 1992). For the present study, therefore, I selected highly successful dyslexic adults with a mean age of 45 years (age range: 26 to 75).

**PROCEDURES AND INSTRUMENTS**

*Clinical interviews.* Using Gilligan's clinical interview methodology (Attanucci 1988), I conducted detailed face-to-face retrospective interviews (three to nine hours long) with each participant. Whenever possible, interviews were conducted in the familiar setting of the person's home or workplace. Twenty interview questions were used to guide the interviews in a semistructured, open-ended format (see Fink 1995/1996 for interview protocol). Care was taken to avoid asking questions in a manner likely to influence participants' responses. Participants recollected their literacy and learning history in a developmental framework, school grade by school grade, content area by content area. Typical questions asked included: "What is your earliest memory of learning differently from other children?" and "What specific strategies did you use for reading, writing, spelling, learning multiplication tables, history, science, and so forth, in first grade, second grade, etc.?" Each interview was audiotaped and written out in its entirety by a trained transcriber in order to preserve descriptive detail and ensure accuracy. I coded interview transcripts according to multiple dimensions of cognitive and affective development. These included experiences of humiliation and frustration with learning, experiences of jubilation and joy in learning, topic(s) and type(s) of first books read, ages and circumstances of early memories regarding reading, and relationships with important people, among others. To check for reliability, data were also coded and analyzed by an independent psychologist, who analyzed one quarter of the transcripts for topics of self-selected reading and one third for ages of development of basic fluency.

*Additional background information.*   To verify interview information, I collected additional biographical data from various sources. These included a detailed *curriculum vita* from each participant, diagnostic school and clinical reports (when available), information from parents and spouses (when available), information from public sources such as *Who's Who in America*, journal articles, book chapters, full-length books, and works of art created and published by each participant.

*Literacy measures.*   Formal and informal literacy tests were administered to each participant on an individual basis. Assessment instruments included:

1. The *Diagnostic Assessments of Reading with Trial Teaching Strategies* (DARTTS) (Roswell and Chall 1992), an untimed, nationally normed instrument that spans beginning through advanced literacy levels (ceiling = 12th grade). One of its main objectives is to assess a student's relative strengths and weaknesses in reading in order to help plan an individualized reading program.

2. The *Nelson-Denny Reading Test of Vocabulary, Reading Comprehension, and Reading Rate* (ND), Form H (Brown et al. 1993), a college reading test that measures reading ability through postgraduate levels. It is a timed, nationally normed test designed to provide an objective ranking of student ability in vocabulary development, silent reading comprehension, and reading rate.

3. The *Pig Latin Test* (adapted by Fink from Lefly 1997), an informal instrument containing 48 items and administered in an untimed format. It assesses awareness of, and ability to manipulate, phonemes and syllables, along with other phonological skills.

4. The *Florida Nonsense Passages* (adapted from Finucci 1974 by Gross-Glenn et al. 1990), an informal jabberwocky-style instrument that entails reading nonsense words embedded in otherwise meaningful paragraphs. It assesses both reading speed and accuracy.

5. The *Graded Nonword Reading and Spelling Test* (Snowling et al. 1996), an untimed measure of the ability to read and spell novel letter strings. Initially designed for use with children, it is also considered suitable for adults with reading difficulties.

*Questionnaire.* The Adult Reading History Questionnaire (ARHQ) (Lefly 1997; Lefly and Pennington in review) was administered to assess the existence and severity of dyslexia and gain further insight regarding literacy development. The ARHQ has been highly correlated with adult diagnostic criteria in Pennington's familial dyslexic sample ($r = .61 - .73$; $p < .001$); these correlations are higher than those of other adult self-report validity studies (Lefly and Pennington in review, pp. 9–10). Lefly and Pennington used a cutoff point of .30 to determine the existence of dyslexia. All 60 participants with dyslexia in the present study had ARHQ scores well above .30, as shown in table II. (Mean for total individuals with dyslexia = .60, $SD$ = .09, range = .38 -.82). By this criterion, all participants with dyslexia in the present study had "severe" dyslexia.

## RESEARCH QUESTIONS

The following questions guided the present study:
1. How, when in development, and under what conditions do highly successful men and women with dyslexia develop literacy?
2. What literacy levels do they achieve?
3. Do successful individuals with dyslexia continue to show jagged profiles of literacy strengths and weaknesses in adulthood?
4. How do the adult reading abilities, habits, and attitudes of successful individuals with dyslexia compare with those of nondyslexic control participants?

## TABLE II. PERFORMANCE ON LITERACY TESTS AND ADULT READING HISTORY QUESTIONNAIRE.*

| | Nondyslexic Controls (n = 10) | Individuals with Dyslexia | | | Contrasts** | |
| | | Fully Compensated (n = 17) | Partially Compensated (n = 43) | Total Dyslexics (n = 60) | Controls v. Total Dys. | Full v. Partial |
|---|---|---|---|---|---|---|
| **DARTT** (% adults obtaining GE < 12th grade)*** | | | | | | |
| Word Recognition | 0 | 0 | 30.2 | 21.7 | .103 | .010 |
| Oral Rdg. Accuracy | 0 | 0 | 55.8 | 40.0 | .014 | .001 |
| Silent Comp'n | 10 | 0 | 6.9 | 5.0 | .528 | .264 |
| Spelling | 40 | 0 | 79.0 | 57.0 | .327 | <.001 |
| Word Meaning | 0 | 0 | 6.9 | 5.0 | .470 | .264 |
| **Nelson-Denny** | | | | | | |
| Vocabulary | | | | | | |
| raw score $M$ (SD) | 79(.6) | 75.9(4.4) | 73.9(5.0) | 73.5(6.3) | .008 | .155 |
| GE $M$ | 18.9 | 17.5 | 16.9 | 16.9 | | |
| GE range | 18.9–18.9 | 14.6–18.9 | 11.6–18.9 | 11.6–18.9 | | |
| Comprehension | | | | | | |
| raw score $M$ (SD) | 75.2(4.4) | 70.5(3.9) | 67.7(5.6) | 68.7(6.7) | .004 | .056 |
| GE $M$ | 18.9 | 18.6 | 17.1 | 17.1 | | |
| GE range | 16.4–18.9 | 13.2–18.9 | 9.6–18.9 | 9.6–18.9 | | |
| Rate (% with s.s. < 180) | 0 | 0 | 33.0 | 23.3 | .088 | .007 |
| % using extended time | 0 | 53 | 60 | 58 | .001 | .594 |

(Continues)

TABLE II. PERFORMANCE ON LITERACY TESTS AND ADULT READING HISTORY QUESTIONNAIRE.* (cont.)

| | Nondyslexic Controls (n = 10) | Individuals with Dyslexia | | | Contrasts** | |
| | | Fully Compensated (n = 17) | Partially Compensated (n = 43) | Total Dyslexics (n = 60) | Controls v. Total Dys. | Full v. Partial |
|---|---|---|---|---|---|---|
| **Adult Reading History Questionnaire** | | | | | | |
| Total Score M (SD) | .07(.04) | .57(.09) | .61(.09) | .60(.09) | .0001 | .126 |
| range | .01–.15 | .38–.75 | .38–.82 | .38–.82 | | |
| **Florida Passages** | | | | | | |
| # seconds M (SD) | 25.3(8.4) | 78.5(17.8) | 106.7(38.9) | 98.7(36.5) | .0001 | .0060 |
| range | 17–50 | 51–112 | 51–225 | 51–225 | | |
| # errors M (SD) | 1.5(1.0) | 8.8(3.0) | 14.5(6.0) | 12.9(5.9) | .0001 | .0004 |
| range | 0–4 | 4–13 | 4–27 | 4–27 | | |
| **Pig Latin Test** | | | | | | |
| # correct M (SD) | 44.2(5.6) | 40.4(7.5) | 30.0(11.9) | 33.0(11.8) | .005 | .002 |
| range | 30–48 | 24–48 | 1–47 | 1–48 | | |
| **Graded Nonword Tests** | | | | | | |
| Reading M (SD) | 19.8(.4) | 17.1(1.9) | 15.0(3.5) | 15.6(3.3) | .0002 | .0231 |
| range | 19–20 | 13–20 | 6–20 | 6–20 | | |
| Spelling M (SD) | 18.8(1.3) | 16(2.4) | 13.0(4.6) | 13.8(4.3) | .0007 | .0136 |
| range | 16–20 | 11–20 | 2–19 | 2–20 | | |

*   Full data set available upon request (participants' identities withheld)
**  Observed probability levels from the statistical contrasts; the first column of contrasts shows comparisons between the non dyslexic comparison group and the total number of individuals with dyslexia; the second column of contrasts shows comparisons between fully compensated and partially compensated individuals with dyslexia.
*** GE = grade equivalent; maximum performance on the DARTT is twelfth grade level (Roswell and Chall 1992).

5. How do the experiences of males and females with dyslexia differ?

6. What are the implications of the results of this study for theory, research, educational, and clinical practice?

# RESULTS

## INTERVIEW RESULTS

*When did basic fluency develop?* The 60 successful men and women with dyslexia developed basic fluency, or relative smoothness in reading connected text, substantially later than normally developing readers. Most of them developed basic fluency between ages 10 and 11 (three to three-and-one-half years later than nondyslexic controls). There were no significant gender differences regarding this variable. Intercoder reliability for the age variable was 100 percent.

Development of basic fluency represented a memorable turning point for many, following years of intense personal frustration and public humiliation. Consequently, development of basic fluency, of beginning to learn to read and "getting it," was an "Ahaa!" experience for many, recalled with vivid emotions and clear memories of a key person at a poignant time.

*Baruj Benacceraf (immunologist):*
My problems were earlier. . . . And from about 11 or 12, I surmounted it; I surmounted my reading problem.

*Lori Boskin (alumni developer):*
Well, I didn't finally start to learn to read until fourth grade. With Mrs. Orenberg. I remember so clearly sitting there with Mrs. Orenberg; she was the first person that took the time to teach me.

*How did literacy develop?* Of the 60 successful men and women with dyslexia, many had read avidly as children. Some began avid reading before they were fluent at a basic level. Despite ongoing struggles with basic, lower level skills (i.e., letter identification, word recognition, and decoding strategies), neither males nor females had circumvented reading overall; rather, they sought out books in order to learn.

*Ann Brown (educational researcher):*
I became a very avid reader; I read my way through the local library. (Age 13 and up.)

*Florence Hazeltine (gynecologist):*
When I was almost 11, I started to read. . . . And from then on I read all the time. (Age 11 and up.)

*Robert Knapp (gynecologist):*
I went to the library and read a lot on my own. (Age 7 and up.)

*Ronald Davis (biochemist):*
You'd start reading a lot. Because you like it. (Age 8 and up.)

Reading was extremely difficult and laborious for these men and women. So why did they read avidly? And, how did they do it? With few exceptions, literacy development was spurred by a strong desire to know more about a content area of passionate personal interest. Consequently, they read every book and magazine they could find in order to satisfy their curiosity about a particular topic.

*H. Girard Ebert (interior designer):*
I've always been attracted to books and anything that has to do with history, decorative arts, architecture. . . . So I took reading, which was a problem, and turned it around, because it was the only way that I could explore what I was interested in.

*Ronald Davis (biochemist):*
You read science for . . . how things are put together. . . . My interest in chemistry just came from . . . it started with my interest in airplanes in grade school . . . that quickly converted to propellant systems in seventh and eighth grades.

Passionate interest in a topic spurred avid reading that provided the scaffolds necessary to develop literacy skills. A pattern common to most of these 60 individuals' reading histories was that they engaged in a great deal of personal interest reading. Although topics and genres of personal interest varied, fascination with a topic was a common theme.

*Ann Brown (educational researcher):*
I remember reading many historical novels; I read those avidly, particularly about the Tudor and Stuart Periods. Because mainly they were lovely love stories.

*Jane Buchbinder (fiction writer):*
I loved novels. *Harriet the Spy* is the book I remember as a milestone. I also read Judy Blume books, which were really captivating.

*Susan Cobin (headmaster):*
I've always liked biographies. The first book I remember reading was a biography of Franklin Roosevelt. That's the one I remember as a key to reading, a step into reading for me.

*Ronald Davis (biochemist):*
I became fascinated with nitrogen chemistry. So the way to understand that was to start reading chemistry books. So I got organic chemistry books.

*Robert Knapp (gynecologist):*
I always read history books. Beginning in grade school! And even today, I'm a Civil War buff. I love to read about the Civil War.

Through avid reading in a content area of high interest, these individuals with dyslexia developed knowledge of the specialized vocabulary, concepts, themes, questions, typical text structures, and critical issues of a particular field. Extensive reading about a favorite subject enhanced their background knowledge and enabled them to gain practice, which fostered fluency and development of increasingly sophisticated skills. With practice, these men and women developed deep schema knowledge, which supported their literacy development (Anderson 1983). They relied extensively on contextual facilitation to derive meaning from a new text, foraging for context clues in their hunt for new information. These context clues proved relatively reliable in a restricted content area. Through unsolicited remarks explaining how they coped, the men and women with dyslexia reported their use of context as an aid to reading.

*Alexander Goldowsky (museum coordinator):*
I tended to be fairly, you know, context-driven. So I made assumptions very quickly based on context and usually substituted a reasonable word.

*Barbara Bidofsky (special educator):*
I used context a lot to guess at new words.

*Baruj Benacerraf (immunologist):*
Even today, when I can't figure out a word, I guess from context.

Because their ability to decode was often unreliable, participants with dyslexia used decoding strategies along with context clues, but not necessarily effectively. Many felt that in spite of explicit phonics instruction, their ability to decode through the use of phonological strategies remained poor.

*Charlann Simon (speech pathologist):*
To this day, I can't sound out a word.

*Charles Bean (neurologist):*
Phonics doesn't always work. Even though I'll read pho-netically, my phonetic sounds don't always fit with every-body else's.

*Florence Hazeltine (gynecologist):*
I can't sound out anything.

*Annette Jenner (biologist):*
I had phonics training in the resource room, but it never got into my head.

Even in cases where they had mastered many of the sound-symbol relationships of English, they often had difficulty using this knowledge because of ongoing problems with the blending and sequencing of sounds.

*Marlene Hirschberg (arts administrator):*
I could look at the letter and tell you what the sound was, but I couldn't put it together into a word.

Contextual guessing strategies were more reliable than phonological decoding strategies for many of these men and women with dyslexia.

*Susan Marlett (artist):*
I cannot figure out how to pronounce a word based on its letters; I always guess it wrong. But I can figure out what words mean from the words around them.

Participants reported that it was easier to guess and cor-rectly predict a word when the schema of a particular topic was familiar. Schema knowledge provided the conceptual scaffolds that supported optimal reading skills about a topic of interest. By focusing on a single domain of knowledge, many of the individ-uals with dyslexia became virtual "little experts" about their fa-vorite topic, sometimes beginning at an early age. For some, early reading interests later developed into high-powered careers; for others, early reading interests developed into lifelong hobbies.

***How did experiences of males and females differ?*** A salient finding that emerged from this study was that personal interests played a pivotal role in the literacy development of these men and women with dyslexia. There were clear gender differences in

personal reading interests. As children, the individuals interviewed chose both fiction and nonfiction that embraced their
specific interests. Of the 30 women with dyslexia, 23 preferred
fiction whereas 7 preferred nonfiction. Of the 30 men with
dyslexia, 14 preferred fiction and 16 preferred nonfiction. Gender
differences in topics of personal interest reading were statistically
significant ($\chi^2 = 5.71$, $p = .017$). Table III summarizes findings related to gender and topics of high interest reading.

Women, more often than men, noted the "pull" of reading
materials related to developmental self-identity and relational
issues provided in novels.

*Priscilla Sanville (arts educator):*
I read as many Nancy Drew mysteries as I could find in the
library. And I was amazed that I could be so locked in a
book; it was like the discovery of how a book could take me
somewhere different and take me into a world and characters that I could identify with.

The men, more often than women, were drawn into factual
information-loaded materials provided by nonfiction texts. Six
males with dyslexia, but only one female, read avidly during
childhood about social studies. The same pattern emerged with
regard to scientific reading. As children, five males with dyslexia,
compared to only two females, were avid science readers. These
numbers, while small, mirror the reading interests of nondyslexic
children (Whitehead and Maddren 1974, pp. 24–25).

Most important for both males and females with dyslexia in
this study was the specificity of their interest-driven reading.

## TABLE III. EARLY READING INTERESTS REPORTED BY MEN AND WOMEN WITH DYSLEXIA.*

| Women n = 30 | | Men n = 30 | |
|---|---|---|---|
| Novels | 23 | Novels | 14 |
| Biographies | 2 | Biographies | 2 |
| Science | 2 | Science | 5 |
| Social Studies | 1 | Social Studies | 6 |
| Cooking | 1 | Auto mechanics | 1 |
| No Data | 1 | Sailing | 1 |
| | | Poetry | 1 |

*Gender differences in topics of high-interest reading were statistically sig-
nificant (chi square = 5.71, $p = .017$).

Through highly focused avid childhood reading in specialized disciplines and genres, they developed deep background knowledge, becoming conversant with domain-specific vocabulary, concepts, themes, questions, and typical text structures. Repetition and practice within a content domain facilitated optimal skill development.

## CURRENT LITERACY ASSESSMENT RESULTS

*What literacy levels did successful men and women with dyslexia develop?* As adults, nearly all of the men and women with dyslexia demonstrated most of the salient characteristics of Chall's Stage 5, the highest level of literacy development (Chall 1983). This was demonstrated in their high performance on the DARTT, shown in table II. In 95 percent of cases, their knowledge of word meanings and silent reading comprehension levels reached ceiling, or as high as the DARTT measures. Only 5 percent of the individuals with dyslexia did not reach ceiling in these skills. Their scores were similar to those of the nondyslexic control participants. Moreover, according to their strong performance on the Nelson Denny, most of the individuals with dyslexia demonstrated the ability to read silently and comprehend text at high collegiate and postgraduate levels that were only slightly lower than those of the nondyslexic control group.

The solid performance of the individuals with dyslexia on both the vocabulary and silent reading comprehension subtests of the DARTT and ND demonstrates their ability as adults to read, understand, make inferences, and create meaning from text. These are all Stage 5 skills. Furthermore, their current utilization and application of reading skills demonstrates Stage 5 performance. Stage 5 entails reading materials that are "highly difficult, specialized, technical, and abstract" (Chall 1983, p. 100). Sylvia Law explained how she reads huge amounts of highly technical legal materials today.

*Sylvia Law (attorney):*
When you're immersed in a field, you kind of know what the forest looks like, and you're looking to see if there's a particular tree in here. So it's easy to just skim and zero in on the important stuff in the law. You know, the most important sentence in a 100 page document, where it says, 'The court says. . . .' So there are a lot of techniques and filtering devices that I use to get through lengthy legal documents.

As Chall points out, the sophisticated Stage 5 reader uses reading for his or her own professional and personal purposes; "reading serves to integrate one's own knowledge with that of others, to synthesize it and to create new knowledge" (Chall 1983, p. 87). The men and women with dyslexia in this study demonstrate all the salient characteristics of Stage 5 except speed and efficiency, which many of them still lack. All of them read materials that are technical, specialized, and abstract. Nearly all do a substantial amount of daily writing in their professions. Moreover, they integrate and synthesize knowledge from other experts with their own knowledge, and create and contribute significantly to the canon of new knowledge in their fields of expertise. Their books and scholarly articles number in the hundreds. The impressive scholarly publications and other creative writings of these men and women with dyslexia provide evidence of their contributions to new knowledge, a hallmark of Stage 5. [1]

*Did jagged profiles of literacy continue?* The 60 adults with dyslexia showed strengths in components of literacy that Chall (1994) has called higher level "meaning aspects." Higher level meaning aspects include vocabulary knowledge and silent reading comprehension. All but six participants with dyslexia scored at ceiling (12th grade level) on the DARTT in these skills, as shown in figure 1. However, despite the congruence of positive results on vocabulary and reading comprehension subtests of both the DARTT and ND, a distinct subset of individuals with dyslexia showed a pattern of ongoing weaknesses in what Chall (1994) has called lower level, "print aspects" of literacy. Their ongoing weaknesses in "print" components were documented in results from the word recognition, oral reading accuracy, and spelling subtests of the DARTT (see table II).

Distinct groups of highly successful adults with dyslexia emerged from this study. One, a compensated group, revealed few, if any, ongoing weaknesses with subcomponents of reading in adulthood. The compensated group's performance was high

---

[1] Among the men and women with dyslexia are Dr. Baruj Benaccerraf, 1980 Nobel laureate in Immunology and Pathology; Lora Brody, TV/radio personality and author of *Cooking with Memories;* Dr. Donald Francis, AIDS researcher/activist and protagonist of the movie "And the Band Played On;" Dr. Florence Haseltine, author of *Woman Doctor* and *Women's Health* Research; Dr. Robert Knapp, Harvard oncologist and author of *Gynecological Oncology;* Professor Ronald W. Davis, genomics researcher and biochemistry textbook author; George Deem, New York City artist, Susan Brown, New York City filmmaker; and Professor Sylvia Law, N.Y.U. legal scholar and author of books on poverty, health care, welfare, and the law.

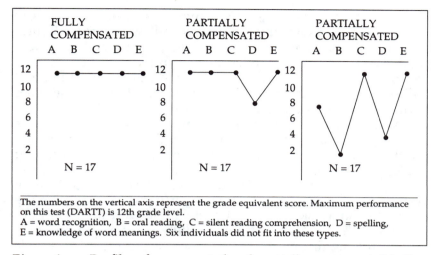

The numbers on the vertical axis represent the grade equivalent score. Maximum performance on this test (DARTT) is 12th grade level.
A = word recognition, B = oral reading, C = silent reading comprehension, D = spelling, E = knowledge of word meanings. Six individuals did not fit into these types.

*Figure 1.    Profiles of compensated and partially compensated individuals with dyslexia.*

across all literacy measures. Seventeen individuals met this criterion, as shown in figure 1. In addition to their ability to comprehend sophisticated text, they demonstrated strong compensation in word recognition, oral reading accuracy, and spelling.

Another group, those with partially compensated dyslexia, showed jagged profiles of literacy strengths and weaknesses. This group consisted of 43 people. With the exception of six individuals, the partially compensated group also met the criteria on the DARTT of scoring at ceiling in knowledge of word meanings and silent reading comprehension. However, the partially compensated group showed lags in other subskills. They lagged behind individuals with compensated dyslexia and nondyslexic controls in word recognition, oral reading accuracy, and spelling. As table II documents, for each of these subskills, the compensated and partially compensated groups differed significantly based on the results of chi square tests, (word recognition, $p = .01$; oral reading accuracy, $p = .001$; spelling, $p < .001$). Therefore, differences in the profiles shown in figure 1 were corroborated by statistical tests.

Partially compensated individuals with dyslexia fell into two categories: one contained those who lagged behind individuals with compensated dyslexia and nondyslexic controls in spelling alone; and another contained those who lagged behind in spelling, word recognition, and oral reading. Figure 1 illustrates the two types of partially compensated, jagged profiles.

One dips only in spelling (15 individuals); the other dips in word recognition and oral reading as well as spelling (22 individuals). The six remaining individuals with partially compensated dyslexia showed similar jagged profiles of strengths and weaknesses; however, their strengths did not reach ceiling and their weaknesses dipped slightly lower than those of the other partially compensated individuals.

When tested as adults and compared with nondyslexic control participants, the individuals with dyslexia performed poorly overall on all measures of phonological and decoding skills, including the Pig Latin Test, the Florida Nonsense Passages Test, and the Graded Nonword Reading and Spelling Tests. An analysis of variance was performed to compare the means for nondyslexic control participants and the total individuals with dyslexia. Differences between the groups were statistically significant on each of these assessments (see table II). For example, on the Florida Nonsense Passages, differences between non-dyslexic controls and the total number of individuals with dyslexia were highly significant, both for speed and accuracy ($p = .0001$). On the Pig Latin Test, differences were also significant. Out of 48 items, the mean number correct for nondyslexic controls was 44.2 ($SD = 5.6$); in contrast, the mean for the total individuals with dyslexia was only 33.0 ($SD = 11.8$), $p = .005$. These results, taken together, attest to ongoing difficulties of the individuals with dyslexia with phonological skills such as blending, sequencing, and manipulating language sounds and symbols.

Table II summarizes the results of all the literacy tests administered and shows three main findings:

1. On every measure of literacy, nondyslexic controls outperformed individuals with dyslexia;
2. The fully compensated group consistently outperformed both of the partially compensated groups; and
3. For individuals with partially compensated dyslexia, ongoing jagged profiles of literacy strengths and weaknesses persisted in adulthood.

*Did reading rate distinguish compensated from partially compensated readers?* Participants were instructed that I would record how many questions they had completed on the ND at the end of the standard test time, but that if they had not completed the test at the end of the standard time, they could continue under an extended time condition. All nondyslexic control participants completed the ND within the standard time. In contrast, 58 percent of the total individuals with dyslexia used extended time. These differences, shown in table II, were highly significant ($p = .001$).

In addition, on the one-minute reading rate subtest of the ND, 33 percent of partially compensated individuals had scaled scores less than 180, indicating reading rates that were slower than those of both compensated individuals and nondyslexic controls (see table II). A chi square test comparing compensated and partially compensated individuals' reading rates showed that differences in rate were highly significant ($p = .007$). Thus, in many cases, rate further distinguished compensated from partially compensated readers. Comparisons of test scores of those who took the ND with standard versus extended time showed that those who took the test with extended time performed well overall, but not as well as those who took the test within the standard time. Based on comparisons of individuals' scores with standard versus extended time conditions, it was apparent that, without the accommodation of extended time, many individuals with dyslexia would have scored lower on the ND.

## QUESTIONNAIRE RESULTS

*How did the adult reading habits and attitudes of the groups compare?* By adulthood, 25 men and 26 women with dyslexia reported positive reading attitudes, asserting that they valued and enjoyed reading a great deal. All nondyslexic control participants reported having a strong positive attitude. Therefore, overall reading attitudes of individuals with dyslexia and nondyslexic controls were similar.

When questioned about the extent of their current reading, there was a slight trend for individuals with dyslexia of both types—compensated and partially compensated—to report less reading overall than nondyslexic controls. Participants in all categories reported doing a great deal of work-related reading and, specifically, more reading for work than reading for pleasure. All nondyslexic control participants reported doing a great deal of work-related reading. In comparison, 88 percent of fully compensated individuals and 67 percent of partially compensated individuals reported doing a great deal of work-related reading (see table IV).

When questioned about the extent of their current reading for pleasure, there were significant differences among the groups. Eighty percent of nondyslexic control participants said they engaged in a great deal of reading for pleasure. This compared with only 53 percent of the fully compensated group and 37 percent of the partially compensated group. Table IV shows that nondyslexic controls and both groups of individuals with dyslexia read numer-

TABLE IV. ADULT SELF-REPORTED READING HABITS, USING SCALE OF 0 TO 4 FROM THE ADULT READING HISTORY QUESTIONNAIRE.*

| | Nondyslexic Controls (*n* = 10) | Individuals with Dyslexia | | | Contrasts** | |
| | | Fully Compensated (*n* = 17) | Partially Compensated (*n* = 43) | Total Dyslexics (*n* = 60) | Controls v. Total Dys. | Full v. Partial |
|---|---|---|---|---|---|---|
| **Work-related Reading** | | | | | | |
| (% reporting a great deal) | 100% | 88% | 67% | 73% | .063 | .101 |
| Mean response (*SD*) | 3.7(.5) | 3.5(1.0) | 3.0(.9) | 3.1(.9) | .0683 | .0652 |
| Range | 3–4 | 0–4 | 1–4 | 0–4 | | |
| **Pleasure Reading** | | | | | | |
| (% reporting a great deal) | 80% | 53% | 37% | 42% | .025 | .265 |
| Mean response (*SD*) | 3.4(.8) | 2.5(1.1) | 2.2(1.3) | 2.3(1.2) | .0081 | .4049 |
| Range | 2–4 | 0–4 | 0–4 | 0–4 | | |
| **Book Reading** | | | | | | |
| Mean response (*SD*) | 3.7(.6) | 2.5(1.2) | 2.4(1.4) | 2.4(1.3) | .0046 | .7966 |
| Range | 2–4 | 0–4 | 0–4 | 0–4 | | |

(*Continues*)

**TABLE IV. ADULT SELF-REPORTED READING HABITS, USING SCALE OF 0 TO 4 FROM THE ADULT READING HISTORY QUESTIONNAIRE.* (cont.)**

| | Nondyslexic Controls (n = 10) | Individuals with Dyslexia | | | Contrasts** | |
| | | Fully Compensated (n = 17) | Partially Compensated (n = 43) | Total Dyslexics (n = 60) | Controls v. Total Dys. | Full v. Partial |
|---|---|---|---|---|---|---|
| **Magazine Reading** | | | | | | |
| Mean response (SD) | 3.2(1.2) | 2.0(1.3) | 2.0(1.4) | 2.0(1.4) | .0113 | 1.0 |
| Range | 0 - 4 | 0 - 4 | 0 - 4 | 0 - 4 | | |
| **Daily News Reading** | | | | | | |
| Mean response (SD) | 3.5(1.0) | 2.9(1.4) | 2.7(1.4) | 2.8(1.4) | .1142 | .6199 |
| Range | 1–4 | 0–4 | 0–4 | 0–4 | | |
| **Sunday News Reading** | | | | | | |
| Mean response (SD) | 3.8(.4) | 2.9(1.0) | 2.7(1.0) | 2.8(1.0) | .0019 | .4879 |
| Range | 0–1 | 1–4 | 0–4 | 0–4 | | |

* (4 = a great deal; 0 = none, or not at all)
** Full data set available upon request (participants' identities withheld)
*** Observed probability levels from the statistical contrasts; the first column of contrasts shows comparisons between the non-dyslexic comparison group and the total number of individuals with dyslexia; the second column of contrasts shows comparisons between fully compensated and partially compensated individuals with dyslexia.

ous books, magazines, and newspapers regularly. However, on average, nondyslexic controls did more of each type of reading than individuals with dyslexia. Nevertheless, of the 30 men and 30 women with dyslexia, 21 men and 20 women read a Sunday newspaper regularly, and 21 men and 16 women read a daily newspaper regularly. These results confirm findings by Finucci and others regarding the reading habits of men with dyslexia (Finucci et al. 1985) and extend the results to include women. Interestingly, there were gender differences in the extent of book reading among adults with dyslexia. Sixteen women with dyslexia, compared to only six men, read more than 10 books per year for pleasure. While the numbers are small, these results fit with data regarding the reading habits of persons without dyslexia; females overall engage in more extensive book reading than males (Finucci et al. 1985).

*What was the role of mentors?*    Although this study was not designed with a focus on mentoring, interesting trends emerged. In elementary school, teachers and tutors played pivotal roles in assisting most of the individuals with dyslexia as they struggled to learn to read and write. Furthermore, parents (especially mothers) provided a strong support system for most participants. William Brewer's memories of his mother were typical.

*William Brewer (psychologist):*
My poor mother—she used to spend endless hours on spelling with me, and then I could take the test the next day. And do okay.

Trends in gender differences emerged with regard to mentoring by extended family members. Six men with dyslexia, compared to only one woman, named a relative such as an aunt, uncle, grandparent, or mother-in-law as a mentor.

*George Deem (graphic artist):*
My aunt was very serious with me, very serious. In college I was taking history and she would see to it that I read every assignment aloud to her so that we could discuss what I was reading.

*Charles Bean (neurologist):*
My uncle was a surrogate father to me in my intellectual life.

*Susan Marlett (artist):*
My mother-in-law Daisy got me to go to college. She's very encouraging about learning, and her approach to learning is very inspiring. She inspired me to go to college. . . . And finish.

Men with dyslexia named mentors more frequently overall than women. Beginning with middle school and continuing throughout their education and into the workplace, men recollected over 30 teachers and colleagues, while women recollected only 15 who stood out as taking a special interest in their academic and professional development. These gender differences, based on small numbers, must be interpreted cautiously; however, these results are similar to gender differences reported in the mentoring literature on nondyslexics (Beaman-Smith and Pacier 1996; Woodd 1997). Ronald Davis' memories of teachers who made a difference for him are illustrative of the powerful role played by mentors.

*Ronald Davis (biochemist):*
My high school biology teacher encouraged me to read more science books and take more science courses. He helped me with my experiments on plants and put me in contact with a biology professor at Eastern Illinois University. Later, when I was a Ph.D. student at Cal Tech, they told me I was gonna flunk out because I kept failing the foreign language tests. But Davidson, my thesis advisor, went to bat for me. He convinced the Graduate Committee to let me do a translation project instead of the language test because I was an unusual circumstance. He wrote me this note: Dear Ron: The Committee decided to accept your translation project for fulfillment of the foreign language requirement. It was the happiest note of my life.

## CONCLUSIONS AND DISCUSSION

Results from this study revealed distinct groups of highly successful adults with dyslexia:  a fully compensated group and two partially compensated groups. Each group's development was augmented by avid reading in a content area of passionate personal interest. Members of each group currently comprehend complex text at Stage 5, the highest level of reading development. Moreover, they create and write sophisticated, provocative texts of their own, as demonstrated by their publication of important books and scholarly articles. Despite these noteworthy strengths and accomplishments, the partially compensated men and women with dyslexia manifest persistent ongoing weaknesses in phonological abilities and processing speed, as shown by their lags in word recognition, oral reading accuracy, spelling, and reading rate. Although they manifest ongoing deficits, they have mastered the ultimate goal of reading—the ability to make meaning from highly sophisticated text.

A second finding from this study was that females with dyslexia preferred fiction whereas males with dyslexia preferred nonfiction. While this result fits with findings in the literature on the reading preferences and interests of persons without dyslexia, it merits further examination in an even larger study of adults with dyslexia. Preferences associated with gender regarding fiction and nonfiction could have important implications for instructors who strive to avoid gender stereotyping. How might teachers lure students with dyslexia into reading through their preferred interests and genres without promoting gender stereotypes? This could be a useful area for new research.

Trends in gender differences in mentoring patterns emerged clearly in middle school and continued into the workplace. These trends would be fruitful and important avenues to follow up in future research, especially considering that these trends in the data were based on small numbers. This study was not designed with a focus on mentoring; however, in a future study, additional questionnaires and interview protocols could be included to investigate more closely subtle and important issues regarding gender, dyslexia, and mentoring.

This study confirms and extends results of previous research on the role of personal interests (Fink 1992, 1993, 1995/96, 1998; Renninger 1992; Schiefele and Krapp 1996) to a larger sample that included a control group and equal numbers of men and women with dyslexia. The model of dyslexia constructed in this study explains how individuals with dyslexia, who in adulthood may continue to lack strong integration of basic, lower level "print" skills, develop higher order, sophisticated "meaning" skills. The model includes four main components:

1. Passionate personal interest in a content area requiring reading;
2. Avid, highly focused reading;
3. Deep schema knowledge; and
4. Contextual strategies.

The finding of domain-specific contextual strategies for reading confirms and extends results from previous research by Blalock (1981) and Bruck (1990), who independently found that adults with dyslexia are extremely skilled at using contextual cues, and that use of context improved their reading speed and accuracy. The 60 successful men and women with dyslexia in this study used domain-specific context and developed Stage 5 skills through scaffolding provided by avid reading in a content area of passionate personal interest. In many cases this occurred in conjunction with systematic phonics instruction. This analysis emphasizes the need for a balanced approach to literacy instruction that includes both "print" and "meaning" aspects. Both systematic phonics and literature-based approaches need to be included simultaneously in a thoughtful, theoretically sound, integrated program of instruction.

This study's identification of three groups of individuals with dyslexia (one compensated and two partially compensated) is consistent with the double-deficit hypothesis, in which phonological deficits and processing speed deficits are "depicted as separable concurrent sources of reading disability whose combined presence leads to the most profound forms of reading impairment" (Bowers and Wolf 1993; Wolf 1997; Wolf and Bowers in review). In this study, the partially compensated individuals with the most jagged profiles fit the double-deficit pattern of profound reading impairment. As adults, these individuals are slower in reading speed and weaker in phonological skills as attested to by their weak word recognition, oral reading, spelling, and reading rate scores. Instructional techniques that have been suggested for ameliorating literacy difficulties in the most severely affected double-deficit readers include increased emphasis on instruction that stresses fluency training to promote automaticity. Theoretical models of reading acquisition have long suggested that development of fluency and automaticity are central components of skilled reading (Adams 1996; LaBerge and Samuels 1974; Perfetti 1977, 1991; Stanovich 1980). However, as Meyer and her colleagues (1997) recently noted, no commercial programs currently exist for fluency training.

I propose here that interest-driven instruction be used to help develop fluency and automaticity. The results of this study suggest that interest-based teaching approaches can provide the necessary practice and exposure to print required for fluency development. The success of these 60 men and women with dyslexia, who developed Stage 5 skills through scaffolding provided by avid reading of high interest texts, argue for integrating solid interest-based approaches as a centerpiece of instruction.

These results indicate the need for teachers to select and provide reading materials based on students' passionate interests.

How can teachers ascertain individual interests? One way is by using individual reading-interest inventories. These questionnaires are easy to administer and easily modified to fit each student's age and developmental stage (Fink 1993, 1998). Another way to ascertain students' interests is to conduct interviews inquiring about students' favorite books, hobbies, movies, and television programs; then gather materials accordingly. The reference book *A to Zoo* (Lima and Lima 1993) lists children's books by topic and can be used used by busy teachers to locate excellent interest-based materials quickly and efficiently. For older students, teachers can consult resources such as *Readers and Writers with a Difference* (Rhodes and Dudley-Marling 1988), which categorizes books by type and focuses on the interests of adolescent readers.

All individuals with dyslexia face terrible obstacles, but being female may add an additional risk factor for reading failure because a girl's reading difficulty may be ignored more often than a boy's (Shaywitz et al. 1997).

*Florence Hazeltine, M.D., Ph.D. (gynecologist):*
I mean, they just forgot about it; they forgot that I couldn't read and ignored me. They didn't worry about me.

Dr. Florence Hazeltine's severe reading difficulties were overlooked by parents and teachers who didn't "worry" about her. She struggled and didn't learn to read until she was almost 11. Eventually, she succeeded, and became Director of the Center for Population Research at the National Institutes of Health and the author of two books and numerous scientific articles. She learned to read and write well by capitalizing on her interests, beginning with her interest in historical novels.

*Florence Hazeltine (gynecologist):*
When I was almost 11, I started to read. I read *The Robe*. . . . And from then on I read books like that a lot. You know, stories about a particular time.

The results of this study should encourage parents, teachers, and clinicians to help girls as well as boys, and women as well as men with dyslexia, to capitalize on their passionate personal interests.

Address Correspondence to: Rosalie P. Fink, Lesley College, 29 Everett Street, Cambridge, MA 02138, e-mail: rfink@mail.lesley.edu

## ACKNOWLEDGMENTS

This research was supported by a Spencer Postdoctoral Research Fellowship awarded to me through the National Academy of Education. I wish to thank the Spencer Foundation and the National Academy of Education for their generous support. I am also grateful to Jeanne Chall, Jane Holmes Bernstein, Kurt Fischer, and Terry Tivnan for their advice. Finally, I wish to thank all of the men and women who participated in the study for sharing their stories with me. Without their enormous courage, candor, and generosity, this study would not have been possible.

*References*

Aaron, P. G. 1997. The impending demise of the discrepancy formula. *Review of Educational Research* 67(4):461–502.

Adams, M. J. 1996. *Beginning to Read: Thinking and Learning About Print.* Cambridge, MA: Massachusetts Institute of Technology.

Anderson, K. G. 1997. Gender bias and special education referrals. *Annals of Dyslexia* 47:151–62.

Anderson, J. R. 1983. *The Architecture of Cognition.* Cambridge, MA: Harvard University Press.

Anderson-Inman, L., and Horney, M. 1996/1997. Computer-based concept mapping: Enhancing literacy with tools for visual thinking. *Journal of Adolescent and Adult Literacy* 40(4):302–6.

Attanucci, J. 1988. In whose terms: A new perspective on self, role, and relationship. In C. Gilligan, J. V. Ward, and J. M. Taylor, eds., *Mapping the Moral Domain.* Cambridge, MA: Harvard University Press, 201–24.

Beaman-Smith, K., and Placier, M. 1996. The interplay of gender in the careers of white female and male senior professors. Paper presented at the Annual Meeting of the Association for the Study of Higher Education. Memphis: TN.

Blalock, J. W. 1981. Persistent problems and concerns of young adults with learning disabilities. In W. M. Cruickshank and A. A. Silver, eds., *Bridges to Tomorrow: The Best of ACDL.* Syracuse, NY: Syracuse University Press, 35–55.

Bowers, P. G., and Wolf, M. 1993. *A "double deficit" hypothesis for developmental reading disorders.* Paper presented at the Society for Research in Child Development. New Orleans: LA.

Brown, J. I., Fischco, V. V., and Hanna, G. 1993. *Nelson-Denny Reading Test, Form H.* Chicago: Riverside.

Bruck, M. 1990. Word recognition skills of adults with childhood diagnoses of dyslexia. *Developmental Psychology* 26(3):439–54.

Chall, J. S. 1983. *Stages of Reading Development.* New York: McGraw-Hill.

Chall, J. S. 1994. Patterns of adult reading. *Learning Disabilities* 5(1):29–33.

Cox, A. R. 1983. Programming for teachers of dyslexics. *Annals of Dyslexia* 33:221–33.

Decker, S. N., Vogler, G. P., and DeFries, J. C. 1989. Validity of self-reported reading disability by parents of reading disabled and control children. *Reading and Writing* 1(4):327–31.

Feldman, E., Levin, B. E., Lubs, H., Rabin, M., Lubs, M. L., Jallad, B., and Kushch, A. 1993. Adult familial dyslexia: A retrospective developmental and psychosocial profile. *Journal of Neuropsychiatry and Clinical Neuroscience* 5:195–99.

Felton, R. H., Naylor, C. E., and Wood, F. B. 1990. Neuropsychological profile of adult dyslexics. *Brain and Language* 39:485–97.

Fink, R. P. 1997. Successful dyslexics: A constructivist study of passionate interest reading. In C. Weaver, ed., *Reconsidering a Balanced Approach to Reading*. Urbana, IL: The National Council of Teachers of English, 387–408

Fink, R. P. 1995/1996. Successful dyslexics: A constructivist study of passionate interest reading. *Journal of Adolescent and Adult Literacy* 39(4):268–80.

Fink, R. P. 1993. How successful dyslexics learn to read. *Teaching Thinking and Problem Solving* 15(5).

Fink, R. P. 1992. Successful dyslexics' alternative pathways for reading: A developmental study (Doctoral dissertation, Harvard Graduate School of Education, 1992). *Dissertation Abstracts International* F4965.

Finucci, J., and Childs, B. 1981. Are there really more dyslexic boys than girls? In A. Ansara, N. Geschwind, and A. Galaburda et al., eds., *Sex Differences in Dyslexia*. Baltimore, Maryland: The Orton Society.

Finucci, J. M., Gottfredson, L. S., and Childs, B. 1985. A follow-up study of dyslexic boys. *Annals of Dyslexia* 35:117–36.

Finucci, J. M., Whitehouse, C. C., Isaacs, S. D., and Childs, B. 1984. Derivation and validation of a quantitative definition of specific reading disability for adults. *Developmental Medicine and Child Neurology* 26(2):143–53.

Flynn, J. M., and Rahbar, M. H. 1993. The effects of age and gender on reading achievement: Implications for pediatric counseling. *Developmental and Behavioral Pediatrics* 14(5):304–7.

Fowler, A. E., and Scarborough, H. S. 1993. Should reading-disabled adults be distinguished from other adults seeking literacy instruction? A review of theory and research (Technical Report #TR93-7). Philadelphia, PA: National Center on Adult Literacy.

Gadsden, V. (ed.). 1991. Literacy and the African-American learner. *Theory into Practice* 31(4):270–78.

Gerber, P. J., Ginsberg, R., and Reiff, H. B. 1992. Identifying alterable patterns in employment success for highly successful adults with learning disabilities. *Journal of Learning Disabilities* 25:475–87.

Gerber, P. J., and Reiff, H. B. 1992. Speaking for Themselves: *Ethnographic Interviews with Adults with Learning Disabilities*. Ann Arbor, MI: University of Michigan.

Gilger, J. W. 1992. Using self-report and parental-report survey data to assess past and present academic achievement of adults and children. *Journal of Applied Developmental Psychology* 13:235–56.

Gilligan, C. 1982. *In a Different Voice: Psychological Theory and Women's Development*. Cambridge, MA: Harvard University Press.

Gillingham, A., and Stillman, B. 1966. *Remedial Training of Children with Specific Disability in Reading, Spelling, and Penmanship* (7th ed.). Cambridge, MA: Educators Publishing Service.

Griesbach, G. 1993. *Dyslexia: Its history, Etiology, and Treatment*. (Report No. CS011300). West Bend, WI: ERIC Document Reproduction Service.

Gross-Glenn, K., Jallad, B. J., Novoa, L., Helgren-Lempesis, V., and Lubs, H. A. 1990. Nonsense passage reading as a diagnostic aid in the study of adult familial dyslexia. *Reading and Writing: An Interdisciplinary Journal* 2:161–73.

Knight, J. 1986. The adult dyslexic in remediation: The ABCs and much more. *Churchill Forum* 8:1–4.

LaBerge, D., and Samuels, S. J. 1974. Toward a theory of automatic information processing in reading. *Cognitive Psychology* 6:293–323.

Ladson-Billings, G. 1994. *The Dreamkeepers.* San Francisco: Jossey-Bass.

Lefly, D. L. 1997. Risk status and phonological processing. Ph.D. diss., University of Denver, Denver, CO.

Lefly, D. L., and Pennington, B. F. (submitted July 1997). Reliability and validity study of the adult reading history questionnaire. *Journal of Learning Disabilities.*

Lefly, D. L., and Pennington, B. F. 1991. Spelling errors and reading fluency in compensated adult dyslexics. *Annals of Dyslexia* 41:143–62.

Leinhardt, G., Seewald, A., and Zigmond, N. 1982. Sex and race differences in learning disabilities classrooms. *Journal of Educational Psychology* 74(6):835–43.

Lima, C. W., and Lima, J. A. 1993. *A to Zoo: Subject Access to Children's Picture Books* (4th ed.). New Providence, NJ: R. R. Bowker Publishers.

Mellard, D., and Byrne, M. 1993. Learning disabilities referrals, eligibility outcomes, and services in community colleges: A four year summary. *Learning Disabilities Quarterly* 16:199–217.

Meyer, M. S., Wood, F. B., Hart, L. A., and Felton, R. H. 1997, November. Selective predictive value of rapid automatized naming within poor readers. Poster presented at the Annual Meeting of the International Dyslexia Association, Minneapolis.

Meyer, A., Pisha, B., and Rose, D. 1991. Process and Product in Writing: Computer as Enabler. In A. M. Bain, L. L. Bailet, and L. C. Moats, eds., *Written Language Disorders: Theory Into Practice.* Austin, TX: PRO-ED.

Morris, G. H. 1983. Adapting a college preparatory curriculum for dyslexic adolescents: Confronting the problems of what to teach. *Annals of Dyslexia* 33:243–50.

Naiden, N. February, 1976. Ratio of boys to girls among disabled readers. *Reading Teacher:* 439–42.

Nass, R. 1993. Sex differences in learning abilities and disabilities. *Annals of Dyslexia* 43:61–77.

Orton Dyslexia Society Research Committee. 1994. Operational definition of dyslexia. *Perspectives* 20(5):4.

Orton, S. T. 1937. *Reading, Writing, and Speech Problems in Children.* London: Chapman and Hall.

Perfetti, C. A. 1977. Language comprehension and fast decoding: Some psycholinguistic prerequisites for skilled reading comprehension. In J. Guthrie, ed., *Cognition, Curriculum, and Comprehension.* Newark, DE: International Reading Association.

Rawson, M. 1968. Developmental Language Disability: *Adult Accomplishments of Dyslexic Boys.* Baltimore, MD: Johns Hopkins University Press.

Renninger, K. A. 1992. Individual interest and development: Implications for theory and practice. In K. A. Renninger, S. Hidi, and A. Krapp, eds., *The Role of Interest in Learning and Development.* Hillsdale, NJ: Lawrence Erlbaum Associates.

Rhodes, L. K., and Dudley-Marling, C. 1988. *Readers and Writers with a Difference.* Portsmouth, NH: Heinemann.

Rose, D. H., and Meyer, A. 1996. Expanding the literacy toolbox: Why we must broaden our definition of literacy and incorporate new media in the classroom (Literacy Paper 11): Scholastic, Inc.

Rose, D. H., and Meyer, A. 1994. The role of technology in language arts instruction. *Language Arts* 71(4):290–94.

Roswell, F. G., and Chall, J. S. 1992. *Diagnostic Assessments of Reading with Trial Teaching Strategies.* Chicago: Riverside.

Scarborough, H. S. 1984. Continuity between childhood dyslexia and adult reading. *British Journal of Psychology* 75:329–48.

Scarborough, H. S. 1989. Prediction of reading disability from familial and individual differences. *Journal of Educational Psychology* 81:101–8.

Schiefele, U., and Krapp, A. 1996. Topic interest and free recall of expository text. *Learning and Individual Differences* 8(2):141–60.

Shaywitz, B., Fletcher, J., and Shaywitz, S. 1994. The conceptual framework for learning disabilities and attention deficit/hyperactivity disorder. *Canadian Journal of Special Education* 9(3):1–32.

Shaywitz, B., Fletcher, J., and Shaywitz, S. January, 1995. Defining and classifying learning disabilities and attention-deficit/hyperactivity disorder. *Journal of Child Neurology* 10(1):50–57.

Shaywitz, S., Towle, V., Keese, D., and Shaywitz, B. 1990. Prevalence of dyslexia in boys and girls in an epidemiologic sample. *Journal of the American Medical Association* 181:143–57.

Snowling, M., Stothard, S., and McLean, J. 1996. *Graded Nonword Reading Test.* Edmunds, England: Thames Valley Test Publishers.

Stanovich, K. E. 1991. Discrepancy definitions of reading disability: Has intelligence led us astray? *Reading Research Quarterly* 26:7–29.

Stanovich, K. E. 1980. Toward an interactive-compensatory model of individual differences in the development of reading fluency. *Reading Research Quarterly* 16:32–71.

Vogel, S. 1990. Gender differences in intelligence, language, visual-motor abilities, and academic achievement in students with learning disabilities: A review of the literature. *Journal of Learning Disabilities* 23(1):44–52.

Vogel, S. A., and Walsh, P. C. 1990. Gender differences in cognitive abilities of learning-disabled females and males. *Annals of Dyslexia* 37:142–65.

Vogel, S. A. 1987. Issues and concerns in college LD programming. In D. J. Johnson and J. W. Blalock, eds., *Adults with Learning Disabilities: Clinical Studies.* Orlando: Grune and Stratton.

Wadsworth, S., DeFries, J., Stevenson, J., Gilger, J., and Pennington, B. 1992. Gender ratios among learning disabled children and their siblings as a function of parental impairment. *Journal of Child Psychiatry* 33:1229–39.

Whitehead, F., and Maddren, W. 1974. Children's reading interests (Schools Council Working Paper No. 52). London, England: University of Sheffield Institute of Education, Schools Council Research Project into Children's Reading Habits.

Wolf, M., and Bowers, P. (submitted January 1998). The "double-deficit hypothesis" for the developmental dyslexias. *Journal of Learning Disabilities.*

Wolf, M. (1997). A provisional, integrative account of phonological and naming-speed deficits in dyslexia: Implications for diagnosis and intervention. In B. Blachman, ed., *Cognitive and Linguistic Foundations of Reading Acquisition: Implications for Intervention Research.* Hillsdale, NJ: Lawrence Erlbaum Associates.

Woodd, M. January 1997. Gender differences in mentoring: A biographical reflection. *Educational Management and Administration* 25:25–34.

# APPENDIX I.

## Professionally Successful Men and Women with Dyslexia

**MEN**

J.William Adams
*Headmaster*
    The Gow School;
    South Wales, New York

S. Charles Bean
*Neurologist*
    Clinical Associate Professor
    Jefferson Hospital
    Philadelphia, Pennsylvania

Baruj Benacerraf
*Immunologist*
    Professor of Immunology
    Chair, Dept. of Pathology
    Harvard Medical School

William Brewer
*Psychologist*
    Professor of Psychology
    University of Illinois;
    Champaign, Ill.

Michael L. Commons
*Psychometrician*
    Lecturer/Research Associate
    Dept. of Psychiatry
    Harvard Medical School

Heriberto Cresto
*Social Worker*
    Latino Health Institute
    Boston, Mass.

Ronald W. Davis
*Biochemist*
    Director, Stanford DNA
    Sequencing/Technology Ctr.
    Professor,
    Stanford University
    School of Medicine
    Stanford, California

George Deem
*Graphic Artist*
    New York City
    Adjunct Professor of Art
    University of Pennsylvania
    Philadelphia, PA

G. Emerson Dickman
*Attorney at Law*
    Maywood, New Jersey

H .Girard Ebert
*Interior Designer and CEO*
    H. Girard Ebert, Inc.
    Baltimore, Maryland

Donald Francis
*Virologist/AIDS Researcher*
    Genentech, Inc.
    Founder & President
    VaxGen, Inc.
    San Francisco, California

Miles Gerety
*Attorney at Law*
    Conn. Public Defender
    Bridgeport, Connecticut

Daniel Gillette
*Learning Specialist*
    Boston Architectural Center

Alexander Goldowsky
*Program Developer*
    New England Aquarium
    Boston, Mass.

David Gordon
*Marketing Consultant*
    Adaptive Computing
    Beverly, Mass.

Philip Hulbig
*Tutor*
    Walpole, Mass.

Robert Knapp
*Gynecologist*
　　Professor and Chair
　　Dept. of Gynecology
　　Harvard Medical School

John Moore
*Social Worker*
　　Boston, Mass.

Jonathan Pazer
*Attorney at Law*
　　Law Offices of Pazer & Epstein
　　New York City

Bart Pisha
*Computer Specialist*
　　Director of Research
　　Center for Applied
　　Special Technology (CAST)
　　Peabody, Mass.

Cruz Sanabria
*Early Childhood Educator*
　　Boston, Mass.

Michael Schweitzer
*General and Vascular Surgeon*
　　Virginia Surgical Specialists
　　Richmond, Virginia

David Selib
*Sales Manager*
　　Reebok International
　　Medfield, Mass.

Larry B. Silver
*Psychiatrist and Writer*
　　Clinical Professor of
　　Psychiatry
　　Georgetown University
　　School of Medicine
　　Washington, DC

James Soberman
*Dentist*
　　Clinical Ass't. Professor
　　of Prosthodontics
　　New York University

Michael Spock
*Co-Director/Researcher*
　　Chapin Hall
　　Center for Children
　　University of Chicago
　　Chicago, Illinois

A. McDonald Vaz
*Writer*
　　Miami Beach, Florida

Michael Van Zandt
*Research Scientist*
　　Institute for
　　Diabetes Discovery
　　Branford, Connecticut

Thomas G. West
*Writer*
　　Visualization Research
　　Institute
　　Washington, DC

Glenn Young
*Learning Disabilities Specialist*
　　Washington State Dept. of
　　Social & Health Services
　　Seattle, Washington

## WOMEN

Hannah Adams
*Elementary School Teacher*
　　Cambridge, Mass.

Tania Baker
*Biochemist*
　　Assistant Professor
　　Mass. Institute of
　　Technology (MIT)

Barbara Bikofsky
*Special Educator*
　　Adjunct Instructor
　　Lesley College
　　Cambridge, Mass.

Lori Boskin
*Director*
   Alumni Relations,
   Special Projects, &
   Promotions
   UCLA School of Law
   Los Angeles, California

Lora Brody
*Cookbook Author*
*TV and Radio Personality*
   Newton, Mass.

Terry Bromfield
*Special Educator*
   Adjunct Ass't. Professor
   Lesley College
   Cambridge, Mass.

Ann L. Brown
*Researcher/Educator*
   Professor of Education
   University of California
   Berkeley, California

Susan E. Brown
*Filmmaker*
   New York City

Jane Buchbinder
*Fiction Writer*
   Boston, Mass.

Susan Cobin
*Administrator/Principal*
   Talmud Torah Day School
   Saint Paul, Minnesota

Ellen Gorman
*Social Worker*
   New Haven Adult
   Education
   New Haven, Connecticut

Stacey Harris
*Attorney at Law*
   Brookline, Mass.

Florence Haseltine
*Gynecologist/Director*
   Ctr. for Population Research
   National Institutes of Health
   Washington, DC

Marlene Hirschberg
*Arts Administrator/Director*
   Jewish Community Center
   Milwaukee, Wisconsin

Melissa Holt
*Head Teacher*
   South Shore Day Care
   Quincy, Mass.

Annette Jenner
*Neurobiologist*
   Biology Teaching Fellow
   Harvard University

Anita Landa
*Educator*
   Associate Professor
   Lesley College
   Cambridge, Mass.

Sylvia Law
*Attorney at Law*
   Professor of Law,
   Medicine, and Psychiatry
   New York University
   School of Law

Nancy Lelewer
*Writer*
*Research Associate in Neurology*
   Harvard Medical School

Joanne Lense
*Social Worker*
   Bronx Lebanon Hospital &
   Knight Education,
   New York City

Susan Marlett
*Artist*
   Clearway Technologies
   Fort Lee, New Jersey
Robin Mello
*Storyteller/Actress*
   Adjunct Instructor
   Tufts Univ. & Lesley College
Fiona Moore
*Social Worker*
   Human Resource Institute
   Brookline, Mass.
Tania Phillips
*Elementary School Teacher*
   Northampton, Mass.
Priscilla Sanville
*Arts Educator*
   Adjunct Ass't. Professor
   Lesley College
   Cambridge, Mass.

Marla Silver
*Social Worker*
   Easton Hospital
   Easton, Pennsylvania
Charlann Simon
*Author and Program Developer*
   Speech/Language &
   Learning Specialist
   Tempe, Arizona
Jane Smith
*Anthropologist*
   American University
   Washington, D. C.
Beth Steucek
*Manager*
   Executive Vice President
   New England Innkeepers
Lezli Whitehouse
*Language Clinician*
   Boston, Mass.

# Index
*(Page numbers in italics indicate material in figures or tables.)*

Specific reading retardation, 28, 48. *See also* Dyslexia
Spelling, 19, 33
Stories, meaning and themes of, 216–18
Student files, release of, 284–85, 287–88
Student teaching by learning-disabled students, 304–305
Stuttering, 7
Successful dyslexic adults, 343–46; academic degrees of, 316; avid reading by, 322–24, 335, 337; literacy levels of, 327–28
Summer camp program: academic achievement and recognition in, 198, 205–207; building self-esteem in, 199–200, 201–205, 208; changes in reading skills during, 207; gains in self-concept during, 201–205; improvements in dyslexic students in, 192; intervention for dyslexic students in, 194, 197–200; psychosocial aspects of, 198–200; tutors in, 197

**T**

Tallal, P., 68
Teachers: induction programs for new, 306–307; standards for new, 300

Teaching. *See* Instruction
Temporal order processing, 68
Themes instruction, 216–18, 218–21; compared to traditional instruction, 224–26, 226–28, 228–30
Thomas, K. V., 77, 80
Torgesen, J. K., 132–33
Tutors in summer camp, 197

**V**

Verbal memory, 117, 122, 129
Videotapes, 313
Visual memory, 82
Visual problems, 156
Visual processing in cerebral cortex of primates, *159*
Vogel, S. A., 297–98, 299

**W**

Warrington, K. E., 184
Writing from dictation, 5, *6*

**Y**

Yule, W., 46

# Annals of Dyslexia
## Information for Contributors

The Annals of Dyslexia is a peer-reviewed interdisciplinary journal dedicated to the understanding and remediation of reading disability. Primary consideration is given to original research papers; we also publish significant reviews and well-documented reports of effective practices. Each manuscript will be evaluated with regard to 1) its general significance for the Annals readership; 2) the specific contribution within the paradigm adopted; 3) the soundness of methodology and interpretation of results; and 4) the clarity and organization of writing. Only papers not previously published will be considered for publication; papers cannot be simultaneously submitted to Annals and other journals. **Please limit manuscript** *text* **to 20 pages not including reference lists, tables, and figures.**

Manuscripts must be submitted by December 15 in order to receive full consideration for publication in the following year. Papers submitted after that time (until January 15) will be considered only if space is available. Manuscripts will be reviewed by the Editor and two other reviewers with expertise in the area to which the topic pertains; the initial review process seldom requires more than 3 months. It is our policy to provide authors such editorial assistance as is necessary to achieve conciseness and clarity in presenting their work; most accepted papers will require some revision. The editorial decision letter will communicate suggestions to the author that should facilitate the preparation of the revision. Strict deadlines must be met in order to meet the once-a-year publication schedule.

The 1982 edition of the *Chicago Manual of Style* is the primary authority used in editing *Annals of Dyslexia*. We recommend that writers refer to it, scrutinizing language, usage, and mechanics in their manuscripts prior to submitting them. The author-date system of text reference and the reference list style should be followed. (Examples are provided in these instructions.) **NOTE: Reference lists, in particular, submitted in APA style will be returned to be resubmitted in the form shown on pages 3 and 4 of this guide.** Tables, figures, and statistical information should follow conventions outlined in Publication Manual of the APA, 4th Edition.

Submit the **original manuscript plus three copies** and retain a copy for your files. Do not staple manuscripts or copies. We also require an **abstract of the paper not to exceed 200 words**. If your paper is accepted, we will ask at a later point for a copy of the computer disk containing the word processing version of your manuscript, including an unformatted ASCII file. Details will be provided at that point.

List your name on the title page, followed by applicable affiliations, exactly as the publication should read. Except for medical doctors, no degrees are used in *Annals*. Please include work and home addresses for correspondence with the author and co-authors (designating the primary address to use), also including phone numbers, fax numbers, and e-mail addresses for each author and co-author as available.

## Preparation of Manuscript

Manuscripts should be double-spaced for text, footnotes, tables, and figure legends. Reference lists should be triple-spaced throughout. All margins, left, right, top and bottom, should be at least one inch wide. Each page should have the author's name and abbreviated title at the left-hand top of the page. *Make the title of the article concise and to the point.* We suggest a three- or four-word running head to facilitate indexing and information retrieval.

A and B headings should be typed on separate lines and should not run into the paragraphs or be italicized (underscored). "A" headings should be centered, and "B" headings should be placed at the left margin. "C" headings should begin at the appropriate paragraph, using capitals and lower case and should be italicized (underscored).

Footnotes should be numbered consecutively in the text, indicated by superscript numbers, and then typed on a separate page labeled *Footnotes.*

References cited in the text should be followed, in parenthesis, by the author's surname (unless it is given in the text of the sentence, as in *a* and *d* below) and the date of the reference. If there are two or more references cited by the same author with the same year of publication, use lowercase letters after the date to distinguish them. Do not use commas preceding publication dates.

*Examples:*

a. The work of Victor Denenberg and his colleagues (1978) is important in this regard.
b. The brain of the rat has been altered as a result of hormone treatments (Diamond, Dowling, and Johnson 1981).
c. In recent years psychologists have referred extensively to metacognition (Brown 1978).
d. Orton provided several case studies which support this position (1928c, 1928e).
e. Satz and his colleagues (Satz and Friel 1973, 1974; Fletcher et al. 1982) undertook a series of studies to investigate the predictive value of kindergarten screening tests.

**Note:** Citations, including the first, of works by more than three authors use the name of the first followed by *et al.*

Illustrations should be original inked drawings in a form suitable for reduction without retouching or redrawing. Suggested size is 8 1/2 x 11 inches. Lettering numerals, and symbols should be large enough so that they will be completely legible after reduction. Photographs should be the original and on glossy paper. Place overlays on all photographs to avoid damage. If only part of the photograph is to be used, indicate that part with penciled lines on the overlay. (Permission must be obtained for any illustrative material previously published in a book or journal.) Legends for illustrations should not be attached, but typed in double space on a separate page and clearly keyed to the illustrations.

Tables should be numbered with Roman numerals and in the order of their mention in the text. Citations in the text to the tables should also be in

Roman numerals. A brief title should be typed directly above each table. Explanatory material for the table should be placed in a footnote.

Figures should be numbered in sequence with Arabic numerals and in the order of their mention in the text. Their citations should be in Arabic numerals in the text. A note in the margin of the text where the figure is mentioned should indicate where the figure is to be placed. Each figure should be identified, either on the back or in the margin, with its number, author's name, and title of manuscript. The legends should be typed in double space and in sequence on a separate page of the manuscript labeled *Figures*; they should not be on the figures.

For all illustrative material—photographs, tables, figures, drawings— place a note in the margin of the text to indicate the approximate placement desired. All typing on or for such material—title, column heading, body of table, etc.—should be double-spaced.

The reference list should include only those references cited in the text.

*Entries in the list should be arranged alphabetically by the author's surname and should not be numbered.* If there is more than one publication by a given author in the same year, the letters a, b, etc. should be added after the date. Please triple-space all entries and follow the style of the examples given below. (DO NOT, however, separate your references into these categories.)

### Book

Bakker, D.J. 1972. *Temporal Order in Disturbed Reading*. Rotterdam: University Press.

### More Than One Publication by a Given Author in the Same Year

Bakker, D.J. 1979a. Perceptual asymmetries and reading proficiency. In *Cognitive Growth and Development*, ed. M. Bortner. New York: Brunner/ Mazel.

Bakker, D.J. 1976b. A set of brains for learning to read. In *Individual Differences and Universals in Language Learning Aptitude*, ed. K.C. Diller. Boston: Newbury House Publishers.

### Edited Book

Benton, A.L., and Pearl, D. eds. 1978. *Dyslexia: An Appraisal of Current Knowledge*. New York: Oxford University Press.

### Chapter in a Book

Bever, T.G. 1975. Cerebral asymmetries in humans are due to the differentiation of two incompatible processes: Holistic and analytic. In *Developmental Psycholinguistics and Communication Disorders*, eds. D. Aaronson and R. Rieber. New York: New York Academy of Sciences.

Buffery, A.W.H., and Gray, J.A. 1972. Sex differences in the development of spatial and linguistic skills. In *Gender Differences: Their Ontogeny and Significance*, eds. C. Ounsted and D.C. Taylor. London: Churchill Livingstone.

### Journal

Geschwind, N. 1979. Asymmetries of the brain: New developments. *Bulletin of the Orton Society* 29:67–73.

Heir, D.B., LeMay, M., Rosenberger, P.B., and Perlo, V.P., 1978. Developmental dyslexia: Evidence for a sub-group with reversal of cerebral asymmetry. *Archives of Neurology* 35:90–92.

***Volume Numbers: Book or Journal***

Kleuber, R. 1971. Mental abilities and disorders of learning. In *Progress in Learning Disabilities*, Vol. II, ed. H.R. Myklebust. New York: Grune and Stratton.

Torgesen, J.K. 1977. Memorization processes in reading-disabled children. *Journal of Educational Psychology* 69(5):571–578.

***Dissertation or Thesis***

Jones, A.J. 1947. Laterality and dominance in preschool deaf children. Ph.D. diss., Northeastern University, Boston.

***Paper Read at a Meeting***

Halpern, E. 1970. Reading success with children with visual-perceptual immaturity. Paper read at 47th Annual Meeting of the American Orthopsychiatric Association, November 1969, San Francisco.

## COMMUNICATIONS AND MANUSCRIPTS

All communications and manuscripts should be sent to:
*Annals of Dyslexia*
The International Dyslexia Association
8600 LaSalle Road
Chester Bldg./Suite 382
Baltimore, MD 21286-2044
(410) 296-0232, ext. 23